# LOG HORIZON

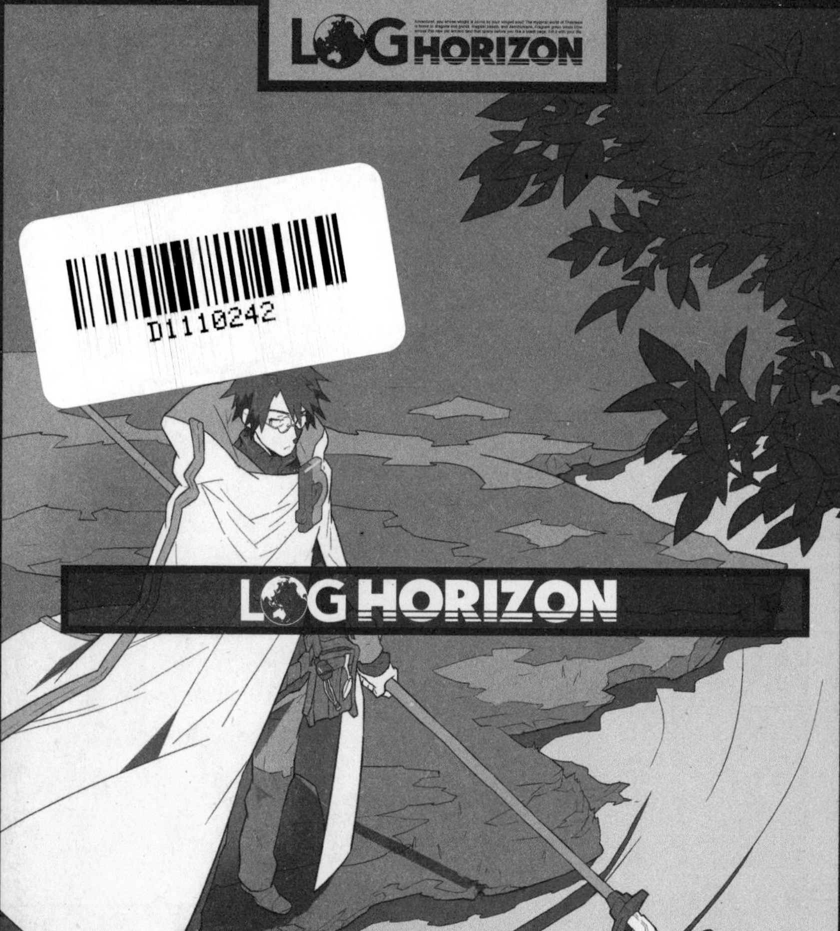



1

ART: KAZUHIRO HARA ORIGINAL STORY: MAMARE TOUNO SUPERVISION: SHOJI MASUDA

## [THE CHARACTERS]

**SHIROE** LEVEL 90

▶ CLASS......ENCHANTER

A veteran player nicknamed "Machiavelli-with-glasses."

・A support-type magic user whose spells are tailored toward amplifying other players' abilities and obstructing monsters.

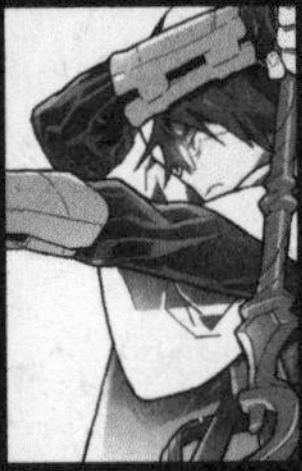

**NAOTSUGU** LEVEL 90

▶ CLASS......GUARDIAN

A cheerful, tough, young guy who's an old friend of Shiroe's. He has special skills related to the defense and protection of others. His resilient optimism means he's usually the life of his party.

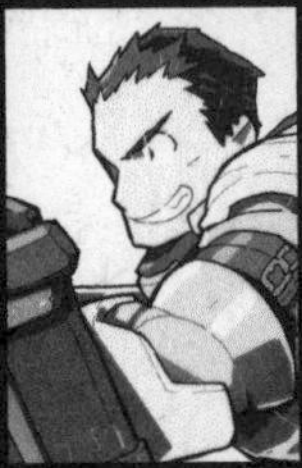

**AKATSUKI** LEVEL 90

▶ CLASS......ASSASSIN

A petite, very pretty, very quiet girl who's an expert at lethal attacks. Since Shiroe saved her, she calls him her liege and has decided to travel with him.

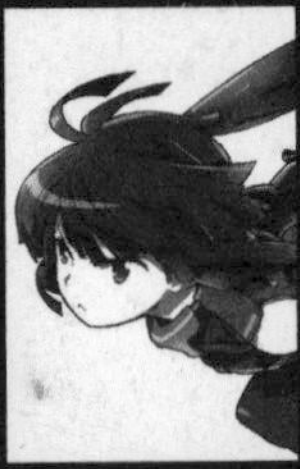

**SERARA** LEVEL 19

▶ CLASS DRUID

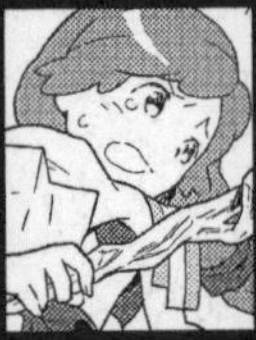

**MARIELLE** LEVEL 90

▶ CLASS CLERIC

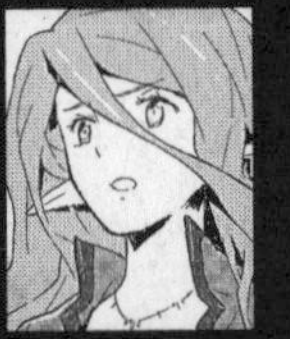

## [STORY]

▶ *Elder Tales* is a venerable, old online RPG. On the day its twelfth expansion pack is released, thirty thousand Japanese players are pulled into the game and trapped there. They have no idea how to get back to their old world, and on top of that, the food in the game doesn't taste like anything! The players lose hope, and the world that used to be fun dissolves into anarchy.

▶ Shiroe, a.k.a. "Machiavelli-with-glasses," is a veteran player based in the town of Akiba. When his friend Marielle tells him one of her guild members has been stranded in the distant town of Susukino, he sets off to rescue the girl...

# [ C O N T E N T S ]

LOG HORIZON 1

▶CHAPTER:01 ANOTHER WORLD

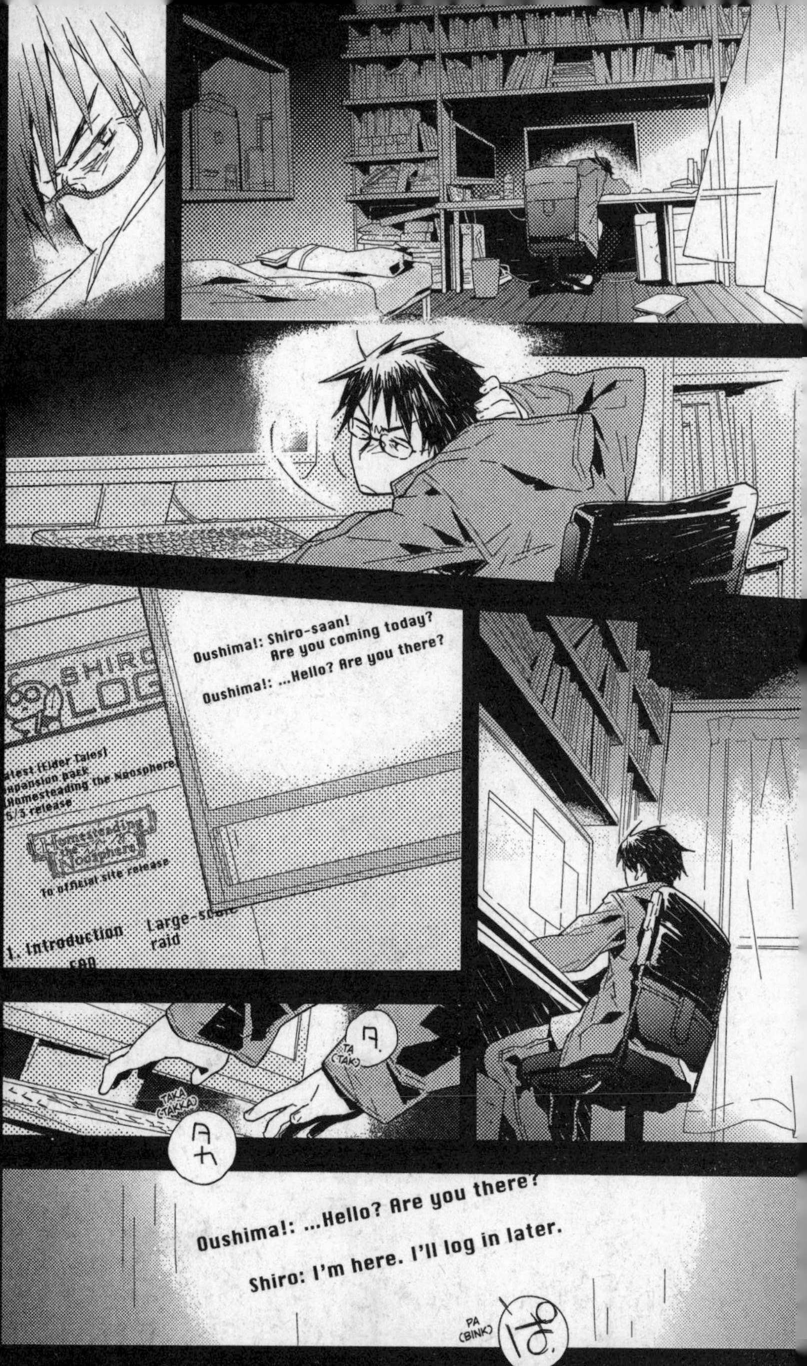
Oushima!: Shiro-saan! Are you coming today?
Oushima!: ...Hello? Are you there?
SHIRO LOG
[Elder Tales]
expansion pack
Homesteading the Noosphere
5/3 release
Homesteading the Noosphere
To official site release
1. Introduction
Large-scale raid
タ.
TA (TAK)
タカ
TAKA (TAKKA)
Oushima!: ...Hello? Are you there?
Shiro: I'm here. I'll log in later.
ぱ.
PA (BINK)

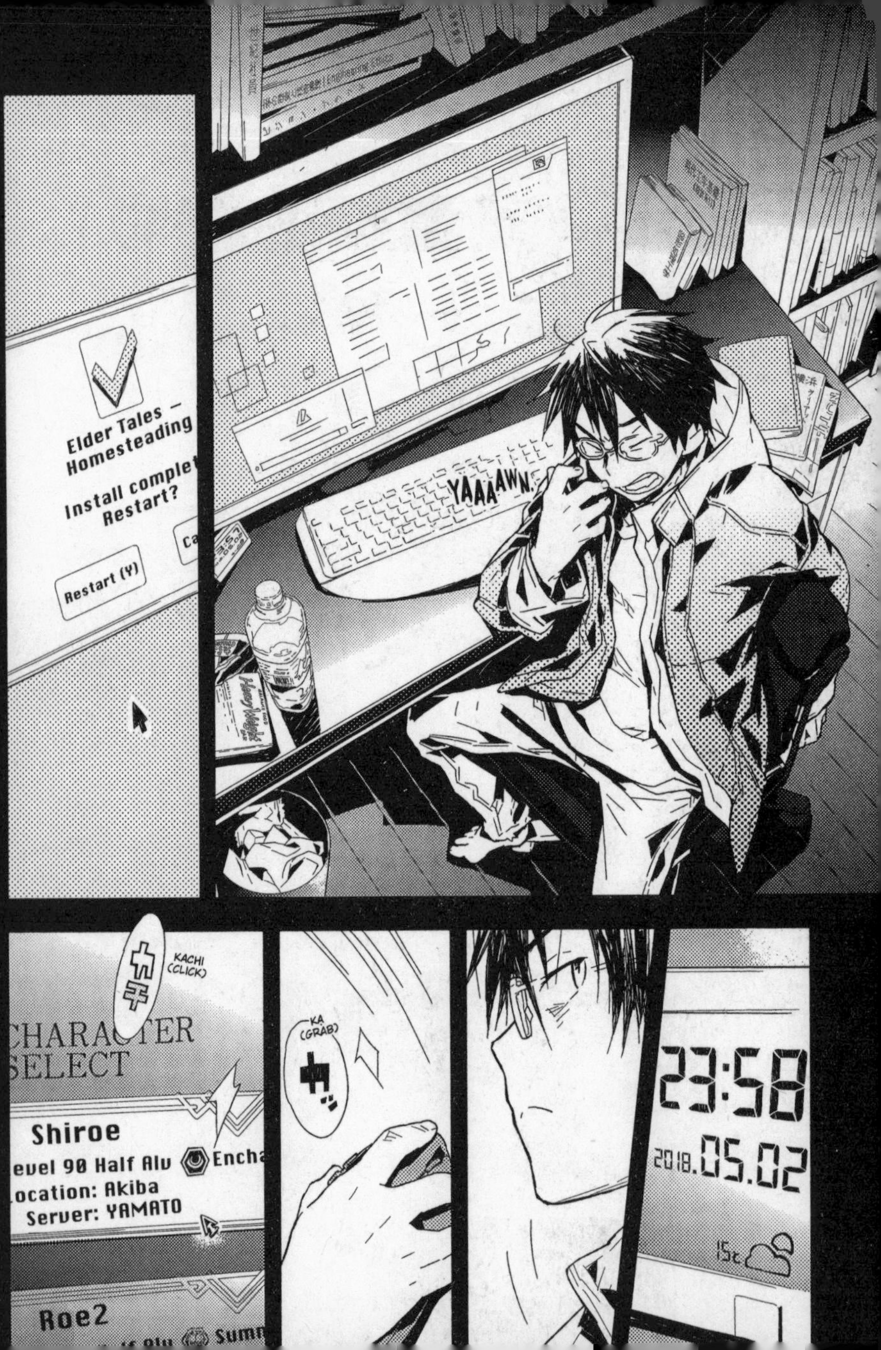
YAAAAWN
Elder Tales — Homesteading
Install complet
Restart?
Restart (Y)
Ca
23:58
2018.05.02
15c
KA (GRAB)
KACHI (CLICK)
CHARACTER SELECT
Shiroe
evel 90 Half Alv
Encha
Location: Akiba
Server: YAMATO
Roe2
Summ

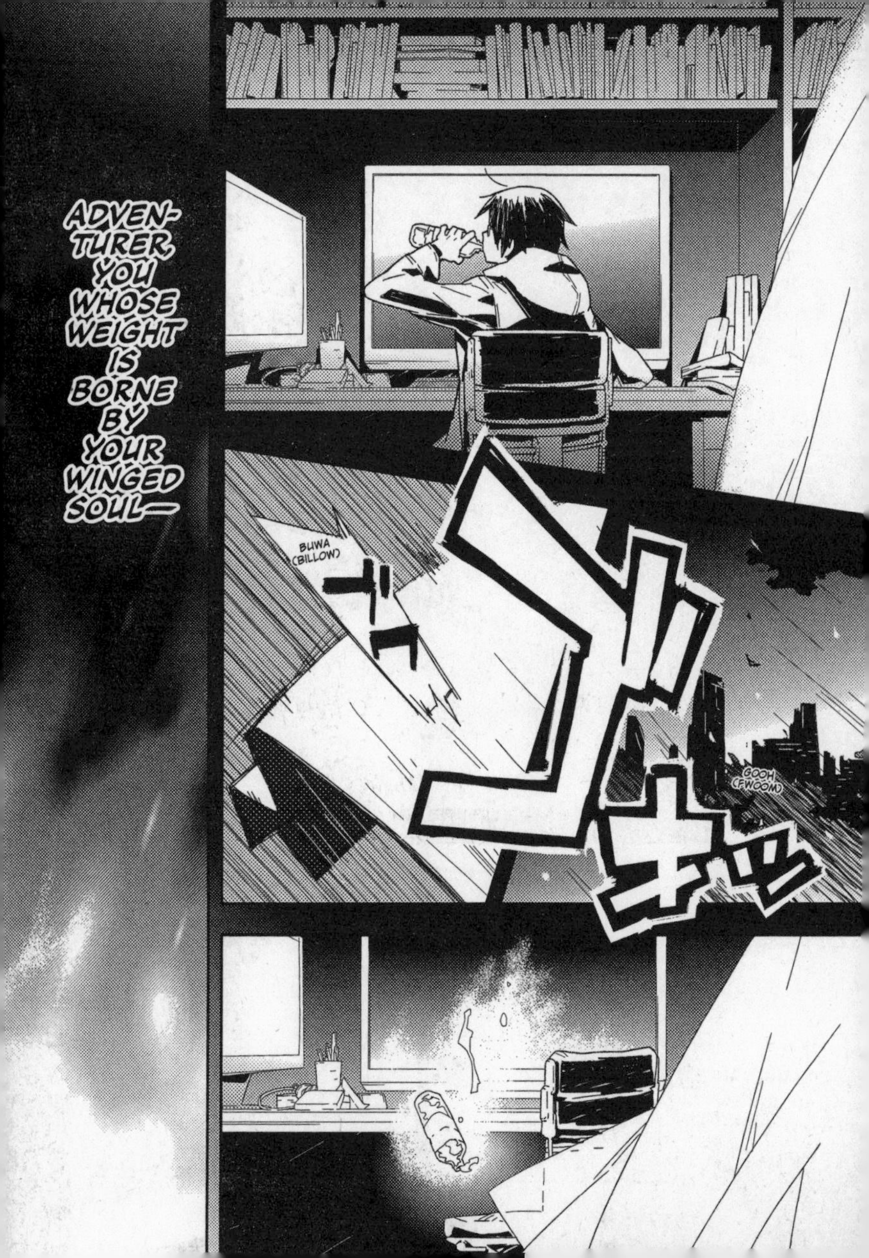
GOOH (FWOOM)
BUWA (BILLOW)
ADVEN-TURER, YOU WHOSE WEIGHT IS BORNE BY YOUR WINGED SOUL—

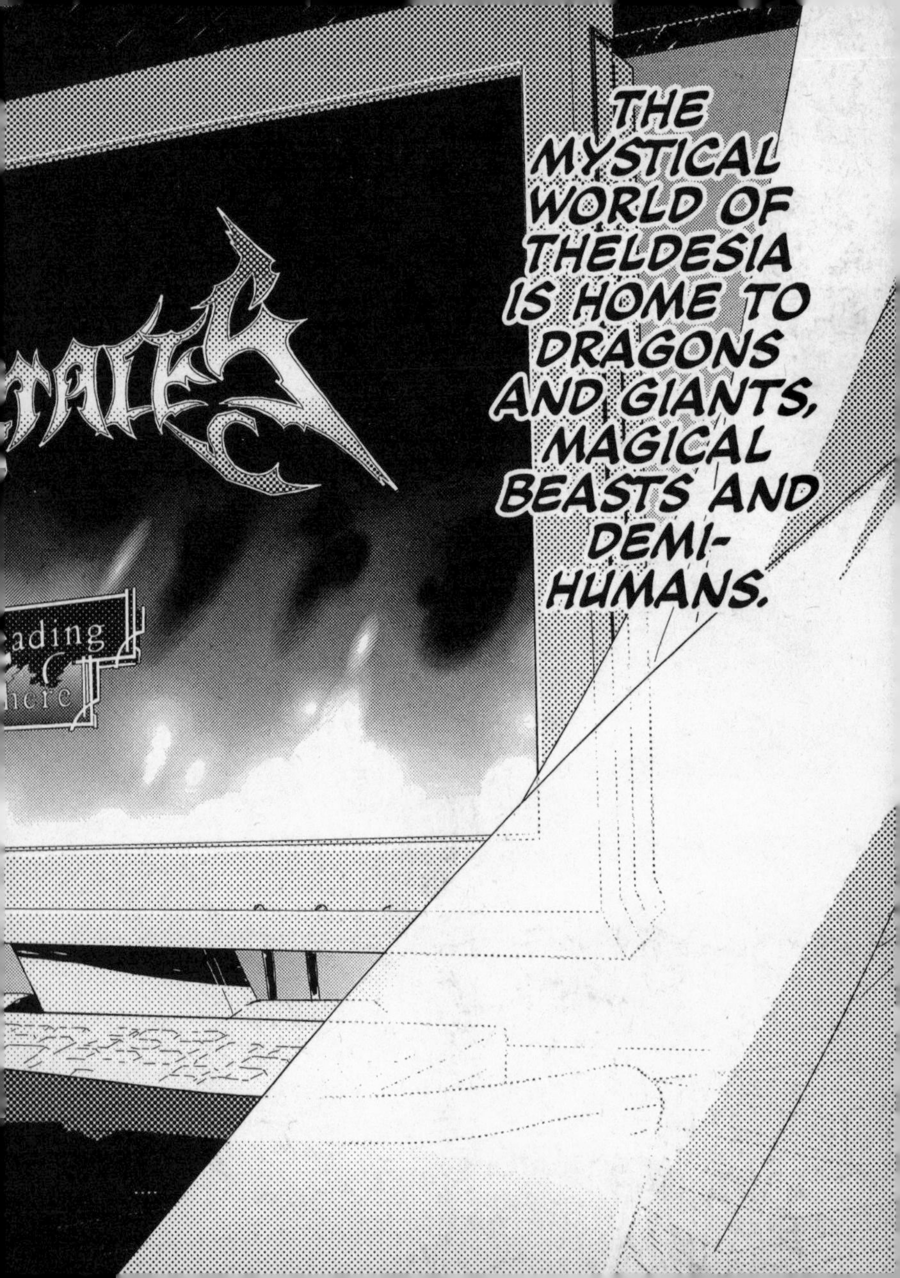
THE MYSTICAL WORLD OF THELDESIA IS HOME TO DRAGONS AND GIANTS, MAGICAL BEASTS AND DEMI-HUMANS.

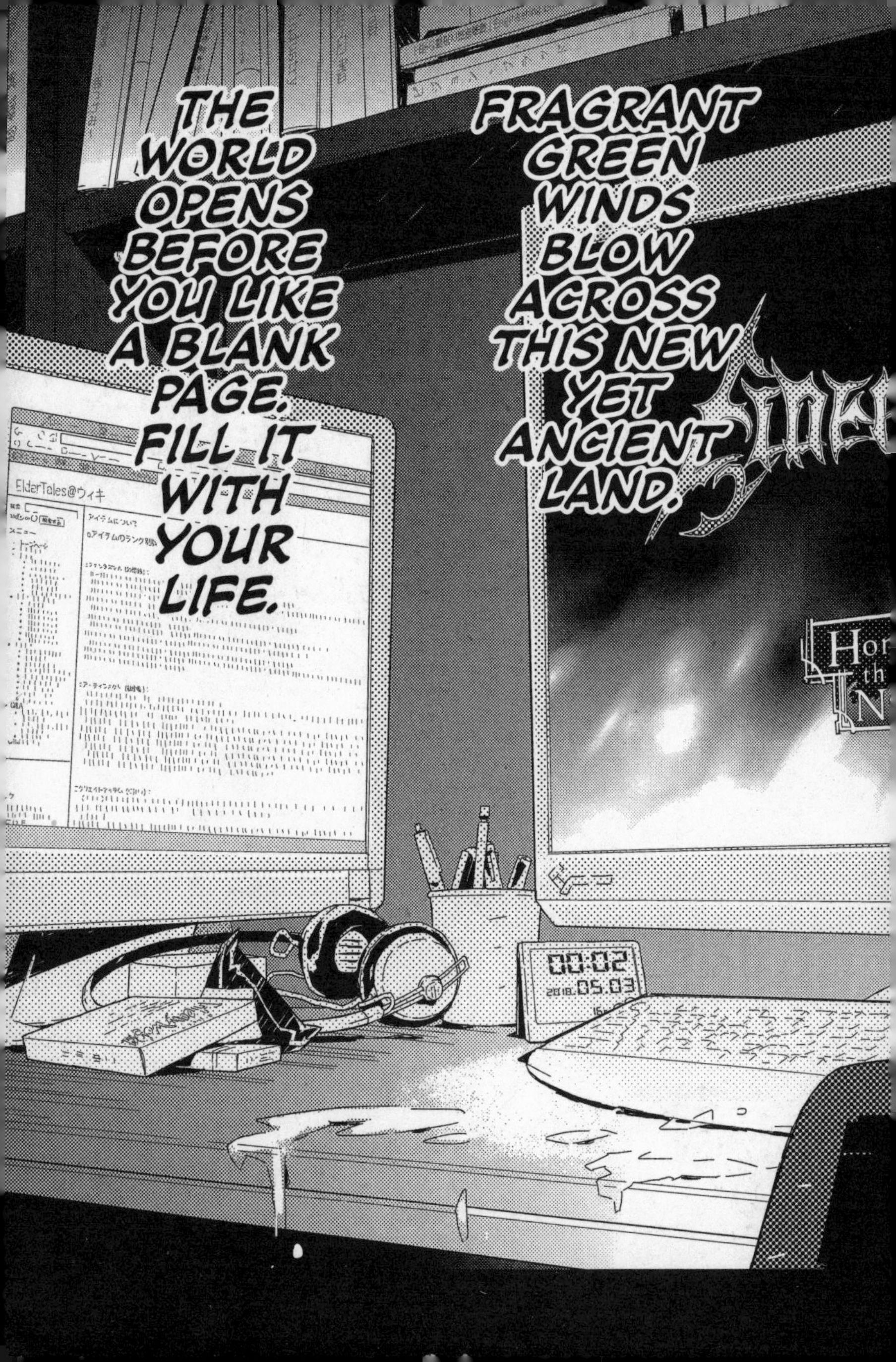
FRAGRANT GREEN WINDS BLOW ACROSS THIS NEW YET ANCIENT LAND.
THE WORLD OPENS BEFORE YOU LIKE A BLANK PAGE. FILL IT WITH YOUR LIFE.
ElderTales@ウィキ
00:02
2018.05.03

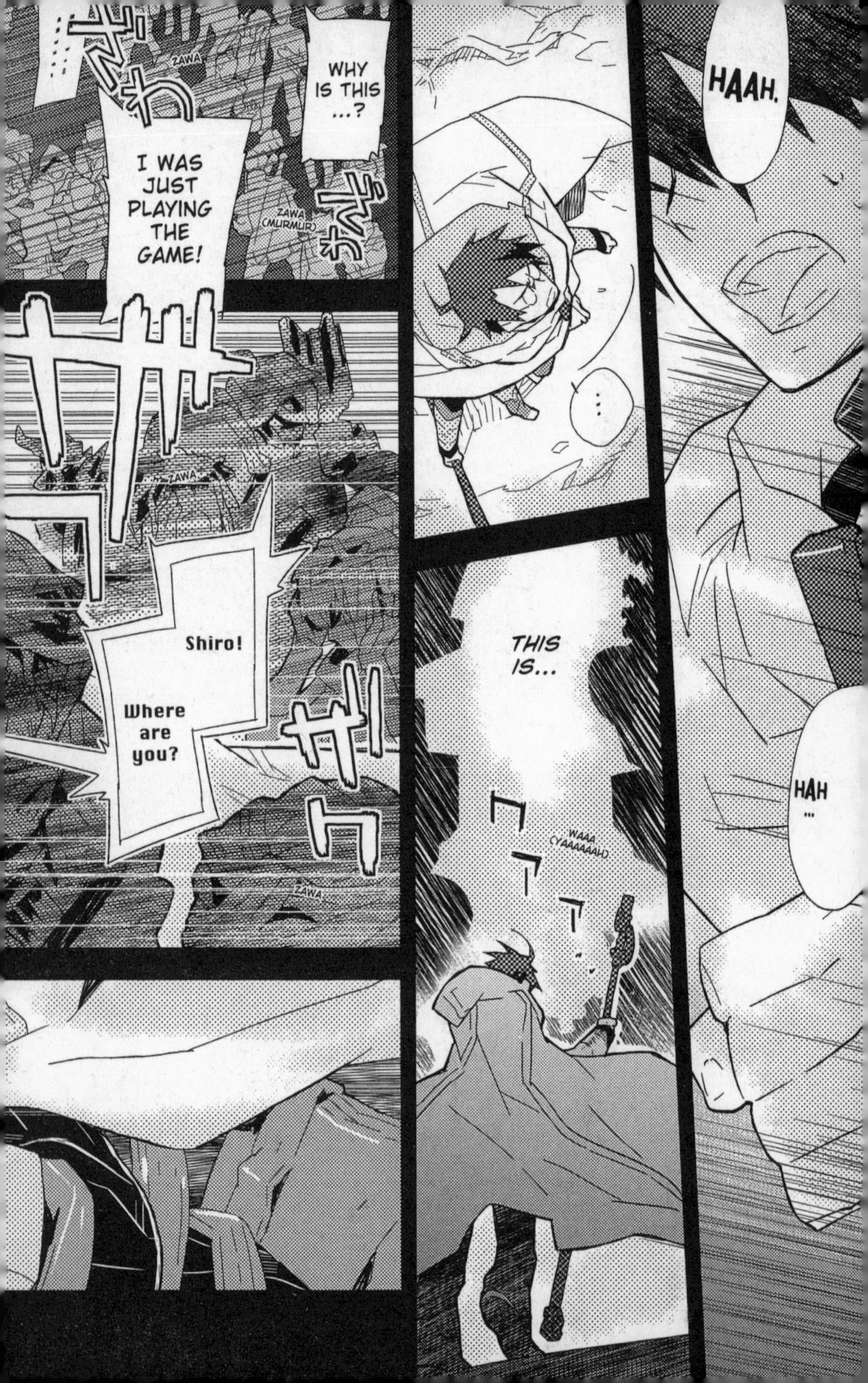
HAAH.
HAH ...
...
THIS IS...
WAAA (YAAAAAAH)
WHY IS THIS ...?
I WAS JUST PLAYING THE GAME!
ZAWA
ZAWA (MURMUR)
ZAWA
Shiro!
Where are you?
ZAWA

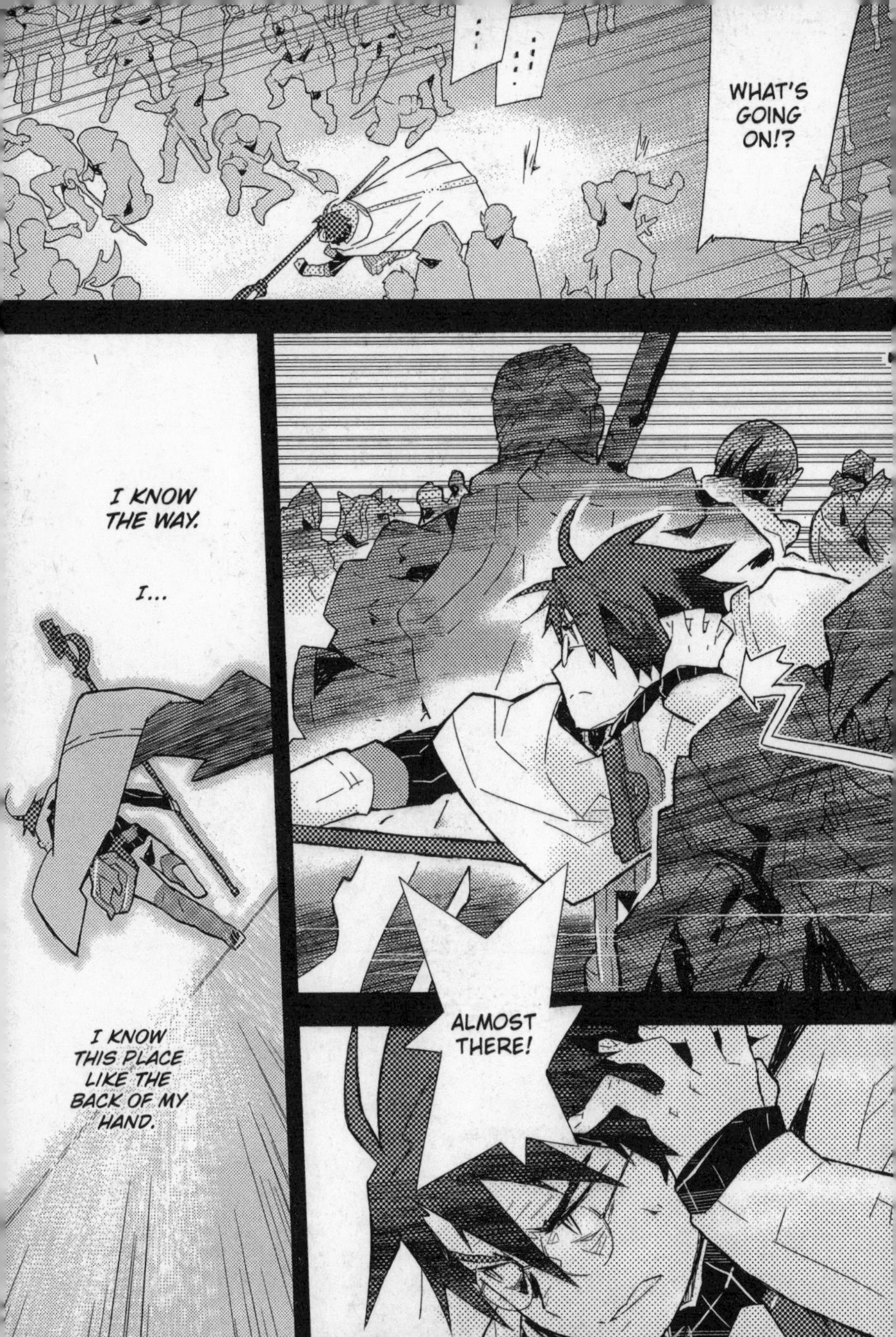
WHAT'S GOING ON!?
ALMOST THERE!
I KNOW THE WAY.
I...
I KNOW THIS PLACE LIKE THE BACK OF MY HAND.

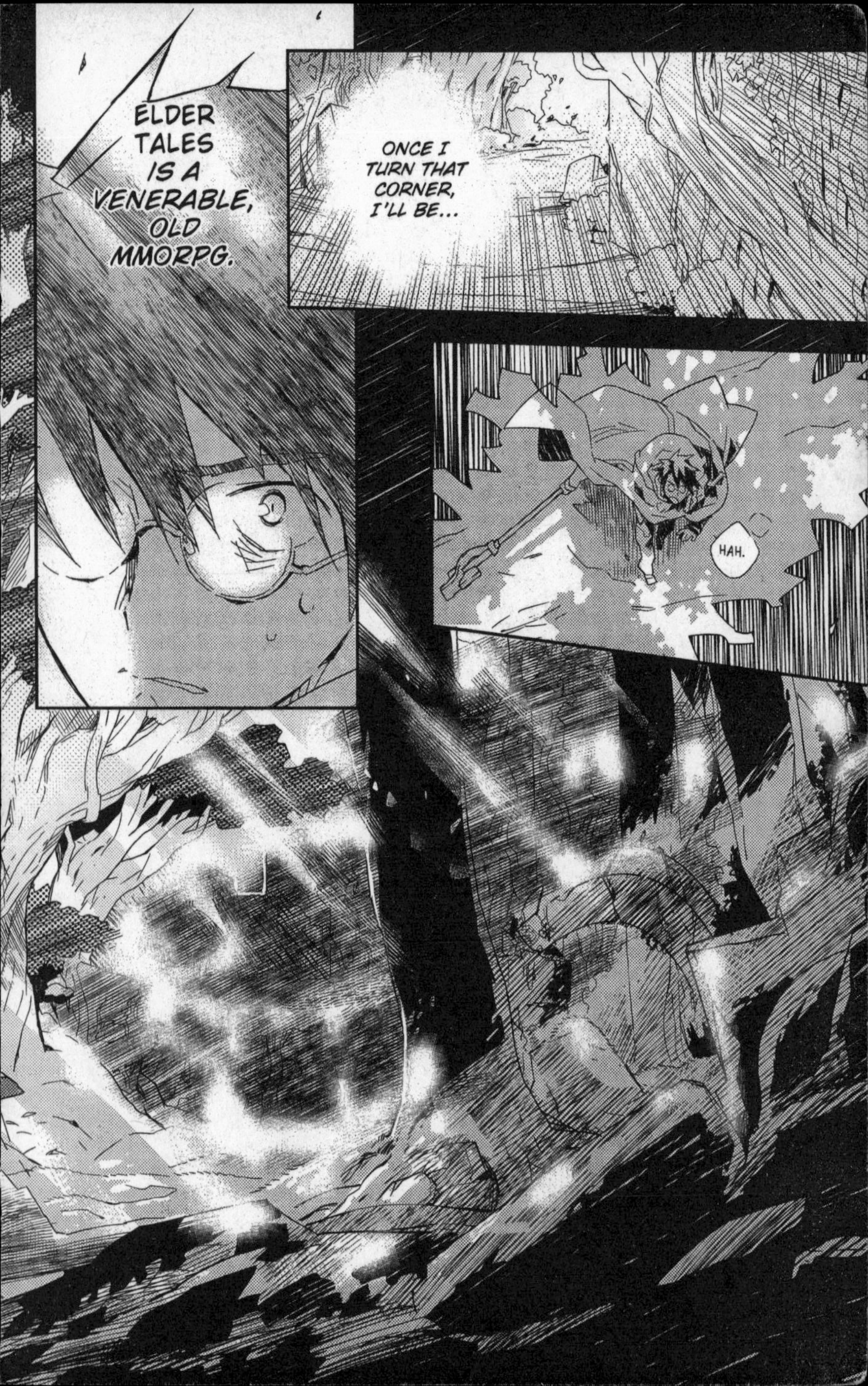
ONCE I TURN THAT CORNER, I'LL BE...
HAH.
ELDER TALES IS A VENERABLE, OLD MMORPG.

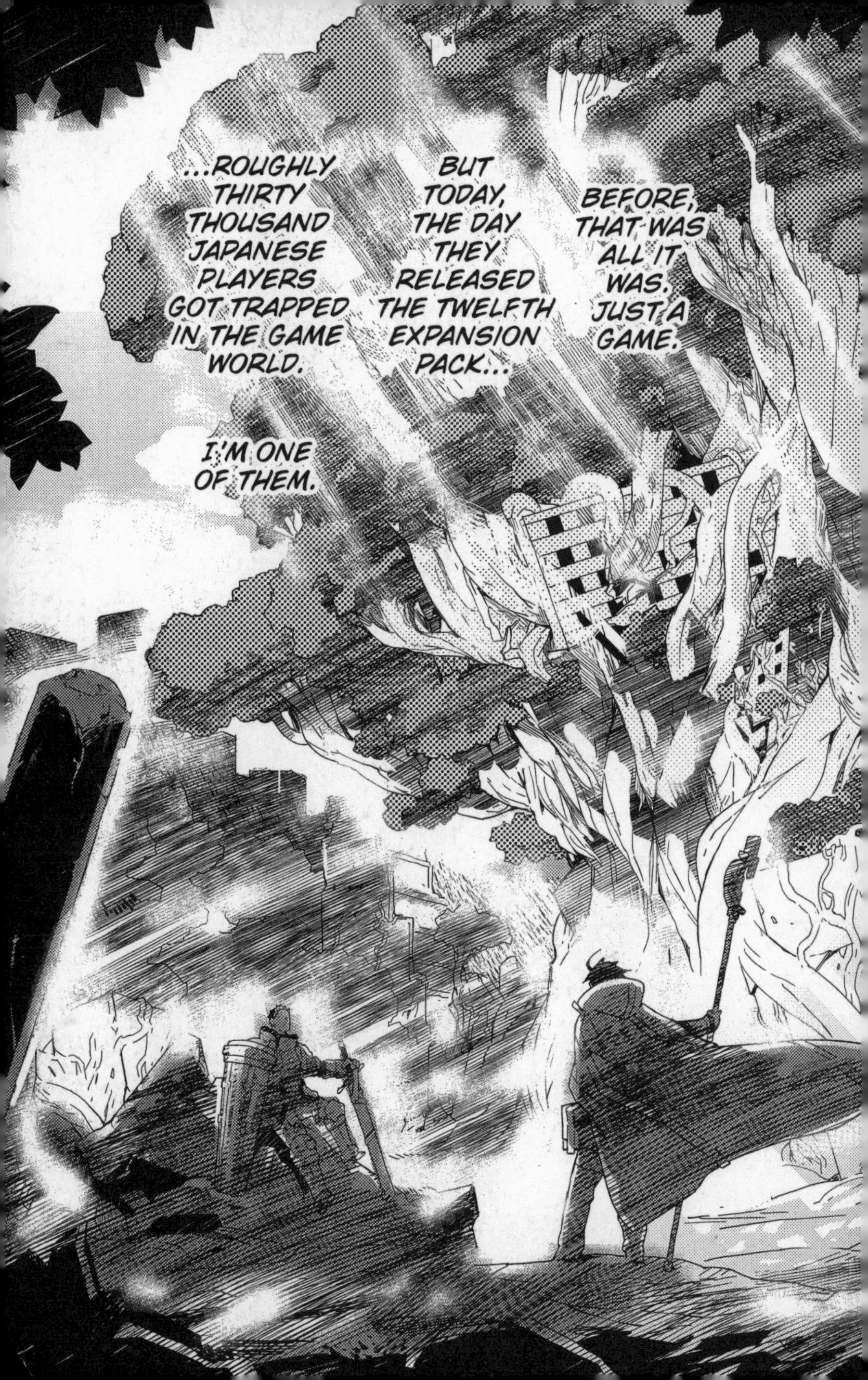
BEFORE, THAT WAS ALL IT WAS. JUST A GAME.
BUT TODAY, THE DAY THEY RELEASED THE TWELFTH EXPANSION PACK...
...ROUGHLY THIRTY THOUSAND JAPANESE PLAYERS GOT TRAPPED IN THE GAME WORLD.
I'M ONE OF THEM.

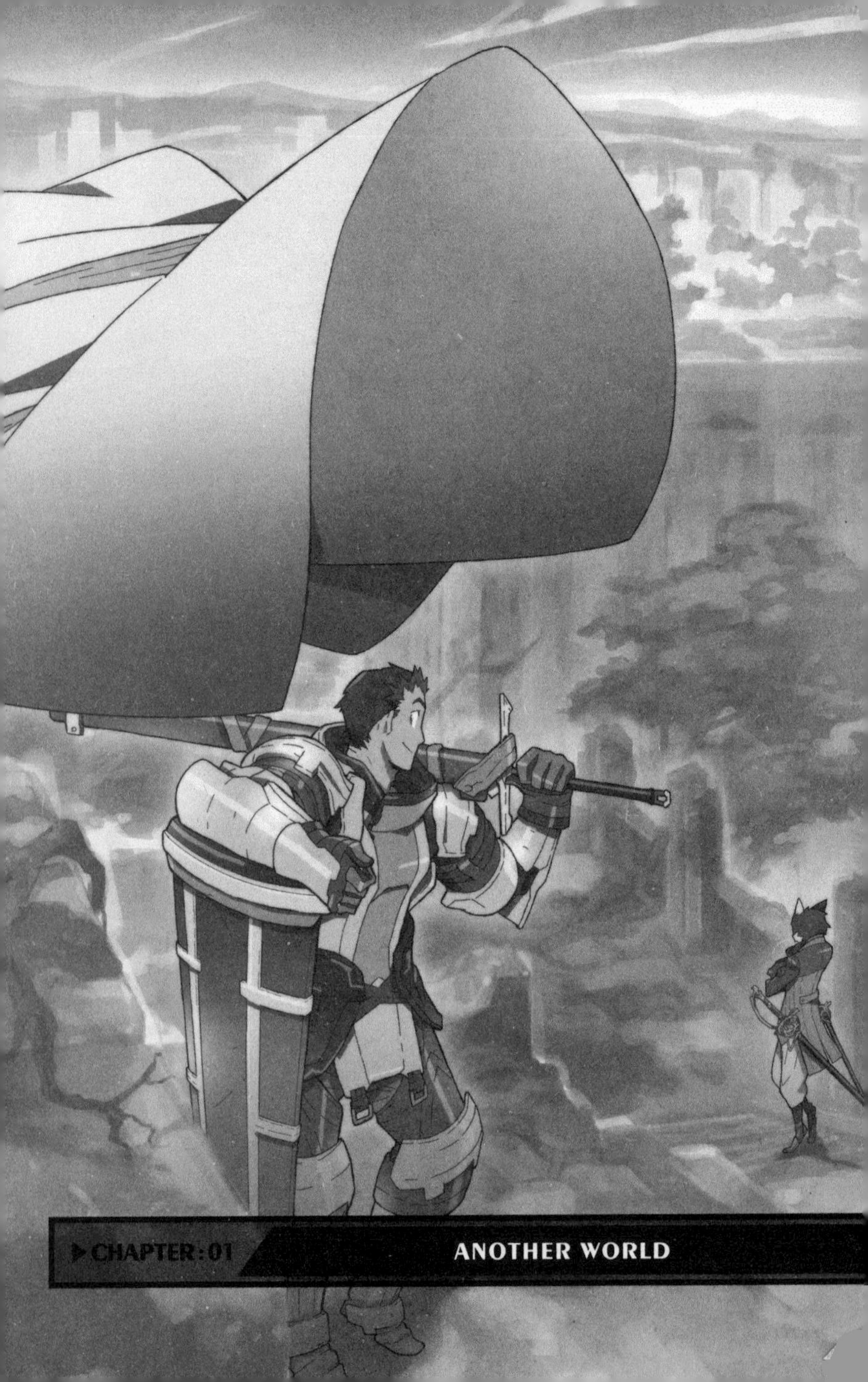
CHAPTER : 01
ANOTHER WORLD

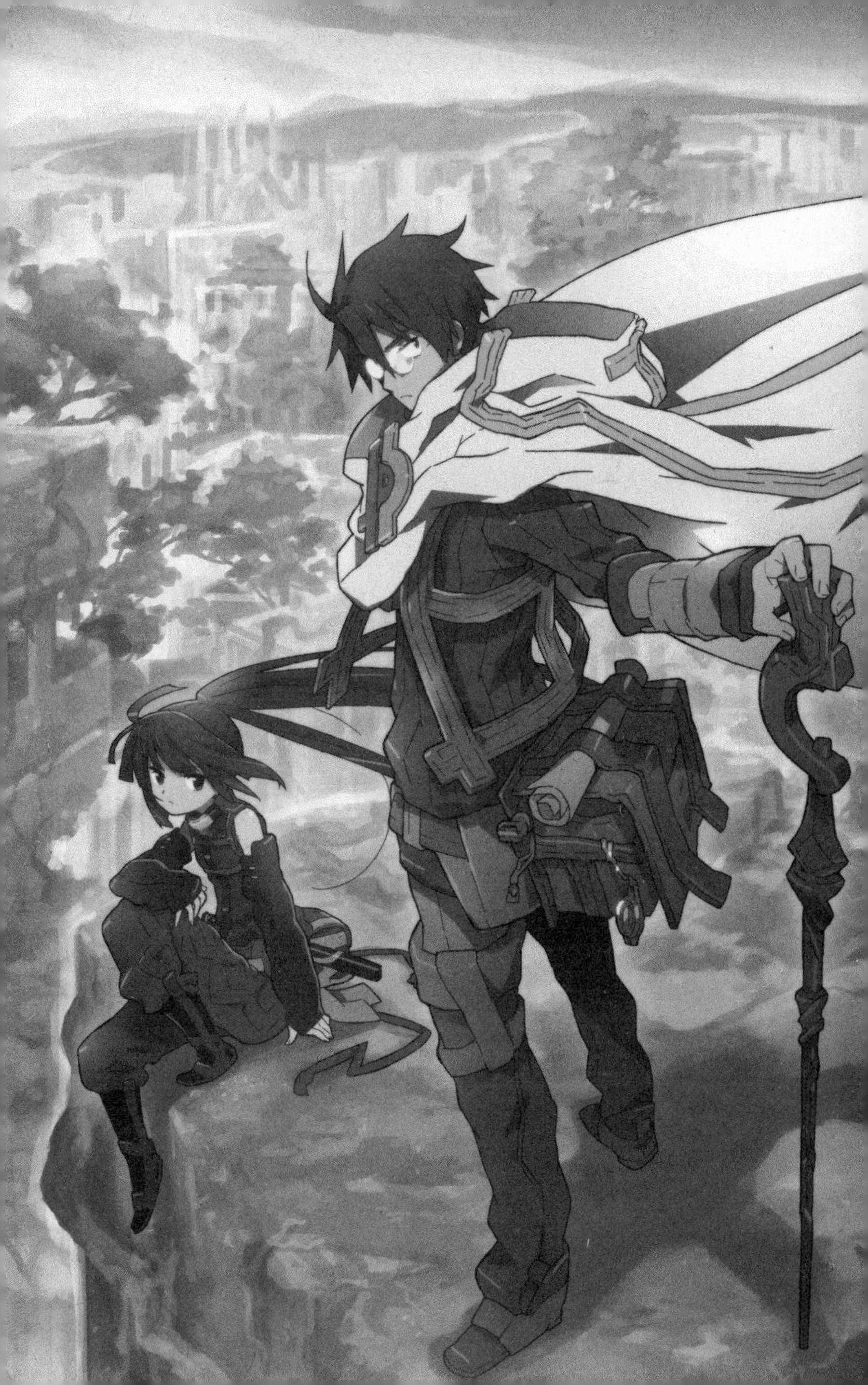

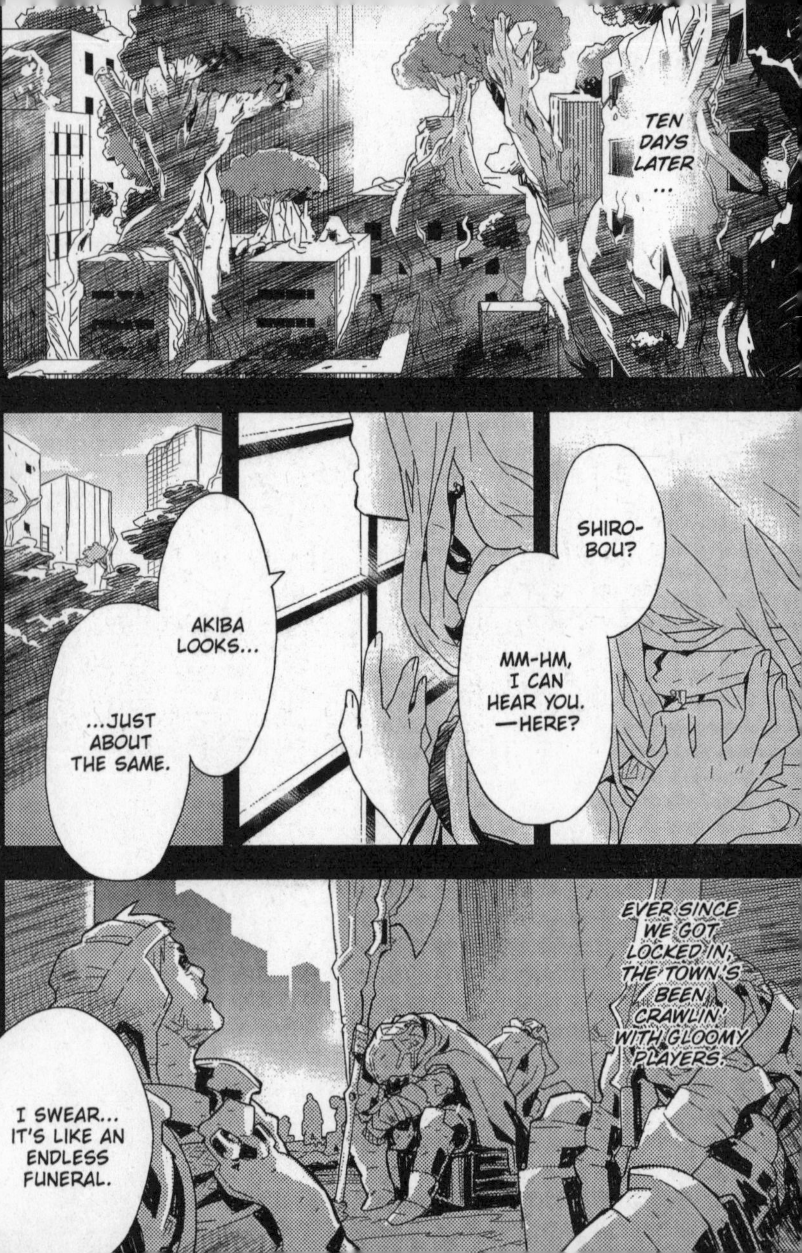
TEN DAYS LATER ...
SHIRO-BOU?
MM-HM, I CAN HEAR YOU. —HERE?
AKIBA LOOKS...
...JUST ABOUT THE SAME.
EVER SINCE WE GOT LOCKED IN, THE TOWN'S BEEN CRAWLIN' WITH GLOOMY PLAYERS.
I SWEAR... IT'S LIKE AN ENDLESS FUNERAL.

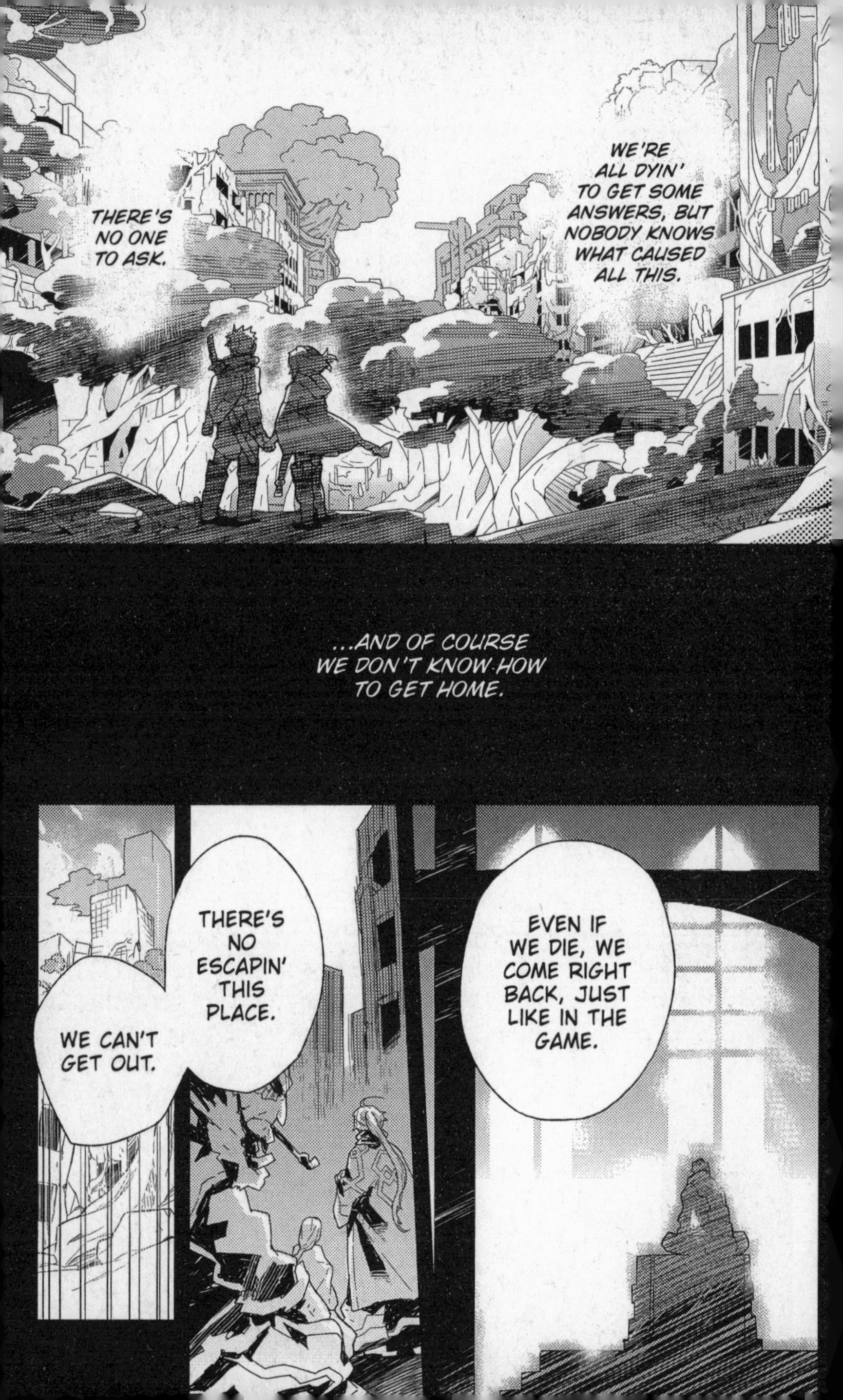
WE'RE ALL DYIN' TO GET SOME ANSWERS, BUT NOBODY KNOWS WHAT CAUSED ALL THIS.
THERE'S NO ONE TO ASK.
...AND OF COURSE WE DON'T KNOW HOW TO GET HOME.
EVEN IF WE DIE, WE COME RIGHT BACK, JUST LIKE IN THE GAME.
THERE'S NO ESCAPIN' THIS PLACE.
WE CAN'T GET OUT.

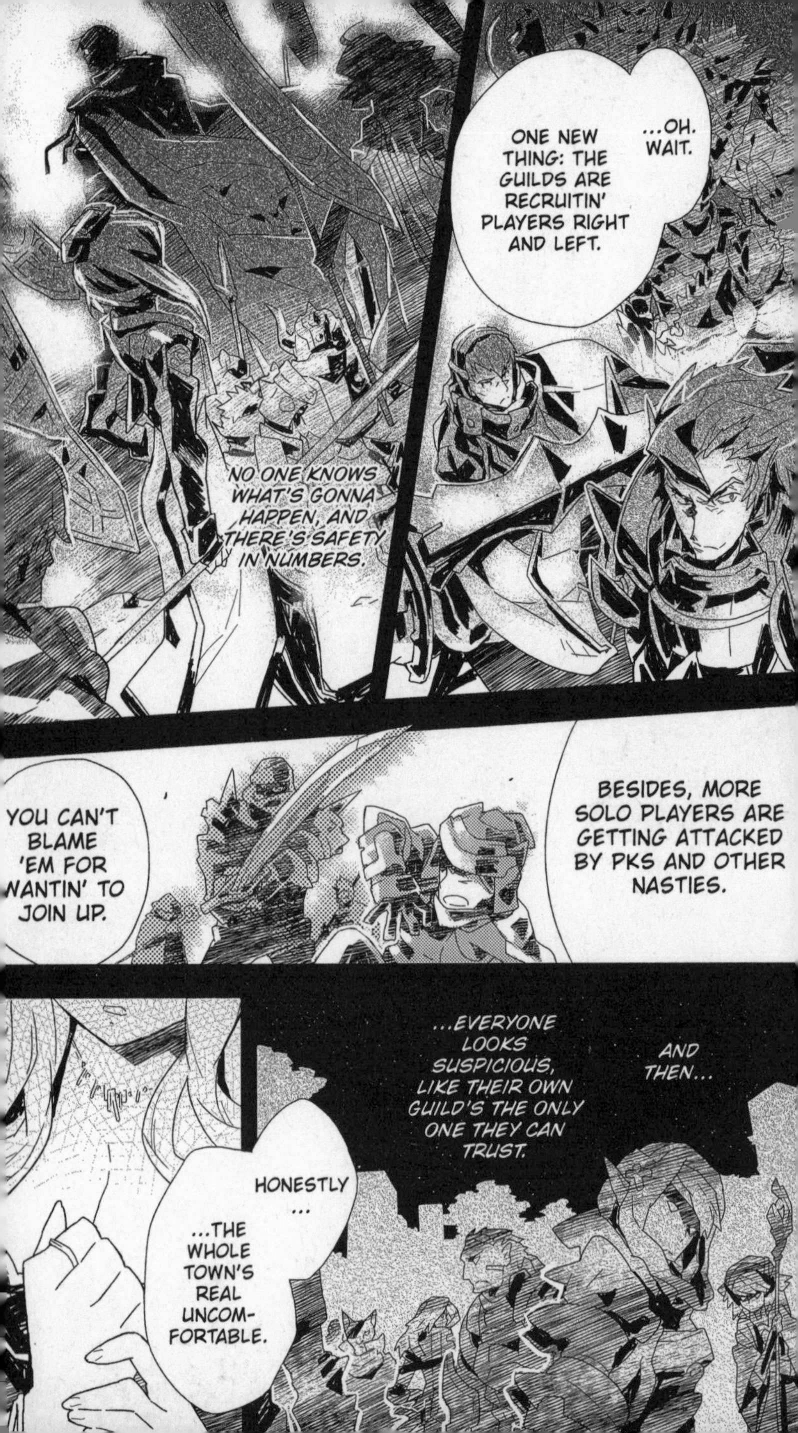
...OH. WAIT.
ONE NEW THING: THE GUILDS ARE RECRUITIN' PLAYERS RIGHT AND LEFT.
NO ONE KNOWS WHAT'S GONNA HAPPEN, AND THERE'S SAFETY IN NUMBERS.
BESIDES, MORE SOLO PLAYERS ARE GETTING ATTACKED BY PKS AND OTHER NASTIES.
YOU CAN'T BLAME 'EM FOR WANTIN' TO JOIN UP.
AND THEN...
...EVERYONE LOOKS SUSPICIOUS, LIKE THEIR OWN GUILD'S THE ONLY ONE THEY CAN TRUST.
HONESTLY ...
...THE WHOLE TOWN'S REAL UNCOMFORTABLE.

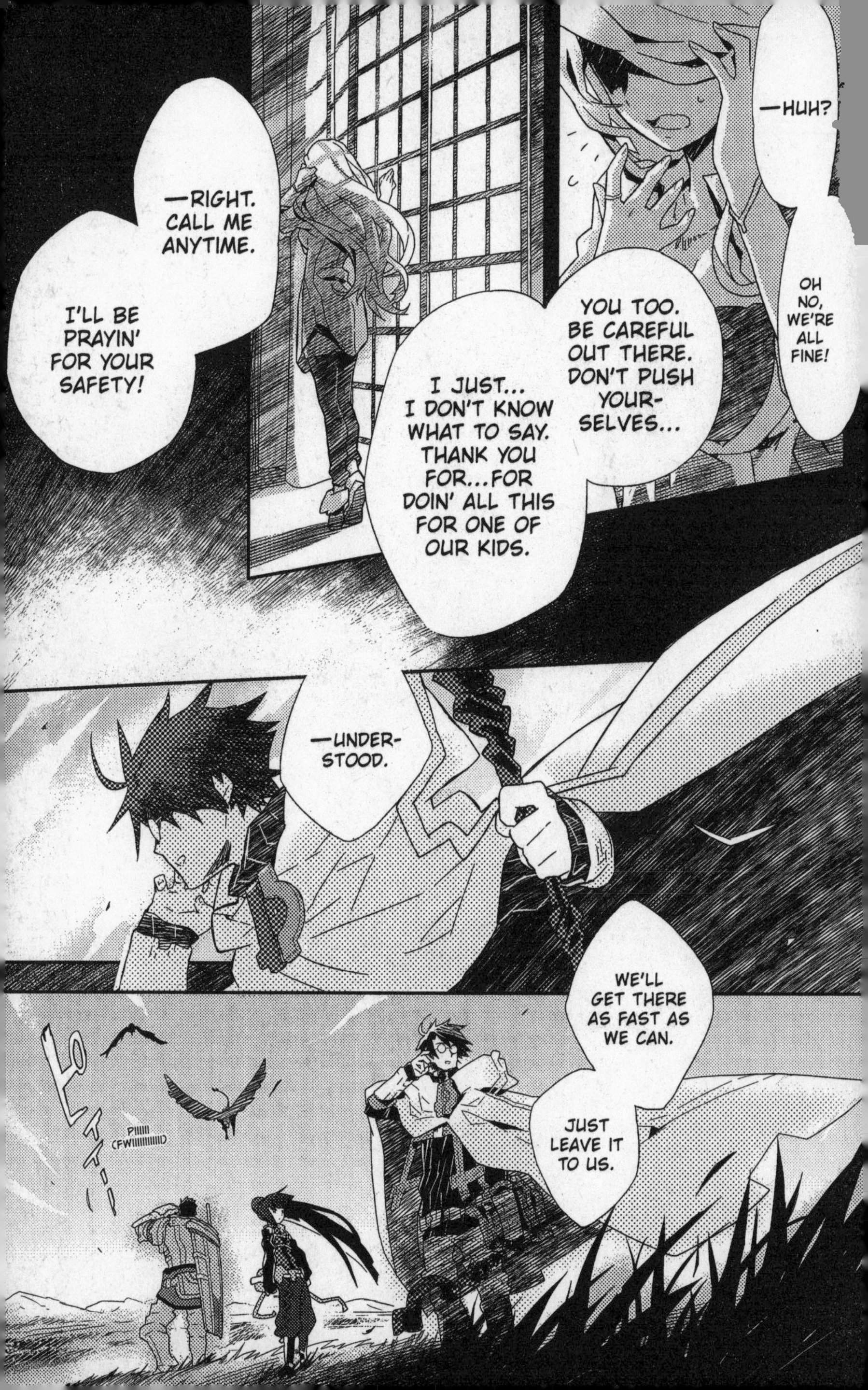
—HUH?
OH NO, WE'RE ALL FINE!
YOU TOO. BE CAREFUL OUT THERE. DON'T PUSH YOURSELVES...
I JUST... I DON'T KNOW WHAT TO SAY. THANK YOU FOR...FOR DOIN' ALL THIS FOR ONE OF OUR KIDS.
—RIGHT. CALL ME ANYTIME.
I'LL BE PRAYIN' FOR YOUR SAFETY!
—UNDER-STOOD.
WE'LL GET THERE AS FAST AS WE CAN.
JUST LEAVE IT TO US.
PIIIIII (FWIIIIIIIIIIID)

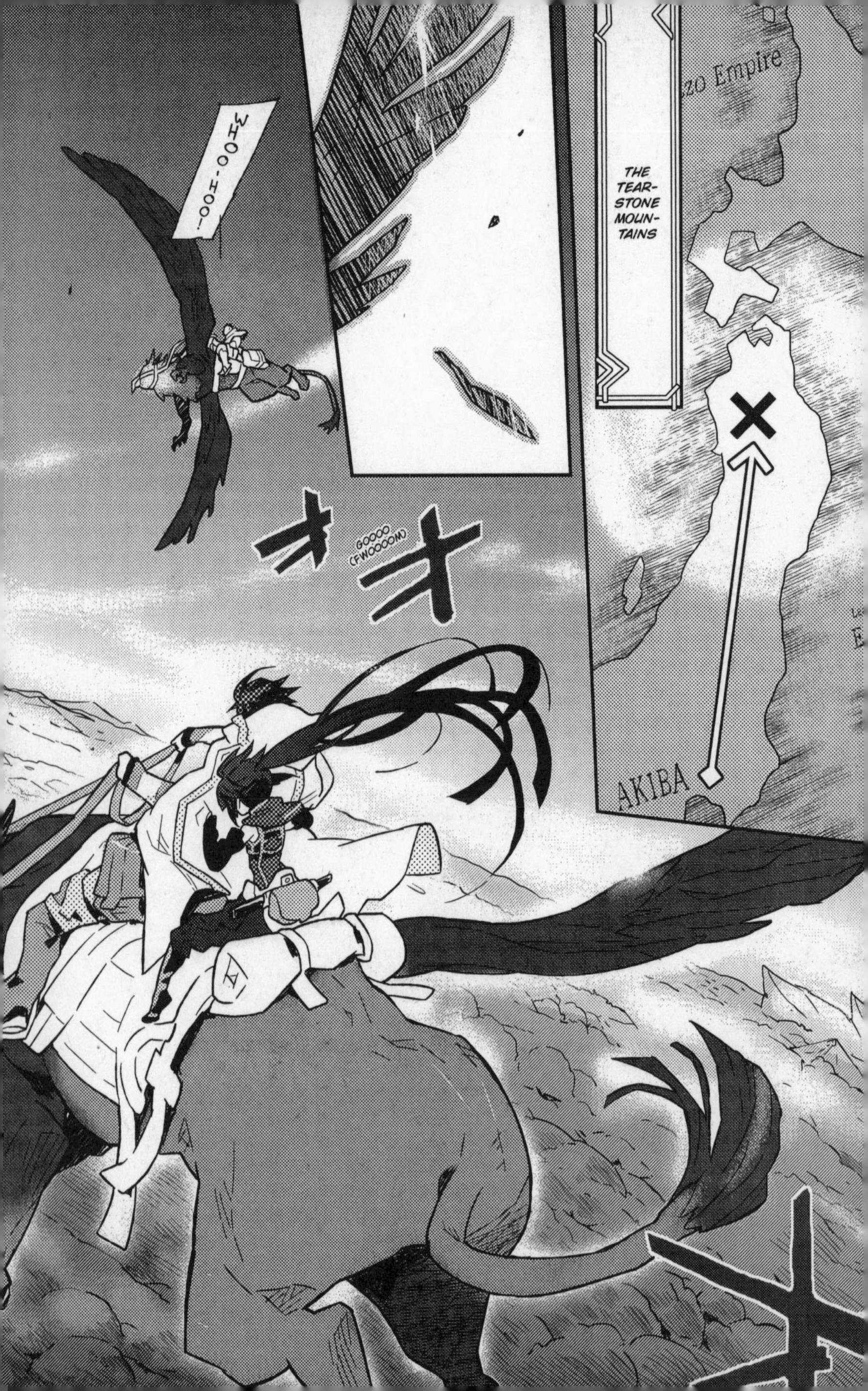
THE TEAR-STONE MOUNTAINS
Empire
AKIBA
WHOO-HOO!
GOOOO (FWOOOOM)

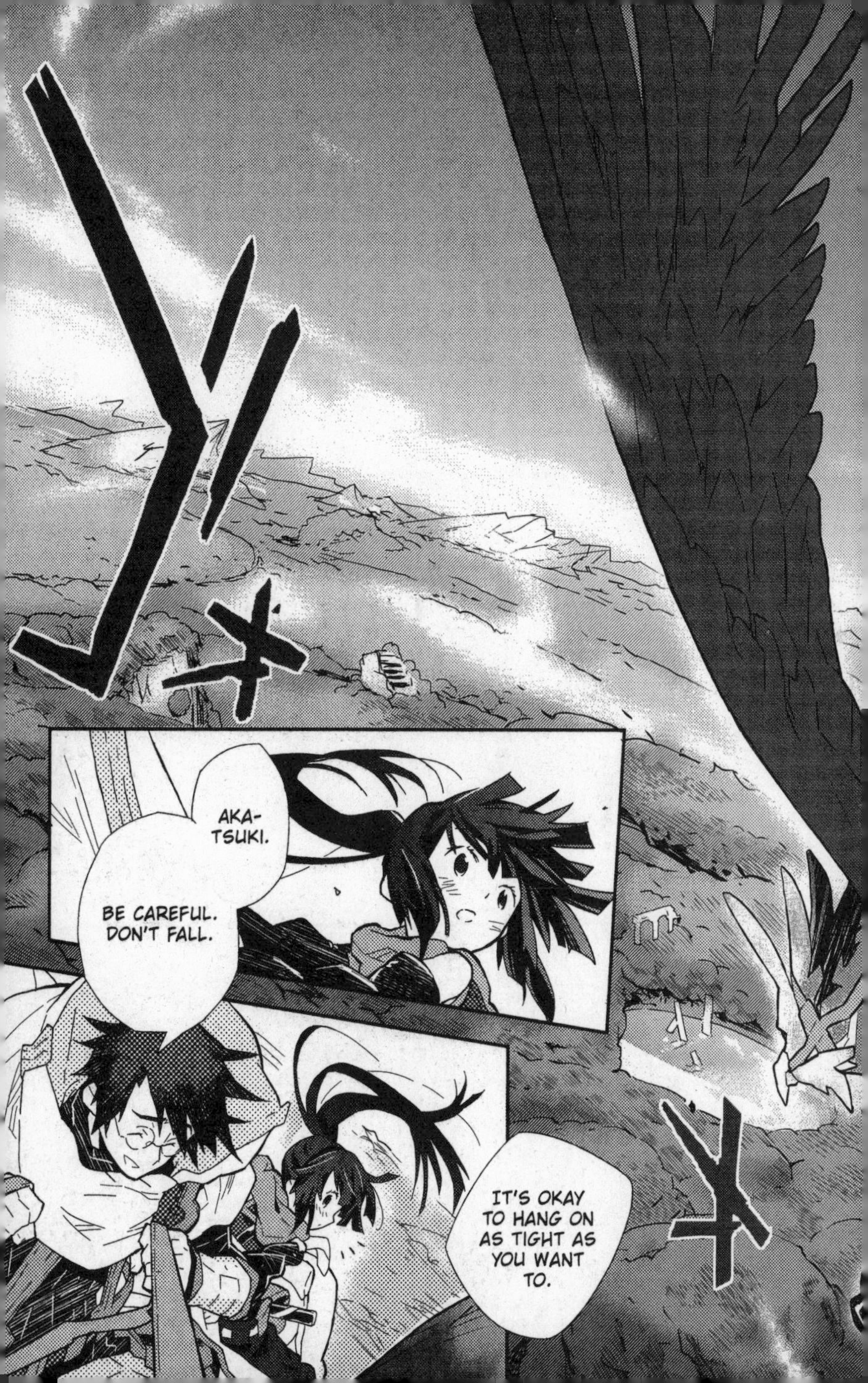
AKA-
TSUKI.
BE CAREFUL.
DON'T FALL.
IT'S OKAY
TO HANG ON
AS TIGHT AS
YOU WANT
TO.

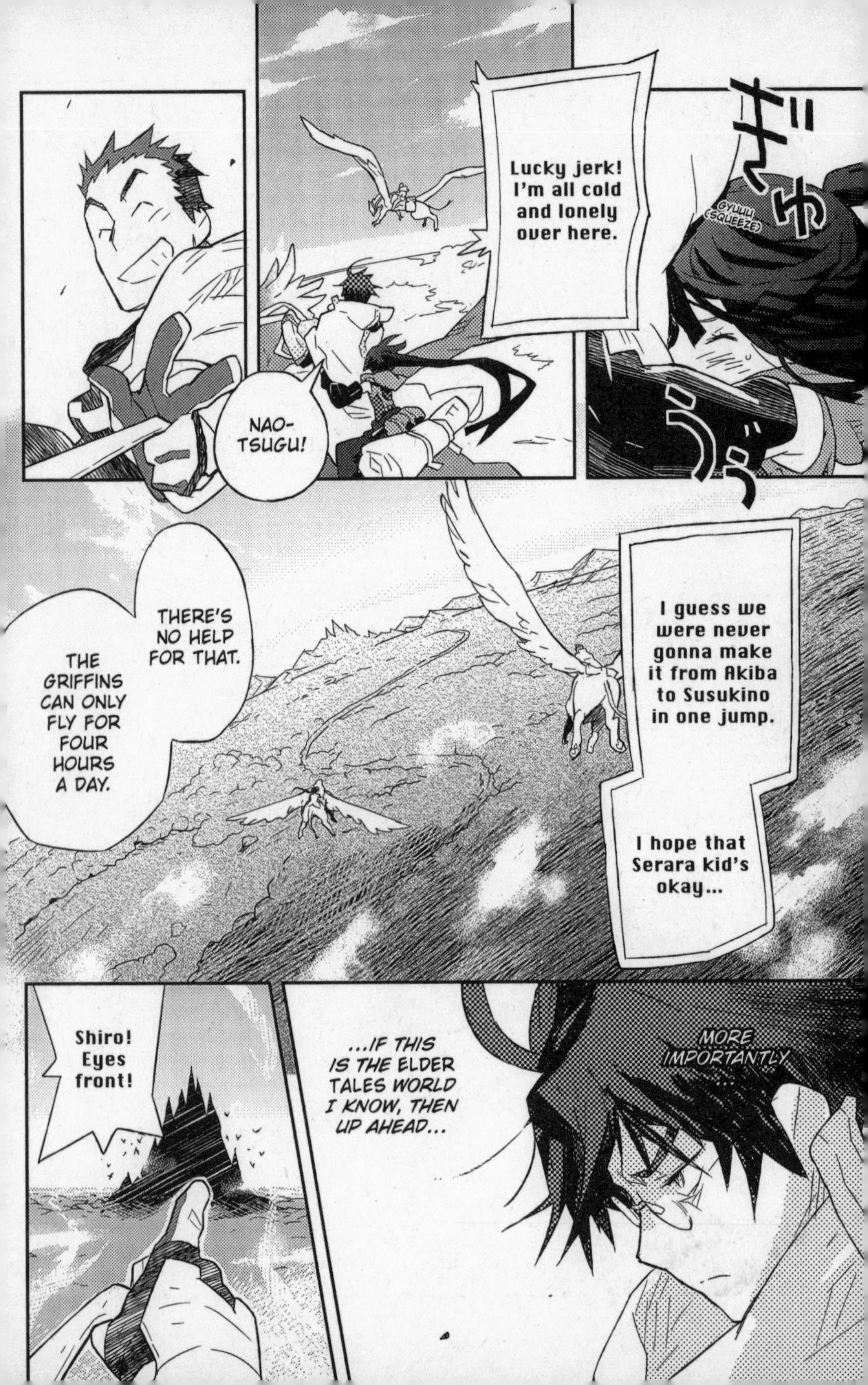
ぎゅ
GYUUU (SQUEEZE)
うぅ
Lucky jerk! I'm all cold and lonely over here.
NAO-TSUGU!
I guess we were never gonna make it from Akiba to Susukino in one jump.
I hope that Serara kid's okay...
THERE'S NO HELP FOR THAT.
THE GRIFFINS CAN ONLY FLY FOR FOUR HOURS A DAY.
MORE IMPORTANTLY
...IF THIS IS THE ELDER TALES WORLD I KNOW, THEN UP AHEAD...
Shiro! Eyes front!

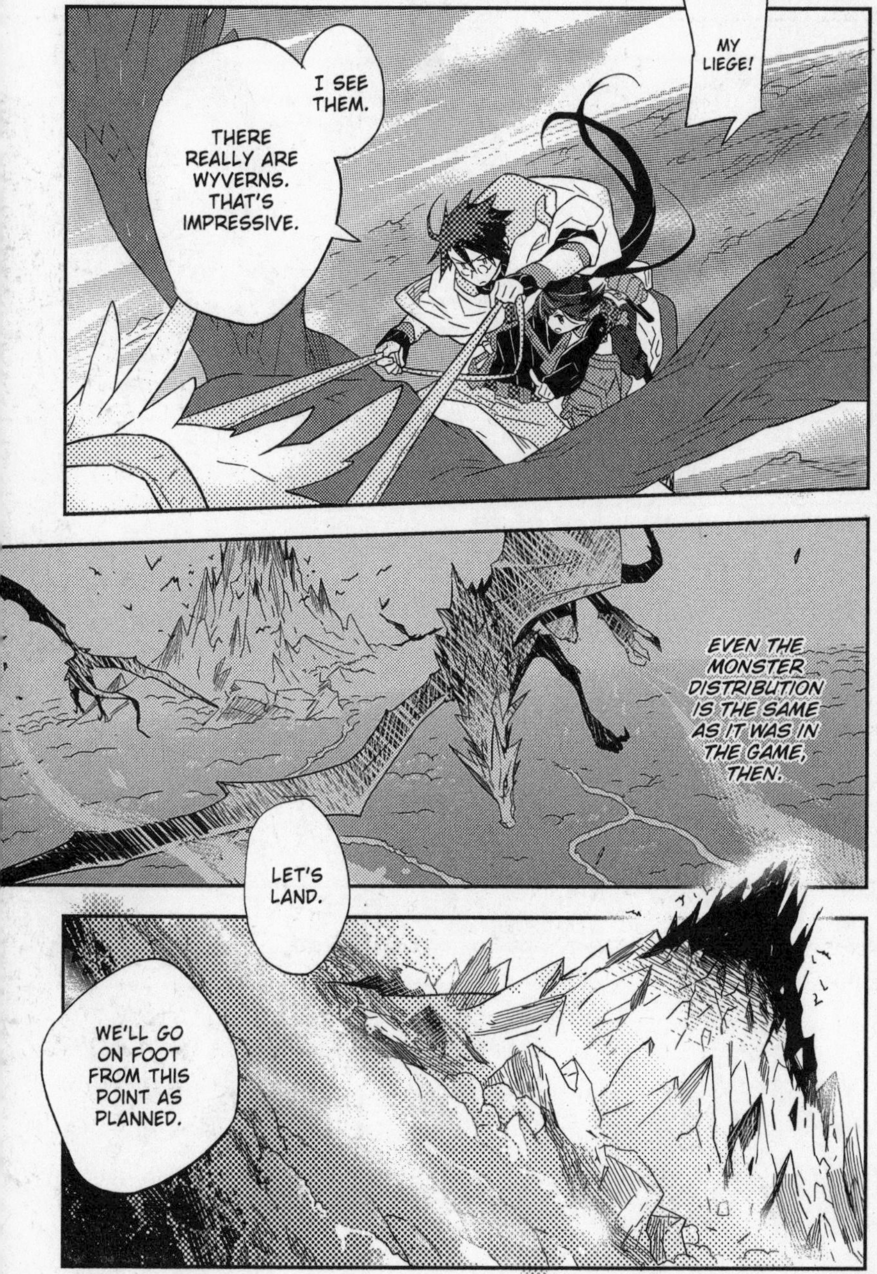
MY LIEGE!
I SEE THEM.
THERE REALLY ARE WYVERNS. THAT'S IMPRESSIVE.
EVEN THE MONSTER DISTRIBUTION IS THE SAME AS IT WAS IN THE GAME, THEN.
LET'S LAND.
WE'LL GO ON FOOT FROM THIS POINT AS PLANNED.

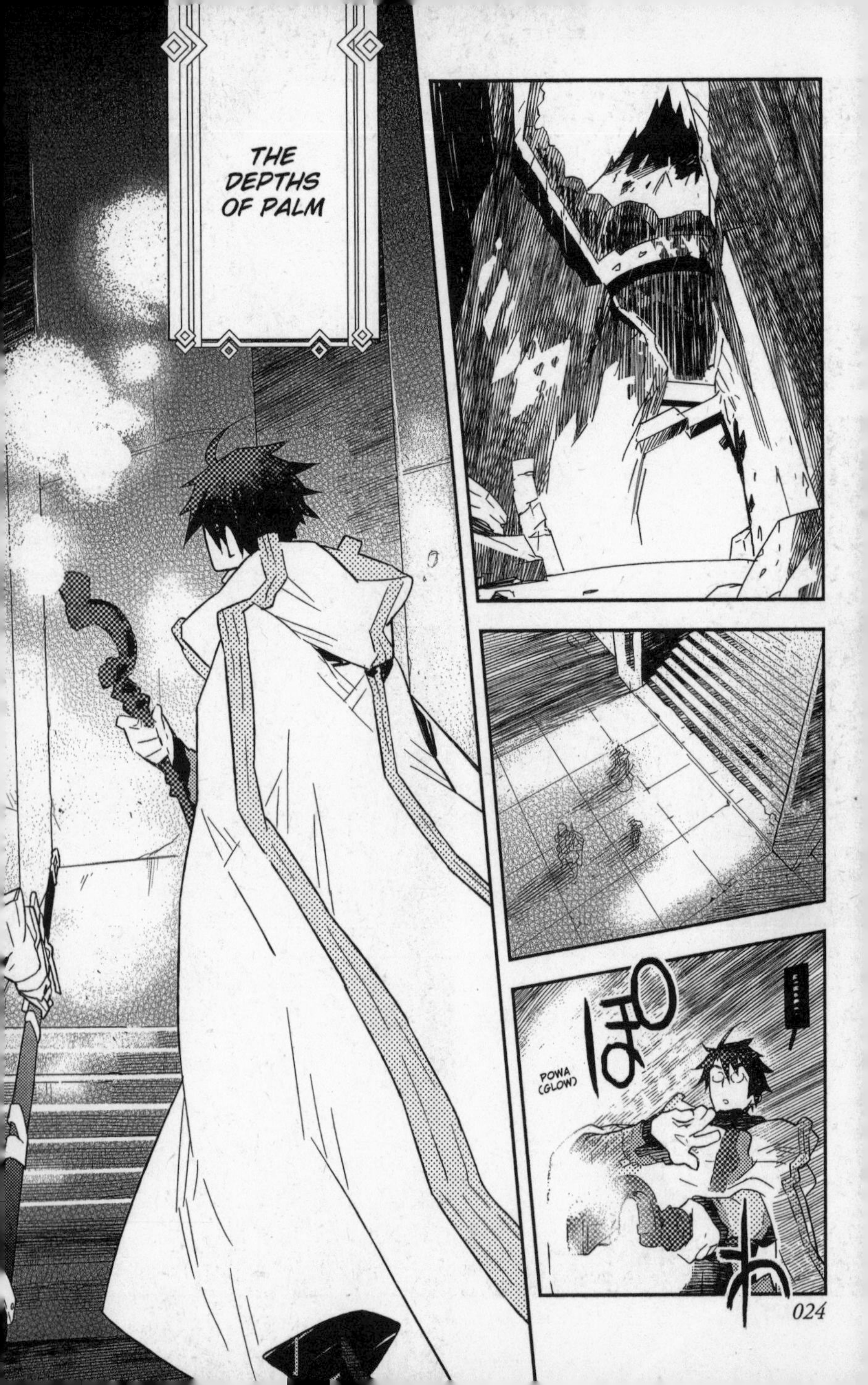
POWA (GLOW)
THE DEPTHS OF PALM

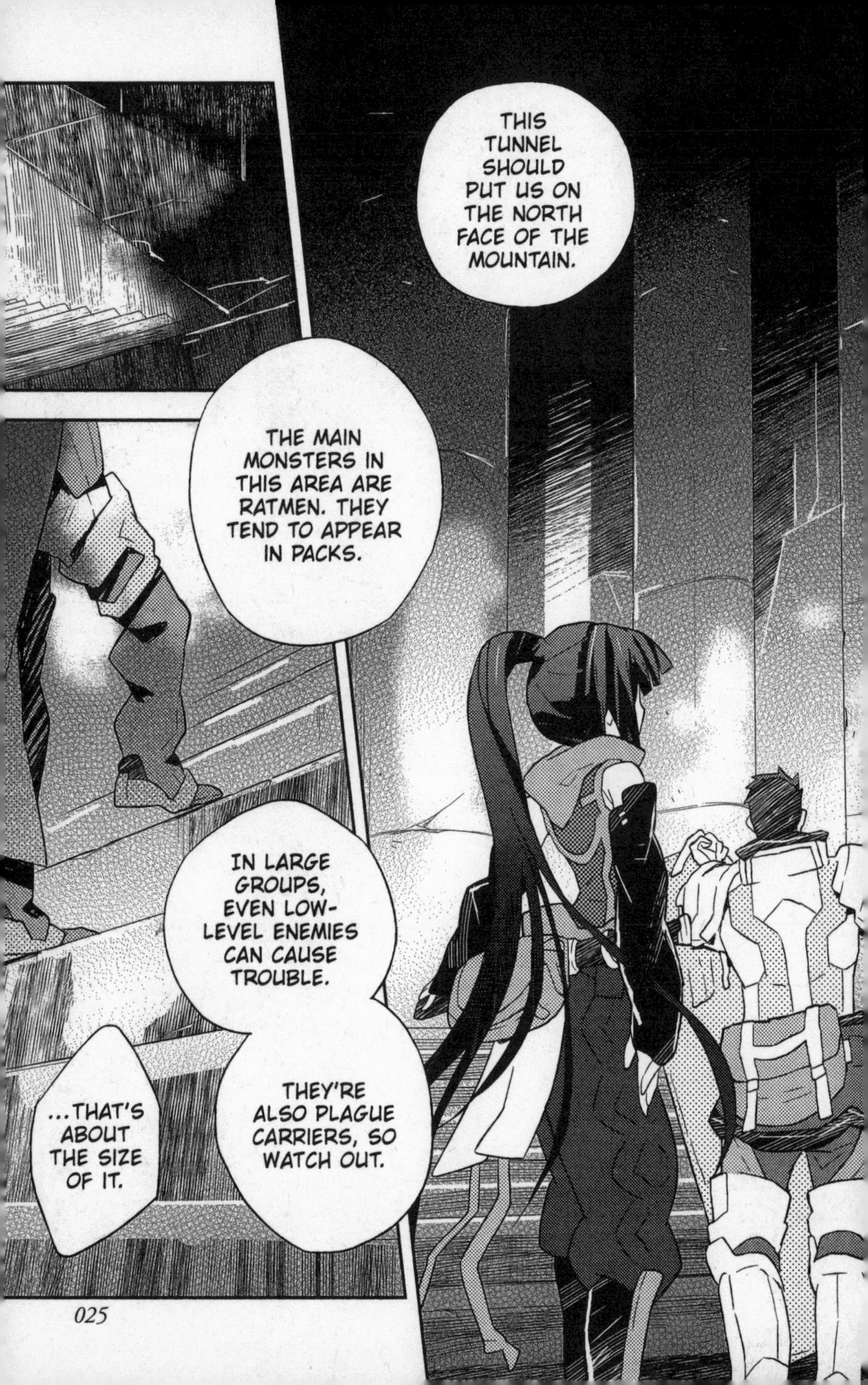
THIS TUNNEL SHOULD PUT US ON THE NORTH FACE OF THE MOUNTAIN.
THE MAIN MONSTERS IN THIS AREA ARE RATMEN. THEY TEND TO APPEAR IN PACKS.
IN LARGE GROUPS, EVEN LOW-LEVEL ENEMIES CAN CAUSE TROUBLE.
THEY'RE ALSO PLAGUE CARRIERS, SO WATCH OUT.
...THAT'S ABOUT THE SIZE OF IT.

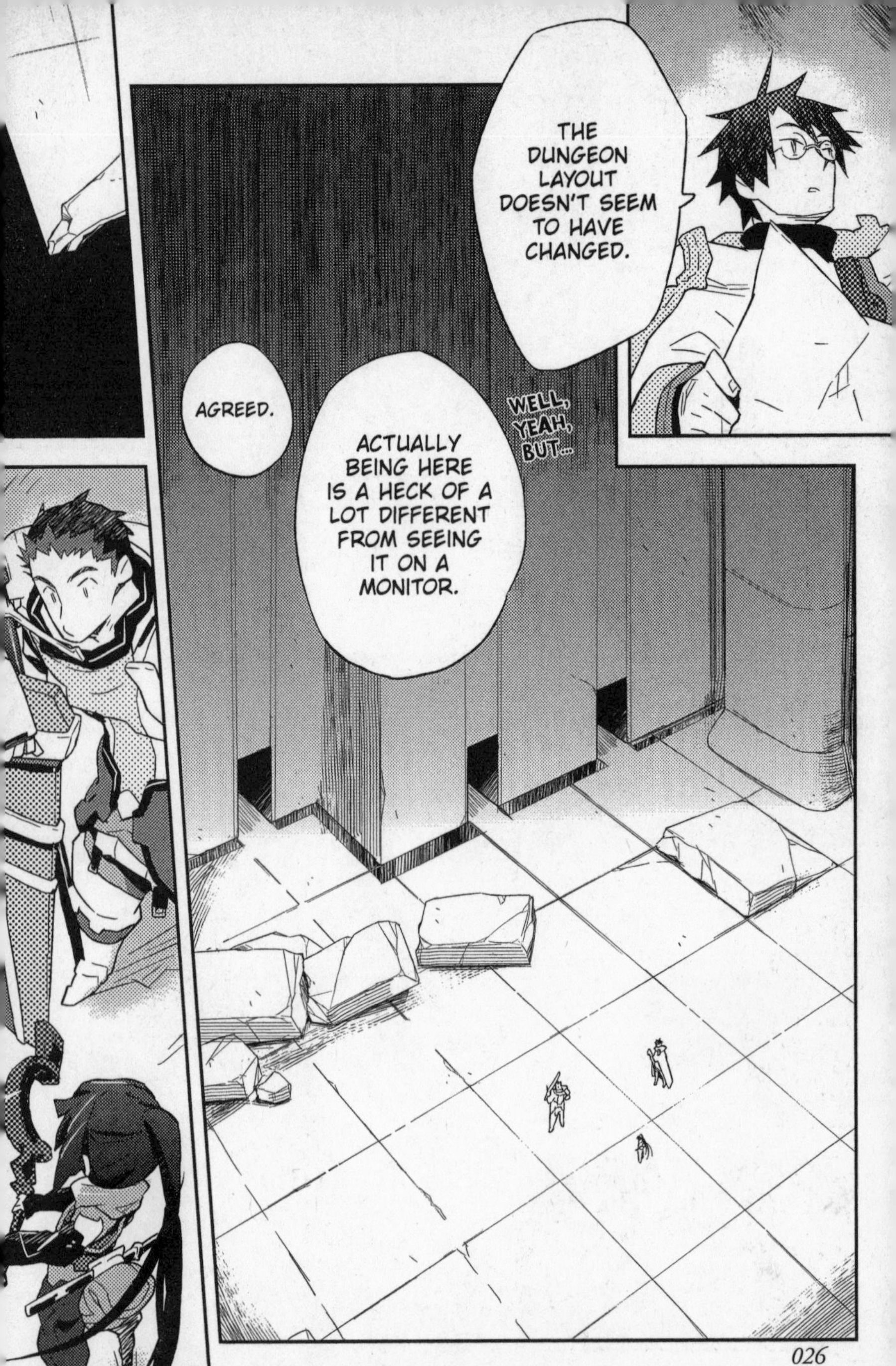
THE DUNGEON LAYOUT DOESN'T SEEM TO HAVE CHANGED.
WELL, YEAH, BUT...
ACTUALLY BEING HERE IS A HECK OF A LOT DIFFERENT FROM SEEING IT ON A MONITOR.
AGREED.

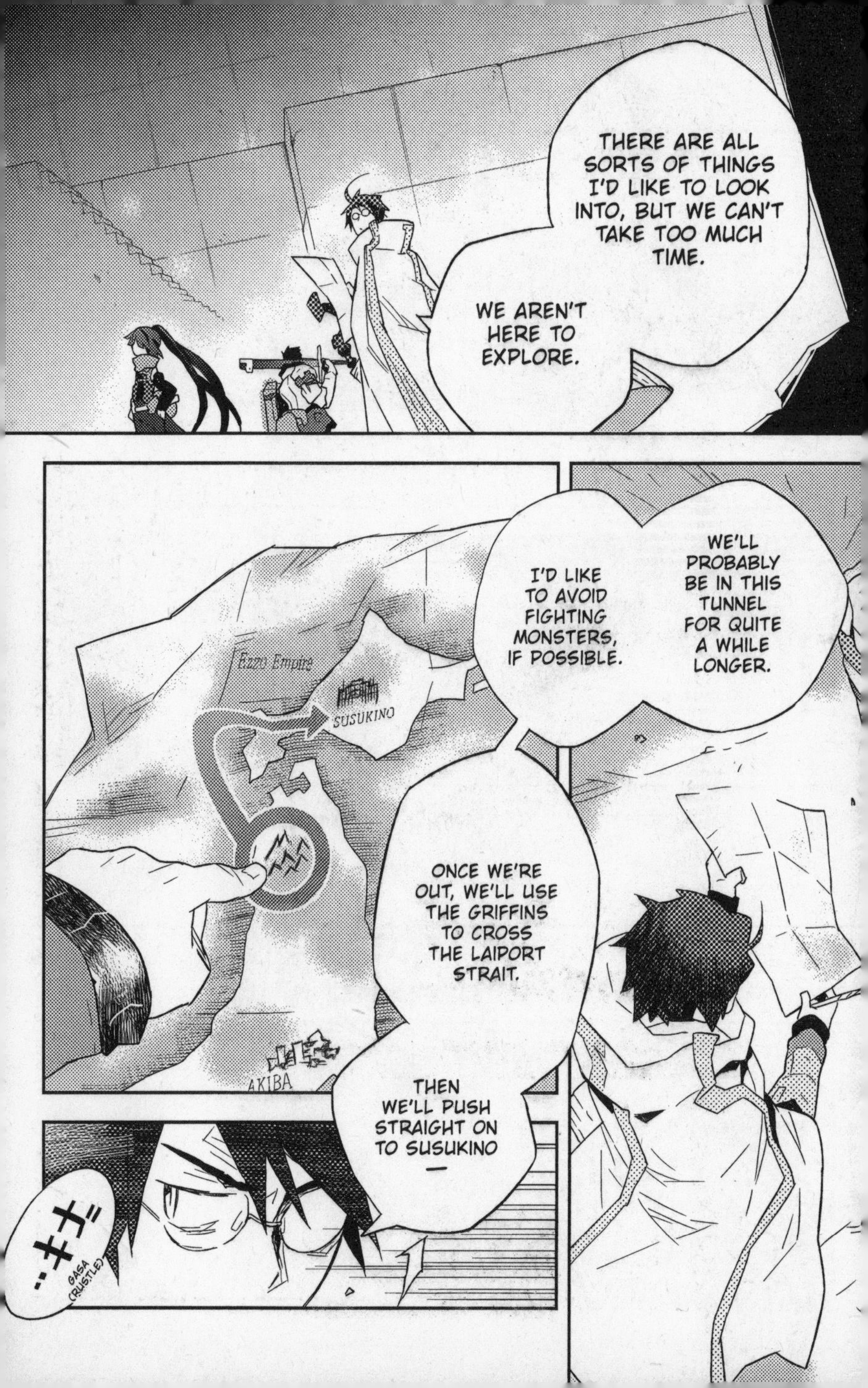
THERE ARE ALL SORTS OF THINGS I'D LIKE TO LOOK INTO, BUT WE CAN'T TAKE TOO MUCH TIME.
WE AREN'T HERE TO EXPLORE.
WE'LL PROBABLY BE IN THIS TUNNEL FOR QUITE A WHILE LONGER.
I'D LIKE TO AVOID FIGHTING MONSTERS, IF POSSIBLE.
Ezzo Empire
SUSUKINO
AKIBA
ONCE WE'RE OUT, WE'LL USE THE GRIFFINS TO CROSS THE LAIPORT STRAIT.
THEN WE'LL PUSH STRAIGHT ON TO SUSUKINO —
GASA (RUSTLE)

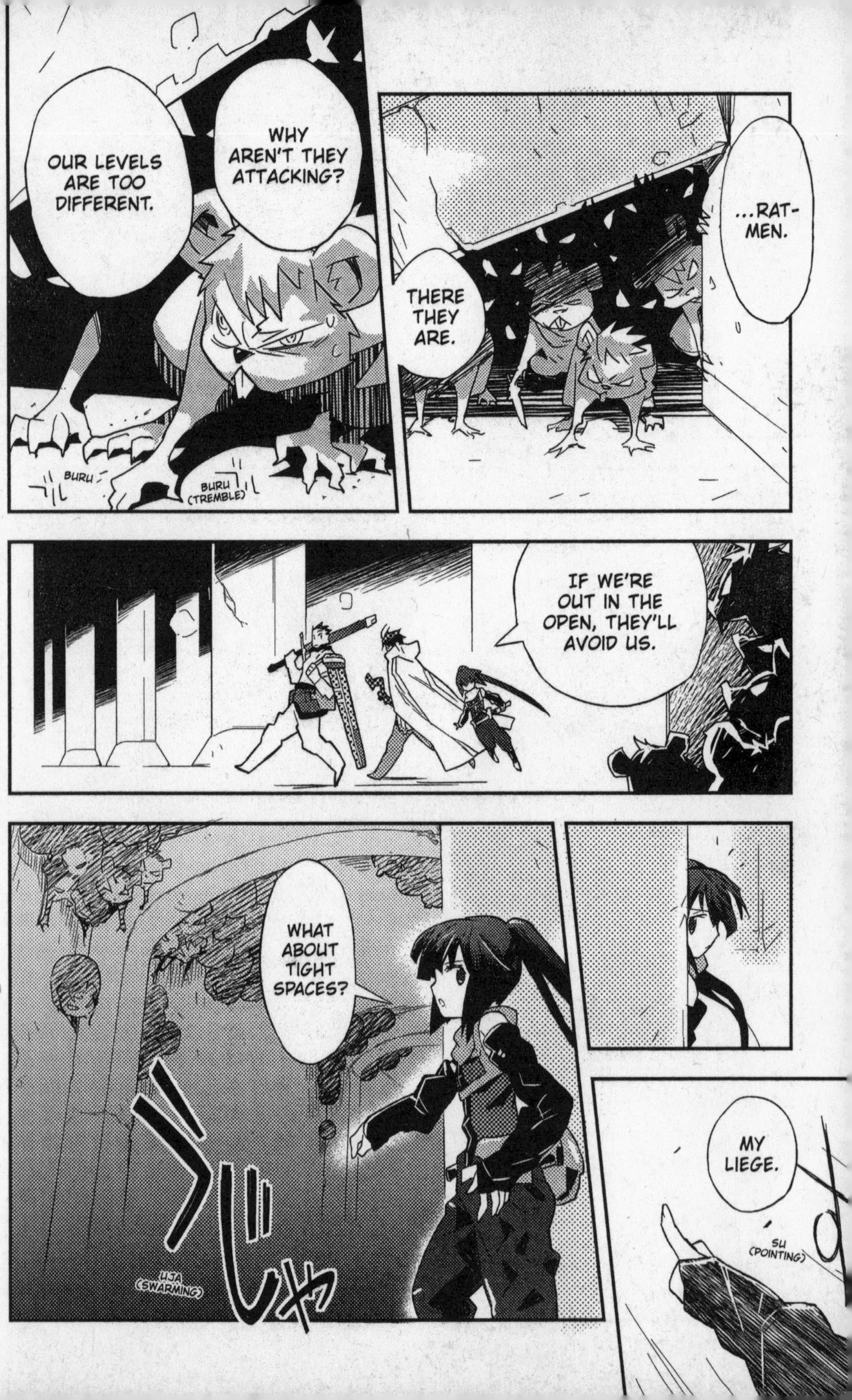
...RAT-MEN.
THERE THEY ARE.
WHY AREN'T THEY ATTACKING?
OUR LEVELS ARE TOO DIFFERENT.
BURU
BURU (TREMBLE)
IF WE'RE OUT IN THE OPEN, THEY'LL AVOID US.
MY LIEGE.
SU (POINTING)
WHAT ABOUT TIGHT SPACES?
うじゃ
UJA (SWARMING)

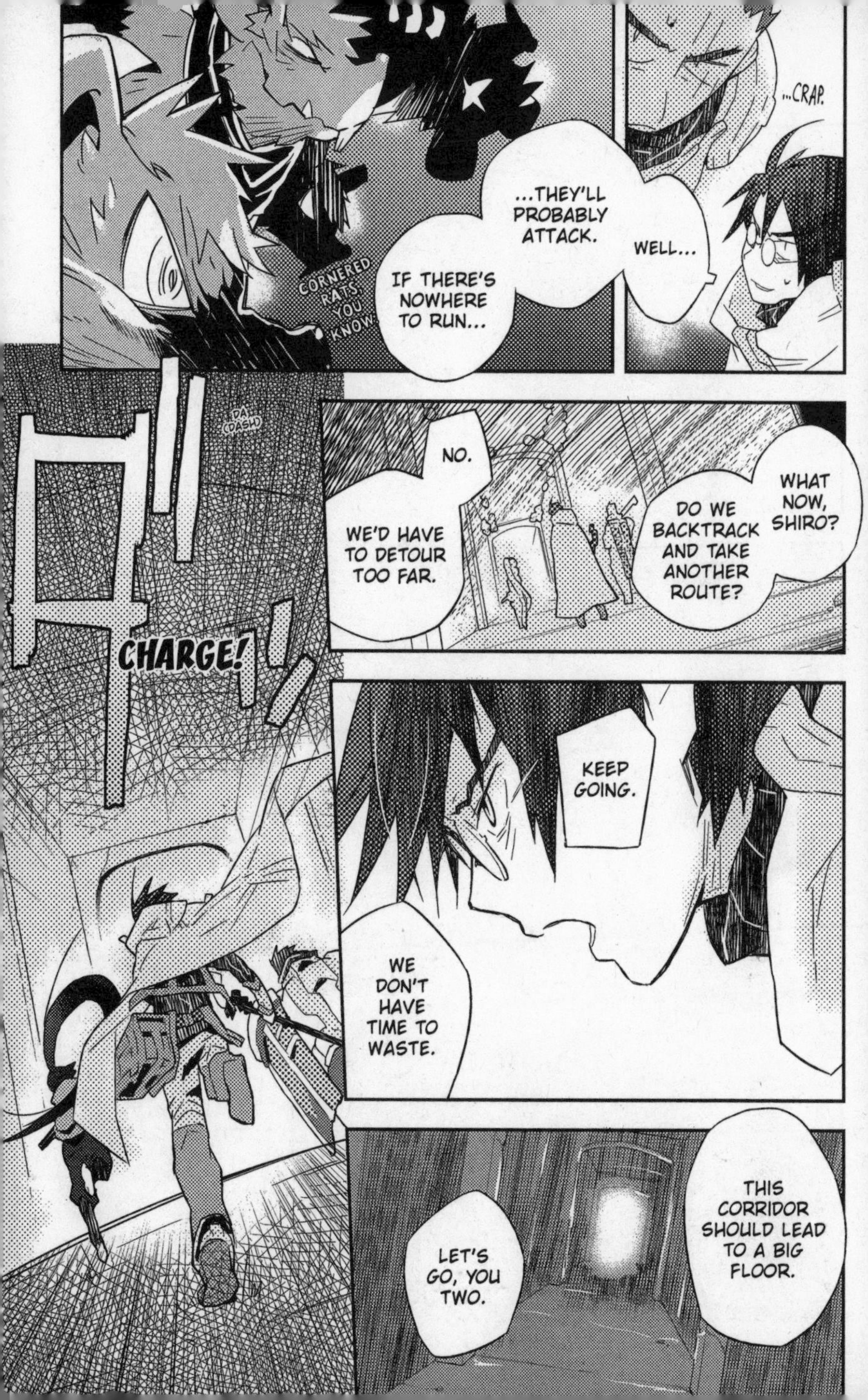
...CRAP.
WELL...
IF THERE'S NOWHERE TO RUN...
...THEY'LL PROBABLY ATTACK.
CORNERED RATS, YOU KNOW
WHAT NOW, SHIRO?
DO WE BACKTRACK AND TAKE ANOTHER ROUTE?
NO.
WE'D HAVE TO DETOUR TOO FAR.
KEEP GOING.
WE DON'T HAVE TIME TO WASTE.
THIS CORRIDOR SHOULD LEAD TO A BIG FLOOR.
LET'S GO, YOU TWO.
DA (DASH)
CHARGE!

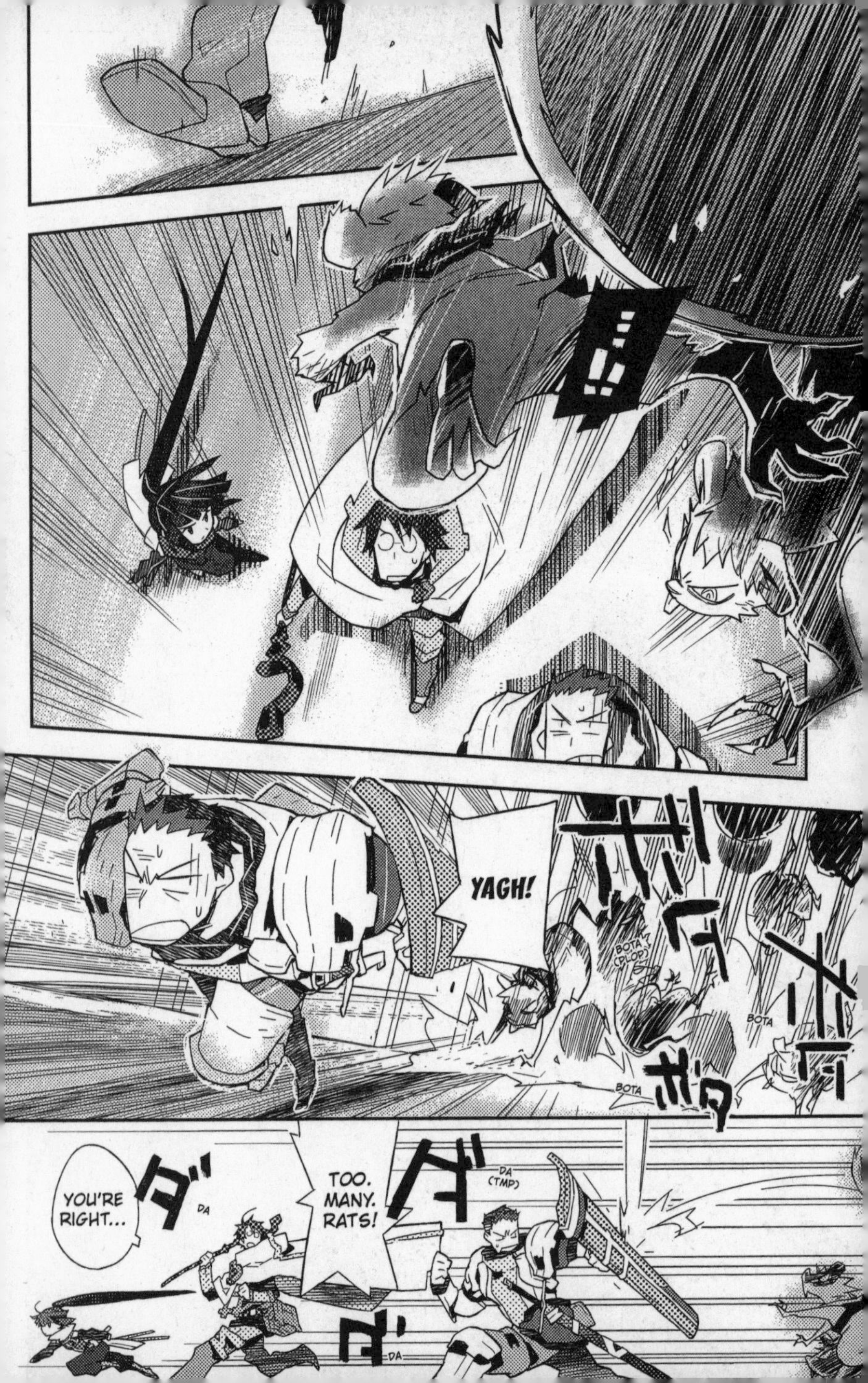
...!!
BOTA (PLOP)
YAGH!
BOTA
BOTA
DA (TMP)
TOO. MANY. RATS!
DA
YOU'RE RIGHT...
DA

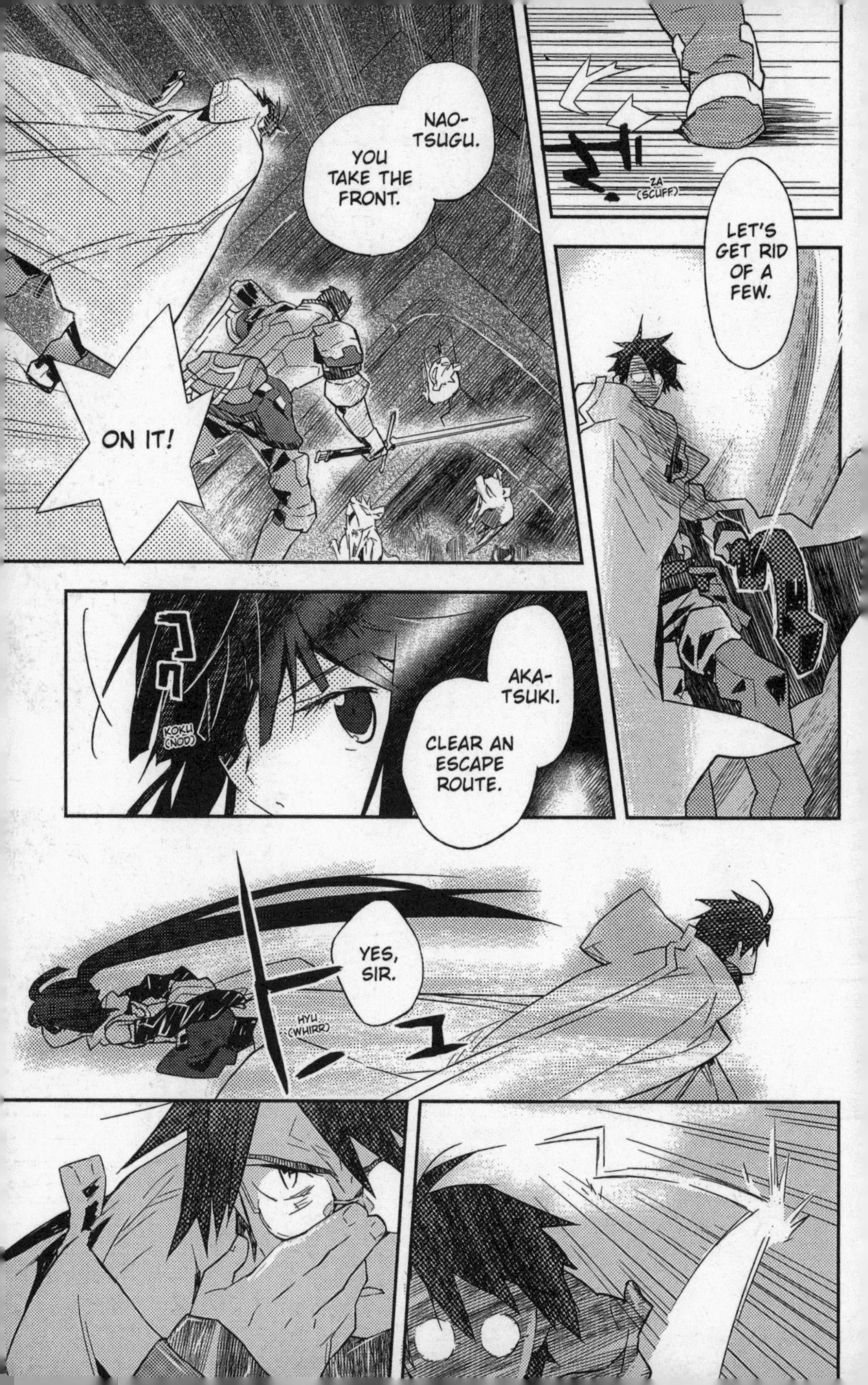
ZA (SCUFF)
LET'S GET RID OF A FEW.
NAO-TSUGU.
YOU TAKE THE FRONT.
ON IT!
AKA-TSUKI.
CLEAR AN ESCAPE ROUTE.
KOKU (NOD)
YES, SIR.
HYU (WHIRR)

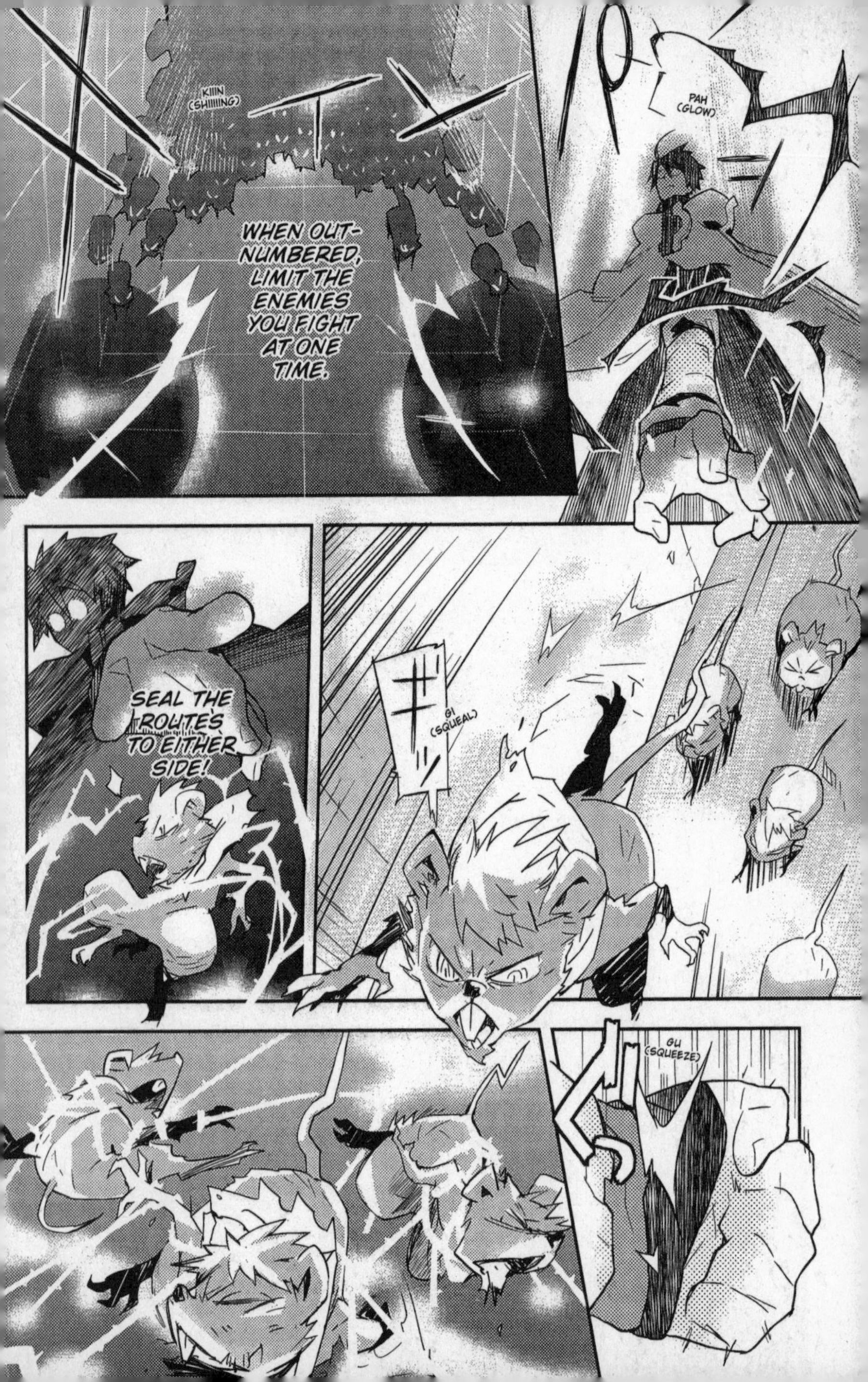
PAH (GLOW)
KIIN (SHIIIING)
WHEN OUT-NUMBERED, LIMIT THE ENEMIES YOU FIGHT AT ONE TIME.
GI (SQUEAL)
SEAL THE ROUTES TO EITHER SIDE!
GU (SQUEEZE)

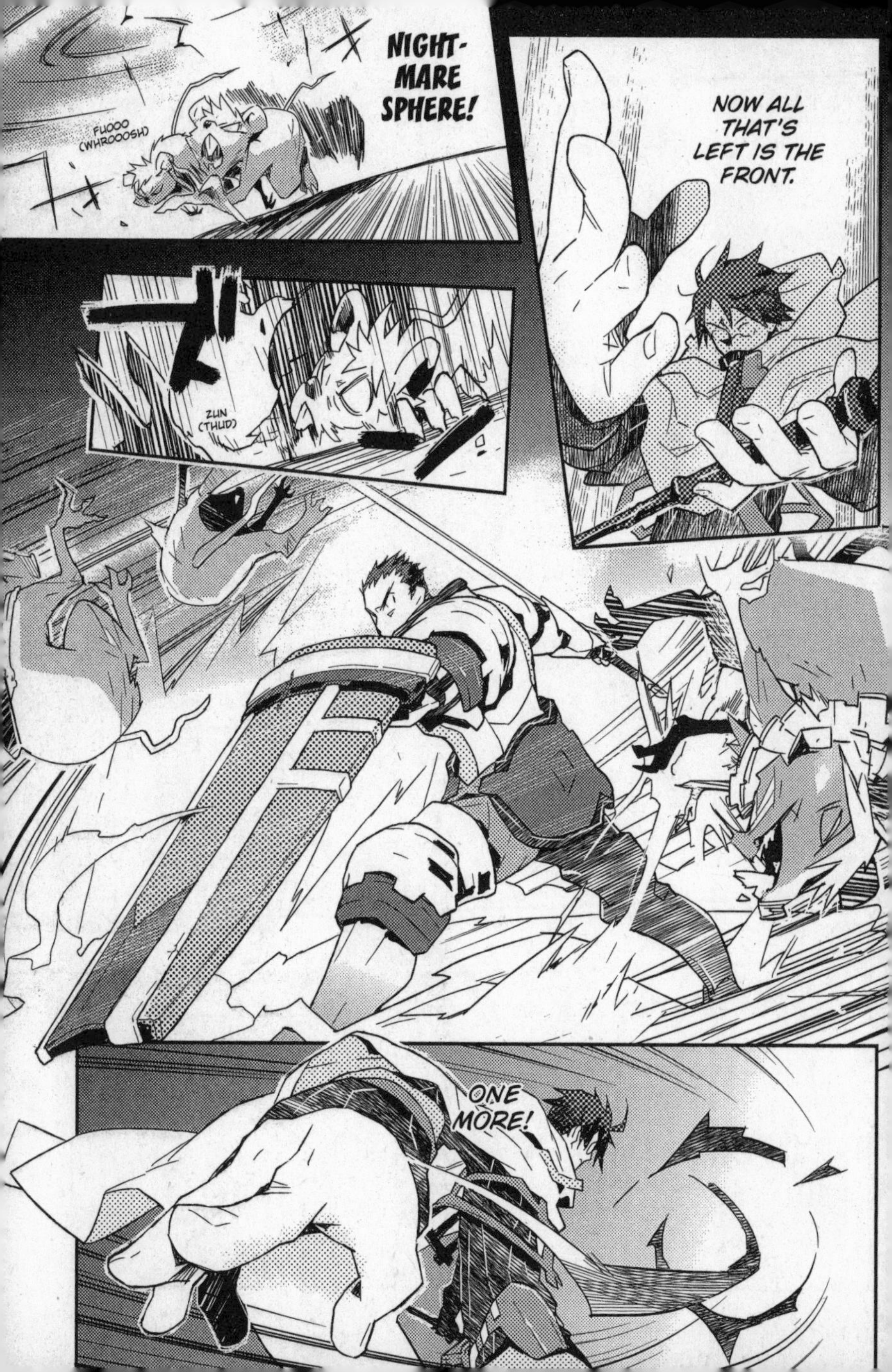
NOW ALL THAT'S LEFT IS THE FRONT.
NIGHT-MARE SPHERE!
FUOOO (WHROOOSH)
ZUN (THUD)
ONE MORE!

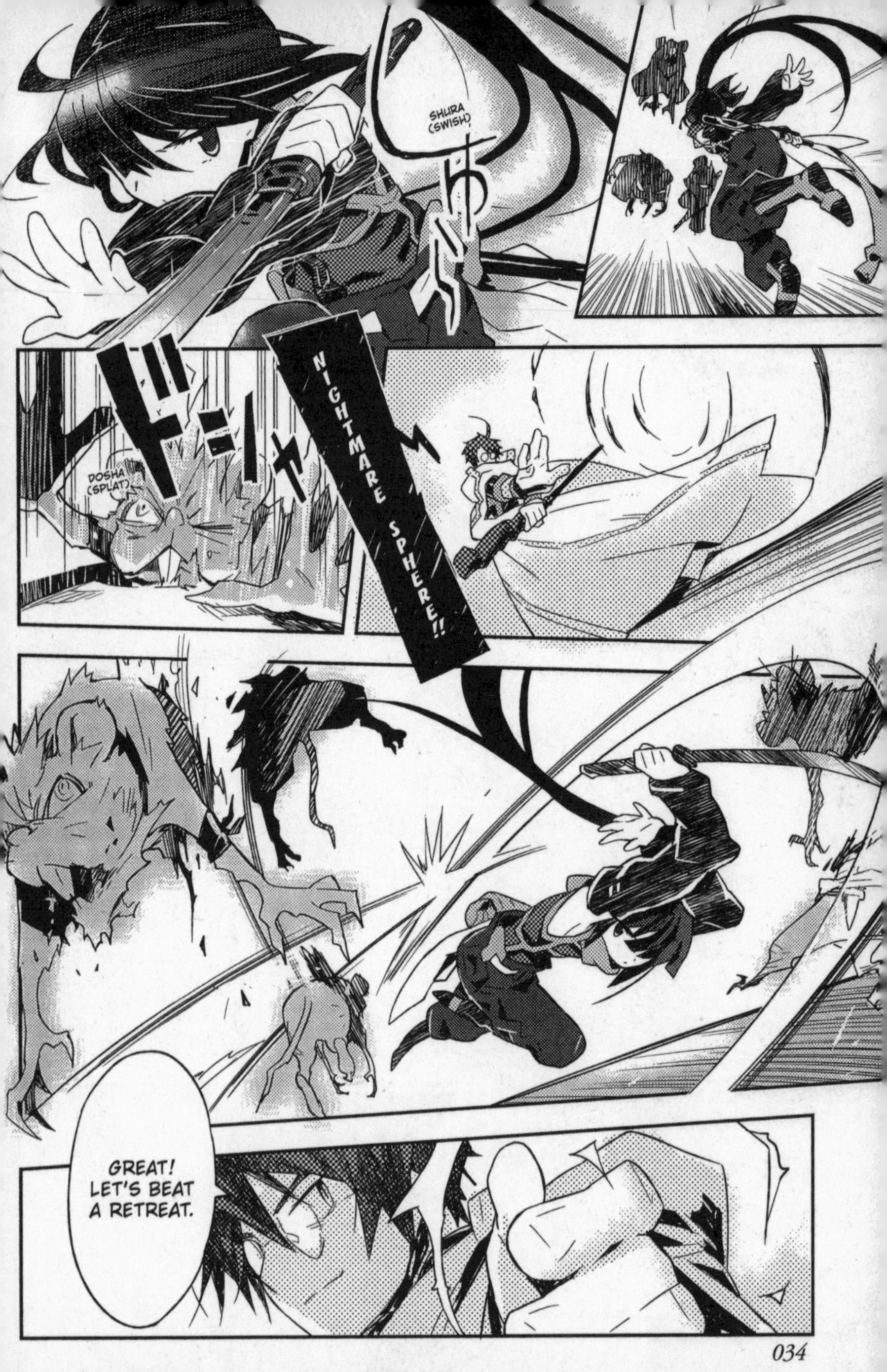
SHURA (SWISH)
NIGHTMARE SPHERE!!
DOSHA (SPLAT)
GREAT! LET'S BEAT A RETREAT.

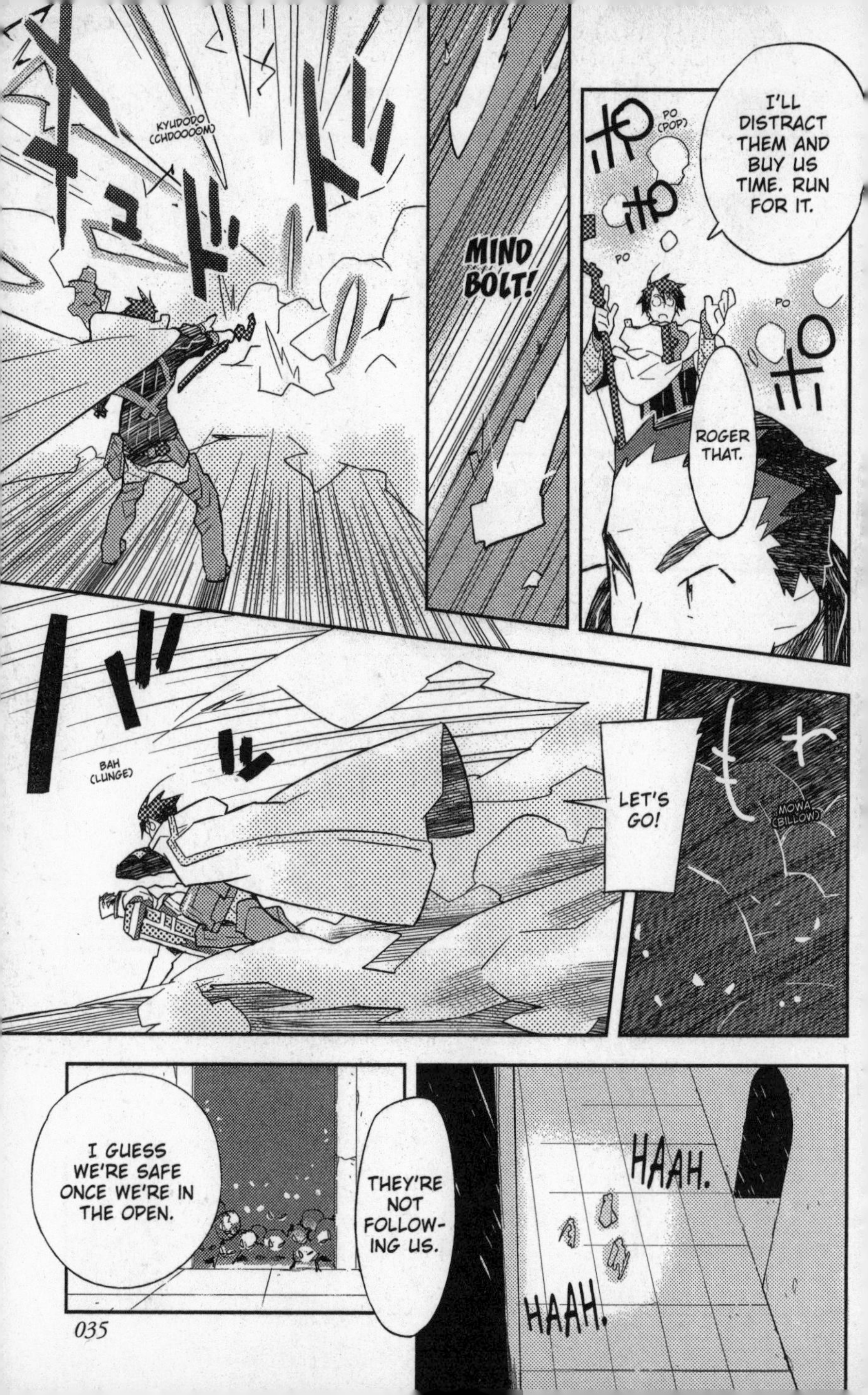
PO (POP)
I'LL DISTRACT THEM AND BUY US TIME. RUN FOR IT.
PO
PO
ROGER THAT.
MIND BOLT!
KYUDODO (CHDOOOOM)
MOWA (BILLOW)
LET'S GO!
BAH (LUNGE)
HAAH.
HAAH.
THEY'RE NOT FOLLOW-ING US.
I GUESS WE'RE SAFE ONCE WE'RE IN THE OPEN.

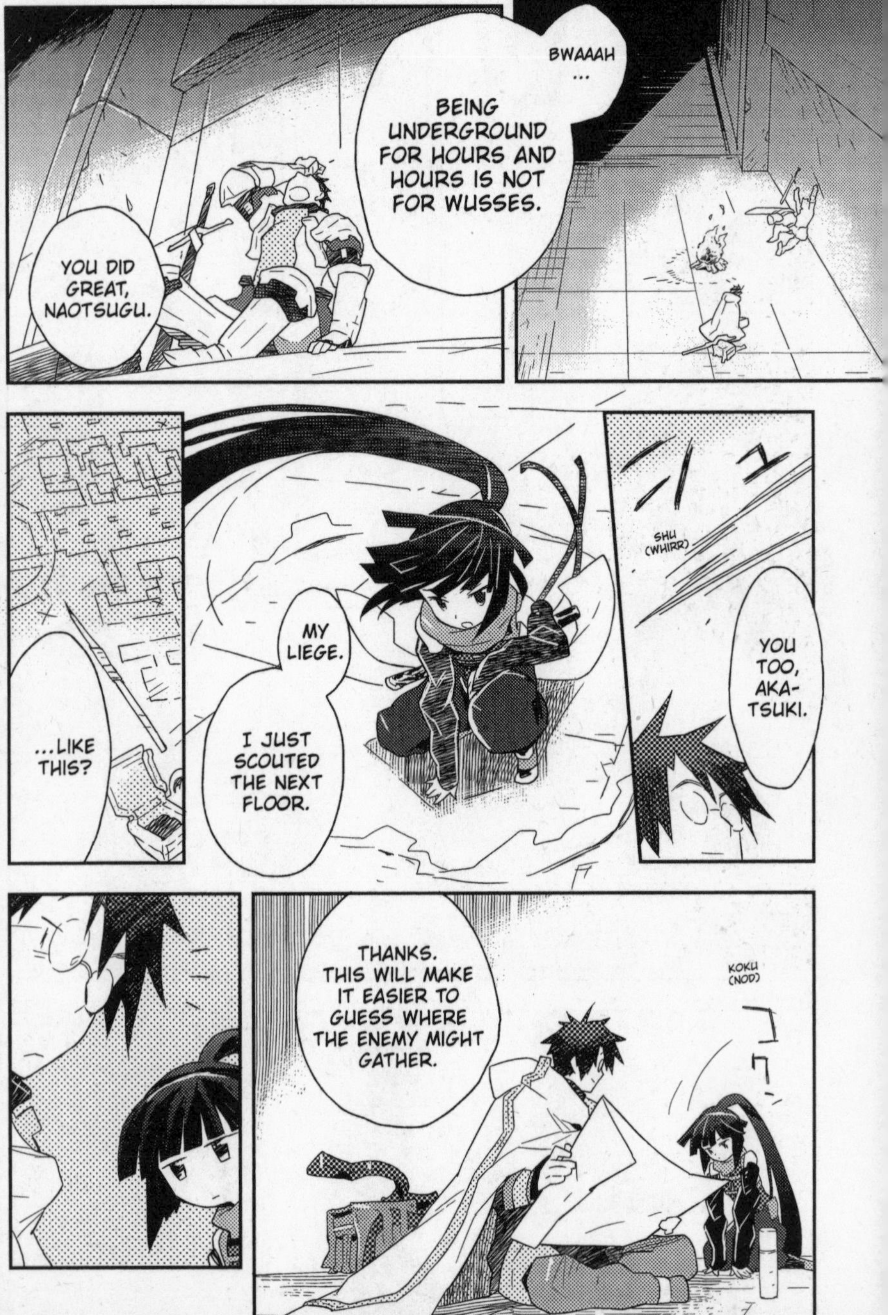
BWAAAH ...
BEING UNDERGROUND FOR HOURS AND HOURS IS NOT FOR WUSSES.
YOU DID GREAT, NAOTSUGU.
SHU (WHIRR)
YOU TOO, AKA-TSUKI.
MY LIEGE.
I JUST SCOUTED THE NEXT FLOOR.
...LIKE THIS?
THANKS. THIS WILL MAKE IT EASIER TO GUESS WHERE THE ENEMY MIGHT GATHER.
KOKU (NOD)

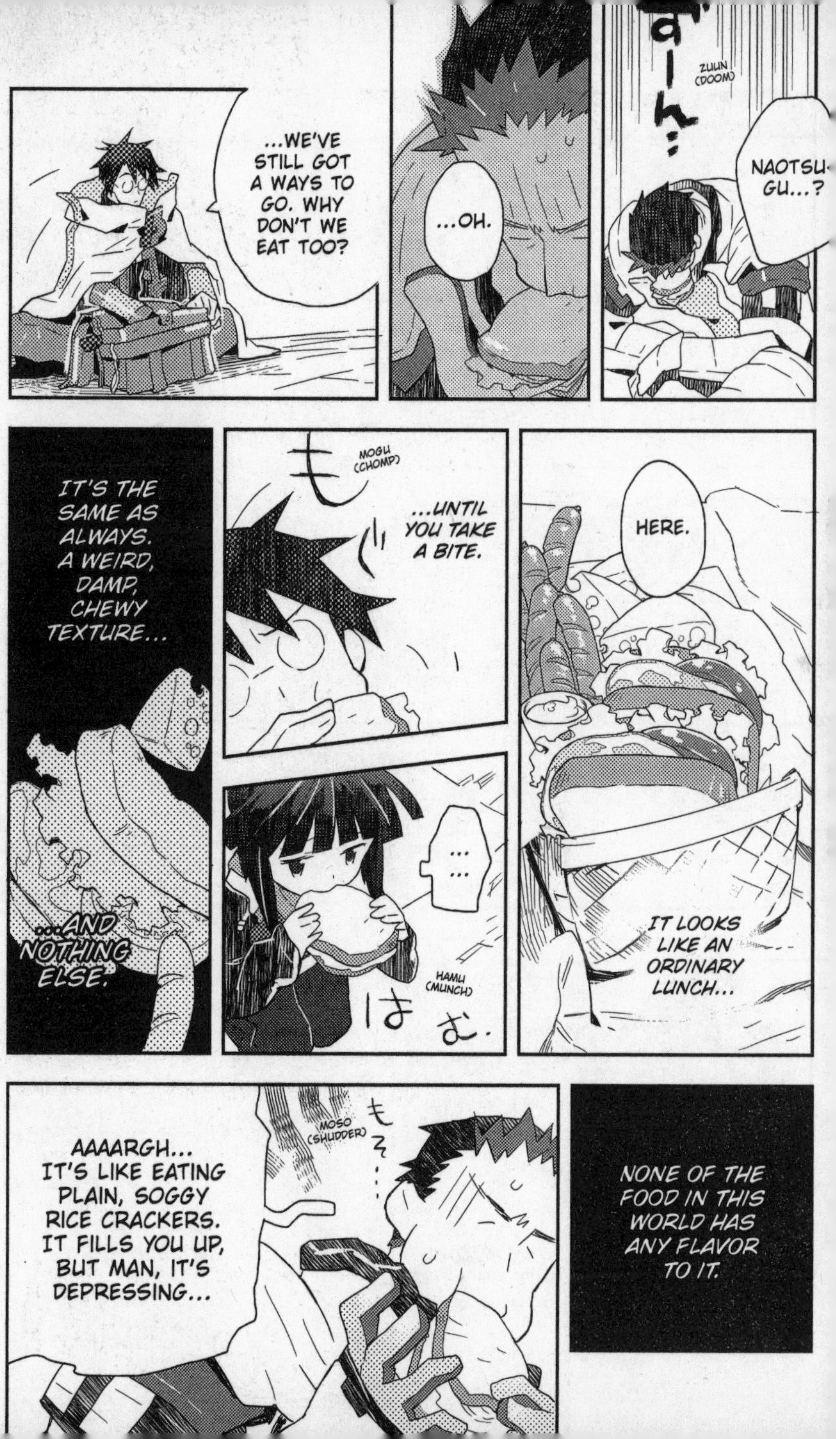
ZUUN (DOOM)
NAOTSUGU...?
...OH.
...WE'VE STILL GOT A WAYS TO GO. WHY DON'T WE EAT TOO?
HERE.
IT LOOKS LIKE AN ORDINARY LUNCH...
MOGU (CHOMP)
...UNTIL YOU TAKE A BITE.
......
HAMU (MUNCH)
IT'S THE SAME AS ALWAYS. A WEIRD, DAMP, CHEWY TEXTURE...
...AND NOTHING ELSE.
NONE OF THE FOOD IN THIS WORLD HAS ANY FLAVOR TO IT.
MOSO (SHUDDER)
AAAARGH... IT'S LIKE EATING PLAIN, SOGGY RICE CRACKERS. IT FILLS YOU UP, BUT MAN, IT'S DEPRESSING...

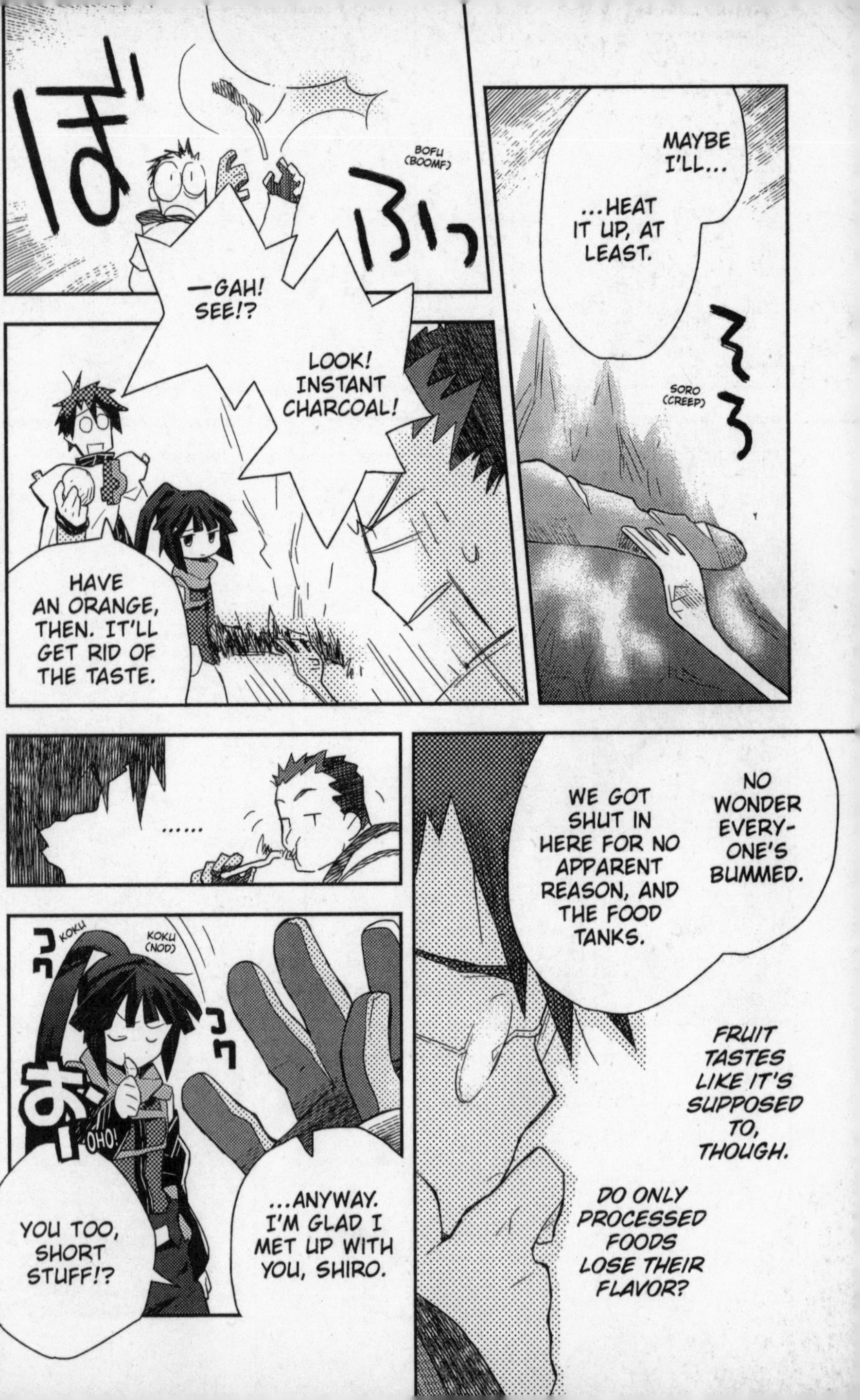
MAYBE I'LL...
...HEAT IT UP, AT LEAST.
SORO (CREEP)
BOFU (BOOMF)
—GAH! SEE!?
LOOK! INSTANT CHARCOAL!
HAVE AN ORANGE, THEN. IT'LL GET RID OF THE TASTE.
NO WONDER EVERYONE'S BUMMED.
WE GOT SHUT IN HERE FOR NO APPARENT REASON, AND THE FOOD TANKS.
FRUIT TASTES LIKE IT'S SUPPOSED TO, THOUGH.
DO ONLY PROCESSED FOODS LOSE THEIR FLAVOR?
......
KOKU
KOKU (NOD)
...ANYWAY. I'M GLAD I MET UP WITH YOU, SHIRO.
OHO!
YOU TOO, SHORT STUFF!?

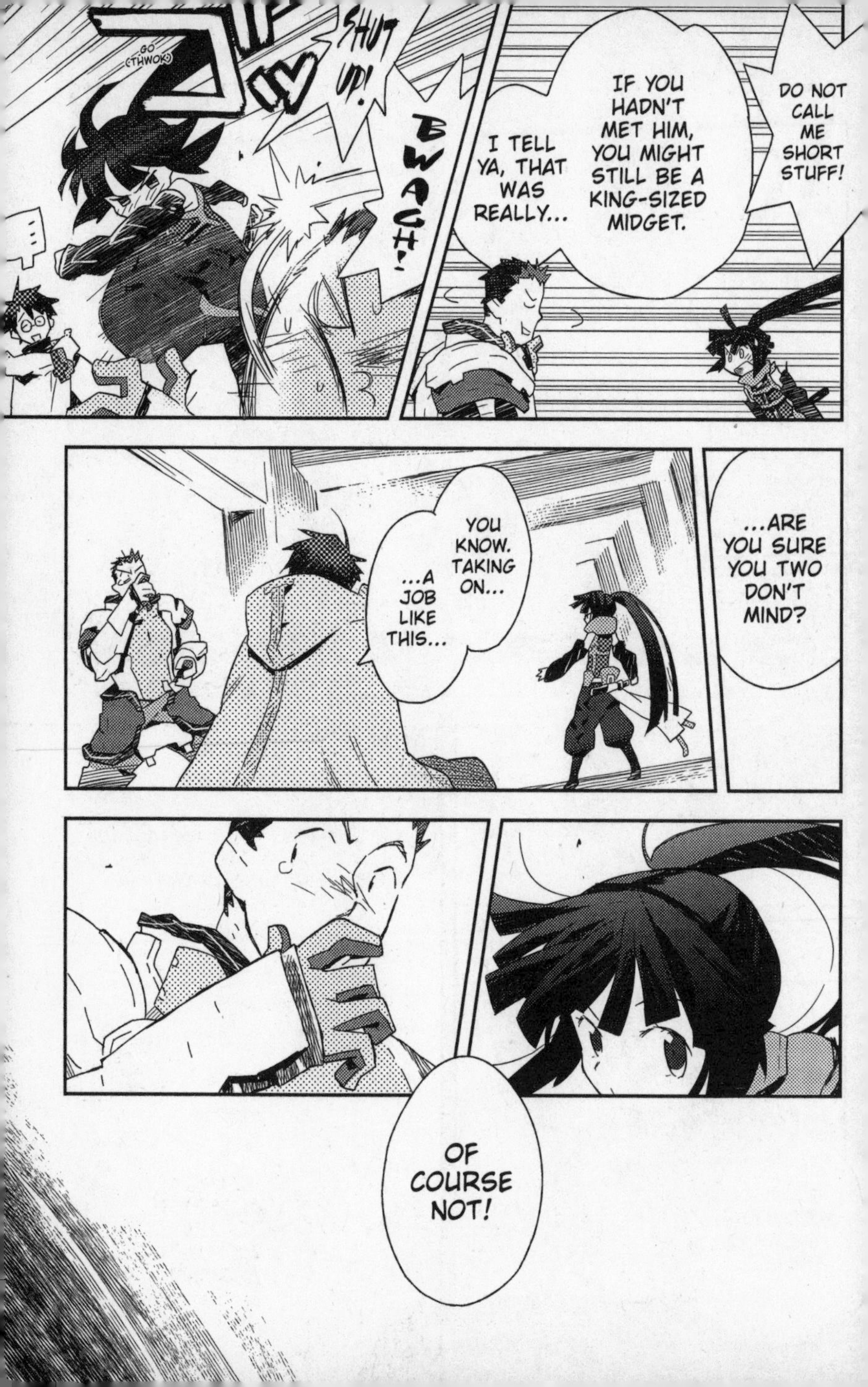
DO NOT CALL ME SHORT STUFF!
IF YOU HADN'T MET HIM, YOU MIGHT STILL BE A KING-SIZED MIDGET.
I TELL YA, THAT WAS REALLY...
SHUT UP!
BWAGH!
GO (THWOK)
...
...ARE YOU SURE YOU TWO DON'T MIND?
YOU KNOW. TAKING ON...
...A JOB LIKE THIS...
OF COURSE NOT!

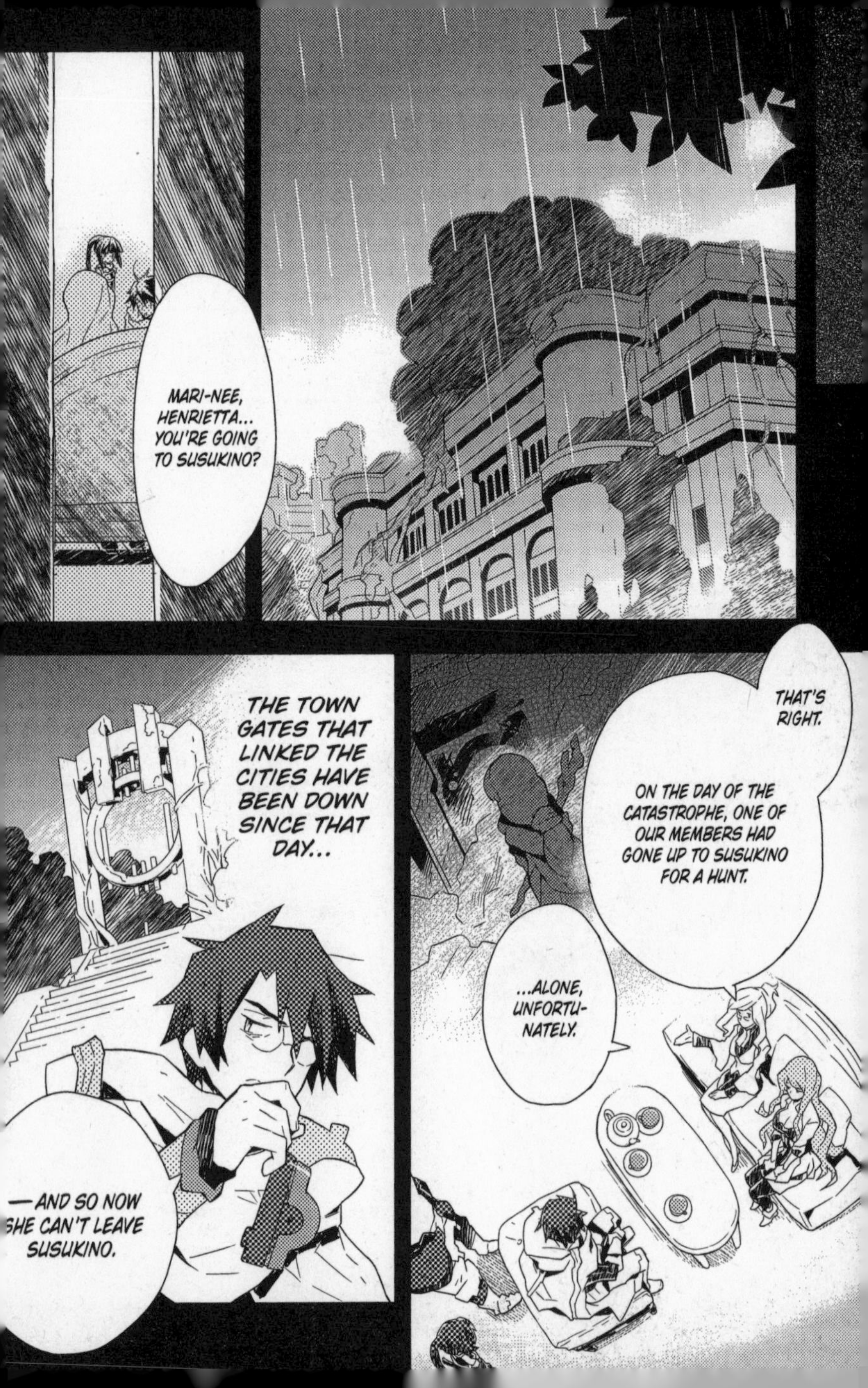
MARI-NEE, HENRIETTA... YOU'RE GOING TO SUSUKINO?
THAT'S RIGHT.
ON THE DAY OF THE CATASTROPHE, ONE OF OUR MEMBERS HAD GONE UP TO SUSUKINO FOR A HUNT.
...ALONE, UNFORTU-NATELY.
THE TOWN GATES THAT LINKED THE CITIES HAVE BEEN DOWN SINCE THAT DAY...
—AND SO NOW SHE CAN'T LEAVE SUSUKINO.

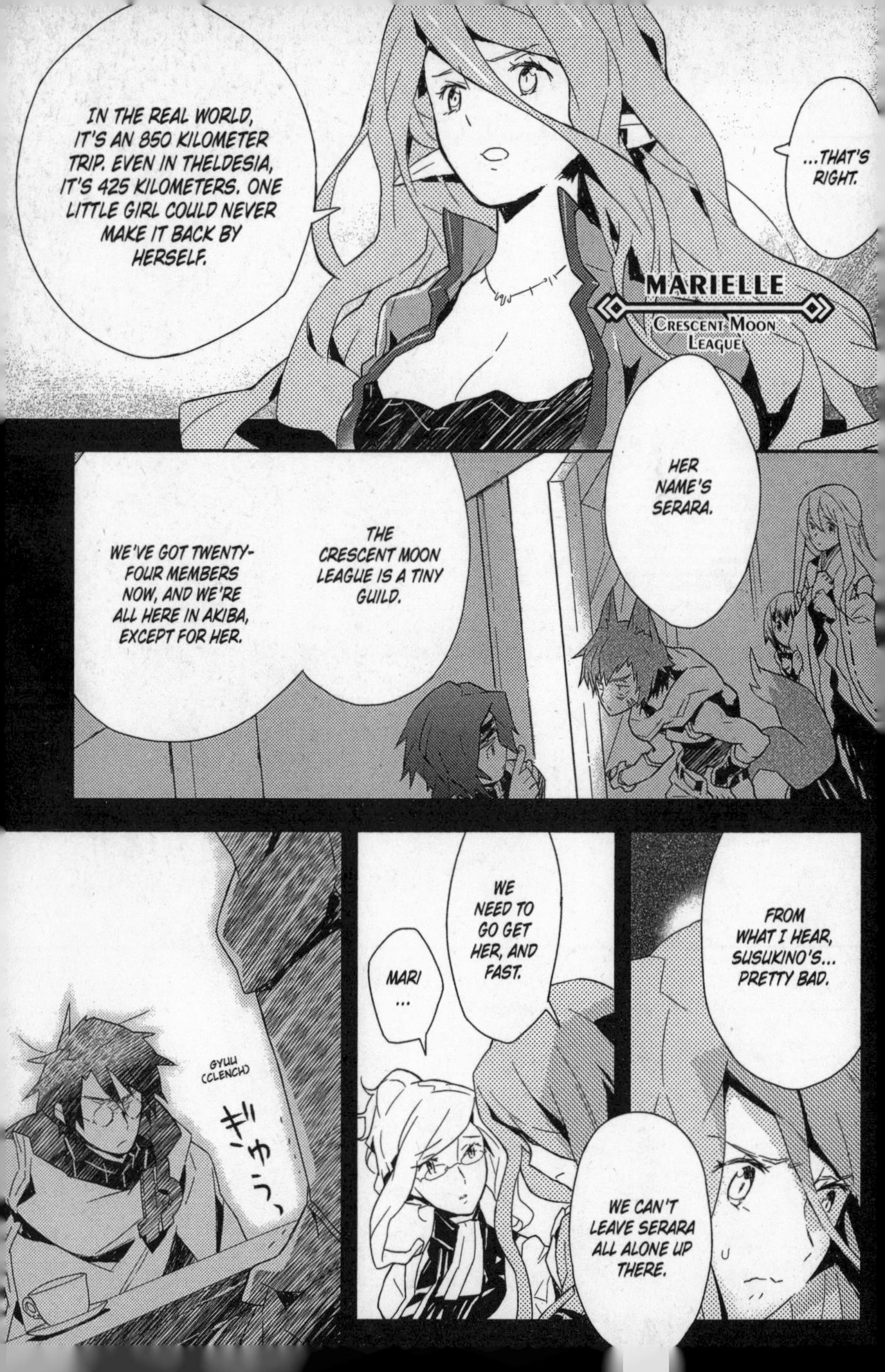
...THAT'S RIGHT.
MARIELLE
CRESCENT MOON LEAGUE
IN THE REAL WORLD, IT'S AN 850 KILOMETER TRIP. EVEN IN THELDESIA, IT'S 425 KILOMETERS. ONE LITTLE GIRL COULD NEVER MAKE IT BACK BY HERSELF.
HER NAME'S SERARA.
THE CRESCENT MOON LEAGUE IS A TINY GUILD.
WE'VE GOT TWENTY-FOUR MEMBERS NOW, AND WE'RE ALL HERE IN AKIBA, EXCEPT FOR HER.
FROM WHAT I HEAR, SUSUKINO'S... PRETTY BAD.
WE CAN'T LEAVE SERARA ALL ALONE UP THERE.
WE NEED TO GO GET HER, AND FAST.
MARI...
GYUU (CLENCH)
ぎゅう、

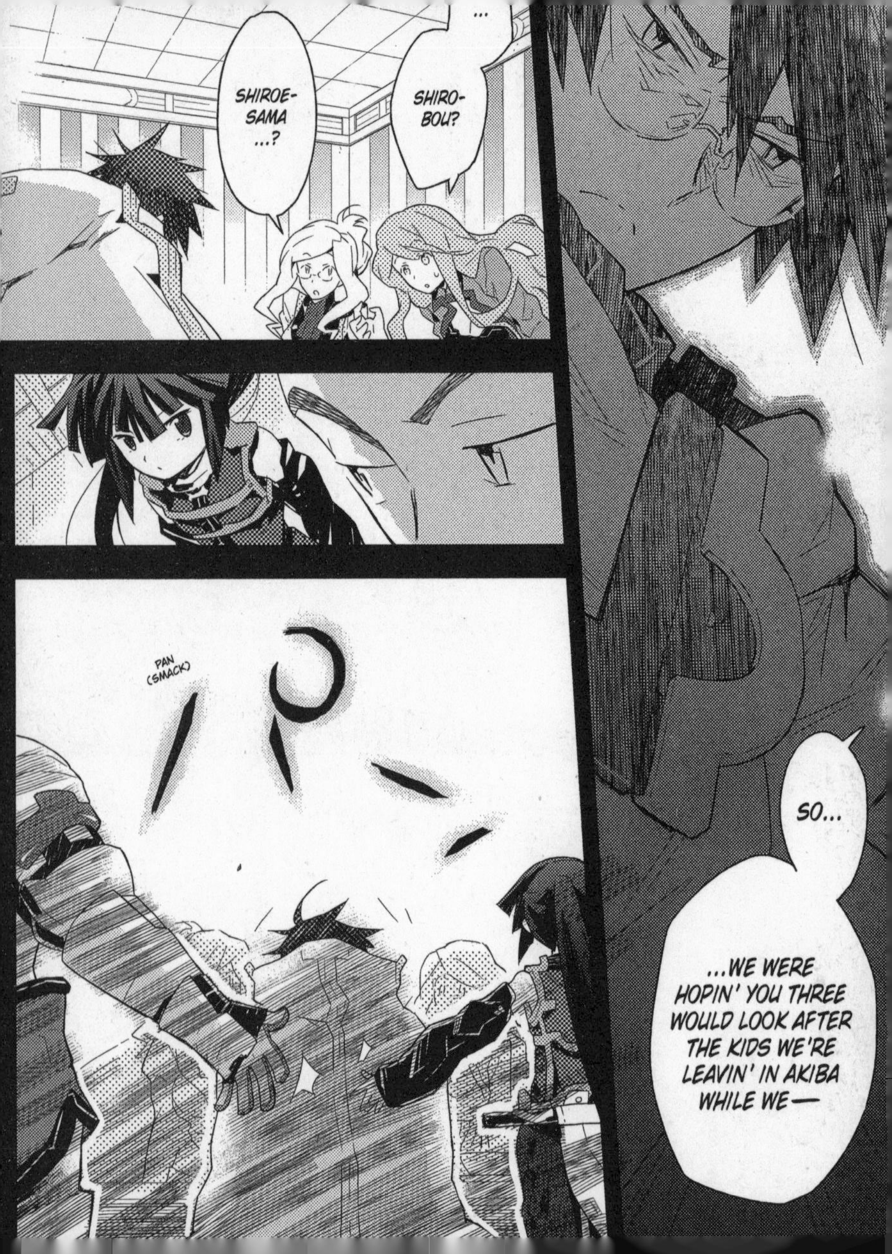
SO...
...WE WERE HOPIN' YOU THREE WOULD LOOK AFTER THE KIDS WE'RE LEAVIN' IN AKIBA WHILE WE—
...
SHIRO-BOU?
SHIROE-SAMA ...?
PAN (SMACK)

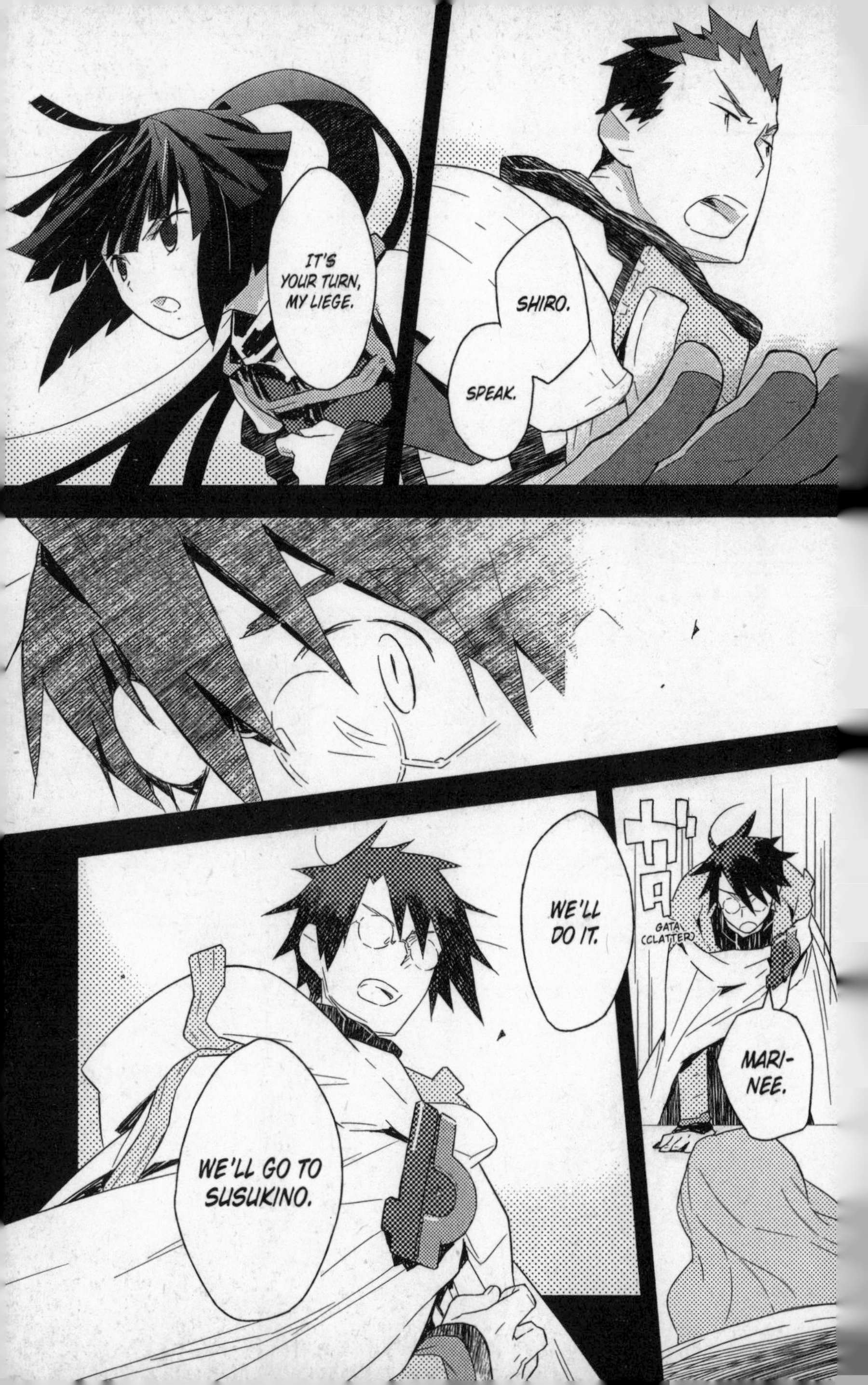
SHIRO.
SPEAK.
IT'S YOUR TURN, MY LIEGE.
GATA (CLATTER)
MARI-NEE.
WE'LL DO IT.
WE'LL GO TO SUSUKINO.

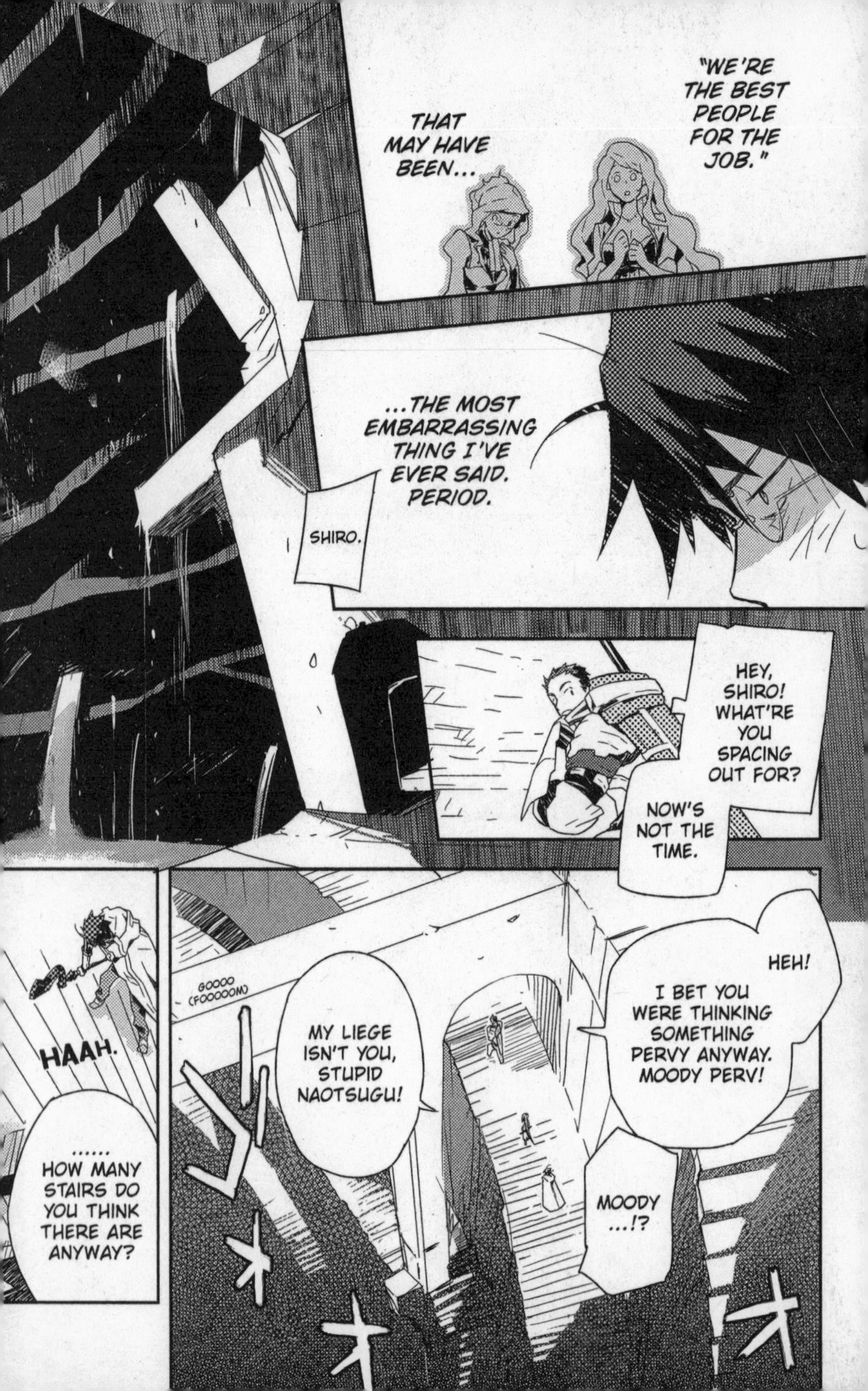
"WE'RE THE BEST PEOPLE FOR THE JOB."
THAT MAY HAVE BEEN...
...THE MOST EMBARRASSING THING I'VE EVER SAID. PERIOD.
SHIRO.
HEY, SHIRO! WHAT'RE YOU SPACING OUT FOR?
NOW'S NOT THE TIME.
HEH!
I BET YOU WERE THINKING SOMETHING PERVY ANYWAY. MOODY PERV!
MOODY ...!?
MY LIEGE ISN'T YOU, STUPID NAOTSUGU!
GOOOO (FOOOOOM)
HAAH.
...... HOW MANY STAIRS DO YOU THINK THERE ARE ANYWAY?

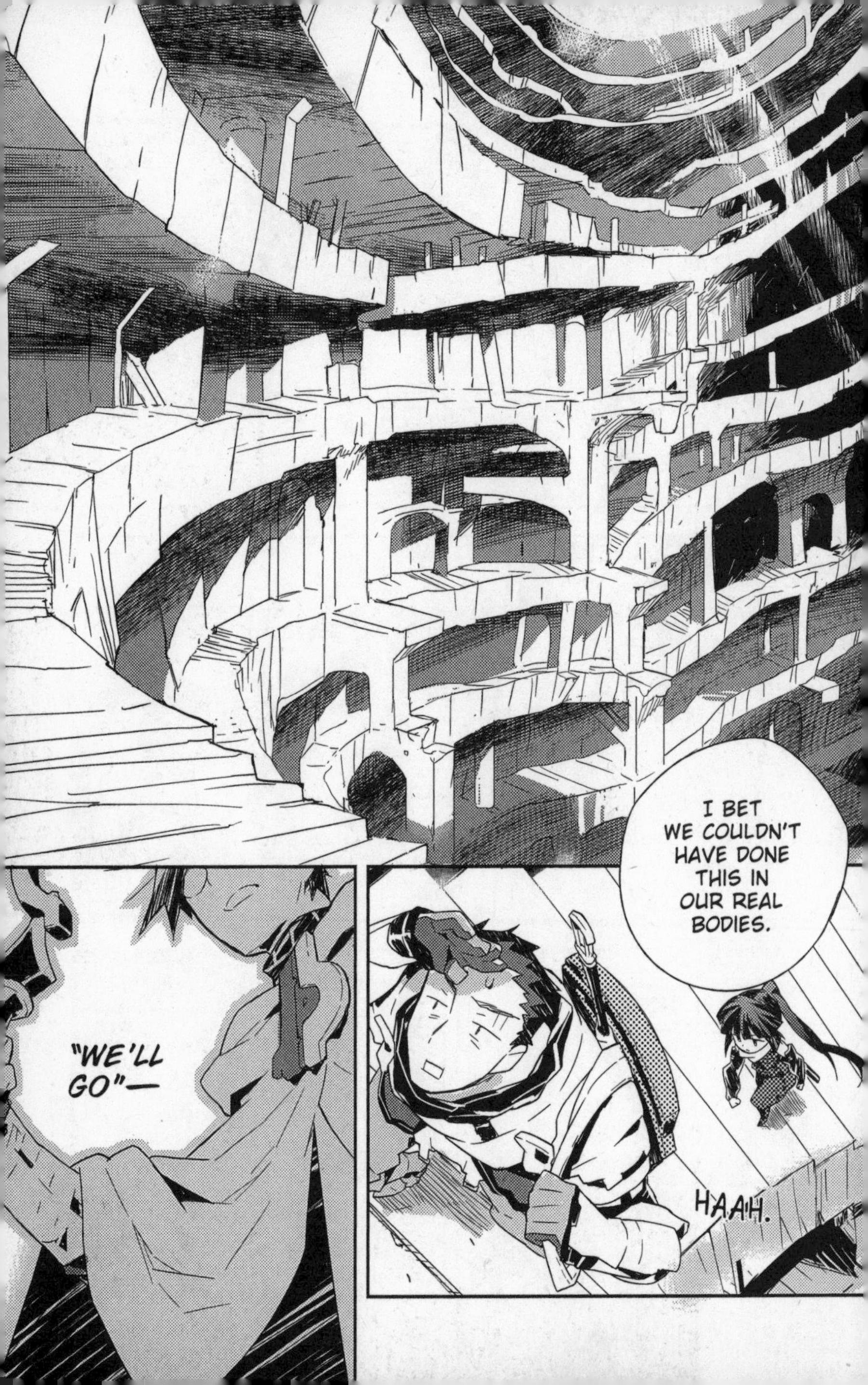
I BET WE COULDN'T HAVE DONE THIS IN OUR REAL BODIES.
HAAH.
"WE'LL GO"—

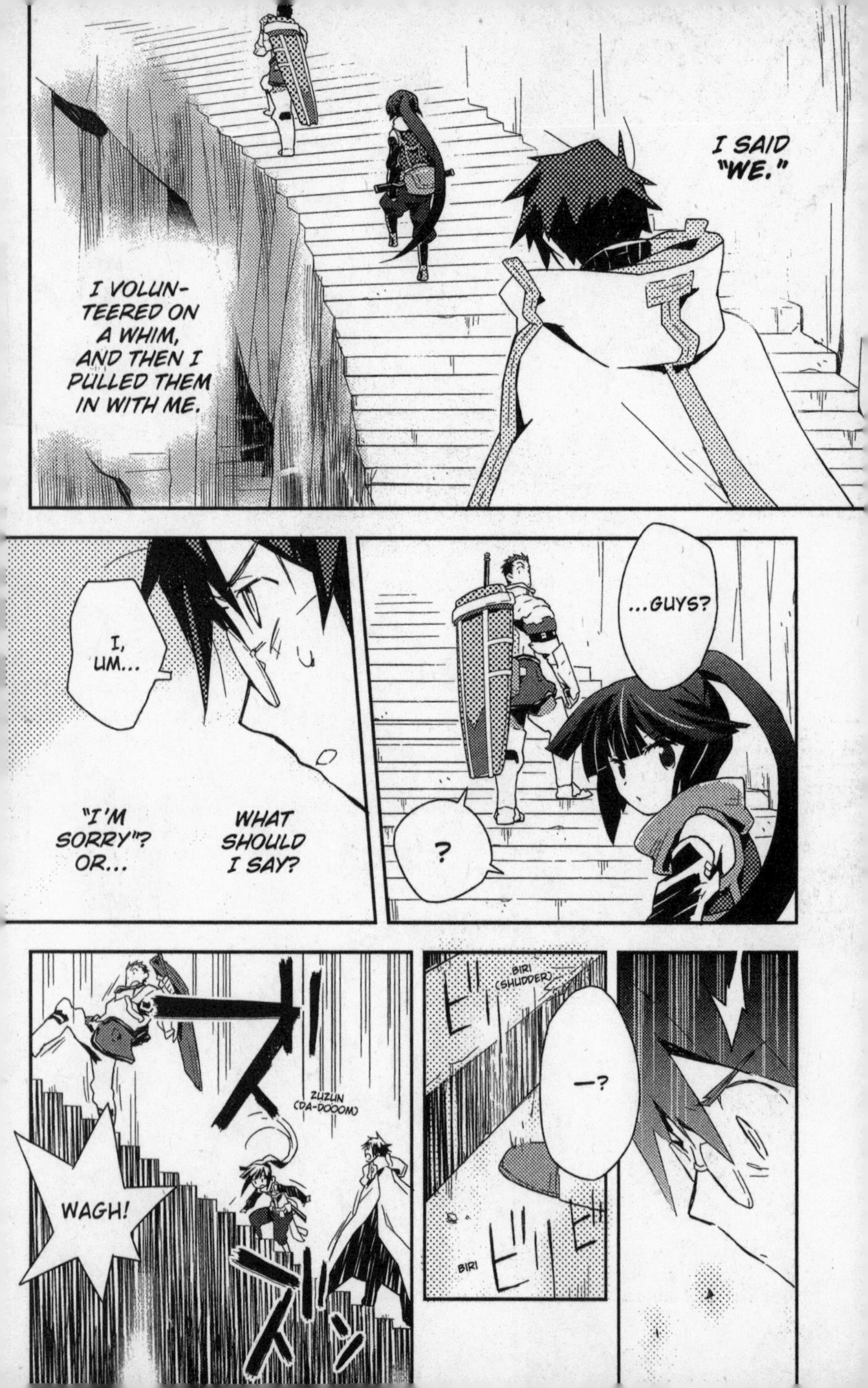
I SAID "WE."
I VOLUN-TEERED ON A WHIM, AND THEN I PULLED THEM IN WITH ME.
...GUYS?
?
I, UM...
WHAT SHOULD I SAY?
"I'M SORRY"? OR...
BIRI (SHUDDER)
—?
BIRI
ZUZUN (DA-DOOOM)
WAGH!

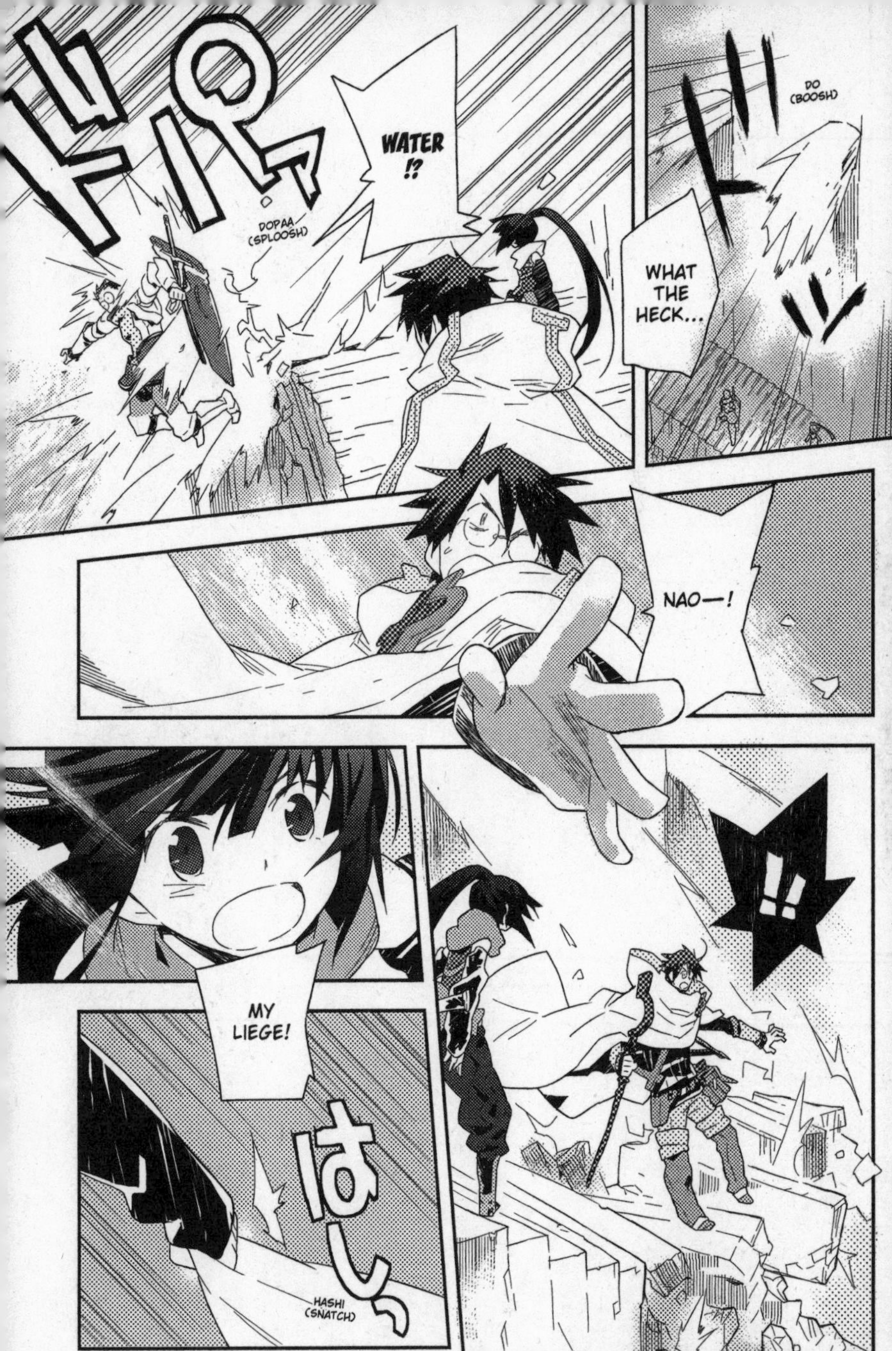

ドッ
DO
(BOOSH)
WHAT THE HECK...
WATER !?
ドパァ
DOPAA
(SPLOOSH)
NAO—!
!!
MY LIEGE!
はしっ
HASHI
(SNATCH)

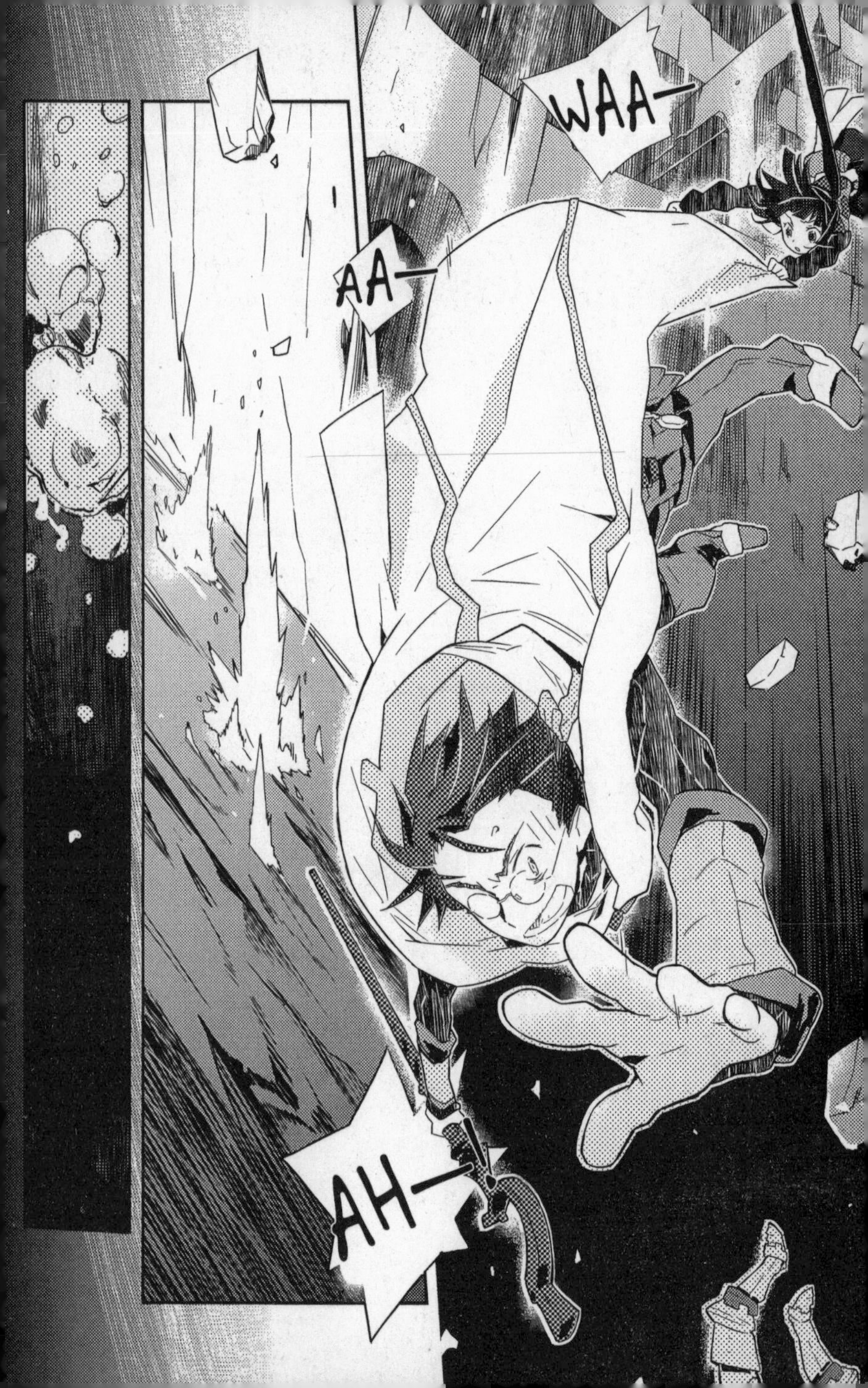
WAA—
AA—
AH—

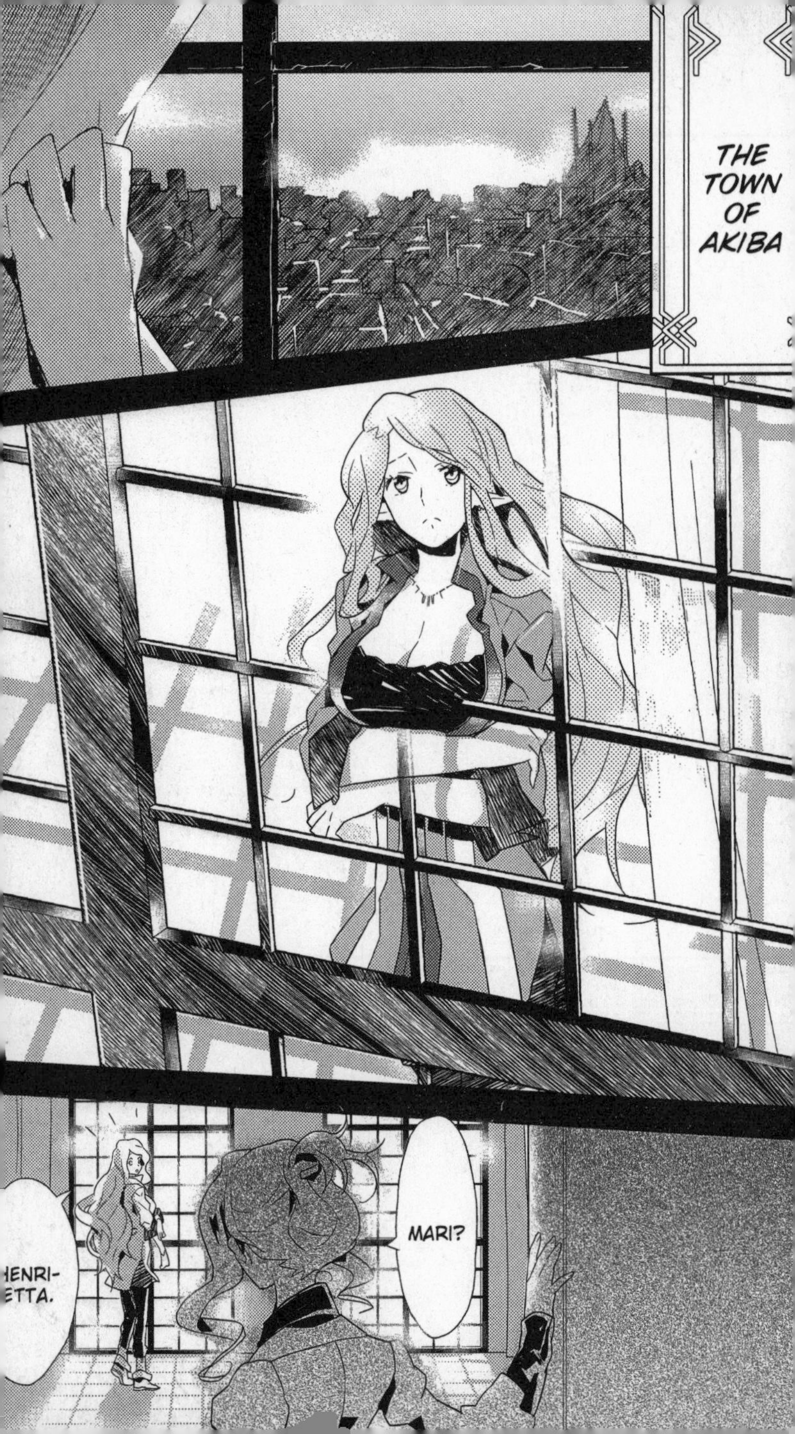
THE TOWN OF AKIBA
MARI?
HENRI-ETTA.

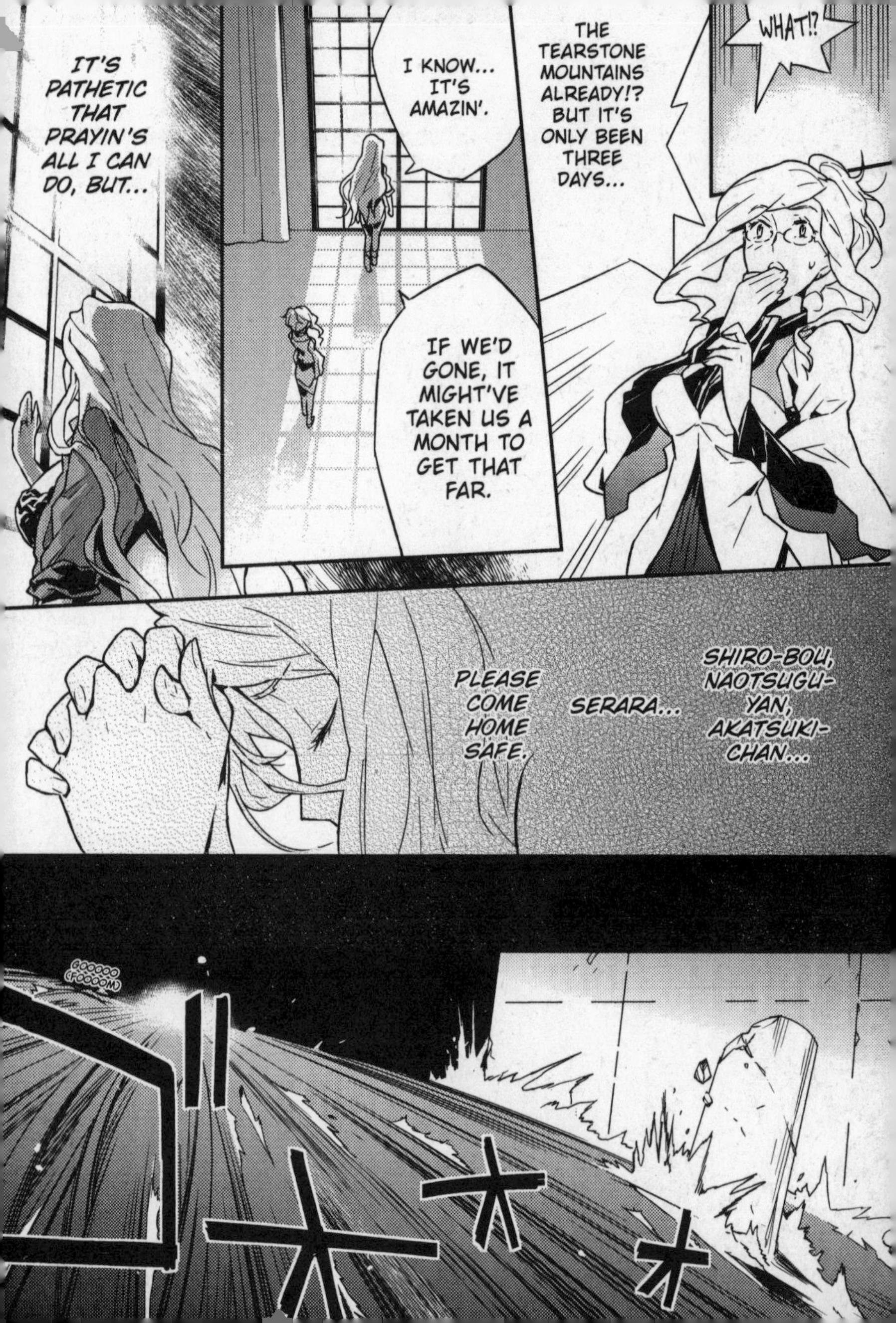
WHAT!?
THE TEARSTONE MOUNTAINS ALREADY!? BUT IT'S ONLY BEEN THREE DAYS...
I KNOW... IT'S AMAZIN'.
IF WE'D GONE, IT MIGHT'VE TAKEN US A MONTH TO GET THAT FAR.
IT'S PATHETIC THAT PRAYIN'S ALL I CAN DO, BUT...
SHIRO-BOU, NAOTSUGU-YAN, AKATSUKI-CHAN...
SERARA...
PLEASE COME HOME SAFE.
GOOOOO (FOOOOM)

KEYWORD ▶ **THE CATASTROPHE**

**AN INCIDENT IN WHICH PLAYERS WERE PULLED INTO THE WORLD OF AN ONLINE GAME AND LEFT UNABLE TO ESCAPE OR EVEN DIE.**

An incident in which players were trapped inside the MMORPG (Massively Multiplayer Online RPG) *Elder Tales*. Players physically live in the game world now. They can't end the game or log out, and they can't communicate with the company that runs the game (the game masters). In this world, ingredient items taste the way they should, but dishes made with them don't taste like anything. Although the food keeps players' bellies full, the pleasure of eating is gone. As in the game, when players die, they are transported to the nearest great temple and resurrected. Players can't just relax and enjoy *Elder Tales* as a game anymore, and more and more of them are getting desperate. The world of *Elder Tales* has turned dark and gloomy.

LOG HORIZON

**KEYWORD ▶ THE HALF-GAIA PROJECT**

**THE VAST MAP OF *ELDER TALES*: A HALF-SIZED REPRODUCTION OF EARTH.**

---

Theldesia, the world of *Elder Tales*, is a replica of the real world, with all its geographical measurements halved. The area that corresponds to Japan is called Yamato, and the town of Akiba—the place where Shiroe first arrived—is Akihabara in Tokyo. The town of Susukino, where the Crescent Moon League guild member is stranded, is the city of Sapporo in Hokkaido. When *Elder Tales* was a game, it was possible for players to travel instantaneously to distant places using the town gates, which let travelers warp between cities. Since the Catastrophe, though, that function has been lost. The distance from Tokyo to Sapporo may be half of what it is in the real world, but in this world, powerful monsters lurk in some areas. It's nearly impossible for a low-level player to travel on foot.

THE TEAR-STONE MOUNTAINS
Eastal
AKIBA

GOOOO (FWOOOOM)

LOG HORIZON

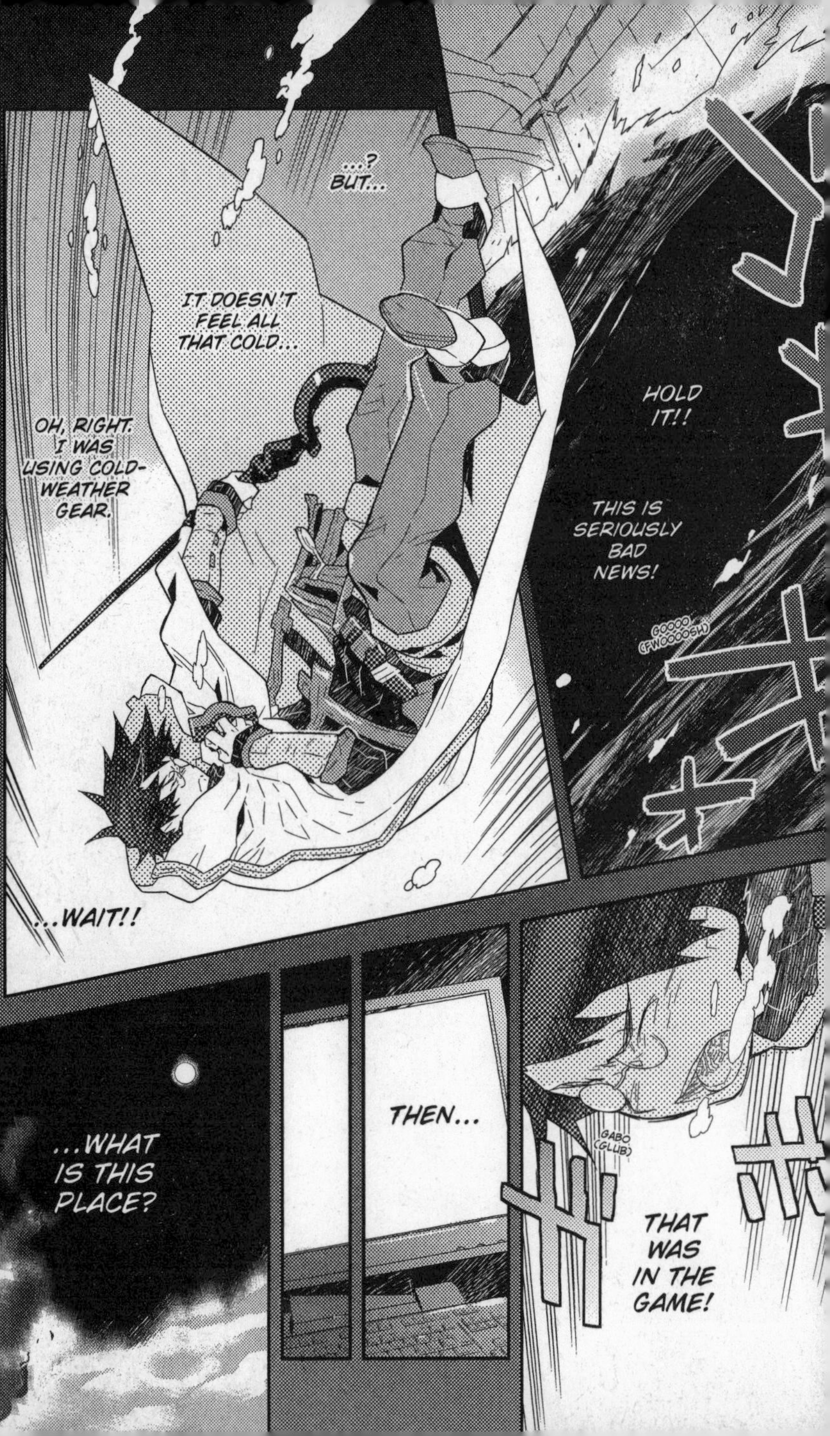
HOLD IT!!
THIS IS SERIOUSLY BAD NEWS!
GOOOO (FWOOOOSH)
...? BUT...
IT DOESN'T FEEL ALL THAT COLD...
OH, RIGHT. I WAS USING COLD-WEATHER GEAR.
...WAIT!!
GABO (GLUB)
THAT WAS IN THE GAME!
THEN...
...WHAT IS THIS PLACE?

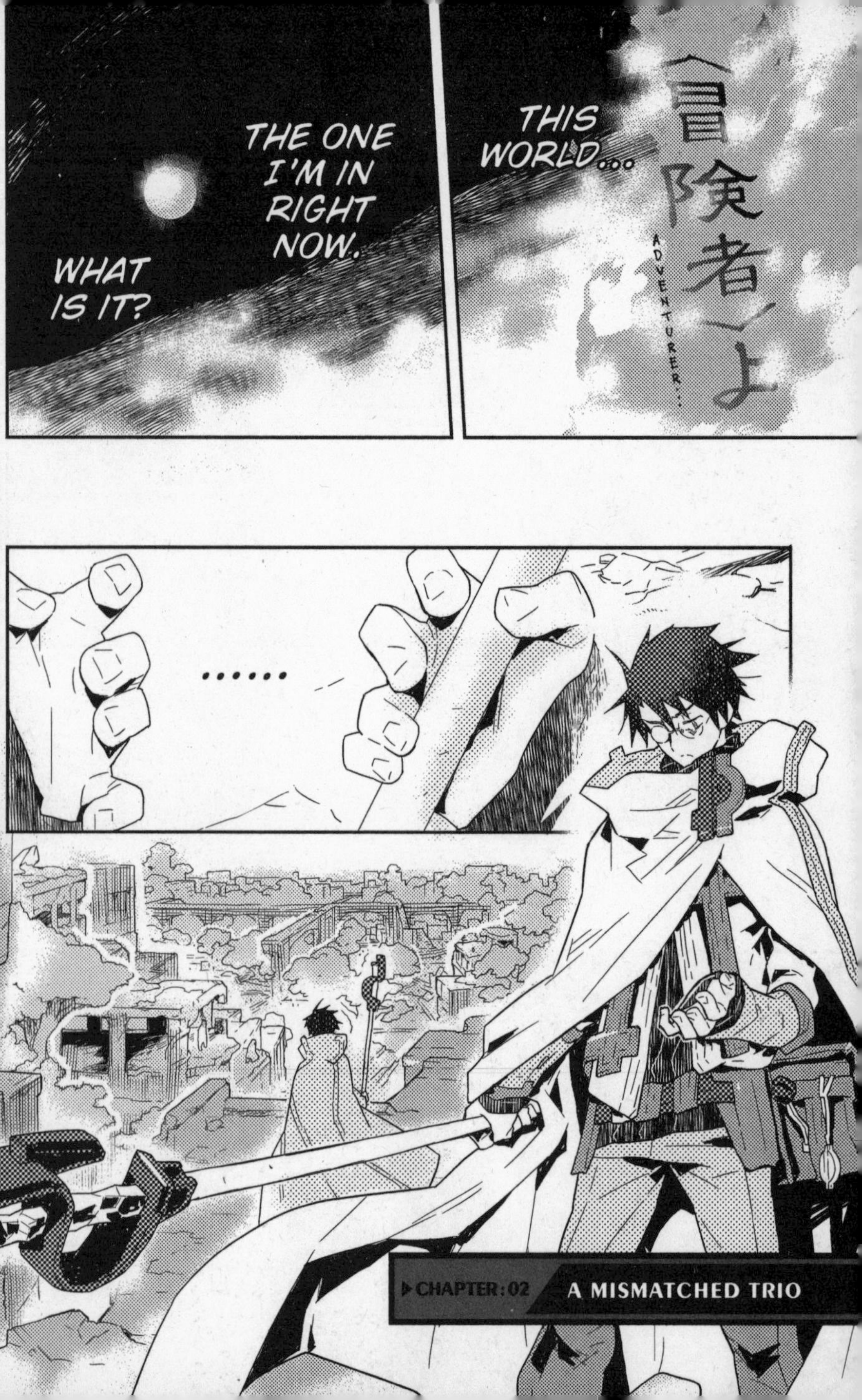
THIS WORLD...
冒険者よ
ADVENTURER...
THE ONE I'M IN RIGHT NOW.
WHAT IS IT?
......
CHAPTER: 02
A MISMATCHED TRIO

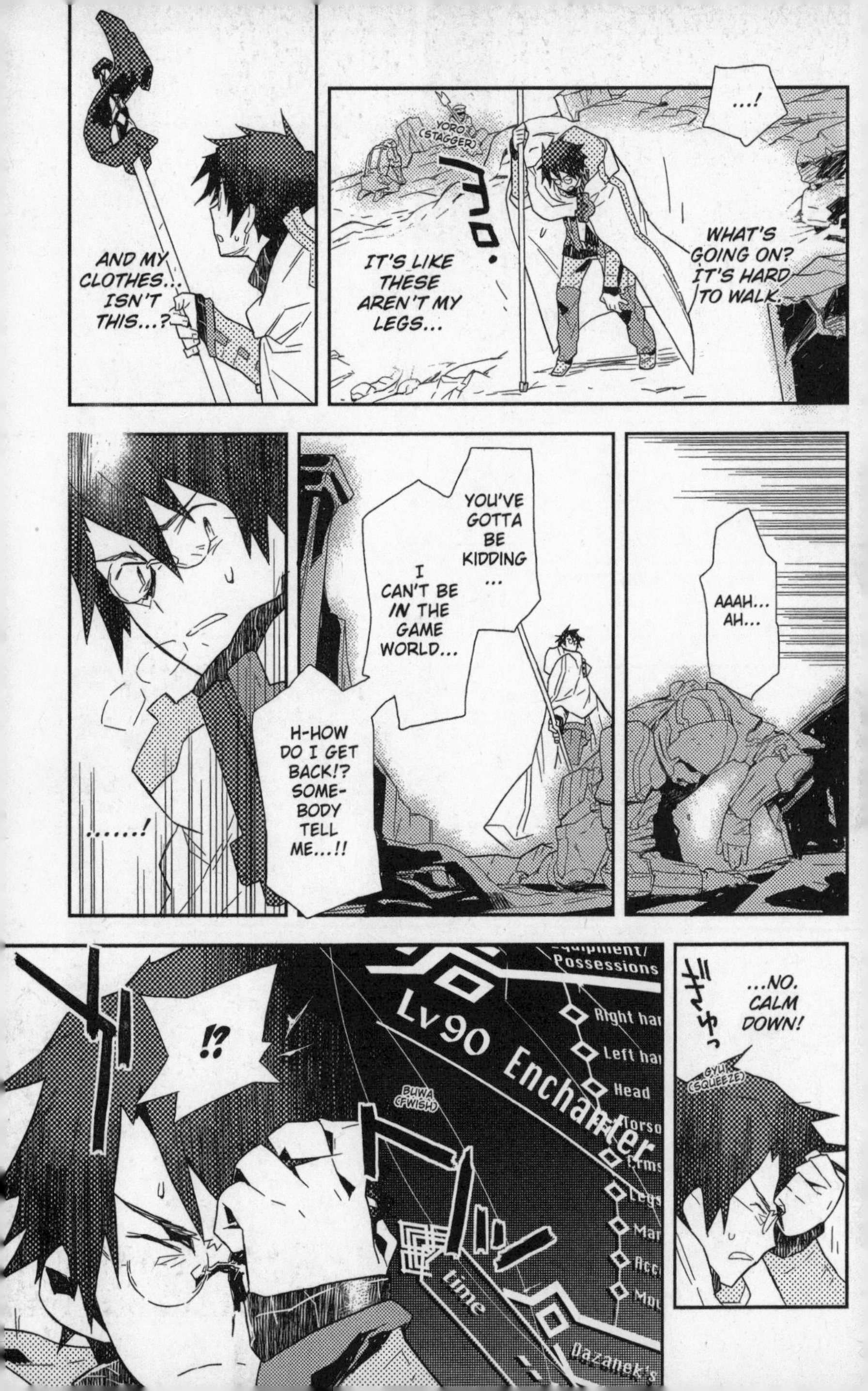
...!
YORO (STAGGER)
WHAT'S GOING ON? IT'S HARD TO WALK.
IT'S LIKE THESE AREN'T MY LEGS...
AND MY CLOTHES... ISN'T THIS...?
AAAH... AH...
YOU'VE GOTTA BE KIDDING...
I CAN'T BE *IN* THE GAME WORLD...
H-HOW DO I GET BACK!? SOME-BODY TELL ME...!!
......!
...NO. CALM DOWN!
GYU (SQUEEZE)
!?
BUWA (FWISH)
Equipment/ Possessions
Lv90 Enchanter
Head
time

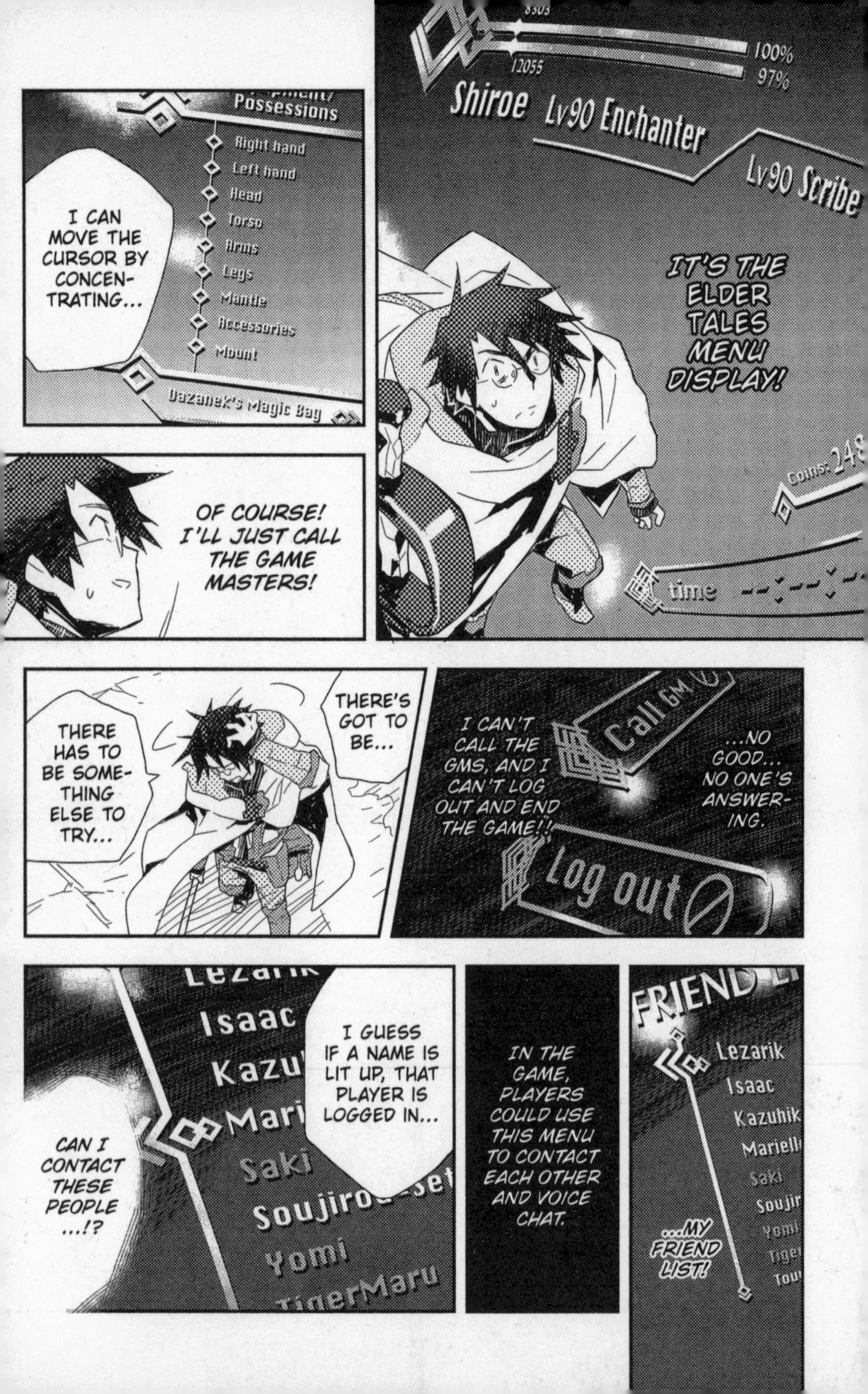

100%
12055
97%
Shiroe
Lv90 Enchanter
Lv90 Scribe
IT'S THE ELDER TALES MENU DISPLAY!
Coins: 248
time
Possessions
Right hand
Left hand
Head
Torso
Arms
Legs
Mantle
Accessories
Mount
I CAN MOVE THE CURSOR BY CONCEN-TRATING...
Dazanek's Magic Bag
OF COURSE! I'LL JUST CALL THE GAME MASTERS!
Call GM
...NO GOOD... NO ONE'S ANSWER-ING.
I CAN'T CALL THE GMS, AND I CAN'T LOG OUT AND END THE GAME!!
Log out
THERE'S GOT TO BE...
THERE HAS TO BE SOME-THING ELSE TO TRY...
Lezarik
Isaac
...MY FRIEND LIST!
IN THE GAME, PLAYERS COULD USE THIS MENU TO CONTACT EACH OTHER AND VOICE CHAT.
Isaac
I GUESS IF A NAME IS LIT UP, THAT PLAYER IS LOGGED IN...
Saki
Yomi
TigerMaru
CAN I CONTACT THESE PEOPLE ...!?

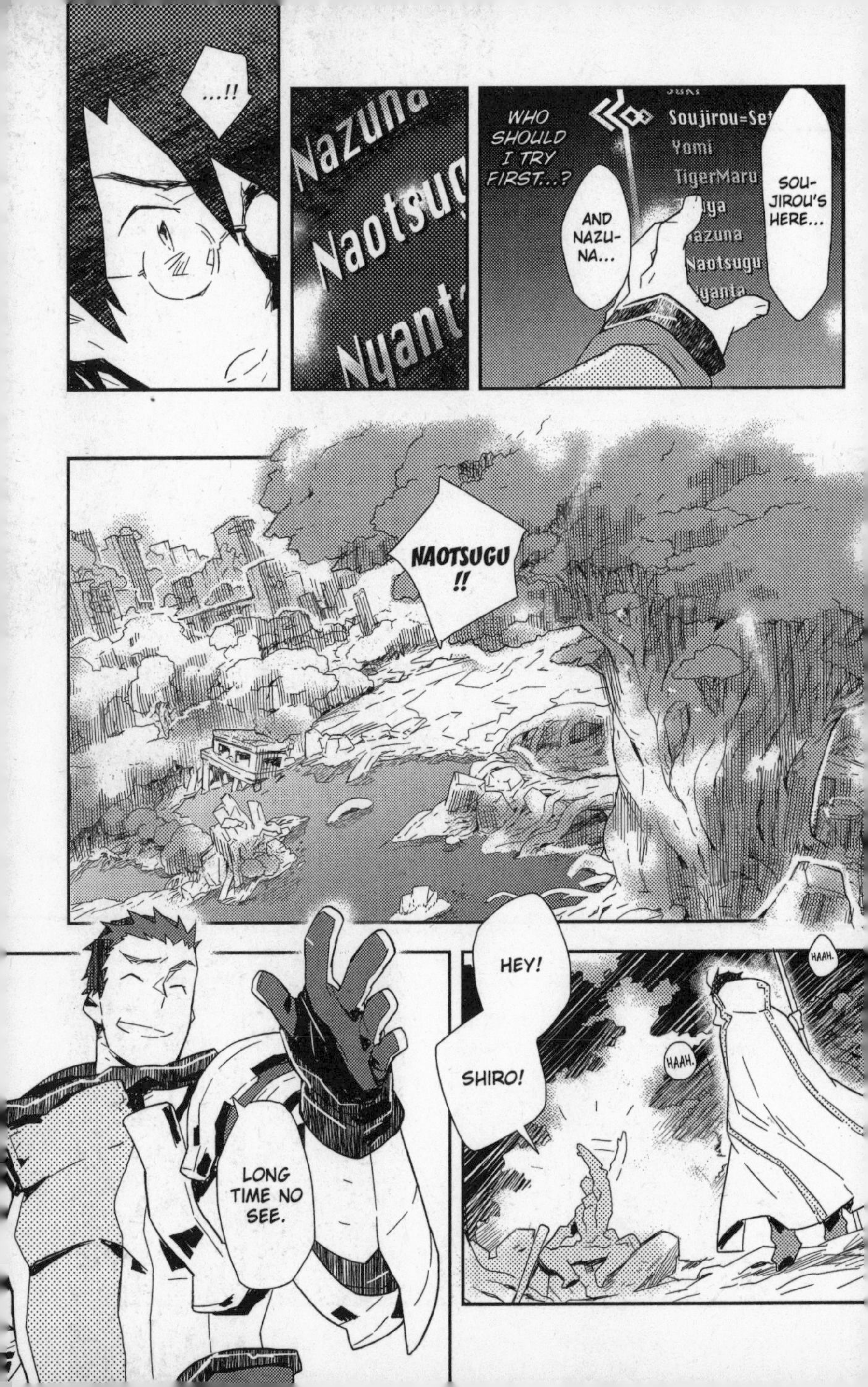
Soujirou=Set
Yomi
TigerMaru
Naotsugu
SOU-JIROU'S HERE...
WHO SHOULD I TRY FIRST...?
AND NAZU-NA...
Nazuna
Naotsugu
...!!
NAOTSUGU!!
HAAH.
HAAH.
HEY!
SHIRO!
LONG TIME NO SEE.

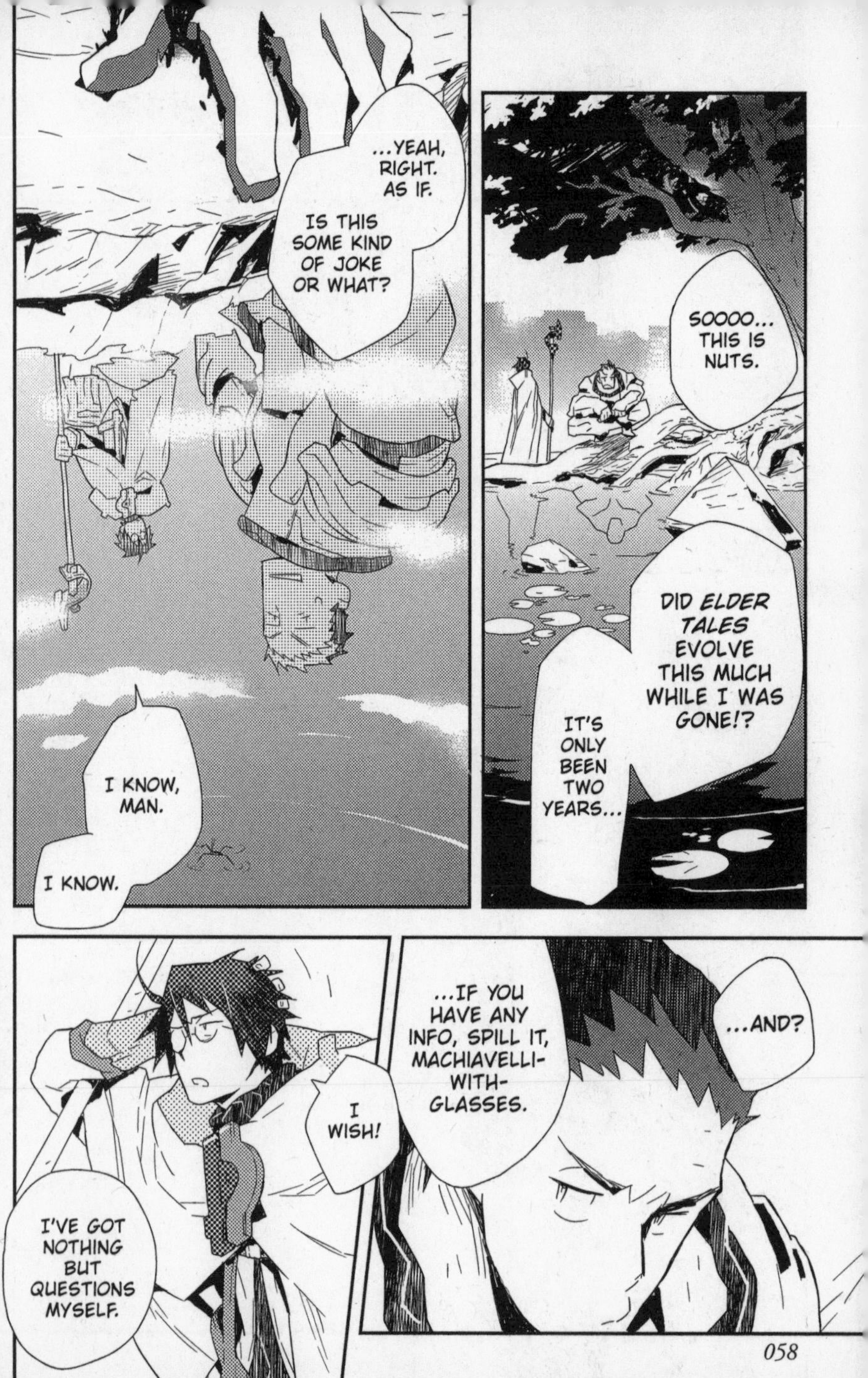
SOOOO... THIS IS NUTS.
DID *ELDER TALES* EVOLVE THIS MUCH WHILE I WAS GONE!?
IT'S ONLY BEEN TWO YEARS...
...YEAH, RIGHT. AS IF.
IS THIS SOME KIND OF JOKE OR WHAT?
I KNOW, MAN.
I KNOW.
...AND?
...IF YOU HAVE ANY INFO, SPILL IT, MACHIAVELLI-WITH-GLASSES.
I WISH!
I'VE GOT NOTHING BUT QUESTIONS MYSELF.

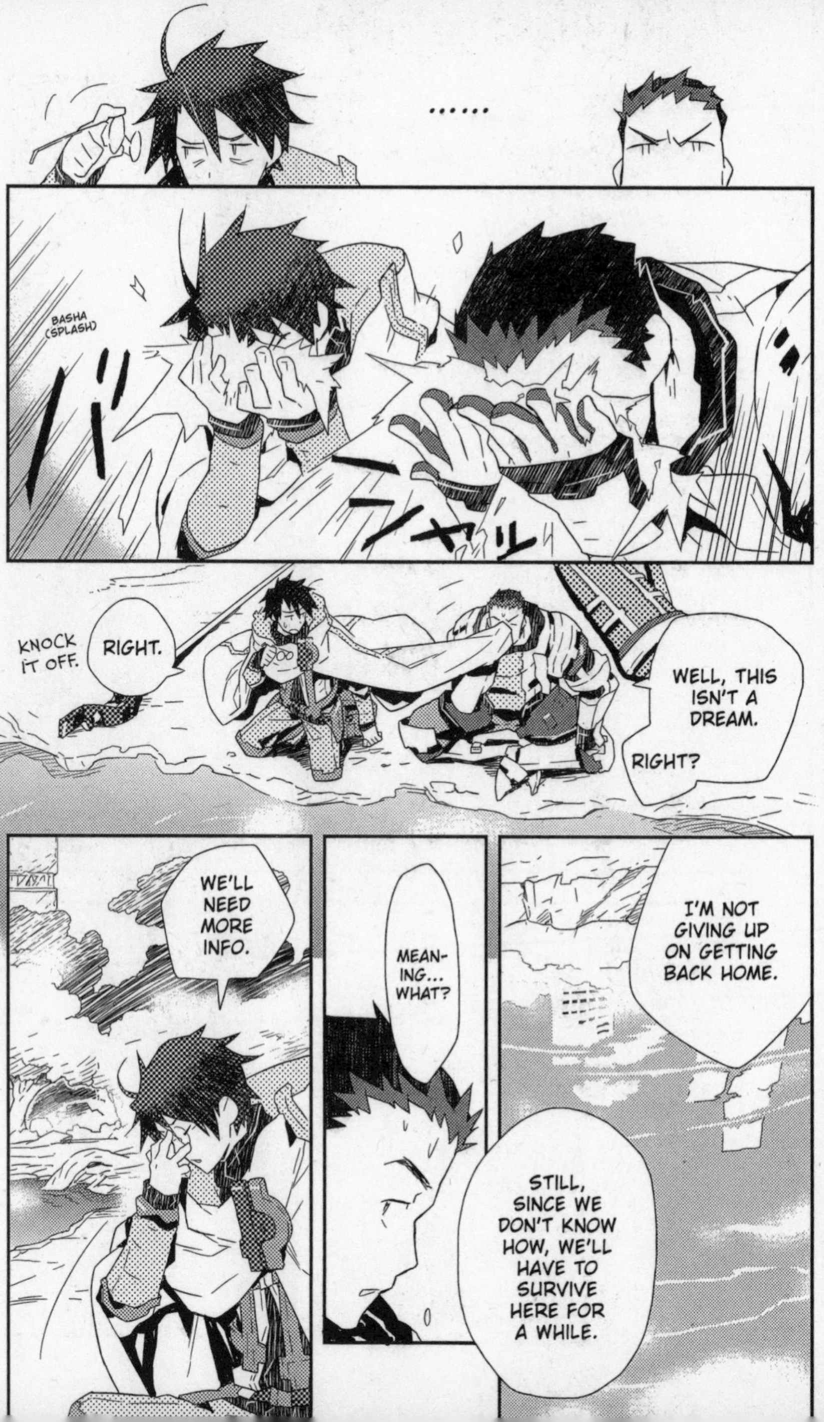
......
BASHA (SPLASH)
WELL, THIS ISN'T A DREAM.
RIGHT?
RIGHT.
KNOCK IT OFF.
I'M NOT GIVING UP ON GETTING BACK HOME.
STILL, SINCE WE DON'T KNOW HOW, WE'LL HAVE TO SURVIVE HERE FOR A WHILE.
MEAN-ING... WHAT?
WE'LL NEED MORE INFO.

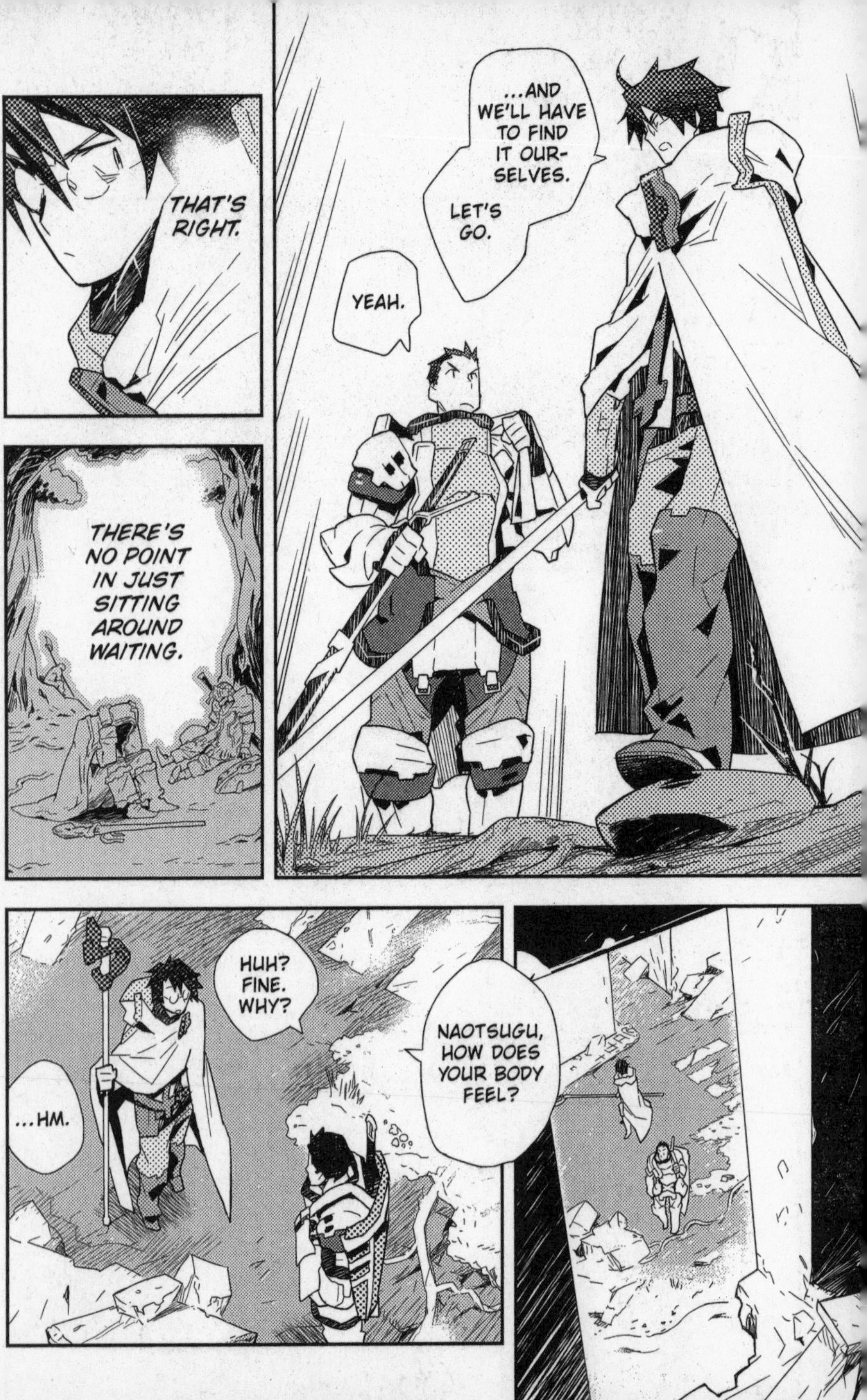
...AND WE'LL HAVE TO FIND IT OUR-SELVES.
LET'S GO.
YEAH.
THAT'S RIGHT.
THERE'S NO POINT IN JUST SITTING AROUND WAITING.
NAOTSUGU, HOW DOES YOUR BODY FEEL?
HUH? FINE. WHY?
...HM.

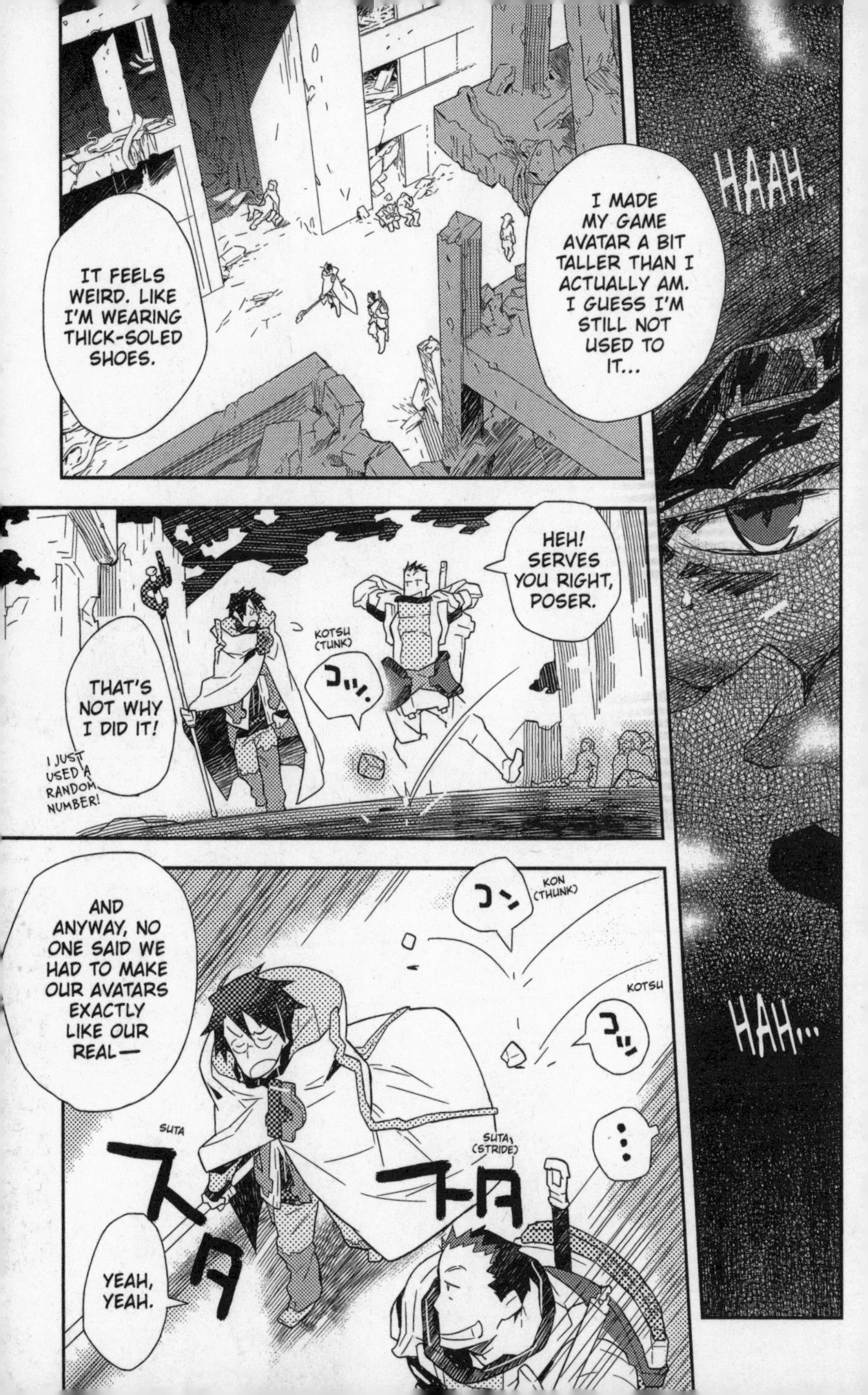
HAAH.
HAH...
I MADE MY GAME AVATAR A BIT TALLER THAN I ACTUALLY AM. I GUESS I'M STILL NOT USED TO IT...
IT FEELS WEIRD. LIKE I'M WEARING THICK-SOLED SHOES.
HEH! SERVES YOU RIGHT, POSER.
KOTSU (TUNK)
コッ.
THAT'S NOT WHY I DID IT!
I JUST USED A RANDOM NUMBER!
KON (THUNK)
コン
AND ANYWAY, NO ONE SAID WE HAD TO MAKE OUR AVATARS EXACTLY LIKE OUR REAL—
KOTSU
コッ
...
SUTA (STRIDE)
スタ
SUTA
スタ
YEAH, YEAH.

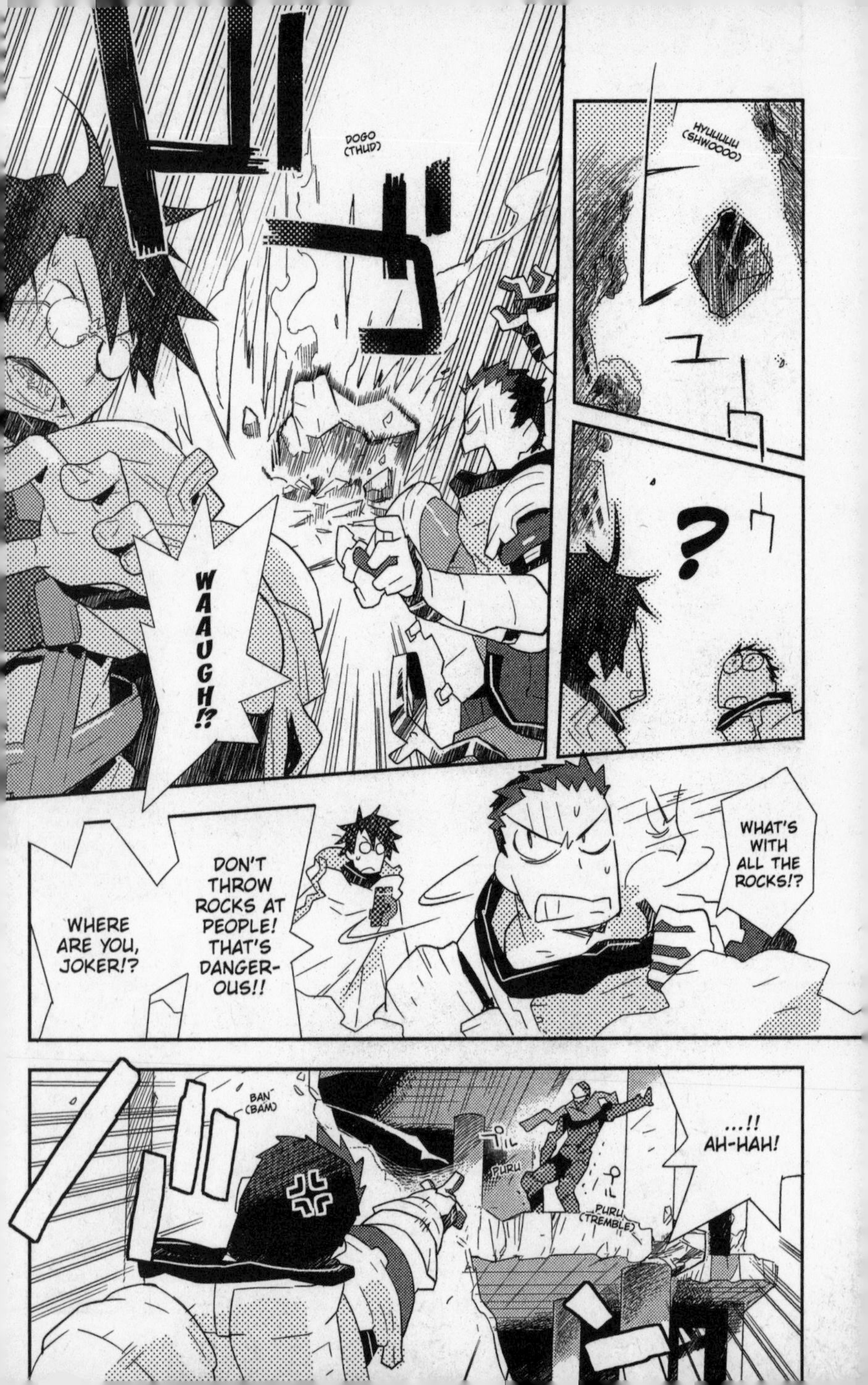
HYUUUUU (SHWOOOO)
?
DOGO (THUD)
WAAAUGH!?
WHAT'S WITH ALL THE ROCKS!?
DON'T THROW ROCKS AT PEOPLE! THAT'S DANGER-OUS!!
WHERE ARE YOU, JOKER!?
...!!
AH-HAH!
PURU
PURU (TREMBLE)
BAN (BAM)

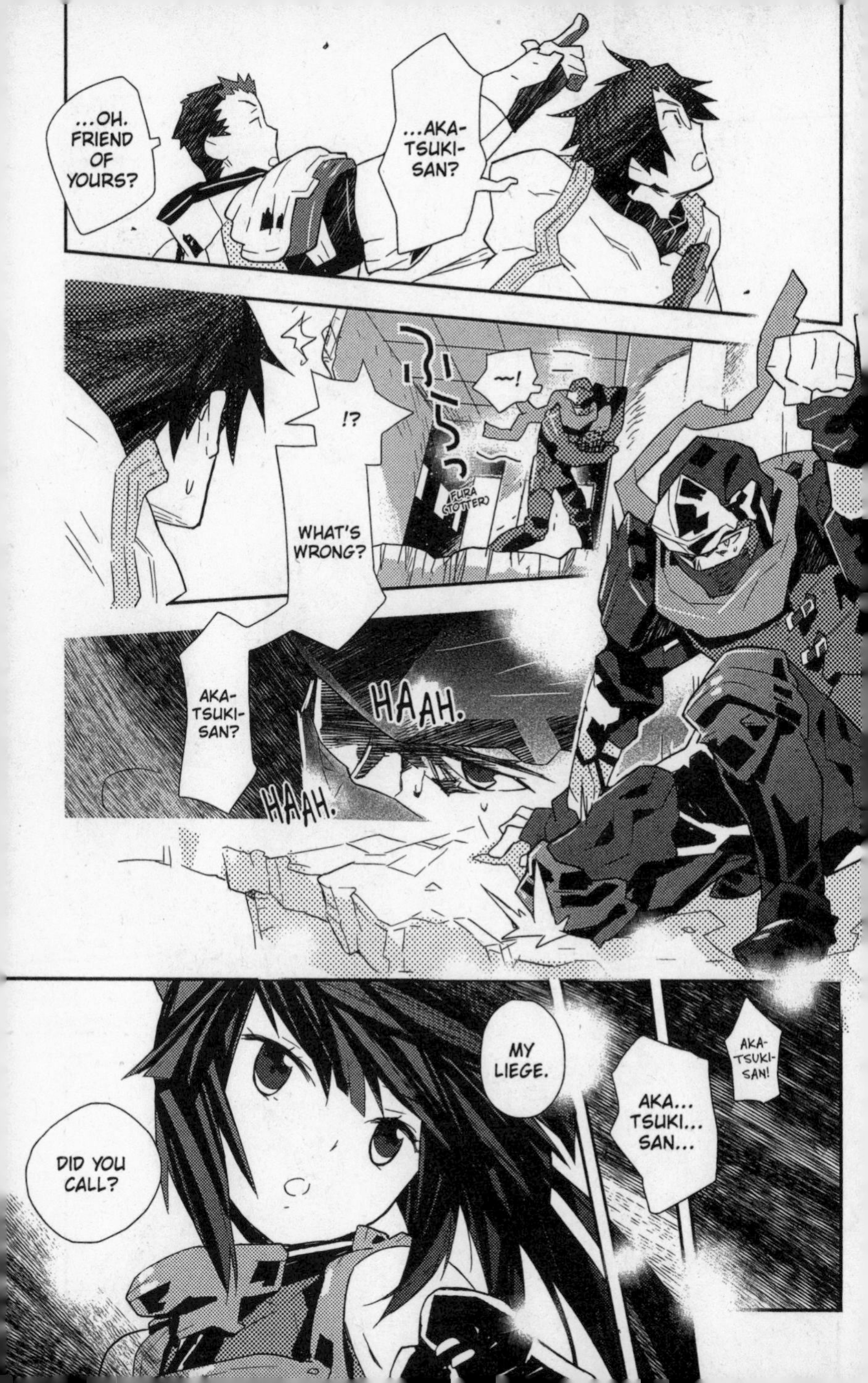

...AKA-TSUKI-SAN?
...OH. FRIEND OF YOURS?
~!
FURA (TOTTER)
!?
WHAT'S WRONG?
HAAH.
AKA-TSUKI-SAN?
HAAH.
AKA-TSUKI-SAN!
AKA... TSUKI... SAN...
MY LIEGE.
DID YOU CALL?

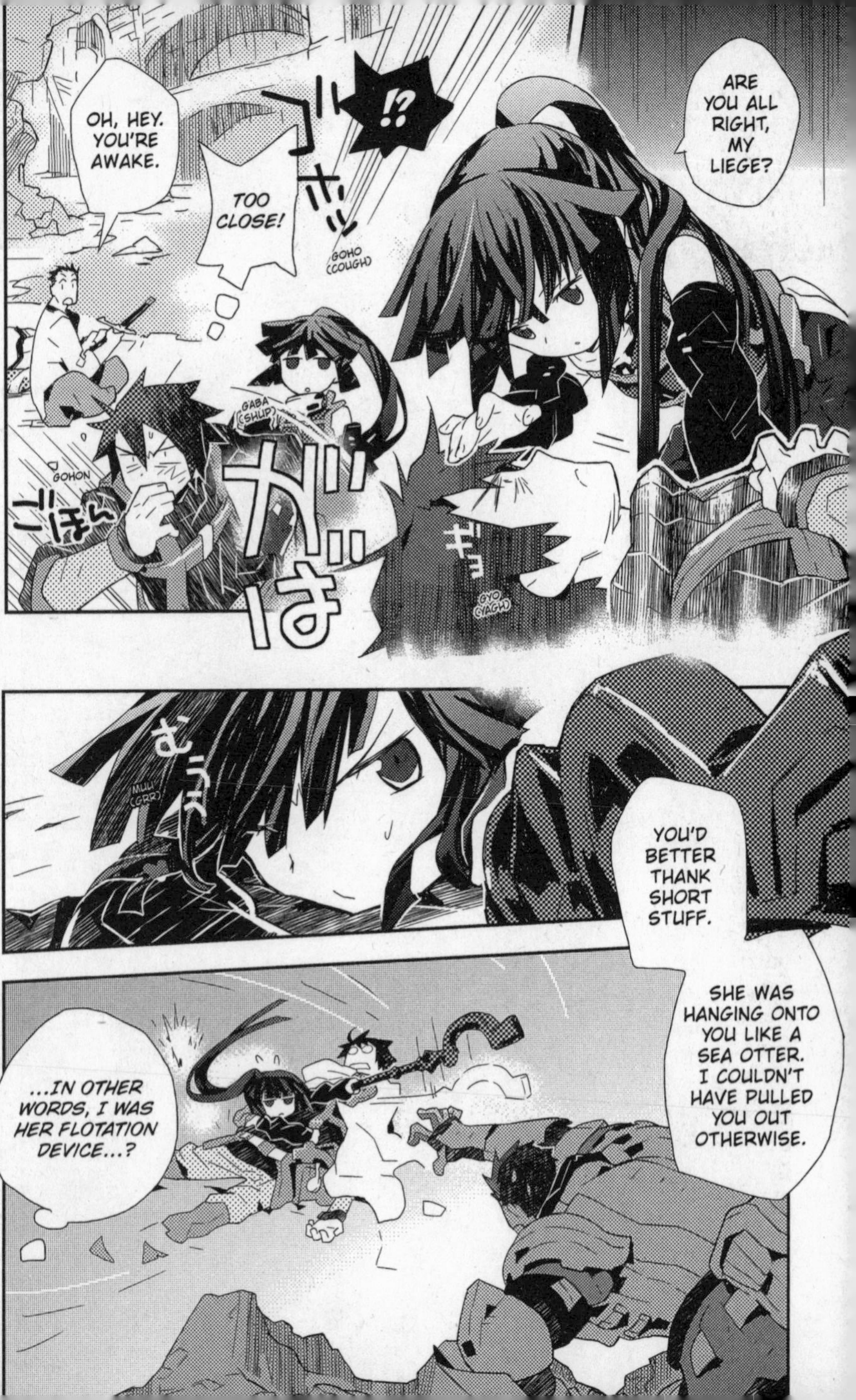
ARE YOU ALL RIGHT, MY LIEGE?
!?
ゴホッ
GOHO (COUGH)
TOO CLOSE!
OH, HEY. YOU'RE AWAKE.
ギョ
GYO (YAGH)
ガバ
GABA (SHUP)
ごほん
GOHON
YOU'D BETTER THANK SHORT STUFF.
MUU (GRR)
SHE WAS HANGING ONTO YOU LIKE A SEA OTTER. I COULDN'T HAVE PULLED YOU OUT OTHERWISE.
...IN OTHER WORDS, I WAS HER FLOTATION DEVICE...?

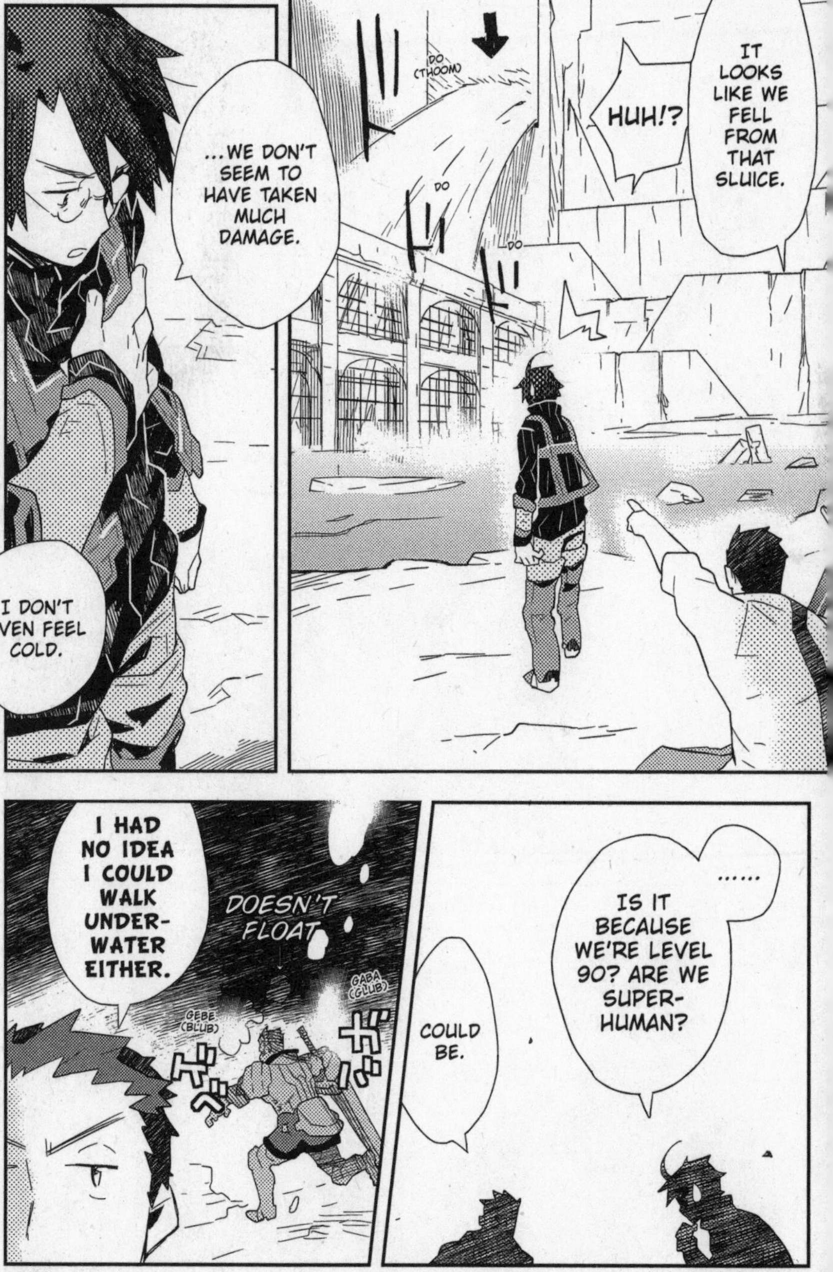
IT LOOKS LIKE WE FELL FROM THAT SLUICE.
HUH!?
DO (THOOM)
DO
DO
...WE DON'T SEEM TO HAVE TAKEN MUCH DAMAGE.
I DON'T EVEN FEEL COLD.
......
IS IT BECAUSE WE'RE LEVEL 90? ARE WE SUPER-HUMAN?
COULD BE.
I HAD NO IDEA I COULD WALK UNDER-WATER EITHER.
DOESN'T FLOAT
GABA (GLUB)
GEBE (BLUB)

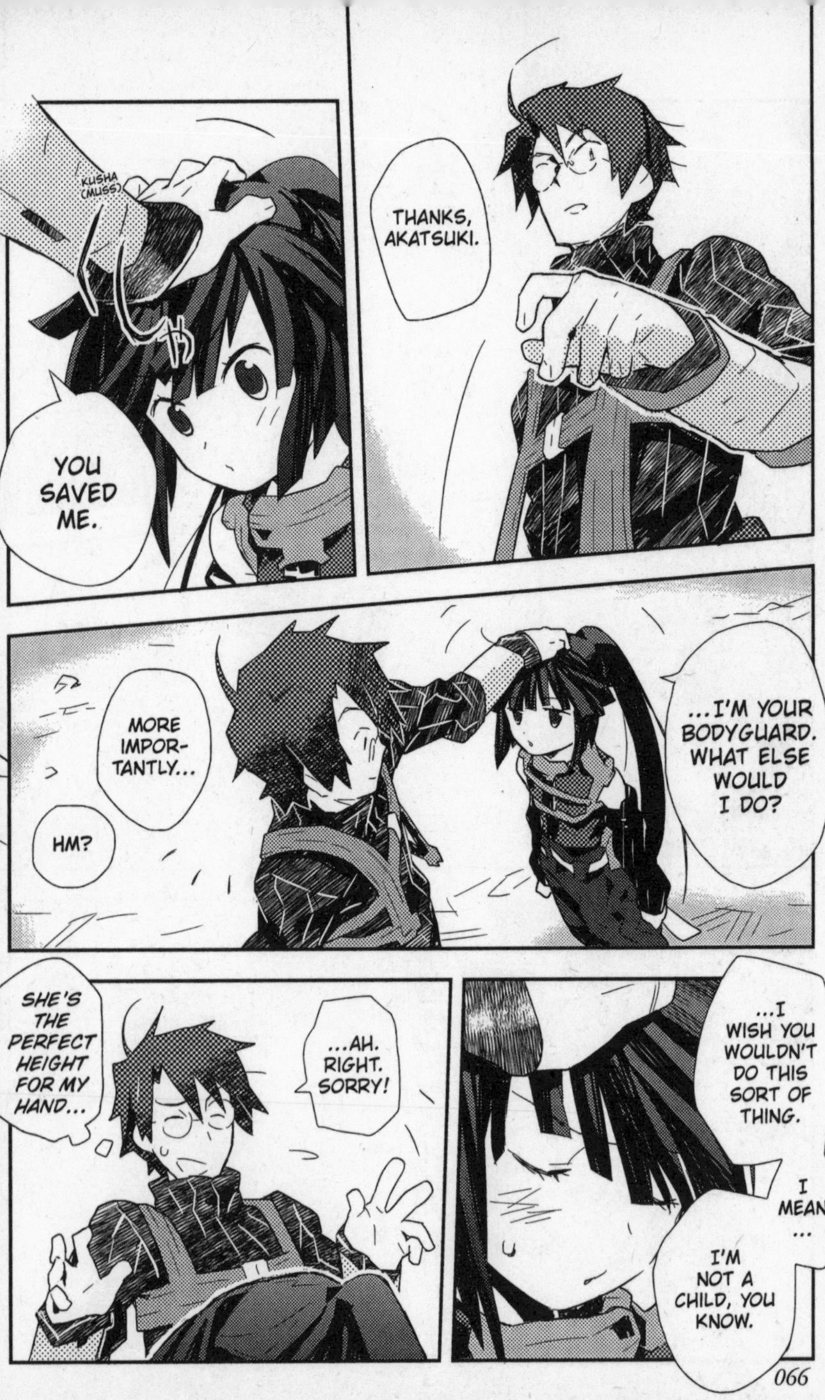
THANKS, AKATSUKI.
KUSHA (MUSS)
YOU SAVED ME.
...I'M YOUR BODYGUARD. WHAT ELSE WOULD I DO?
MORE IMPORTANTLY...
HM?
...I WISH YOU WOULDN'T DO THIS SORT OF THING.
I MEAN...
I'M NOT A CHILD, YOU KNOW.
...AH. RIGHT. SORRY!
SHE'S THE PERFECT HEIGHT FOR MY HAND...

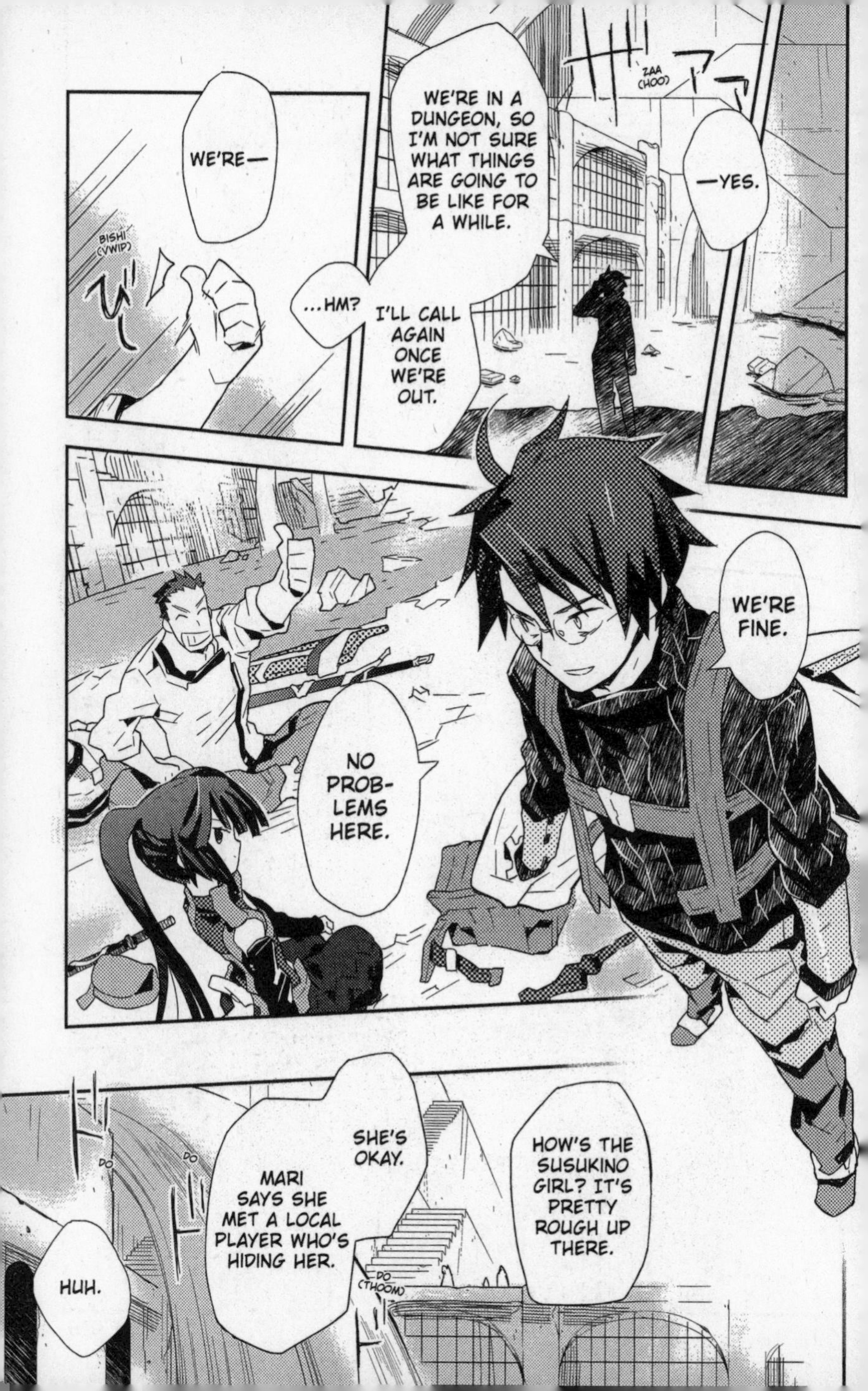
ZAA (HOO)
—YES.
WE'RE IN A DUNGEON, SO I'M NOT SURE WHAT THINGS ARE GOING TO BE LIKE FOR A WHILE.
I'LL CALL AGAIN ONCE WE'RE OUT.
...HM?
BISHI (VWIP)
WE'RE—
WE'RE FINE.
NO PROBLEMS HERE.
HOW'S THE SUSUKINO GIRL? IT'S PRETTY ROUGH UP THERE.
SHE'S OKAY.
DO (THOOM)
MARI SAYS SHE MET A LOCAL PLAYER WHO'S HIDING HER.
DO
DO
HUH.

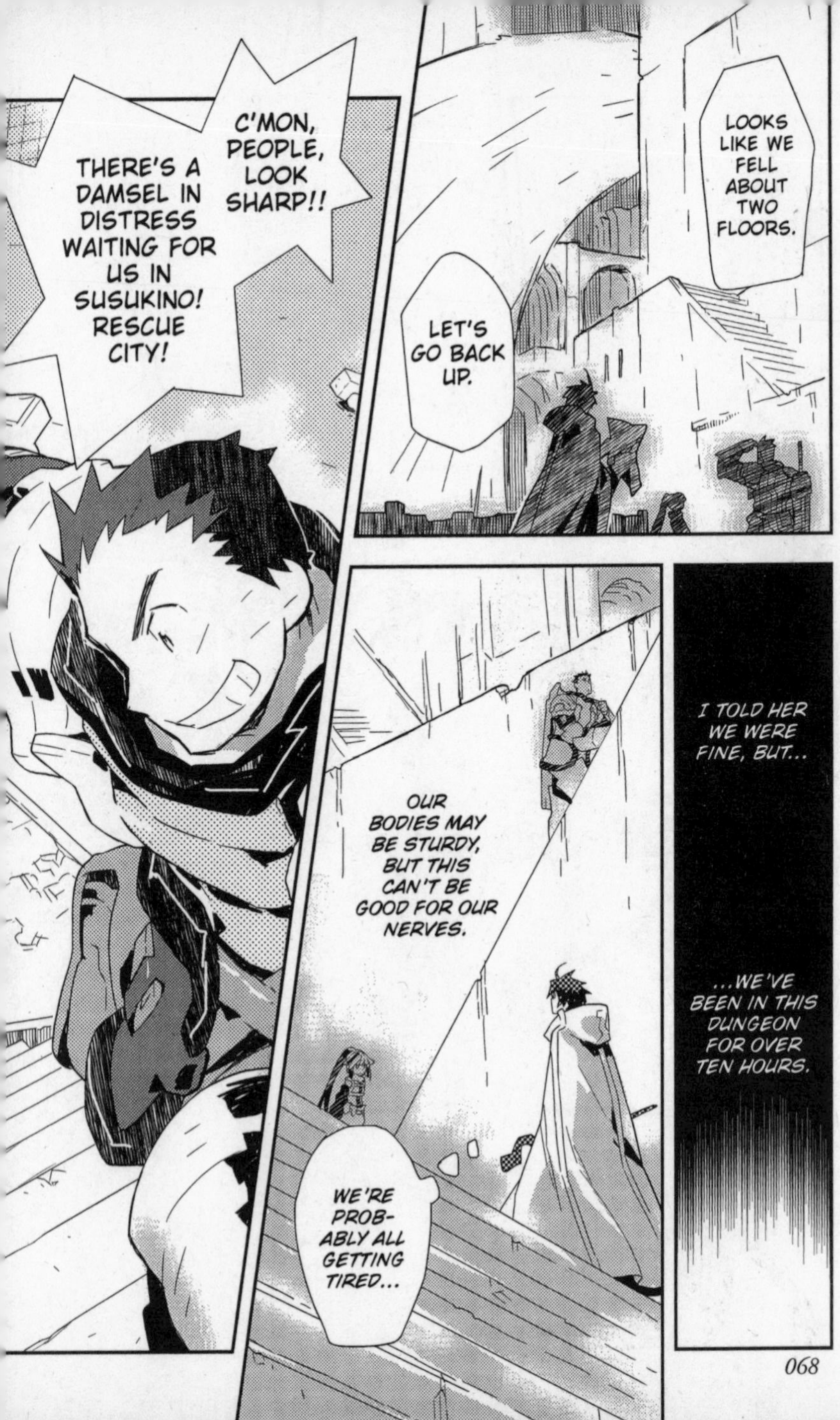
LOOKS LIKE WE FELL ABOUT TWO FLOORS.
LET'S GO BACK UP.
I TOLD HER WE WERE FINE, BUT...
...WE'VE BEEN IN THIS DUNGEON FOR OVER TEN HOURS.
OUR BODIES MAY BE STURDY, BUT THIS CAN'T BE GOOD FOR OUR NERVES.
WE'RE PROB-ABLY ALL GETTING TIRED...
C'MON, PEOPLE, LOOK SHARP!!
THERE'S A DAMSEL IN DISTRESS WAITING FOR US IN SUSUKINO! RESCUE CITY!

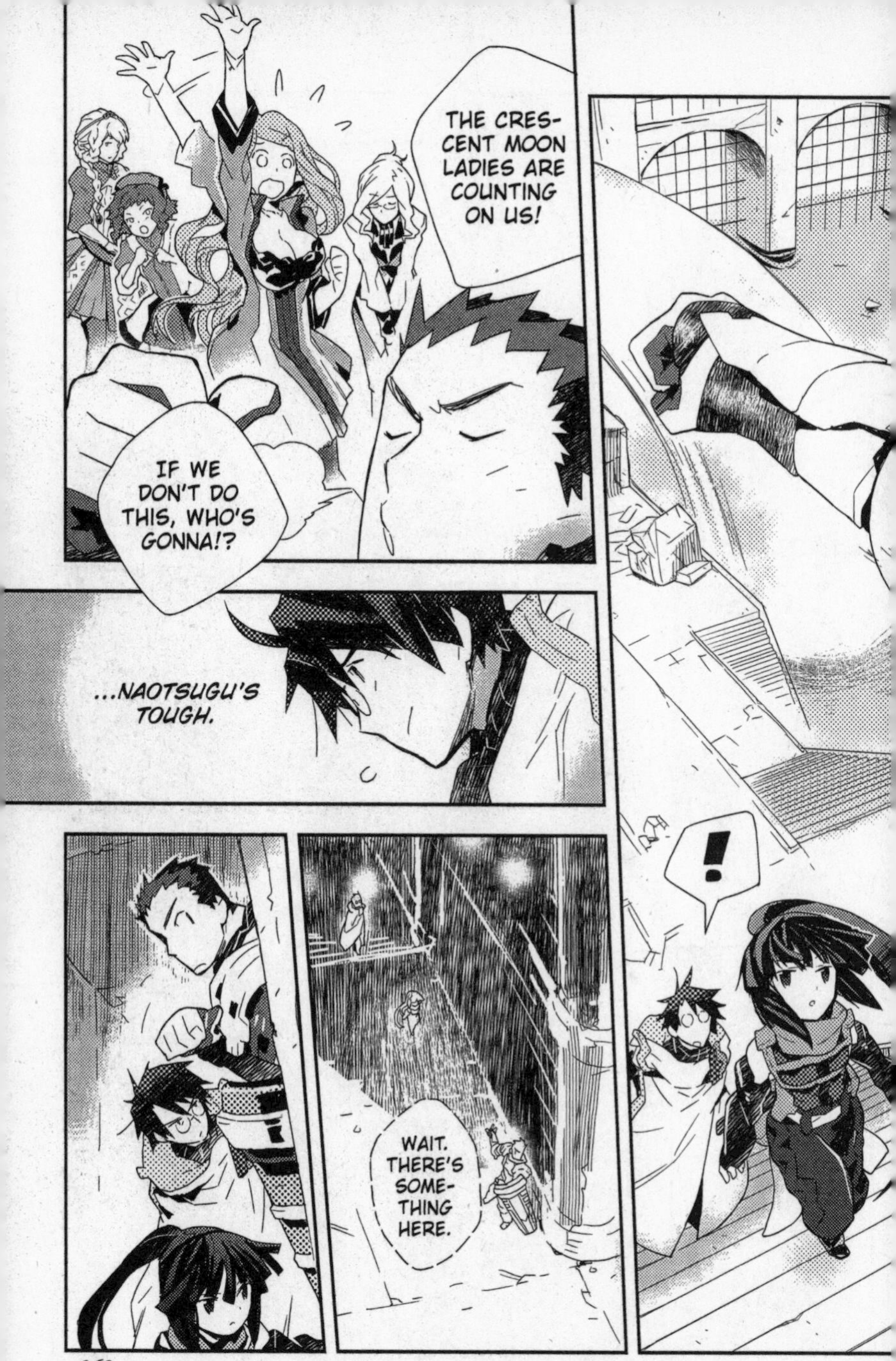
!
THE CRES-CENT MOON LADIES ARE COUNTING ON US!
IF WE DON'T DO THIS, WHO'S GONNA!?
...NAOTSUGU'S TOUGH.
WAIT. THERE'S SOME-THING HERE.

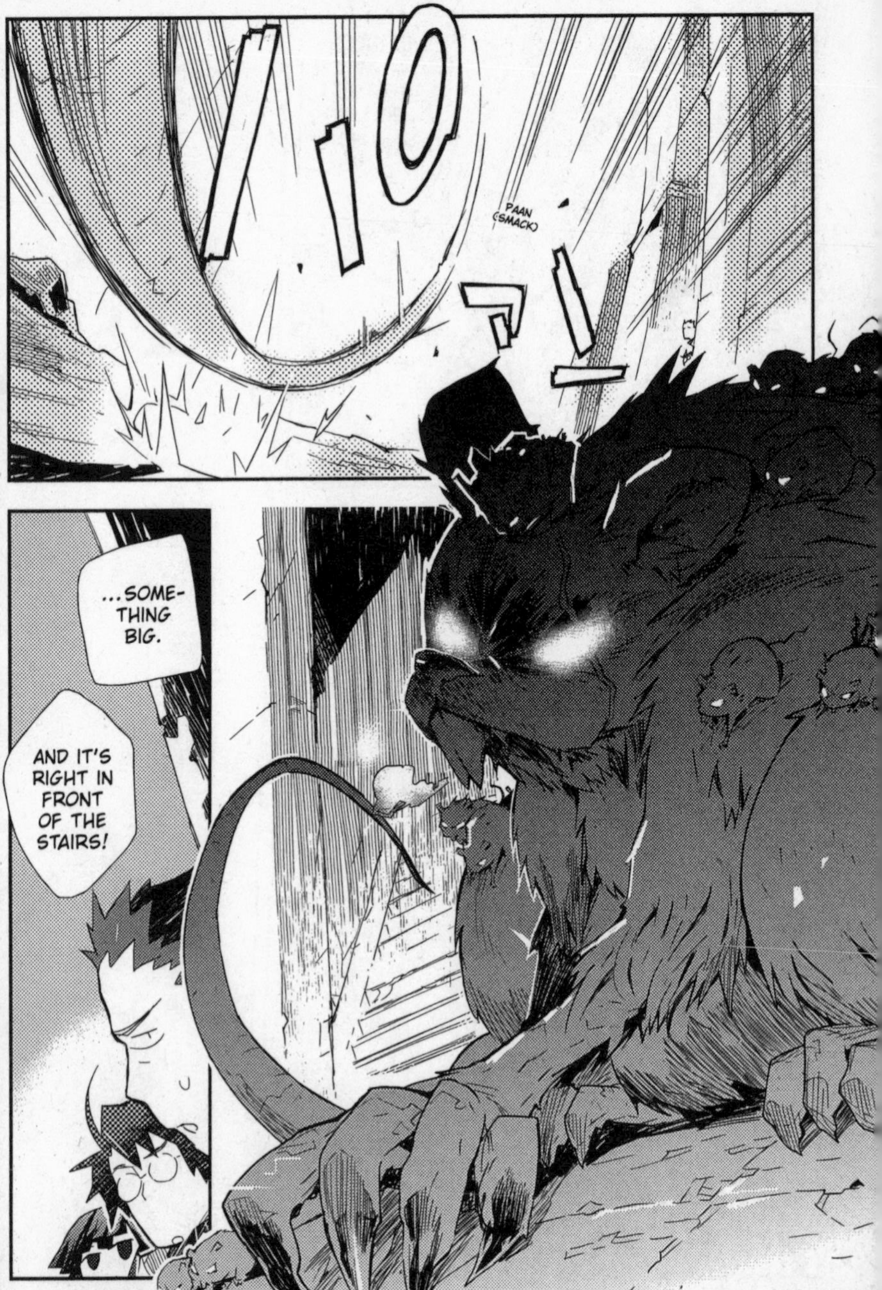
PAAN (SMACK)
...SOME-THING BIG.
AND IT'S RIGHT IN FRONT OF THE STAIRS!

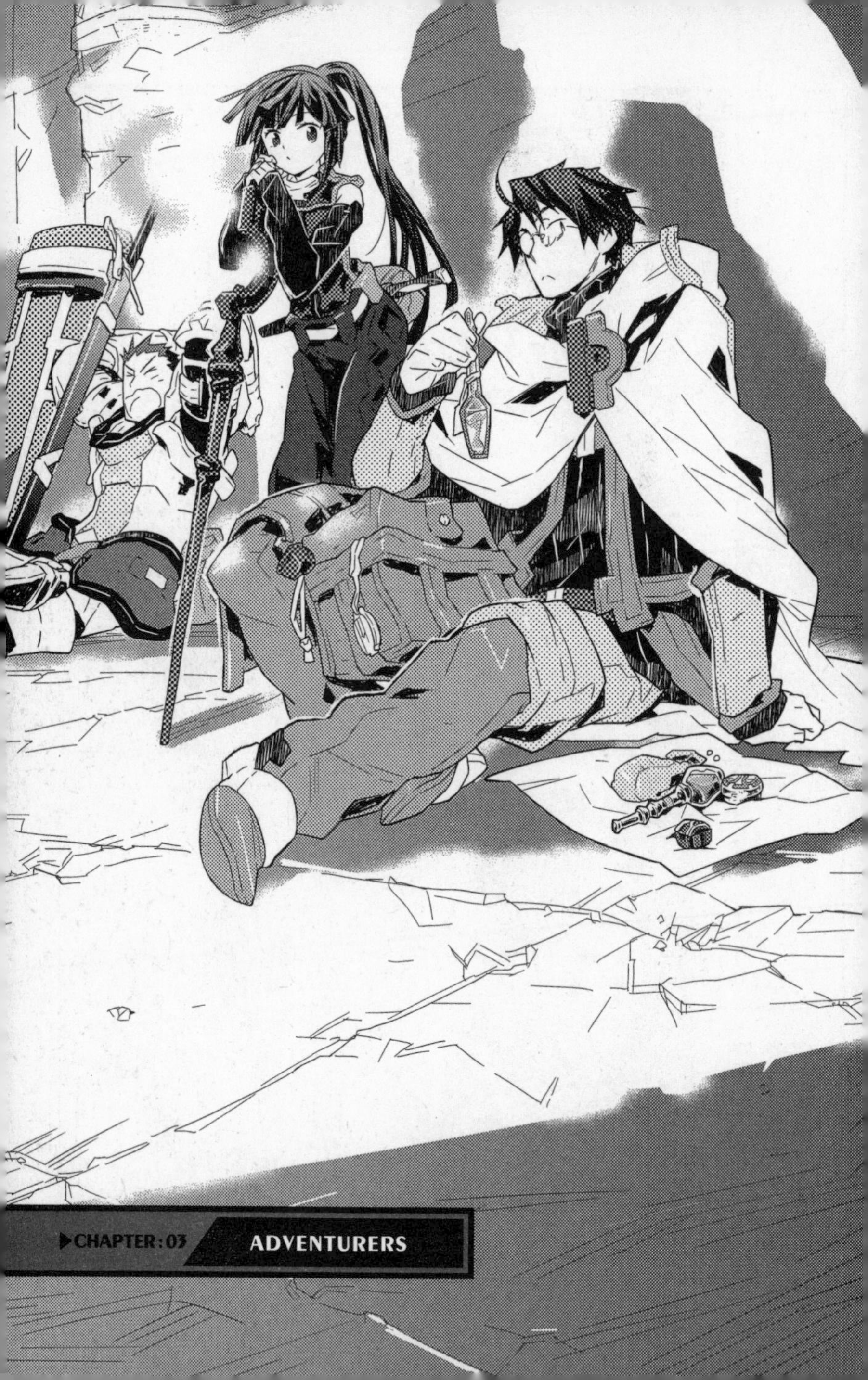

# ▶CHAPTER: 03 ADVENTURERS

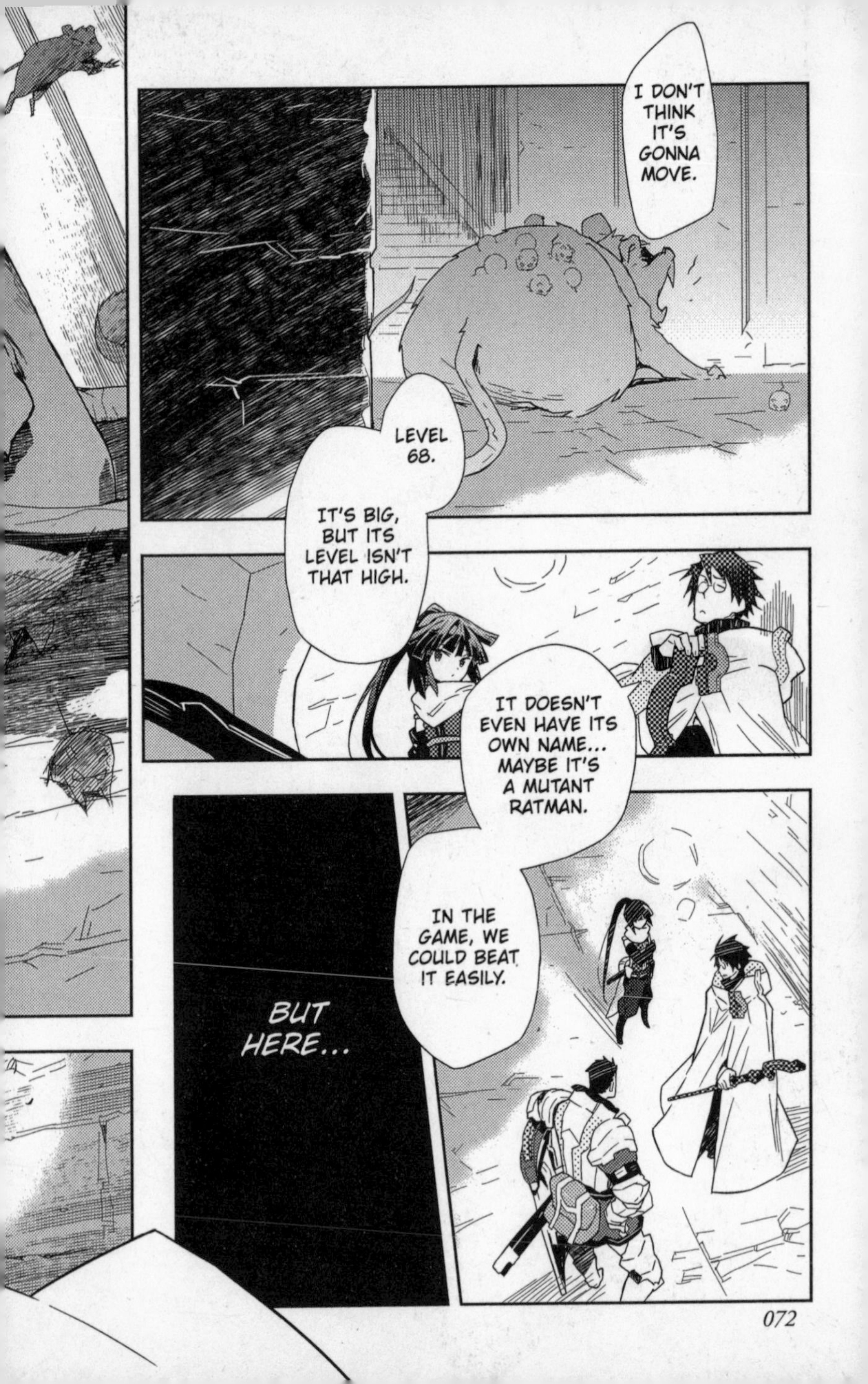
I DON'T THINK IT'S GONNA MOVE.
LEVEL 68.
IT'S BIG, BUT ITS LEVEL ISN'T THAT HIGH.
IT DOESN'T EVEN HAVE ITS OWN NAME... MAYBE IT'S A MUTANT RATMAN.
IN THE GAME, WE COULD BEAT IT EASILY.
BUT HERE...

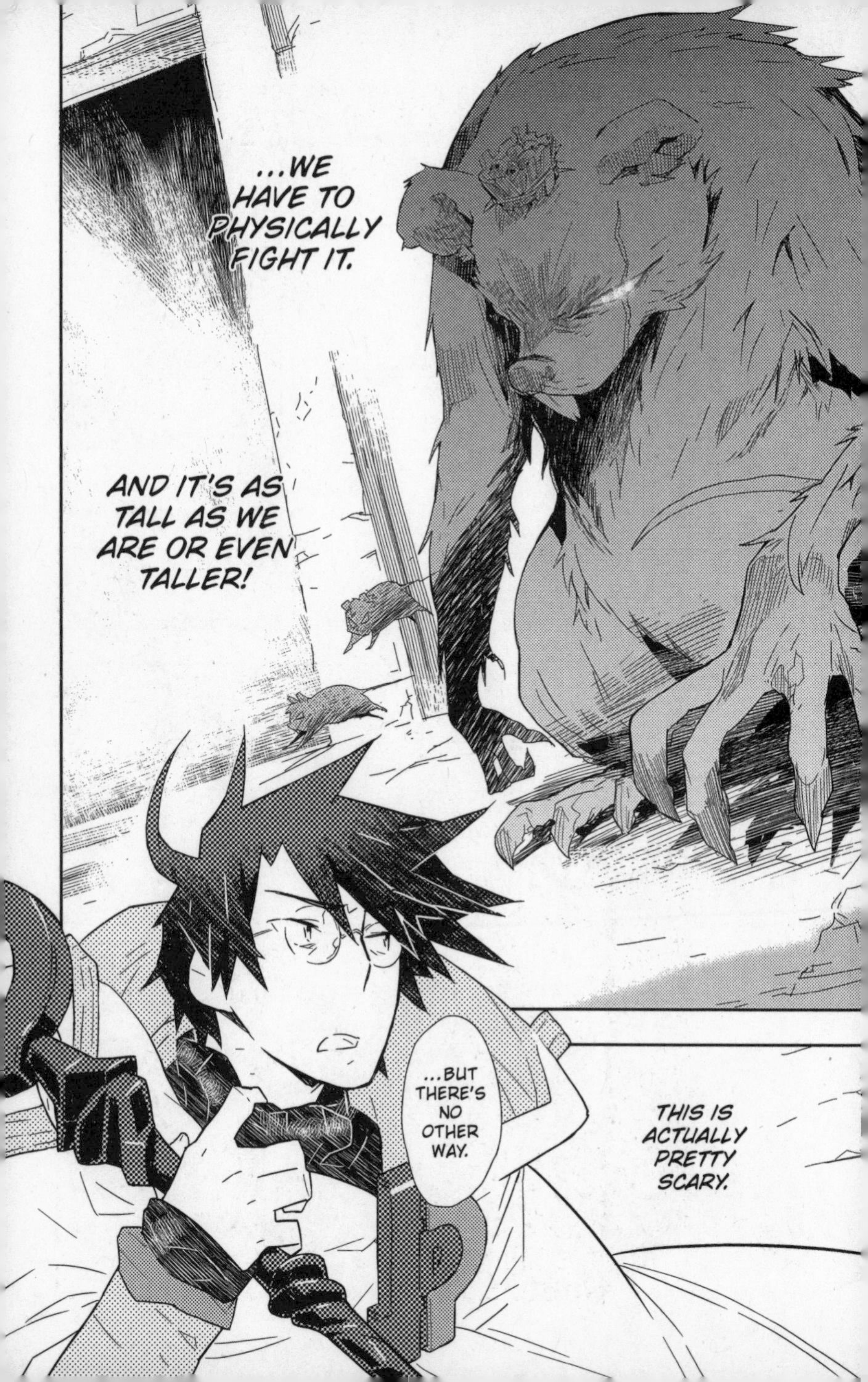
...WE HAVE TO PHYSICALLY FIGHT IT.
AND IT'S AS TALL AS WE ARE OR EVEN TALLER!
THIS IS ACTUALLY PRETTY SCARY.
...BUT THERE'S NO OTHER WAY.

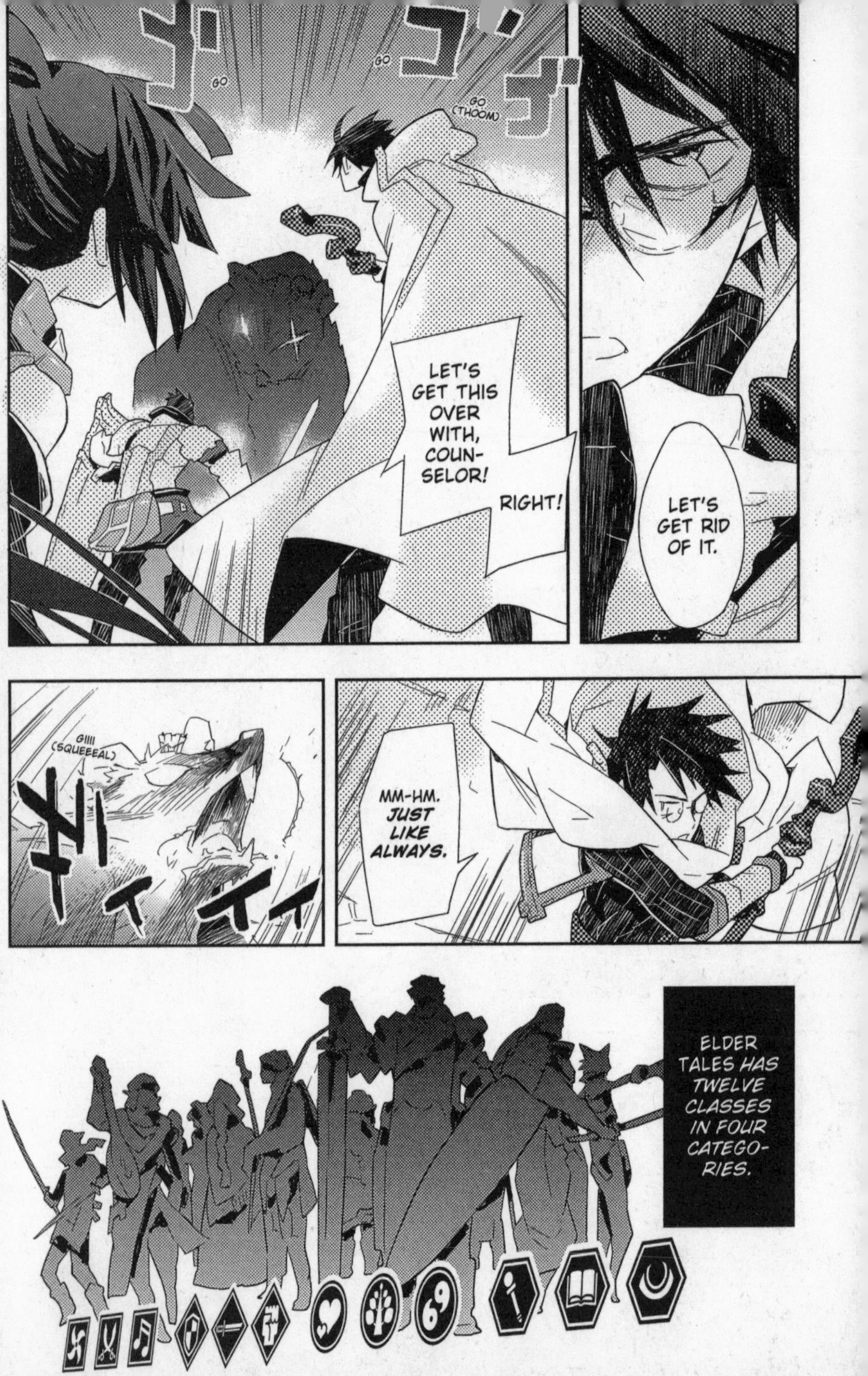
LET'S GET RID OF IT.
GO
GO
GO (THOOM)
LET'S GET THIS OVER WITH, COUN-SELOR!
RIGHT!
MM-HM. JUST LIKE ALWAYS.
GIIII (SQUEEEAL)
ELDER TALES HAS TWELVE CLASSES IN FOUR CATEGO-RIES.

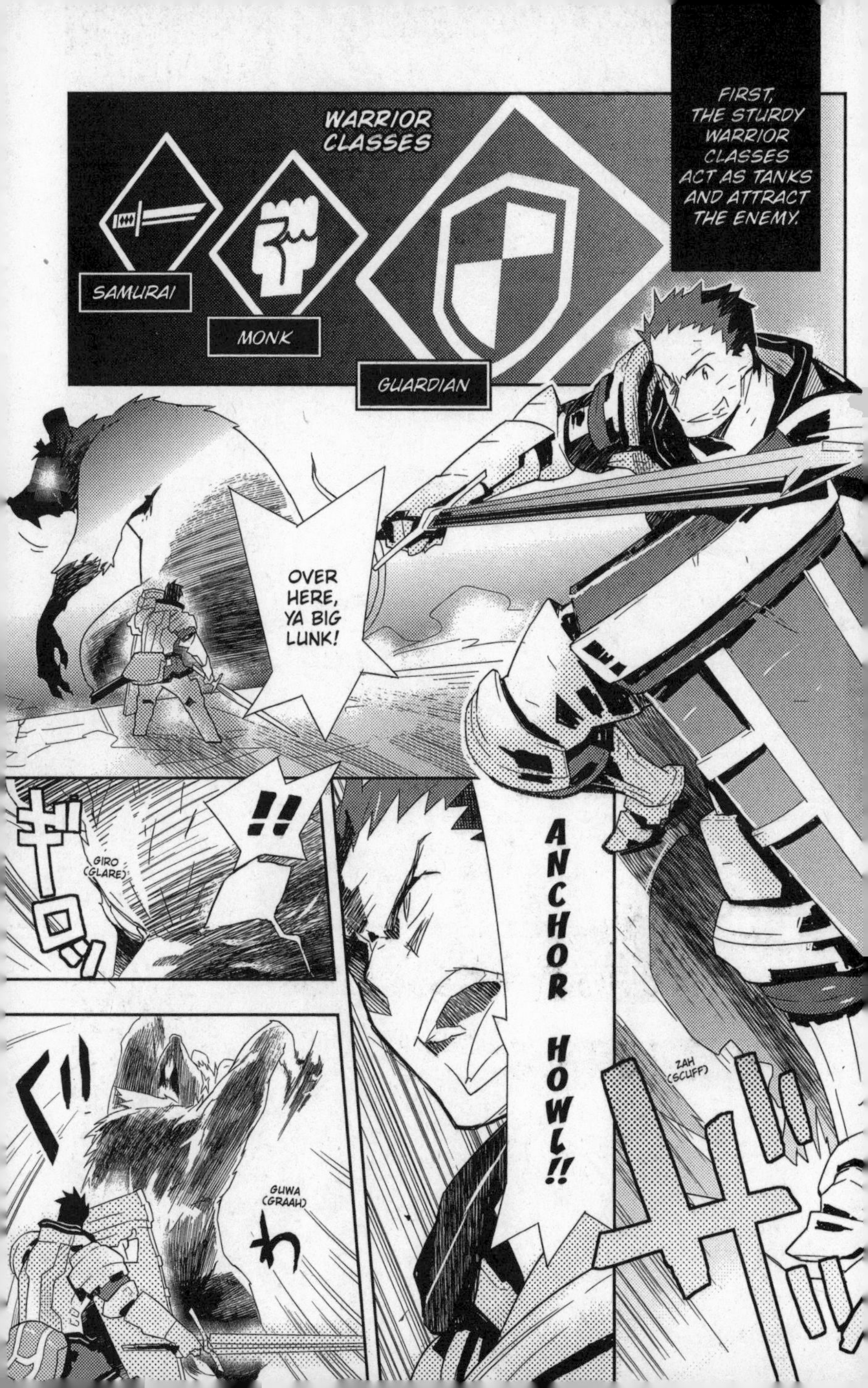

FIRST, THE STURDY WARRIOR CLASSES ACT AS TANKS AND ATTRACT THE ENEMY.
WARRIOR CLASSES
SAMURAI
MONK
GUARDIAN
OVER HERE, YA BIG LUNK!
ANCHOR HOWL!!
ZAH (SCUFF)
!!
GIRO (GLARE)
GUWA (GRAAH)

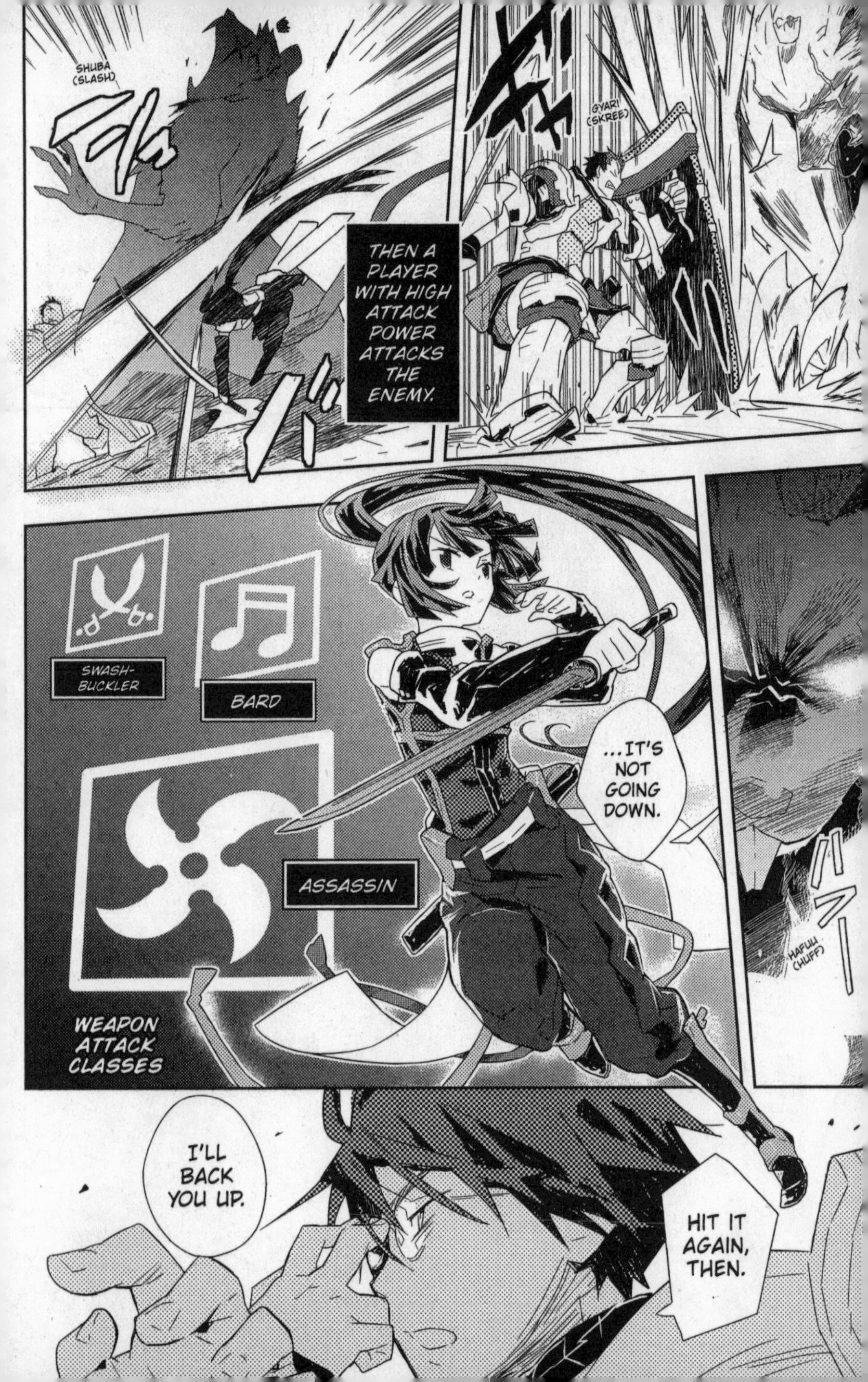
GYARI (SKREE)
THEN A PLAYER WITH HIGH ATTACK POWER ATTACKS THE ENEMY.
SHUBA (SLASH)
HAFUU (HUFF)
...IT'S NOT GOING DOWN.
SWASH-BUCKLER
BARD
ASSASSIN
WEAPON ATTACK CLASSES
HIT IT AGAIN, THEN.
I'LL BACK YOU UP.

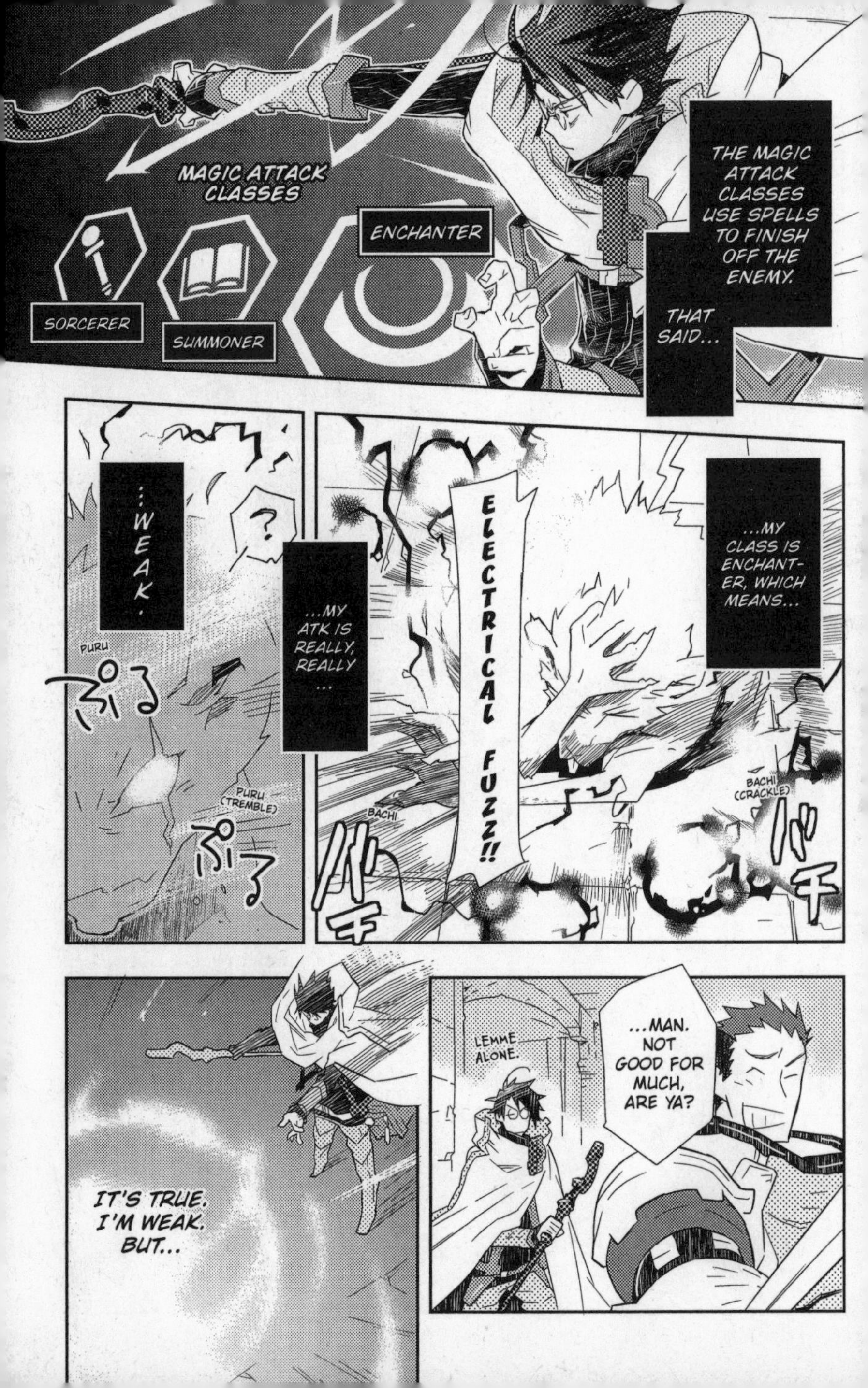
THE MAGIC ATTACK CLASSES USE SPELLS TO FINISH OFF THE ENEMY.
THAT SAID...
ENCHANTER
MAGIC ATTACK CLASSES
SUMMONER
SORCERER
...MY CLASS IS ENCHANTER, WHICH MEANS...
BACHI (CRACKLE)
バチ
ELECTRICAL FUZZ!!
BACHI
バチ
...MY ATK IS REALLY, REALLY ...
...WEAK.
?
PURU
ぷる
PURU (TREMBLE)
ぷる
...MAN. NOT GOOD FOR MUCH, ARE YA?
LEMME ALONE.
IT'S TRUE. I'M WEAK. BUT...

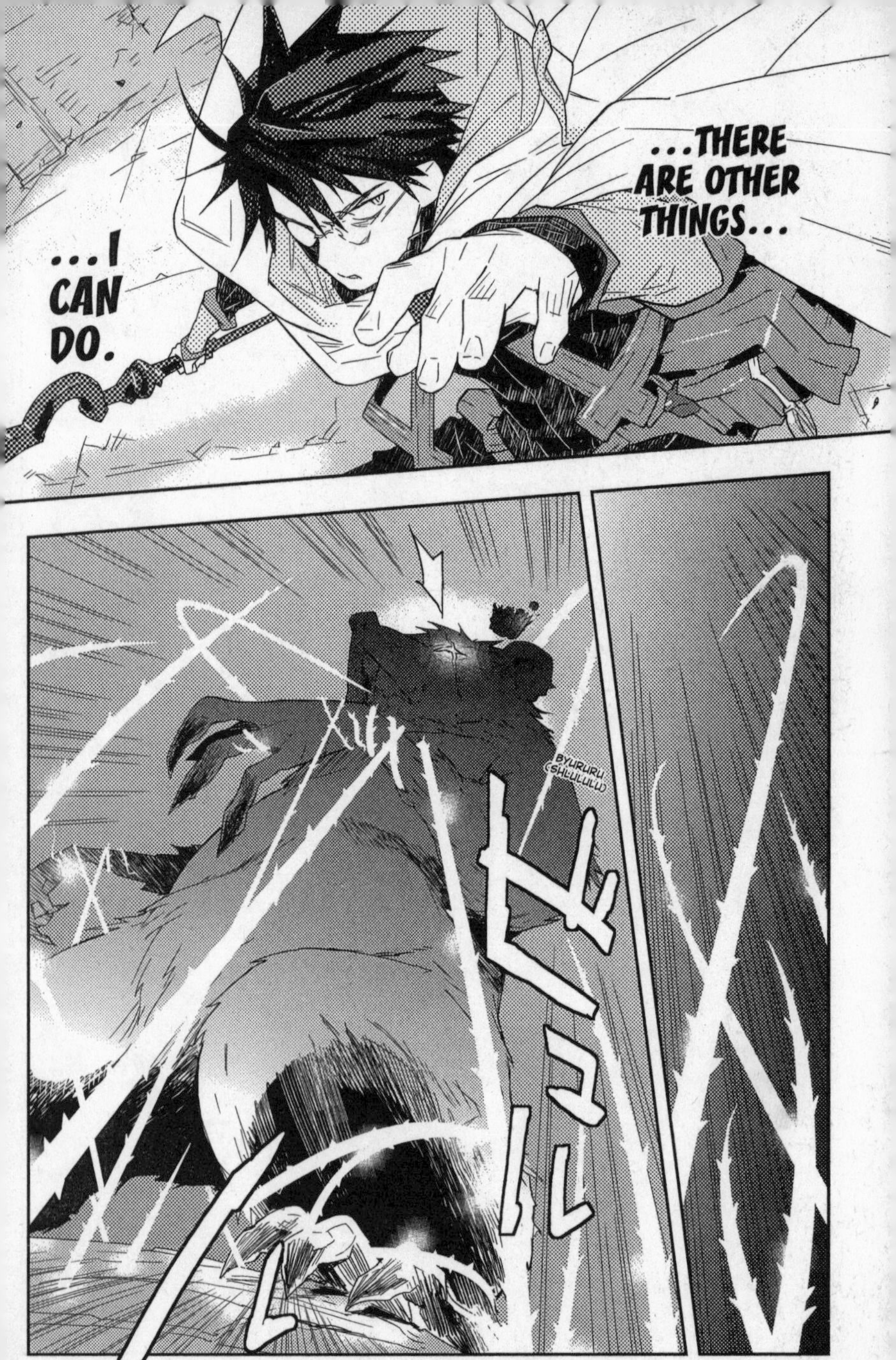
...THERE ARE OTHER THINGS...
...I CAN DO.
BYURURU (SHLULULU)

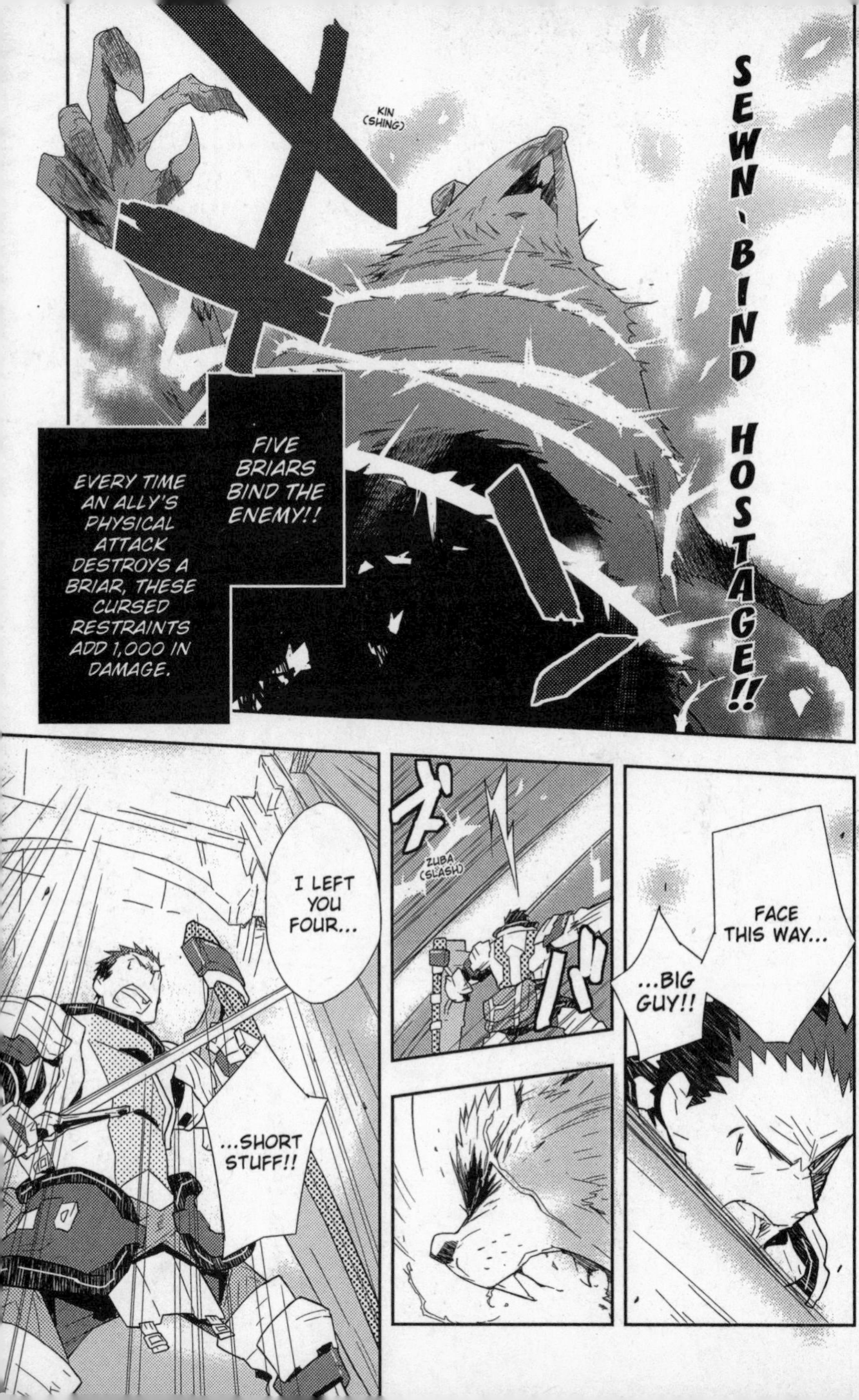
SEWN-BIND HOSTAGE!!
KIN (SHING)
FIVE BRIARS BIND THE ENEMY!!
EVERY TIME AN ALLY'S PHYSICAL ATTACK DESTROYS A BRIAR, THESE CURSED RESTRAINTS ADD 1,000 IN DAMAGE.
FACE THIS WAY...
...BIG GUY!!
ZUBA (SLASH)
I LEFT YOU FOUR...
...SHORT STUFF!!

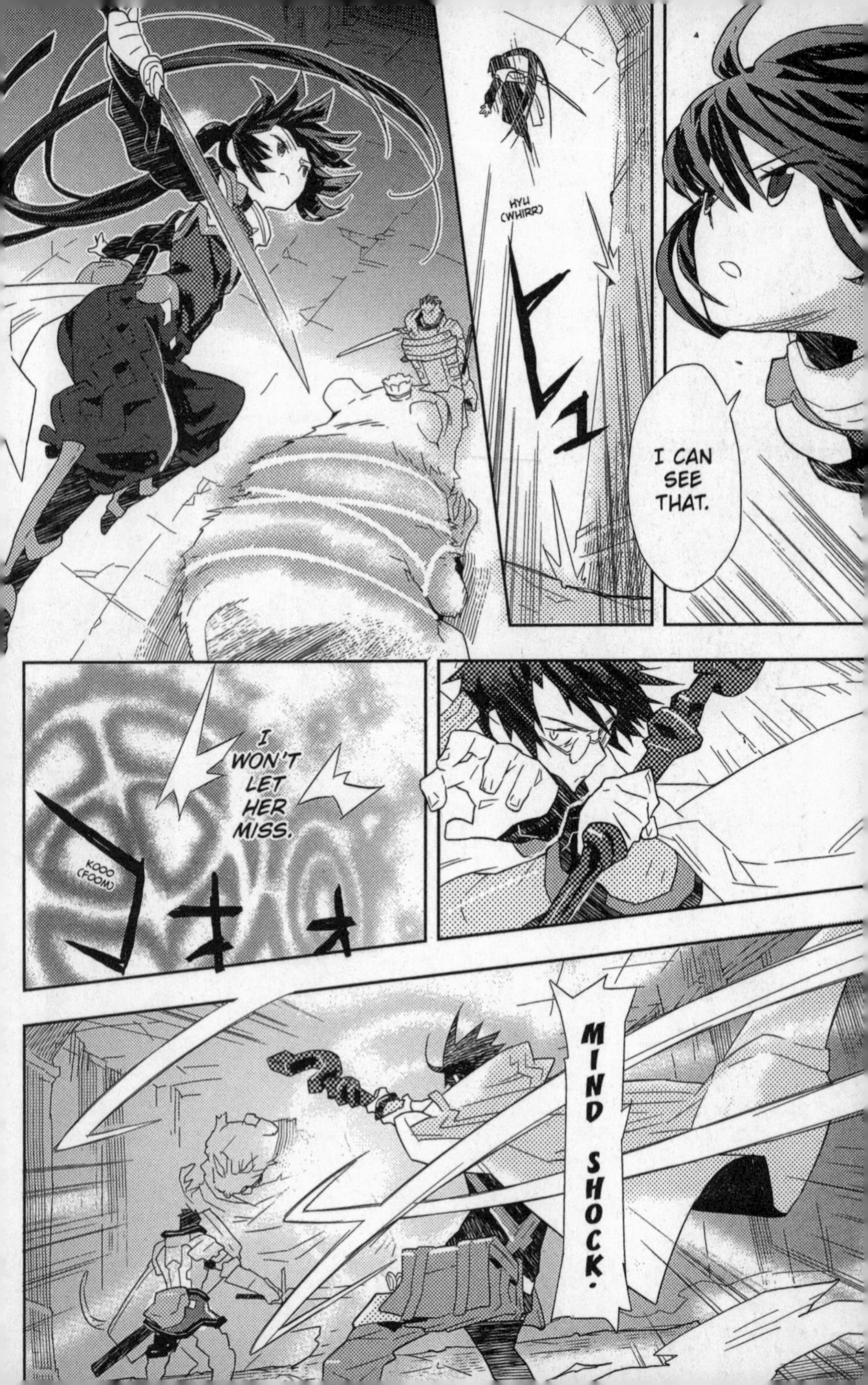
I CAN SEE THAT.
HYU (WHIRR)
I WON'T LET HER MISS.
KOOO (FOOM)
MIND SHOCK.

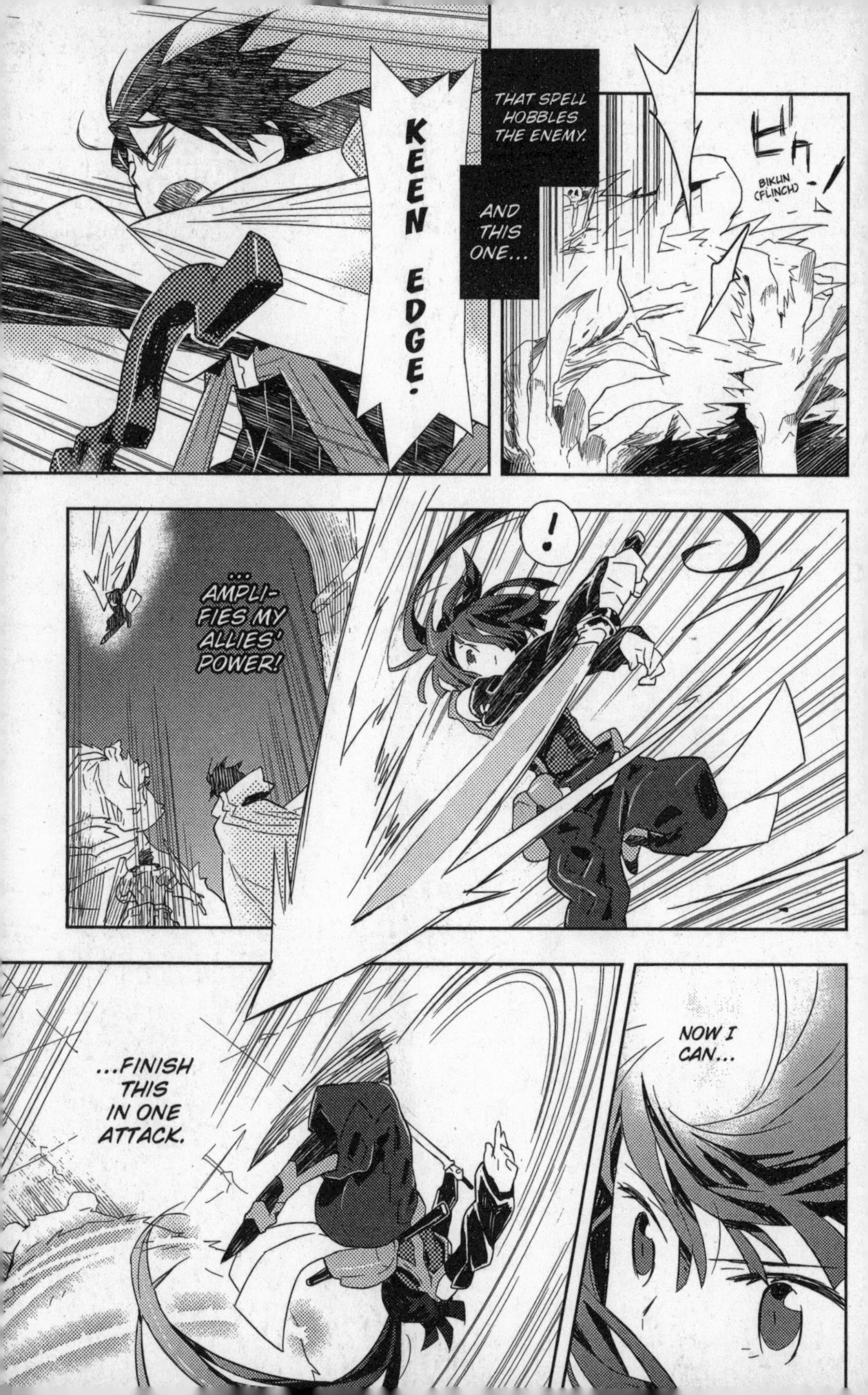
ビクン
BIKUN (FLINCH)
THAT SPELL HOBBLES THE ENEMY.
AND THIS ONE...
KEEN EDGE.
!
...AMPLIFIES MY ALLIES' POWER!
NOW I CAN...
...FINISH THIS IN ONE ATTACK.

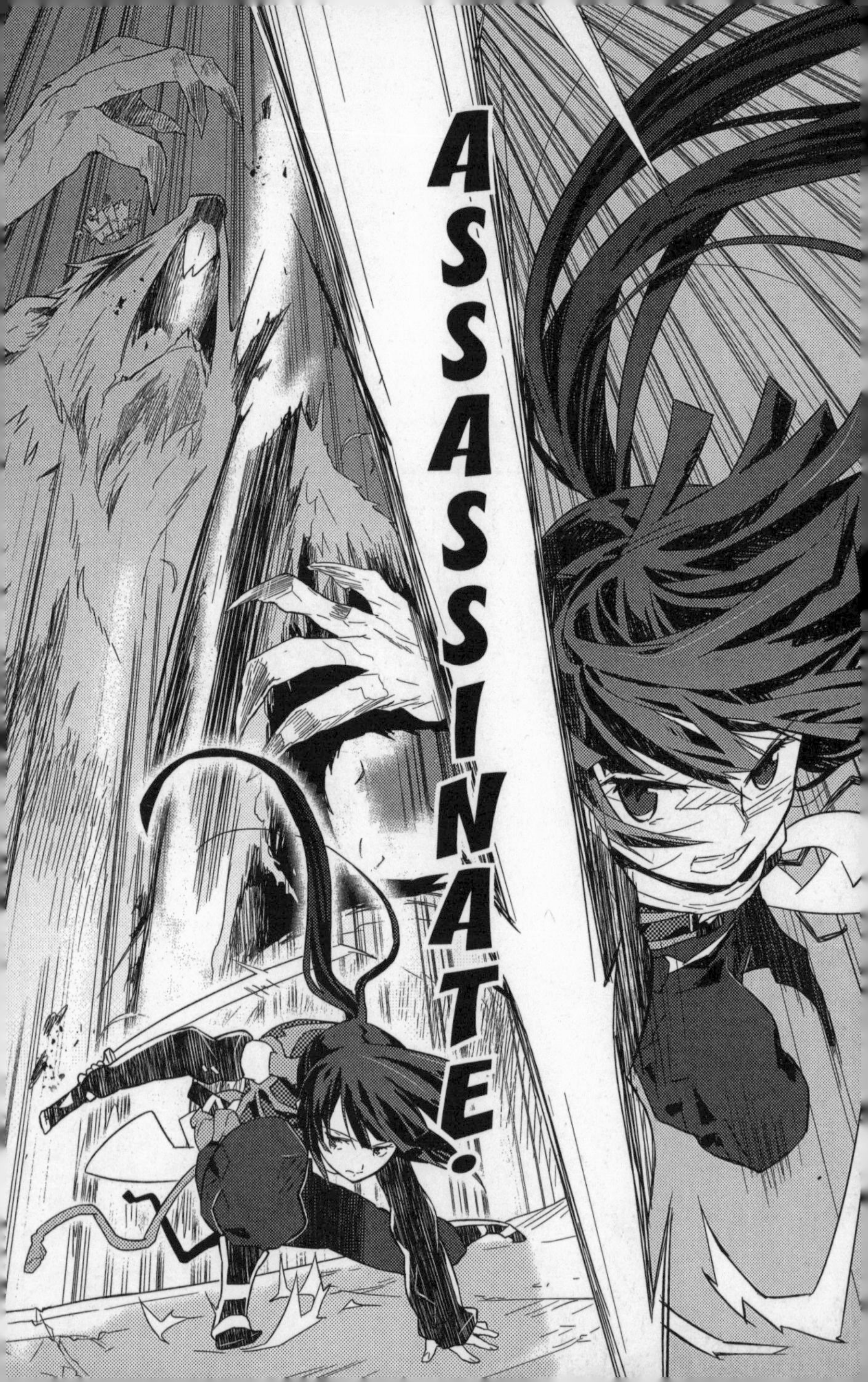
ASSASSINATE!

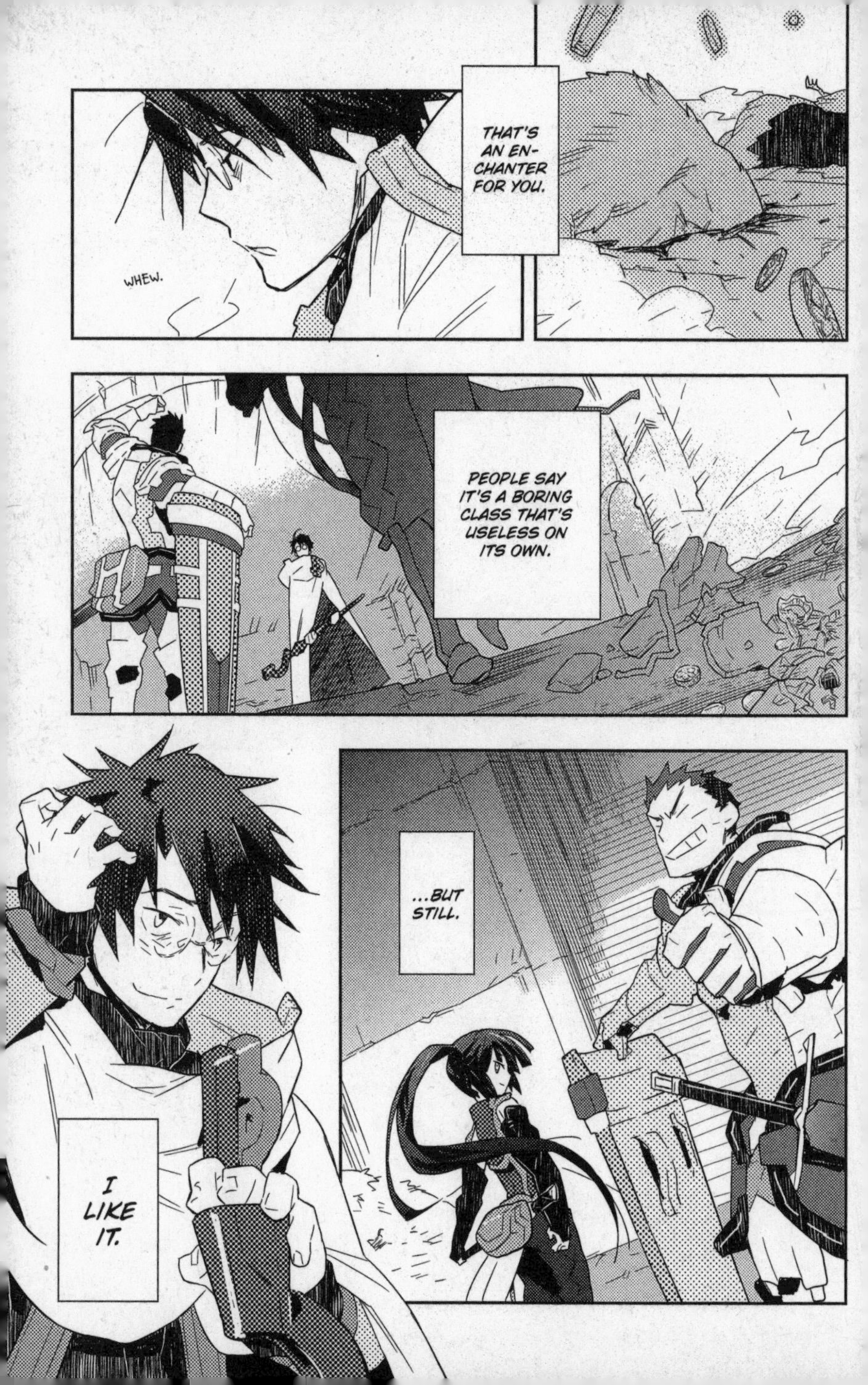
THAT'S AN EN-CHANTER FOR YOU.
WHEW.
PEOPLE SAY IT'S A BORING CLASS THAT'S USELESS ON ITS OWN.
...BUT STILL.
I LIKE IT.

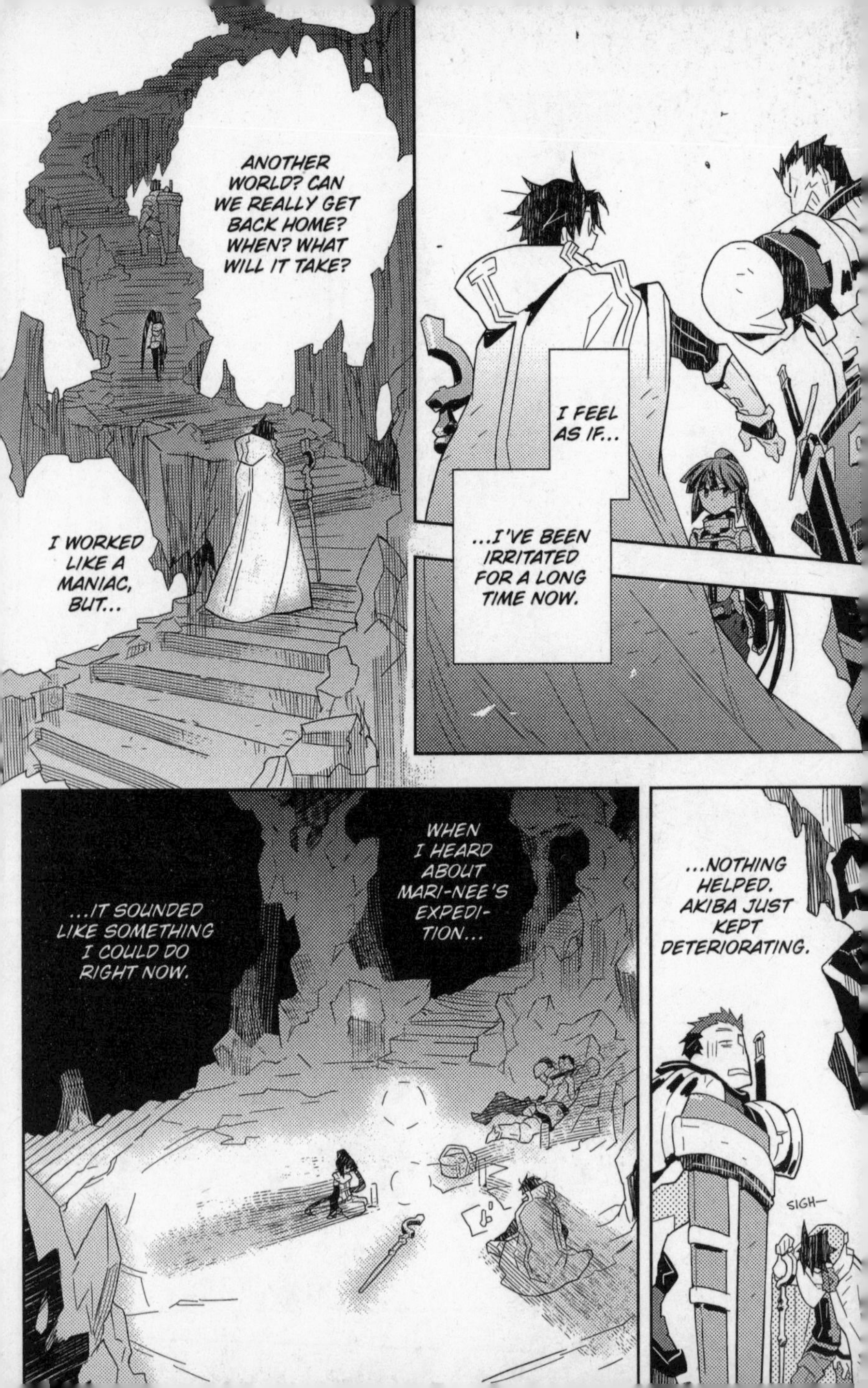
I FEEL AS IF...
...I'VE BEEN IRRITATED FOR A LONG TIME NOW.
ANOTHER WORLD? CAN WE REALLY GET BACK HOME? WHEN? WHAT WILL IT TAKE?
I WORKED LIKE A MANIAC, BUT...
...NOTHING HELPED. AKIBA JUST KEPT DETERIORATING.
SIGH—
WHEN I HEARD ABOUT MARI-NEE'S EXPEDITION...
...IT SOUNDED LIKE SOMETHING I COULD DO RIGHT NOW.

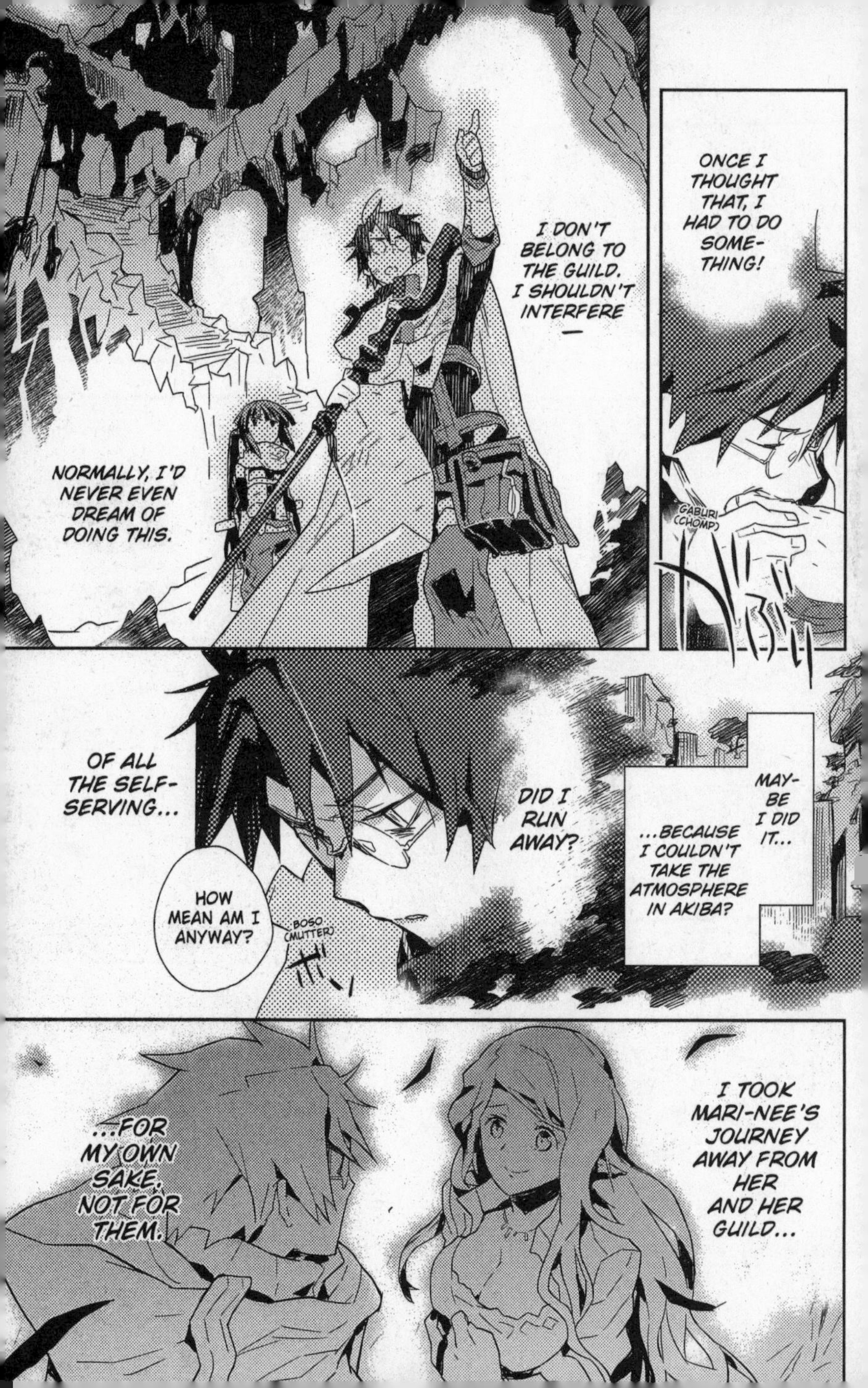
ONCE I THOUGHT THAT, I HAD TO DO SOME-THING!
GABURI (CHOMP)
I DON'T BELONG TO THE GUILD. I SHOULDN'T INTERFERE —
NORMALLY, I'D NEVER EVEN DREAM OF DOING THIS.
MAY-BE I DID IT...
...BECAUSE I COULDN'T TAKE THE ATMOSPHERE IN AKIBA?
DID I RUN AWAY?
OF ALL THE SELF-SERVING...
BOSO (MUTTER)
HOW MEAN AM I ANYWAY?
I TOOK MARI-NEE'S JOURNEY AWAY FROM HER AND HER GUILD...
...FOR MY OWN SAKE. NOT FOR THEM.

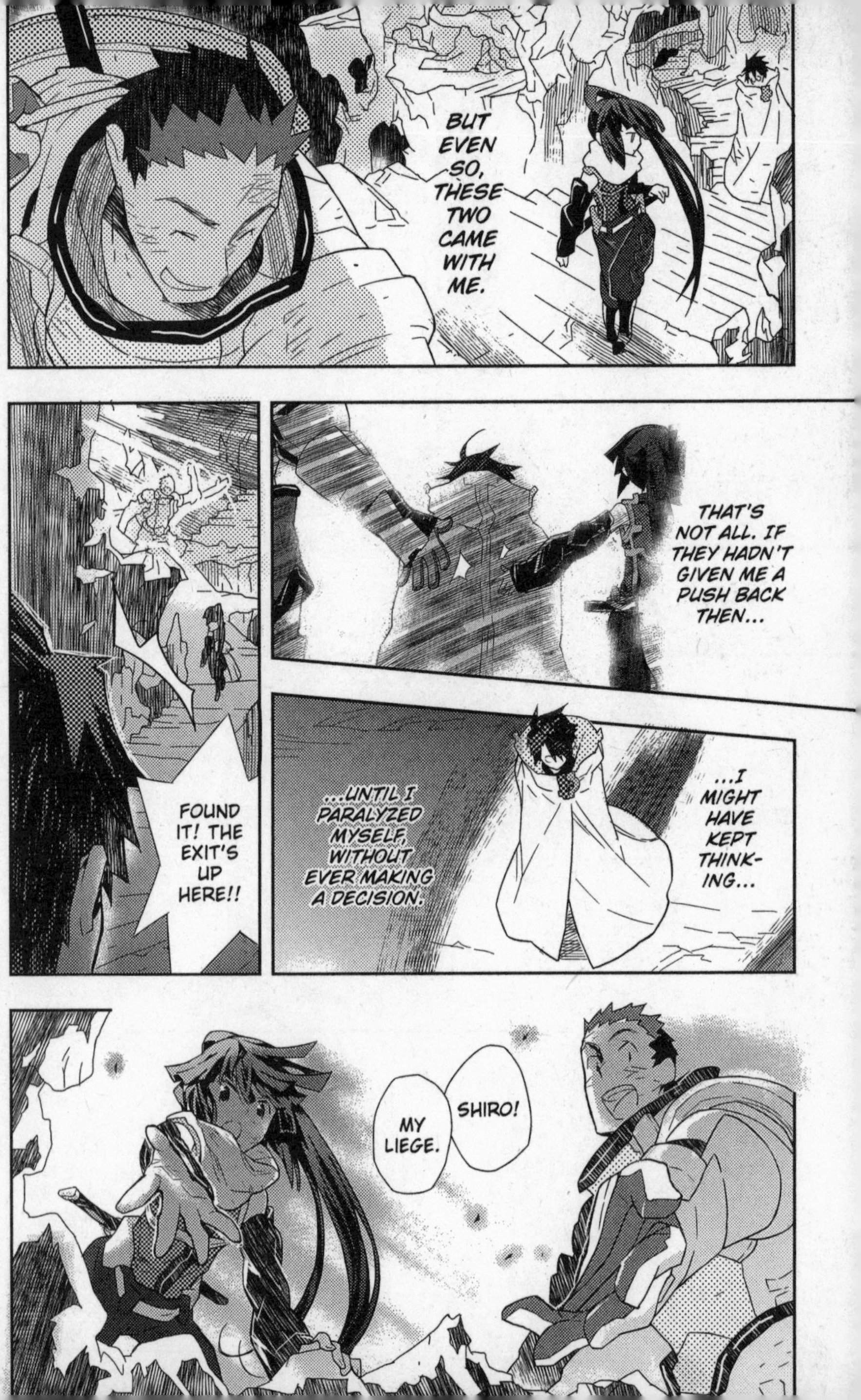
BUT EVEN SO, THESE TWO CAME WITH ME.
THAT'S NOT ALL. IF THEY HADN'T GIVEN ME A PUSH BACK THEN...
...I MIGHT HAVE KEPT THINKING...
...UNTIL I PARALYZED MYSELF, WITHOUT EVER MAKING A DECISION.
FOUND IT! THE EXIT'S UP HERE!!
SHIRO!
MY LIEGE.

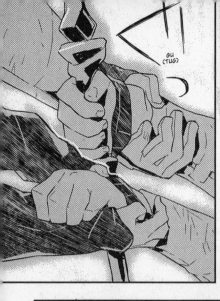

GU
(TUG)

WHAT A COWARD.

I'M SO LAME!

THANKS.

AH HA HA!

ROUGH ON THE EYES, HUH!? WE WERE IN THERE FOREVER!

IT'S SO BRIGHT...

IS IT MORNING?

ザク
ZAKU
(CRUNCH)

THE WIND'S PRETTY COLD.

ゴォキ

ヒュウ

HYUUUU
(CHWOOOOO)

GOOO
(FWOOOM)

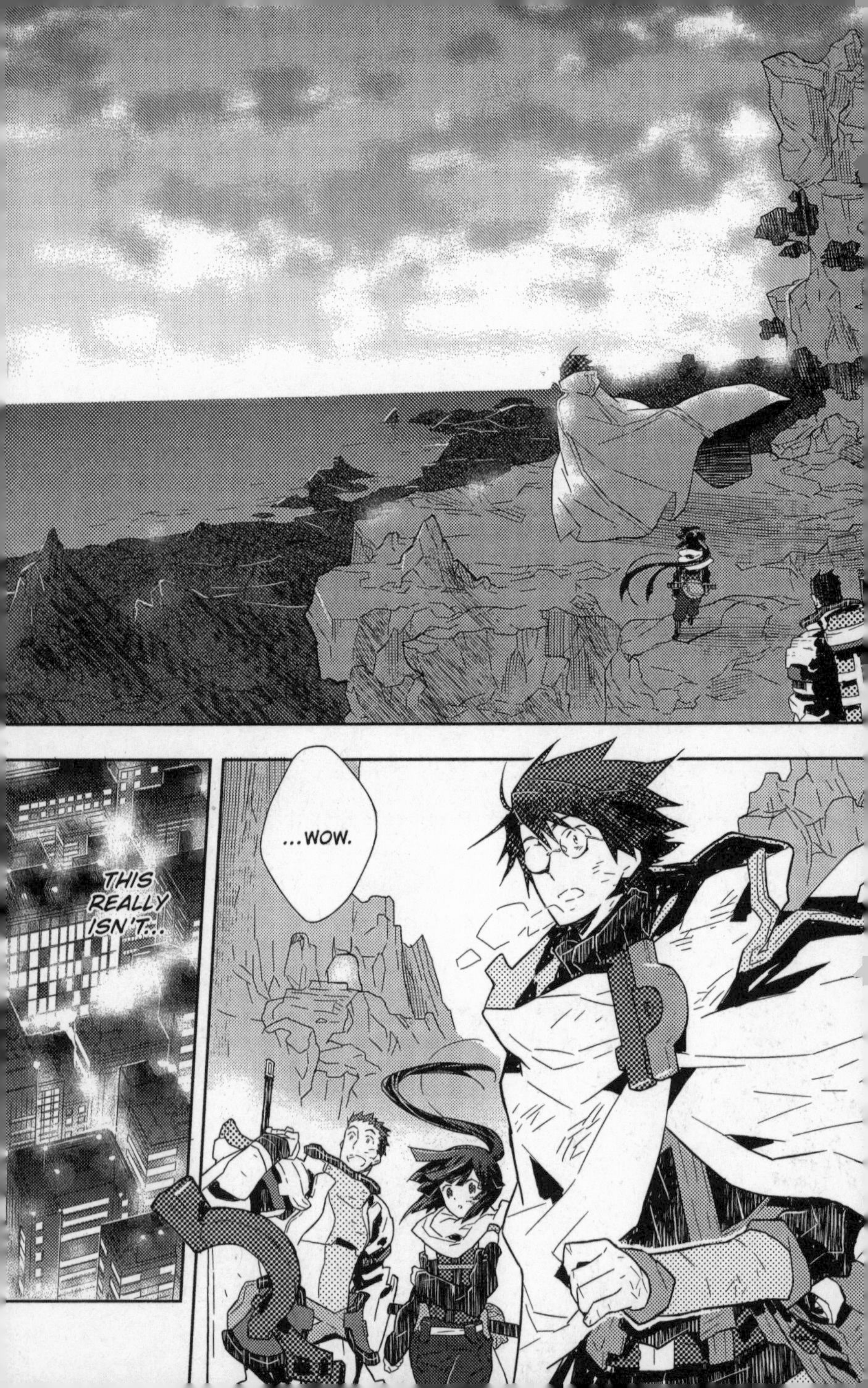
...WOW.
THIS REALLY ISN'T...

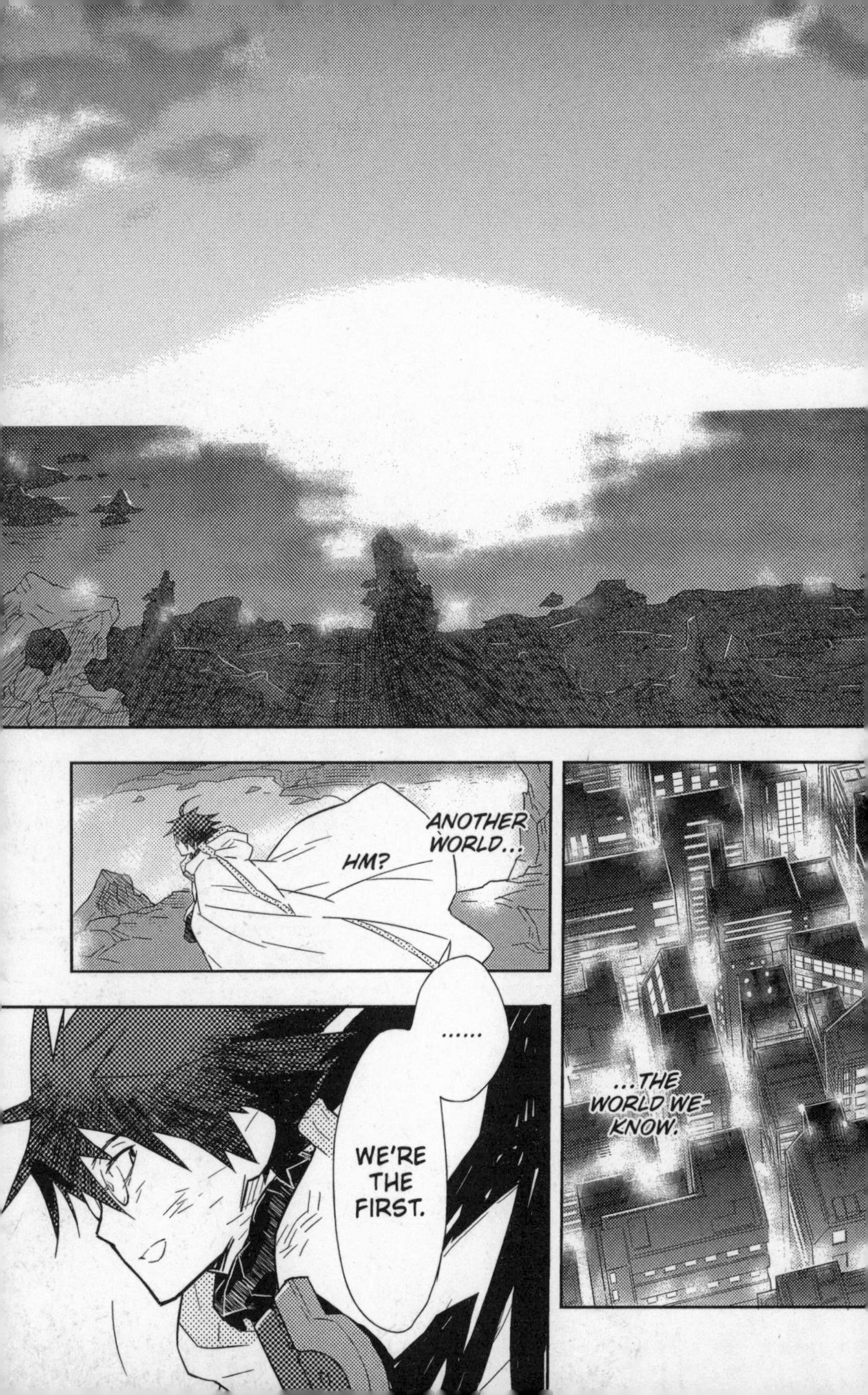
...THE WORLD WE KNOW.
ANOTHER WORLD...
HM?
......
WE'RE THE FIRST.

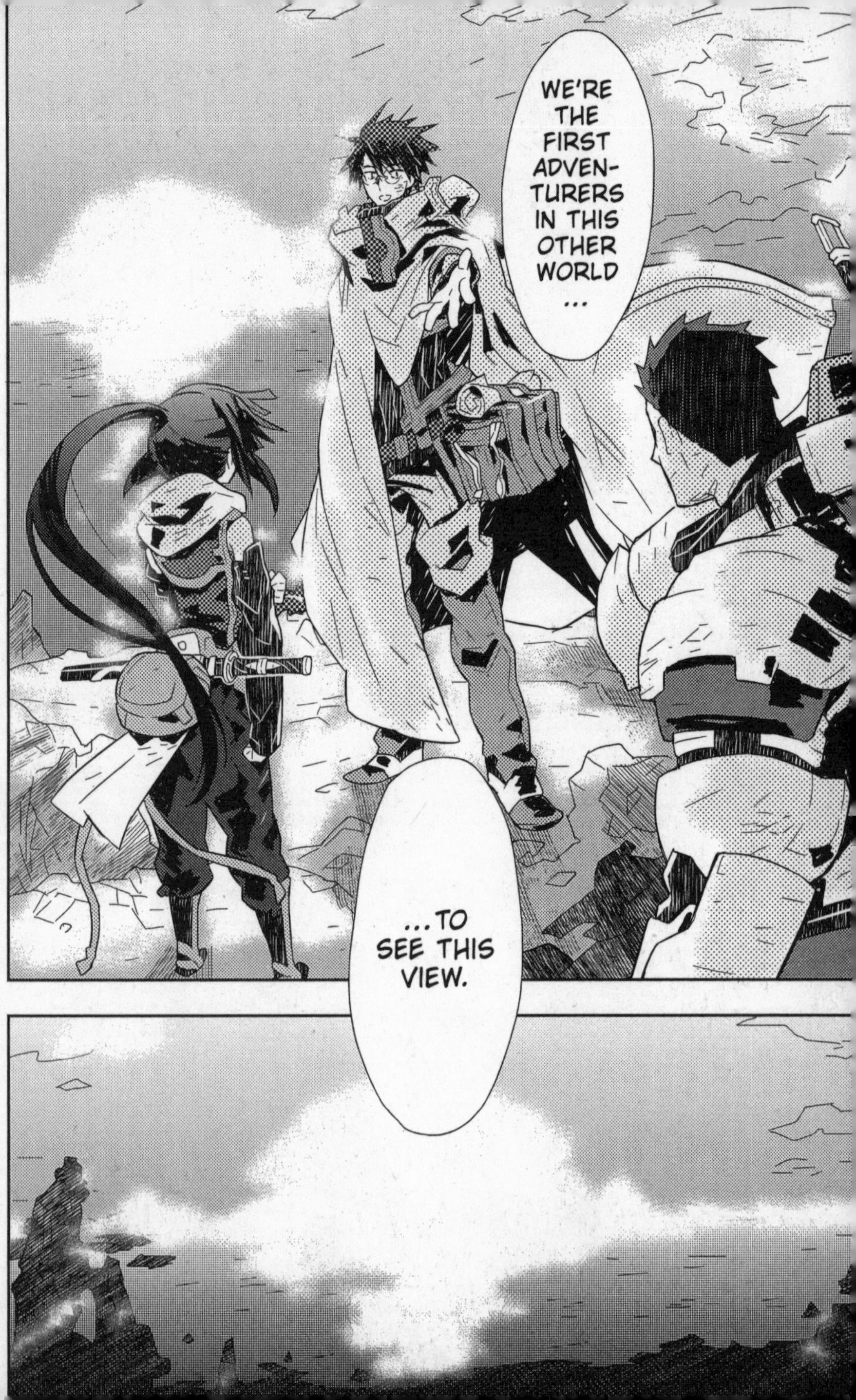
WE'RE THE FIRST ADVENTURERS IN THIS OTHER WORLD ...
...TO SEE THIS VIEW.

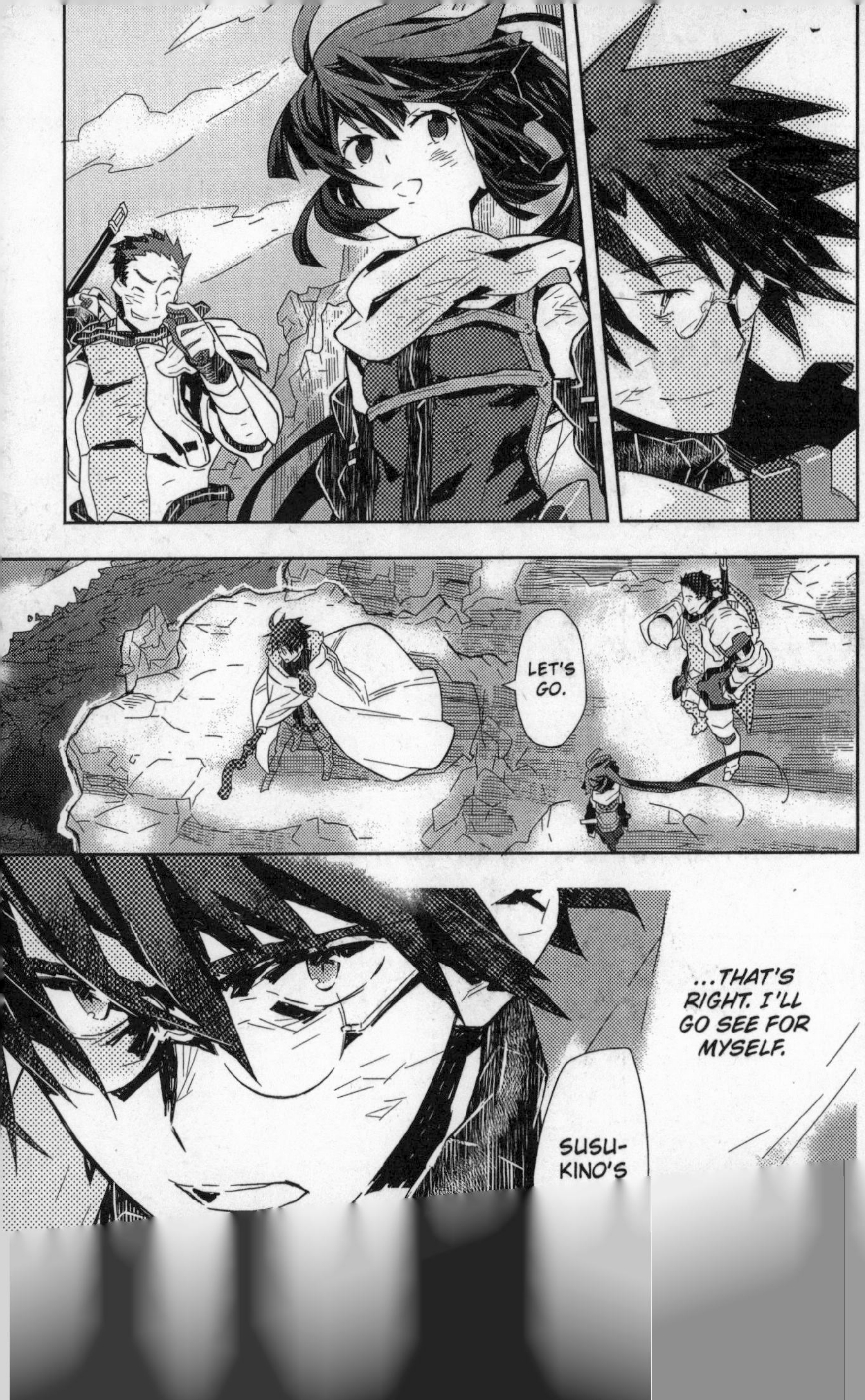
LET'S GO.
...THAT'S RIGHT. I'LL GO SEE FOR MYSELF.
SUSU-KINO'S

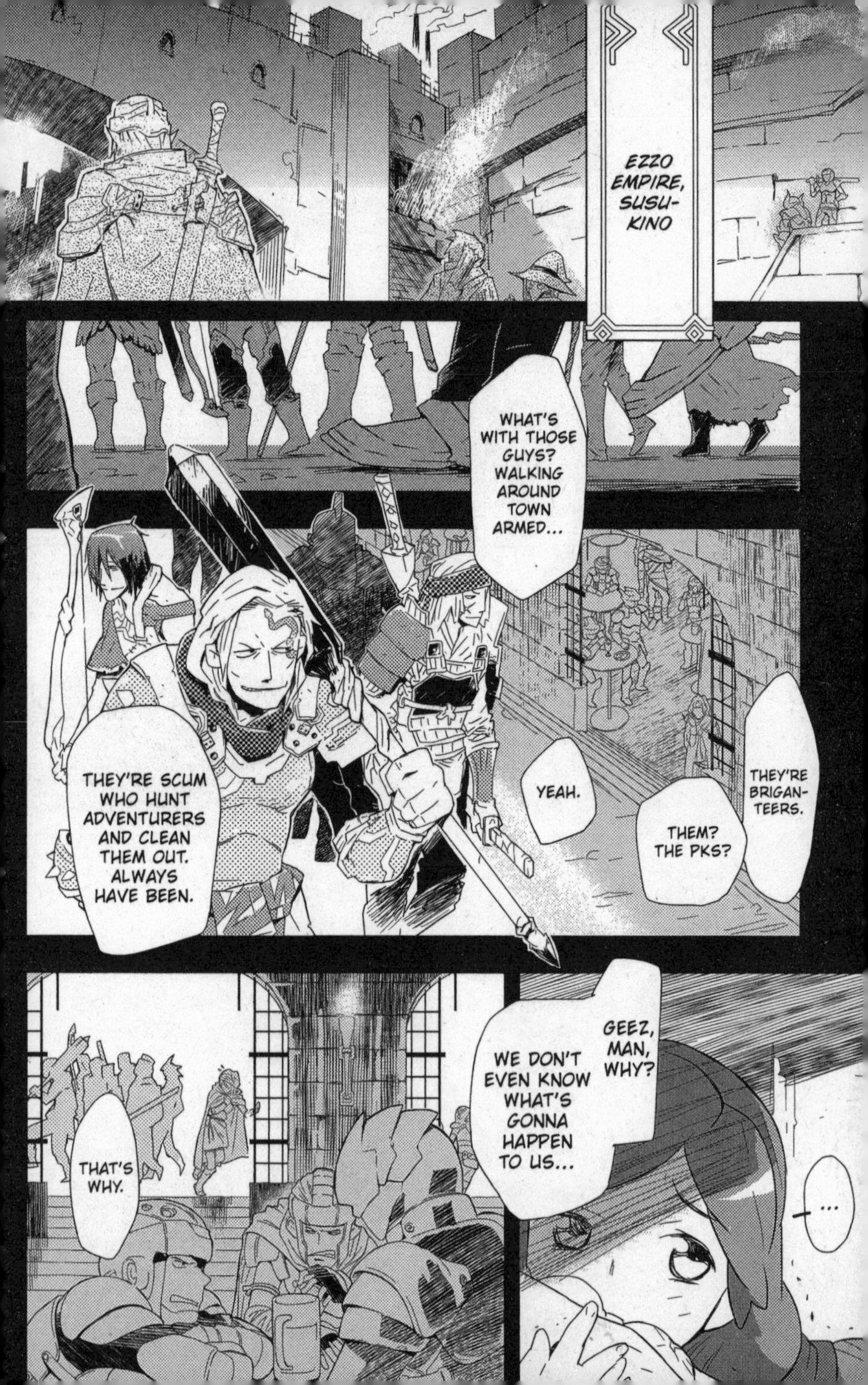
EZZO EMPIRE, SUSUKINO
WHAT'S WITH THOSE GUYS? WALKING AROUND TOWN ARMED...
THEY'RE BRIGANTEERS.
THEM? THE PKS?
YEAH.
THEY'RE SCUM WHO HUNT ADVENTURERS AND CLEAN THEM OUT. ALWAYS HAVE BEEN.
GEEZ, MAN, WHY?
WE DON'T EVEN KNOW WHAT'S GONNA HAPPEN TO US...
...
THAT'S WHY.

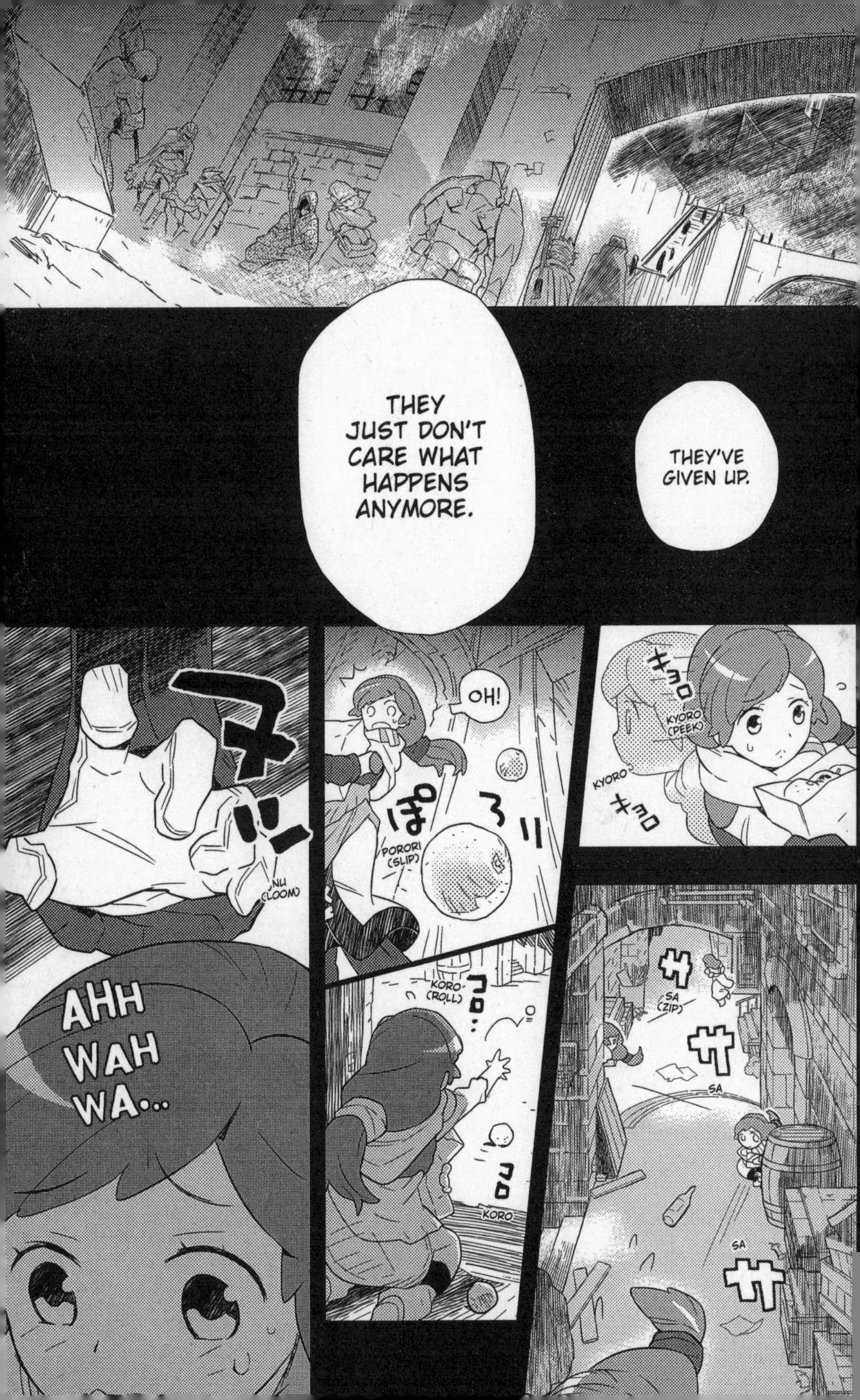

THEY'VE GIVEN UP.
THEY JUST DON'T CARE WHAT HAPPENS ANYMORE.
キョロ
KYORO (PEEK)
KYORO
キョロ
OH!
ぽろり
PORORI (SLIP)
ヌッ
NU (LOOM)
AHH WAH WA...
サ
SA (ZIP)
サ
SA
サ
SA
コロ..
KORO (ROLL)
コロ
KORO

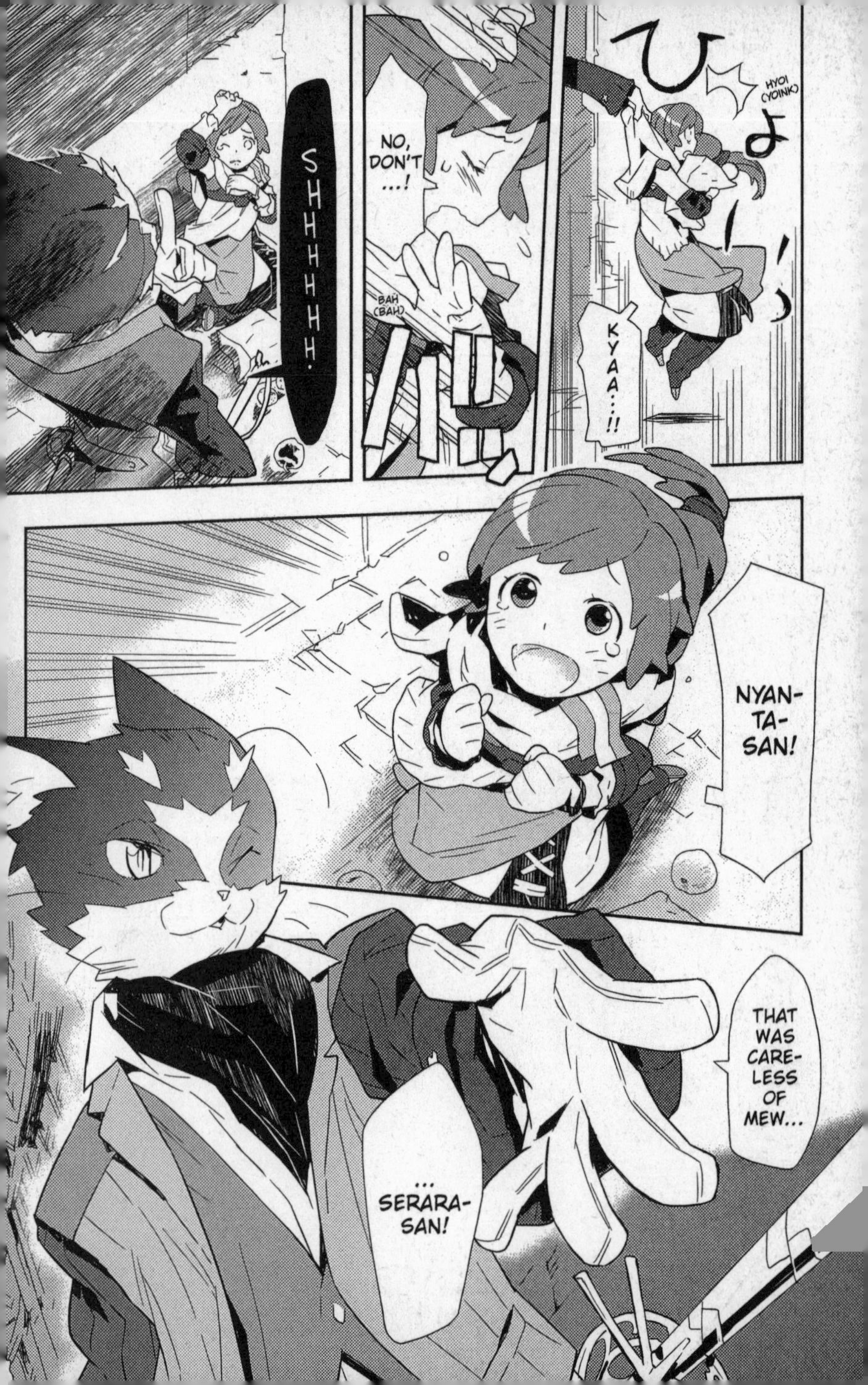
ひょい
HYOI (YOINK)
KYAA...!!
NO, DON'T ...!
BAH (BAH)
SHHHHHH.
NYAN-TA-SAN!
THAT WAS CARELESS OF MEW...
... SERARA-SAN!

# *ELDER TALES* CLASS TABLE 1

## WEAPON ATTACK CLASSES

Three classes whose focus is on weapon-based attacks. In addition to having high Attack Power, they use fighting methods specialized toward offense, such as boosting their companions' combat abilities.

**▶SWASHBUCKLER**
A fast, mobile fighter that attacks with two blades.

**▶BARD**
Skilled at using songs to provide support.

**▶ASSASSIN**
Can deal out lethal damage with a single attack.

### AKATSUKI: ASSASSIN

A focused attacker who is skilled with a wide variety of weapons. Attacks aimed at enemy weak points inflict the greatest physical damage of all the classes. Has many special attack skills that can cause massive damage instantaneously.

## WARRIOR CLASSES

Three classes that boast high HP, Attack Power, and Defense. Their main role is to draw enemy attacks and shield the rest of their party from damage.

**▶SAMURAI**
Has a wide range of techniques. Good at both offense and defense.

**▶MONK**
Strengths include serial attacks, high HP, and high evasive abilities.

**▶GUARDIAN**
Draws attacks with the strongest Defense.

### NAOTSUGU: GUARDIAN

The pillar of the vanguard, with ultimate defensive abilities and an array of techniques to focus enemy attacks on himself. Blocks the enemy's path like a brick wall and draws all attacks to himself, protecting his friends.

# *ELDER TALES* CLASS TABLE 2

## RECOVERY CLASSES

Three classes that are skilled at recovering Health and using techniques to protect their allies. They specialize in life-saving rear guard support, such as recovering HP with magic or blocking damage.

▸ **CLERIC**
Its appeal lies in the strength of its recovery abilities.

▸ **DRUID**
Best at continuous recovery and other types of magical recovery.

▸ **KANNAGI**
Damage obstruction and other preventative recovery techniques.

## MAGIC ATTACK CLASSES

Three classes skilled with magical attacks. Effects are wide-ranging. Some classes use magic to inflict damage directly, others summon spirits and mythical beasts, and still others obstruct movement.

▸ **SORCERER**
Uses offensive magic to inflict damage directly.

▸ **SUMMONER**
Summons and controls mystical beasts and spirits.

▸ **ENCHANTER**
Supports combat by causing abnormal statuses.

### SHIROE: ENCHANTER

A magic user who specializes in using magic itself. Has a vast repertoire of spells, which can boost allies' combat abilities or prevent targets from moving freely. Although the class is unpopular, a skilled Enchanter can control any combat situation to their advantage.

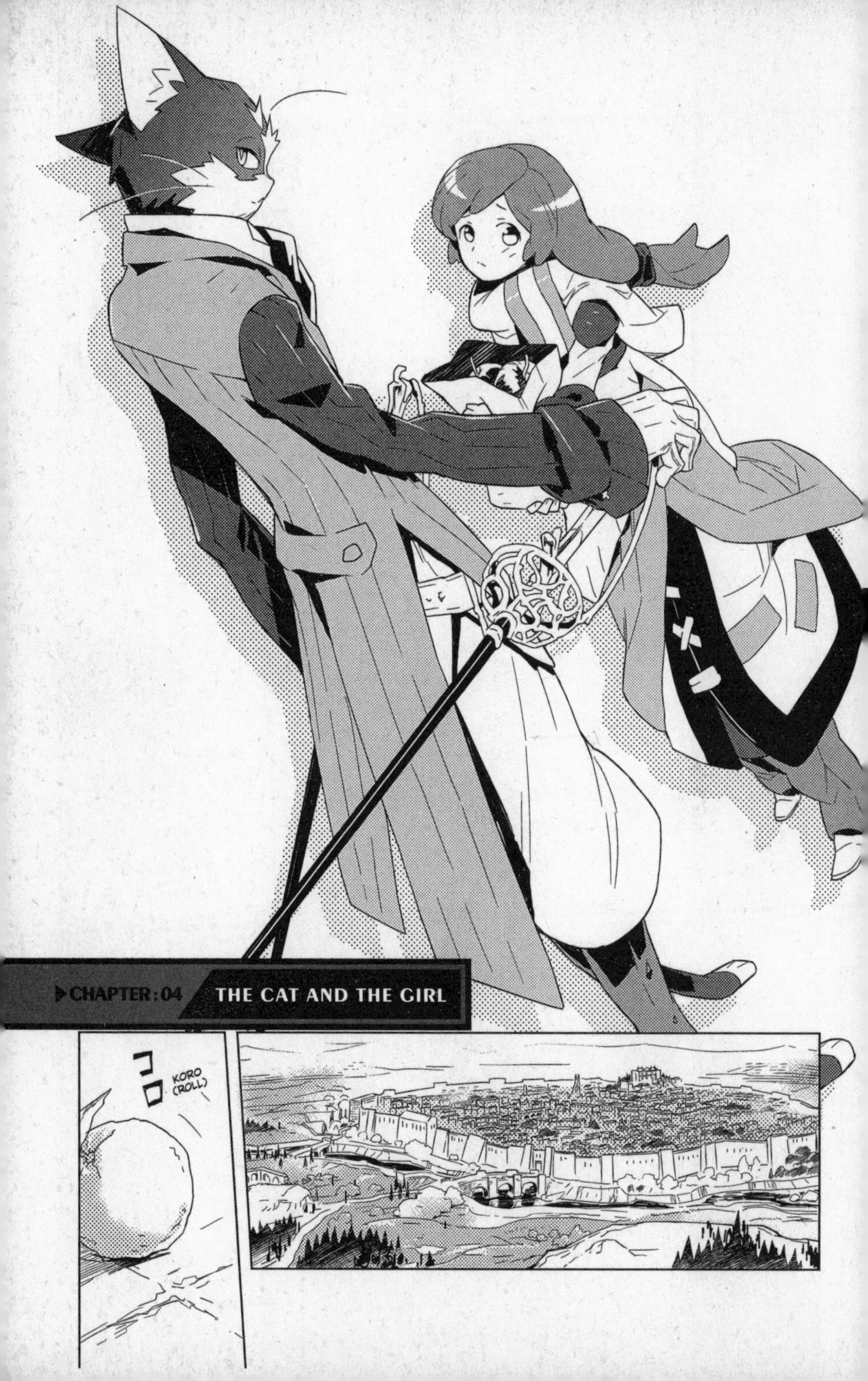
CHAPTER : 04
THE CAT AND THE GIRL
コロ
KORO (ROLL)

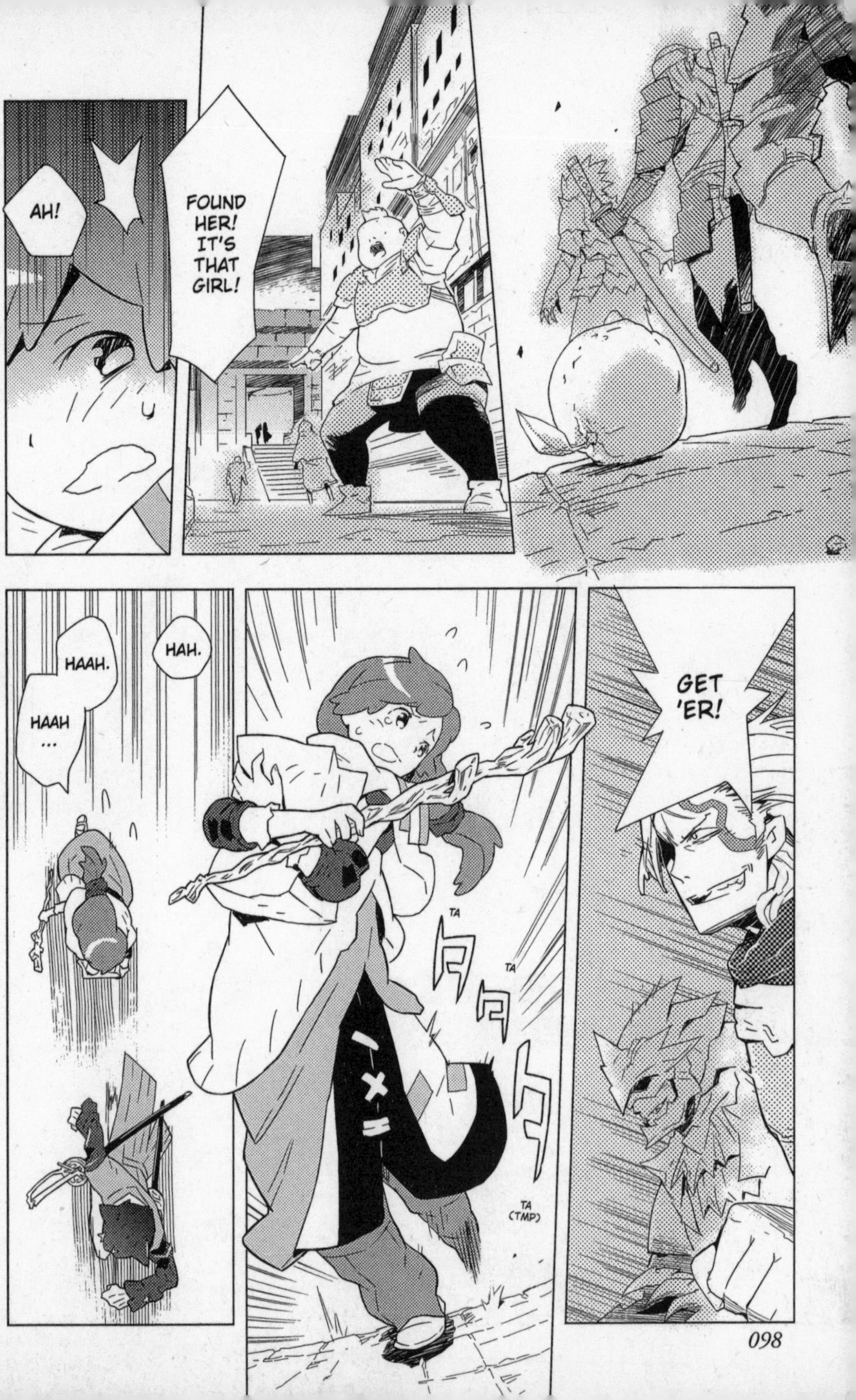
FOUND HER! IT'S THAT GIRL!
AH!
GET 'ER!
TA
TA
TA (TMP)
HAH.
HAAH.
HAAH ...

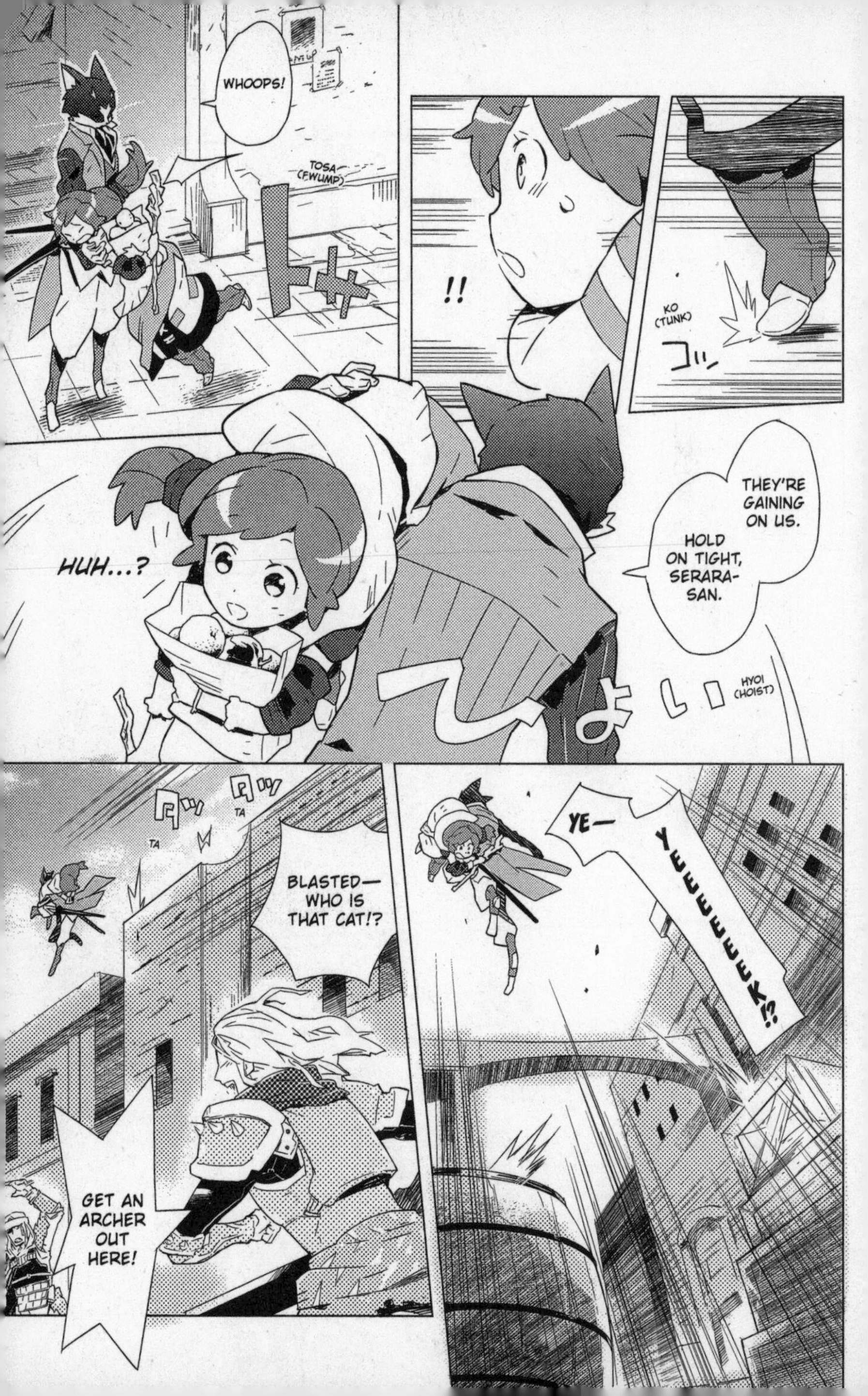
KO
(TUNK)
ゴッ
!!
WHOOPS!
TOSA
(FWUMP)
トサッ
THEY'RE GAINING ON US.
HOLD ON TIGHT, SERARA-SAN.
HYOI
(HOIST)
ひょい
HUH...?
YE—
YEEEEEEEK!?
TA
TA
BLASTED— WHO IS THAT CAT!?
GET AN ARCHER OUT HERE!

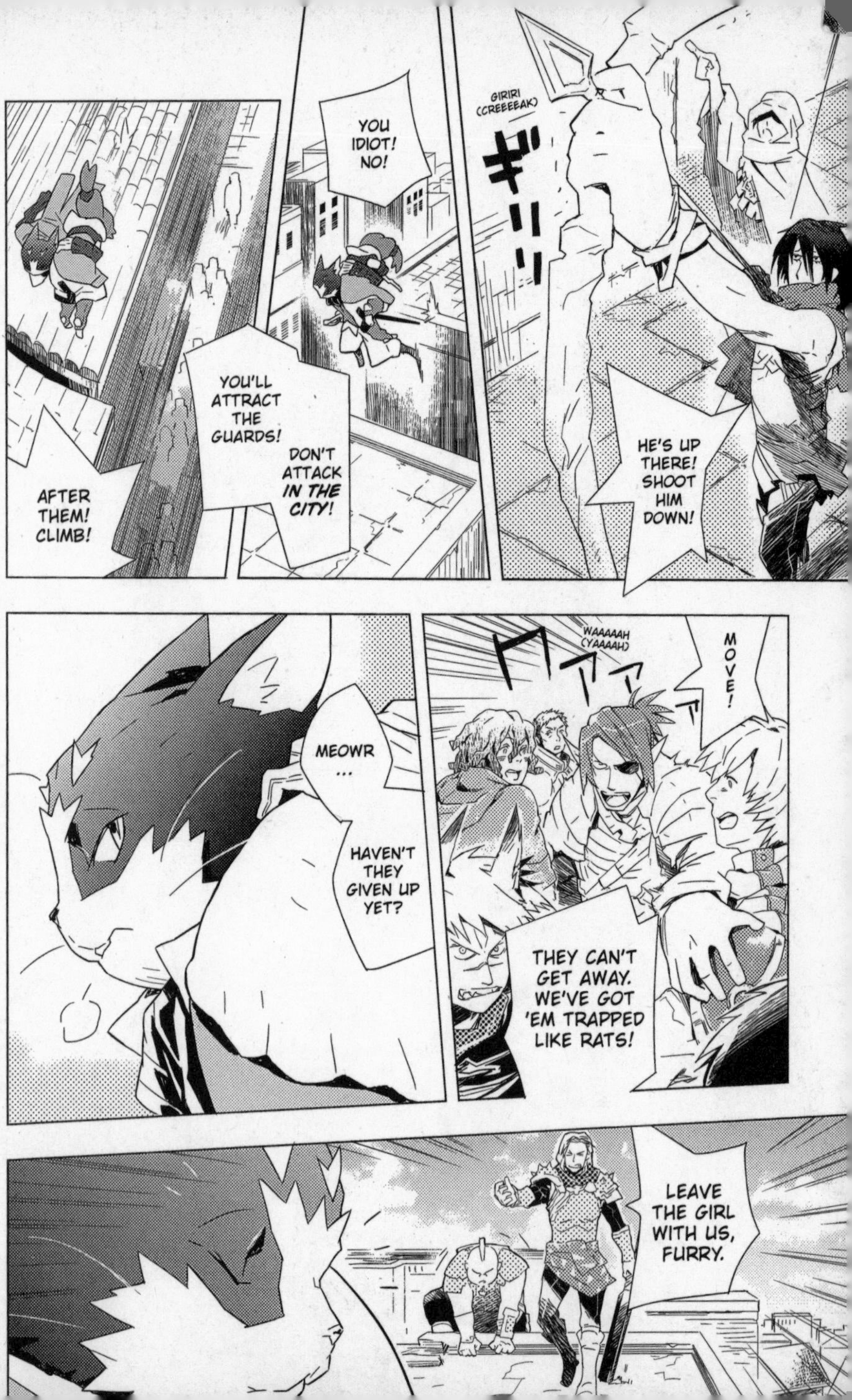
GIRIRI (CREEEEAK)
ギリリ
HE'S UP THERE! SHOOT HIM DOWN!
YOU IDIOT! NO!
DON'T ATTACK *IN THE CITY!*
YOU'LL ATTRACT THE GUARDS!
AFTER THEM! CLIMB!
MOVE!
WAAAAAH (YAAAAH)
THEY CAN'T GET AWAY. WE'VE GOT 'EM TRAPPED LIKE RATS!
MEOWR ...
HAVEN'T THEY GIVEN UP YET?
LEAVE THE GIRL WITH US, FURRY.

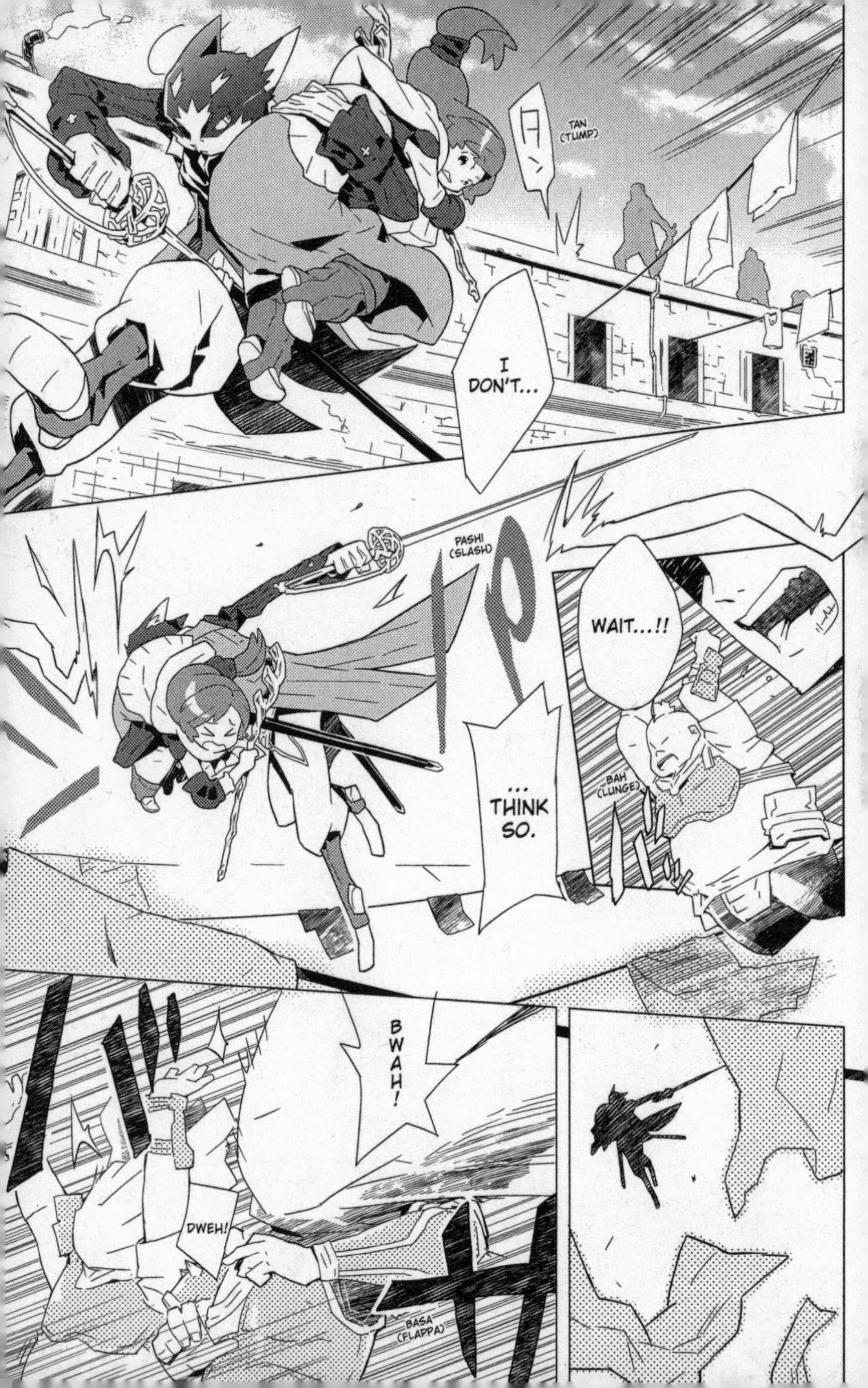
TAN (TUMP)
I DON'T...
WAIT...!!
BAH (LUNGE)
PASHI (SLASH)
...THINK SO.
BWAH!
DWEH!
BASA (FLAPPA)

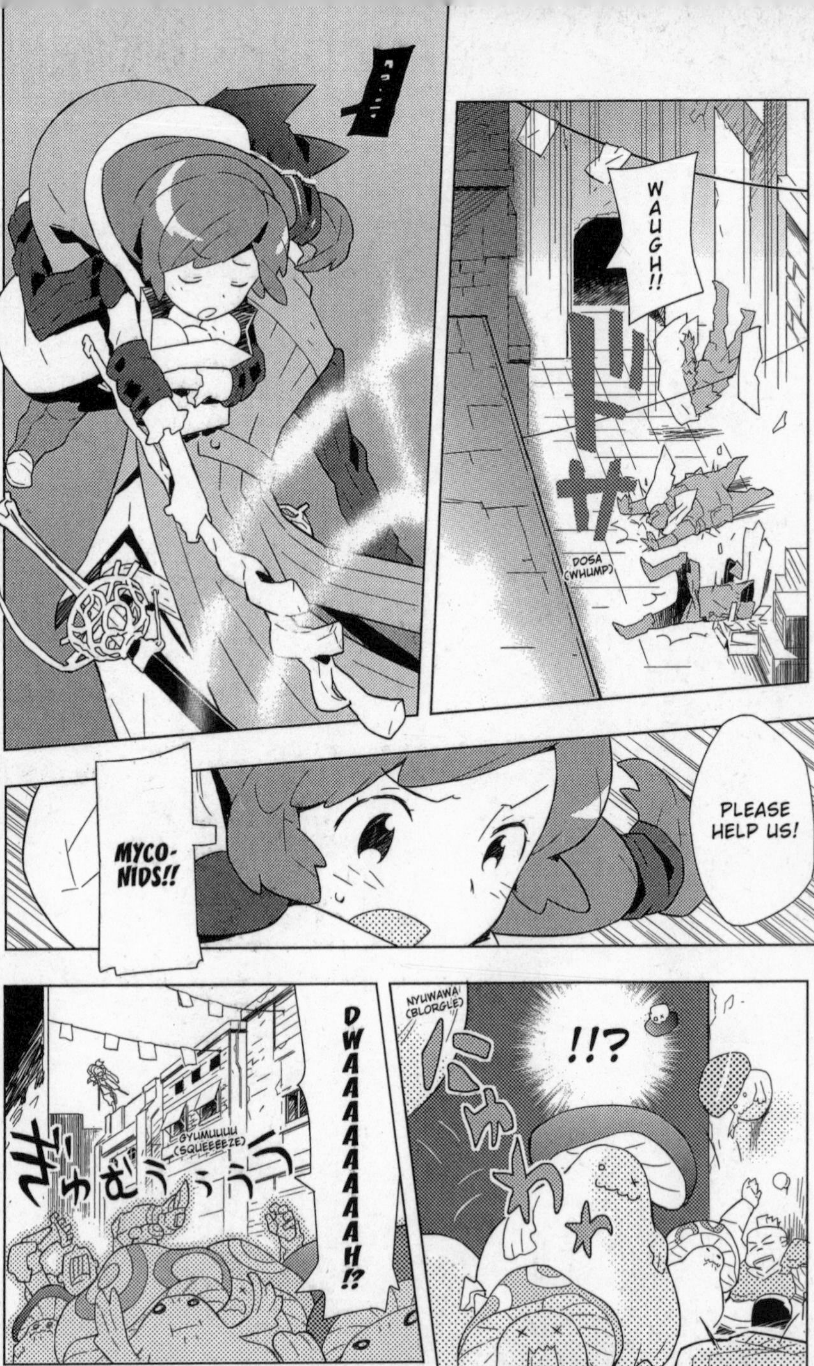
WAUGH!!
DOSA (WHUMP)
PLEASE HELP US!
MYCO-NIDS!!
NYUWAWA (BLORGLE)
!!?
DWAAAAAAAAH!?
GYUMUUUU (SQUEEEEZE)

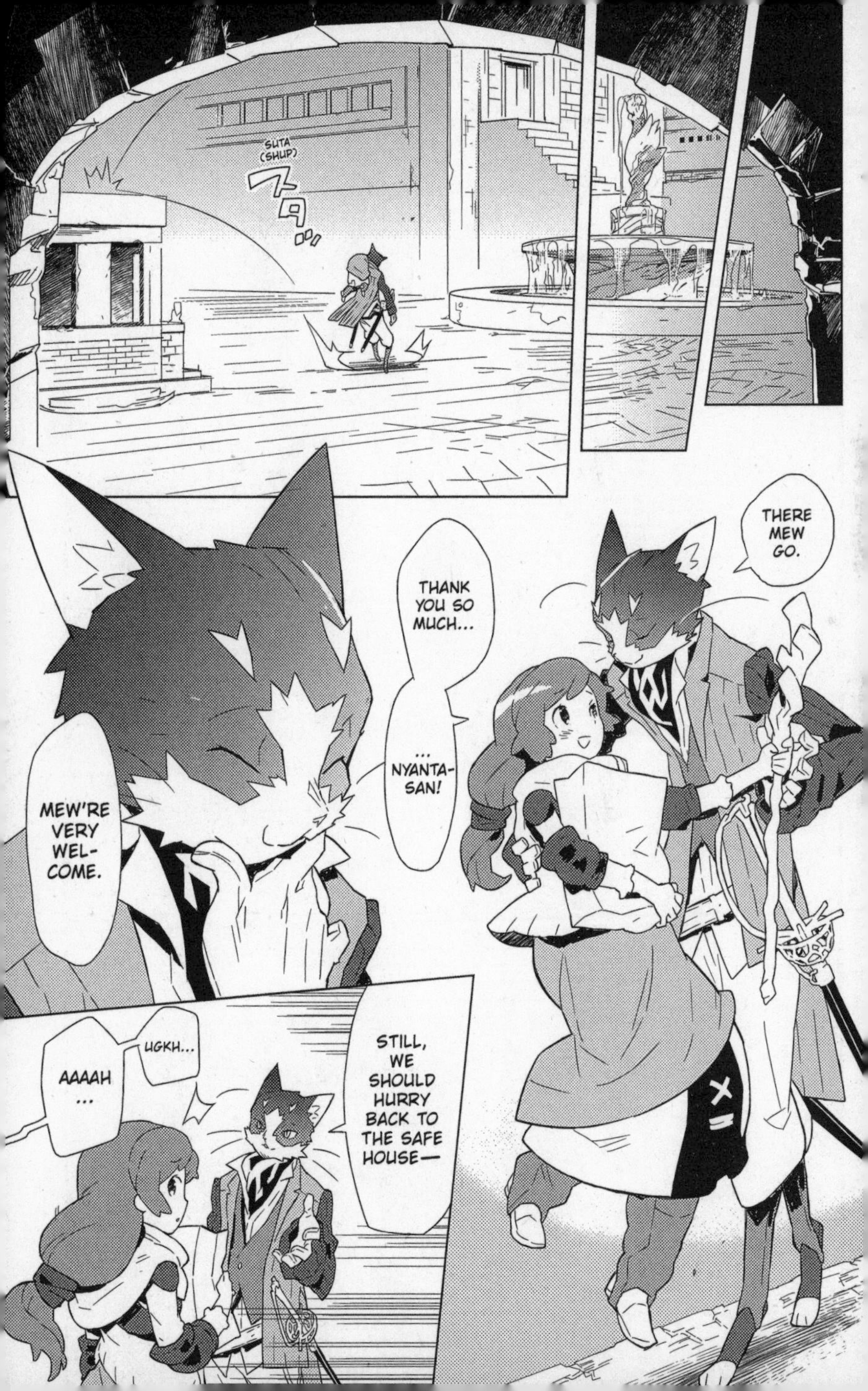
SUTA (SHUP)
スタッ
THERE MEW GO.
THANK YOU SO MUCH...
...NYANTA-SAN!
MEW'RE VERY WEL-COME.
STILL, WE SHOULD HURRY BACK TO THE SAFE HOUSE—
UGKH...
AAAAH ...

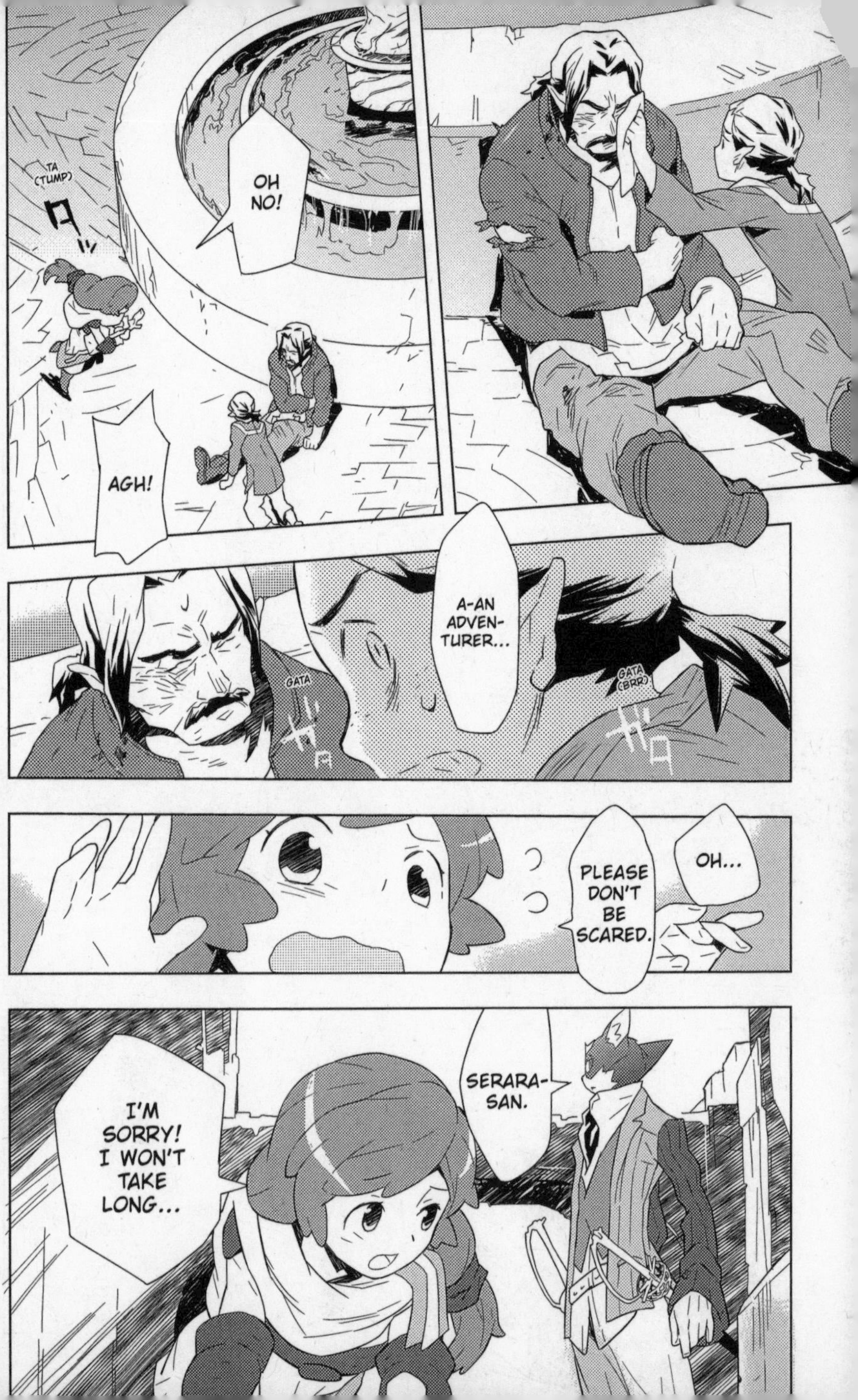
OH NO!
TA (TUMP)
AGH!
A-AN ADVENTURER...
GATA (BRR)
GATA
OH...
PLEASE DON'T BE SCARED.
SERARA-SAN.
I'M SORRY! I WON'T TAKE LONG...

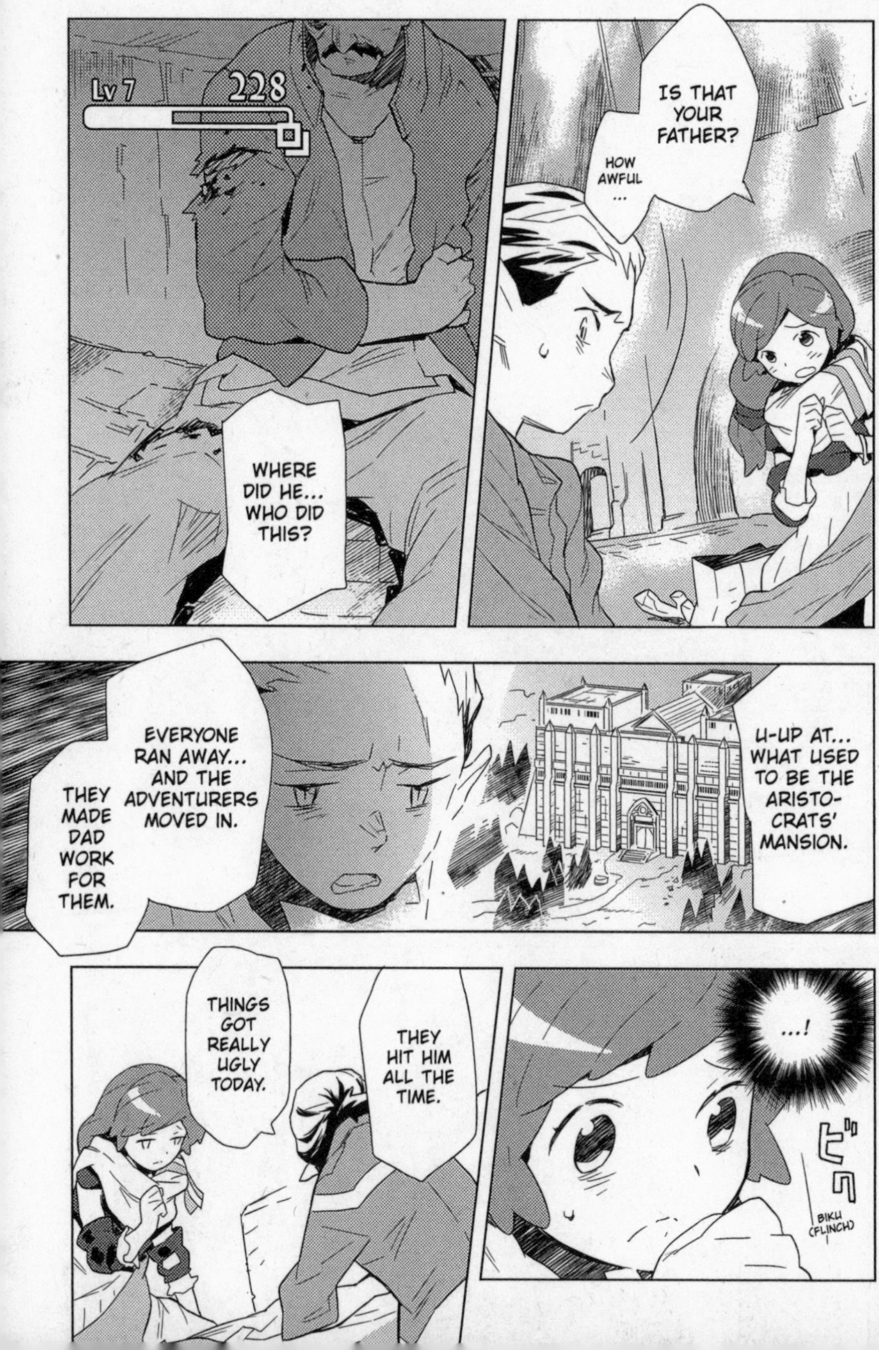
IS THAT YOUR FATHER?
HOW AWFUL...
Lv 7
228
WHERE DID HE... WHO DID THIS?
U-UP AT... WHAT USED TO BE THE ARISTO-CRATS' MANSION.
EVERYONE RAN AWAY... AND THE ADVENTURERS MOVED IN.
THEY MADE DAD WORK FOR THEM.
...!
ビク
BIKU (FLINCH)
THEY HIT HIM ALL THE TIME.
THINGS GOT REALLY UGLY TODAY.

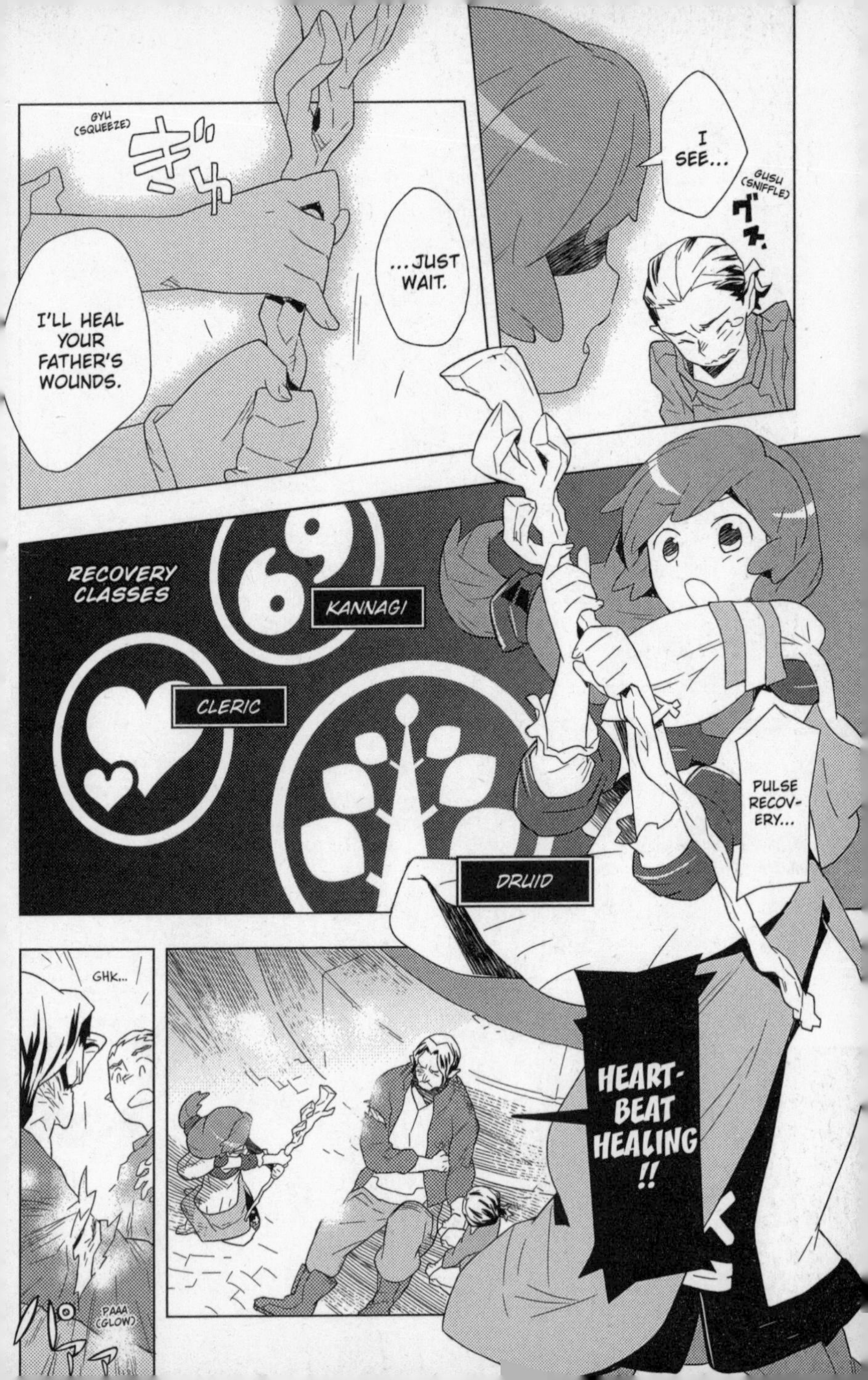
I SEE...
GUSU (SNIFFLE)
...JUST WAIT.
GYU (SQUEEZE)
ぎゅ
I'LL HEAL YOUR FATHER'S WOUNDS.
PULSE RECOVERY...
RECOVERY CLASSES
KANNAGI
CLERIC
DRUID
HEART-BEAT HEALING!!
GHK...
PAAA (GLOW)

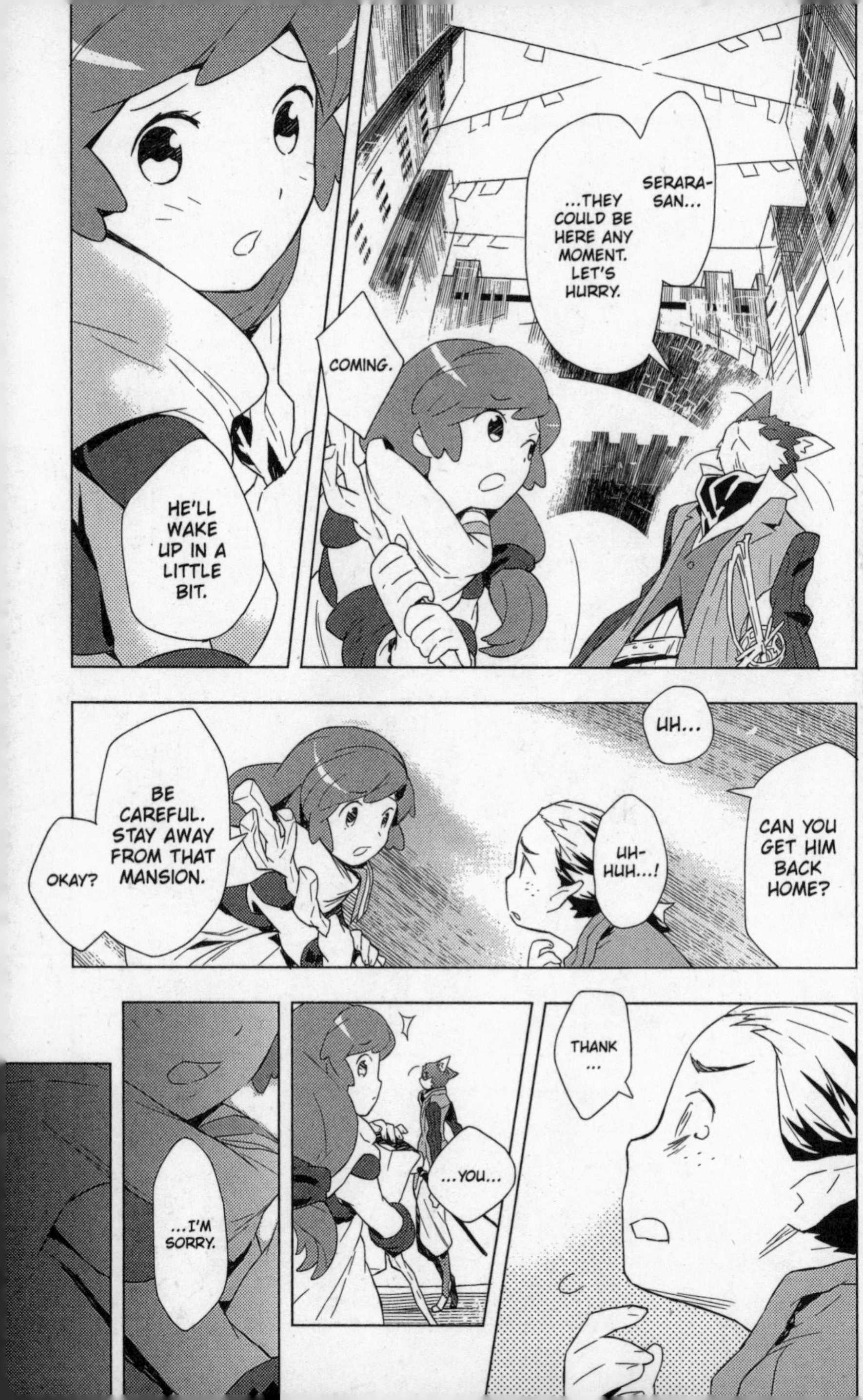
SERARA-SAN...
...THEY COULD BE HERE ANY MOMENT. LET'S HURRY.
COMING.
HE'LL WAKE UP IN A LITTLE BIT.
UH...
CAN YOU GET HIM BACK HOME?
UH-HUH...!
BE CAREFUL. STAY AWAY FROM THAT MANSION.
OKAY?
THANK...
...YOU...
...I'M SORRY.

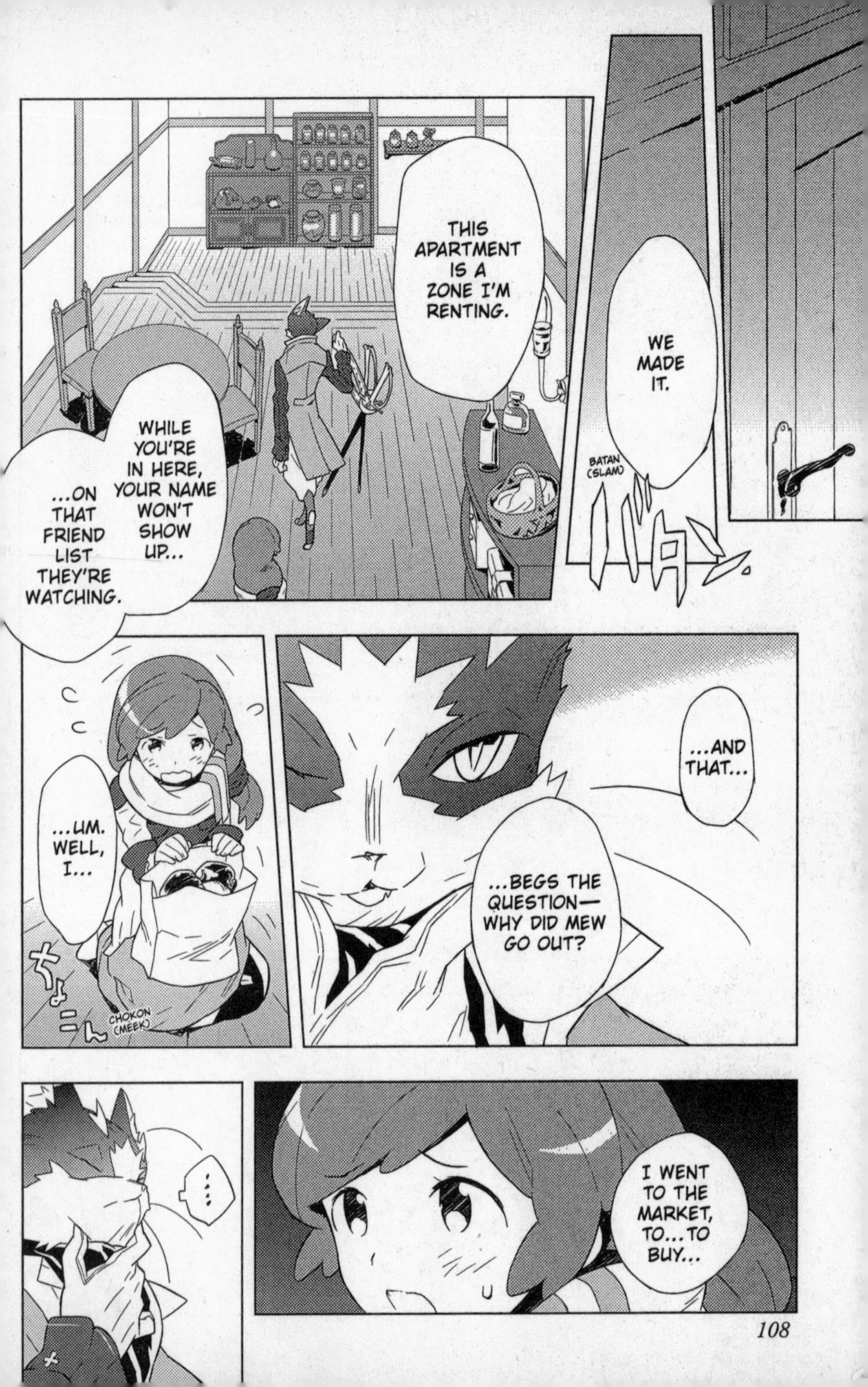
WE MADE IT.
BATAN (SLAM)
THIS APARTMENT IS A ZONE I'M RENTING.
WHILE YOU'RE IN HERE, YOUR NAME WON'T SHOW UP...
...ON THAT FRIEND LIST THEY'RE WATCHING.
...AND THAT...
...BEGS THE QUESTION—WHY DID MEW GO OUT?
...UM. WELL, I...
CHOKON (MEEK)
I WENT TO THE MARKET, TO... TO BUY...
....

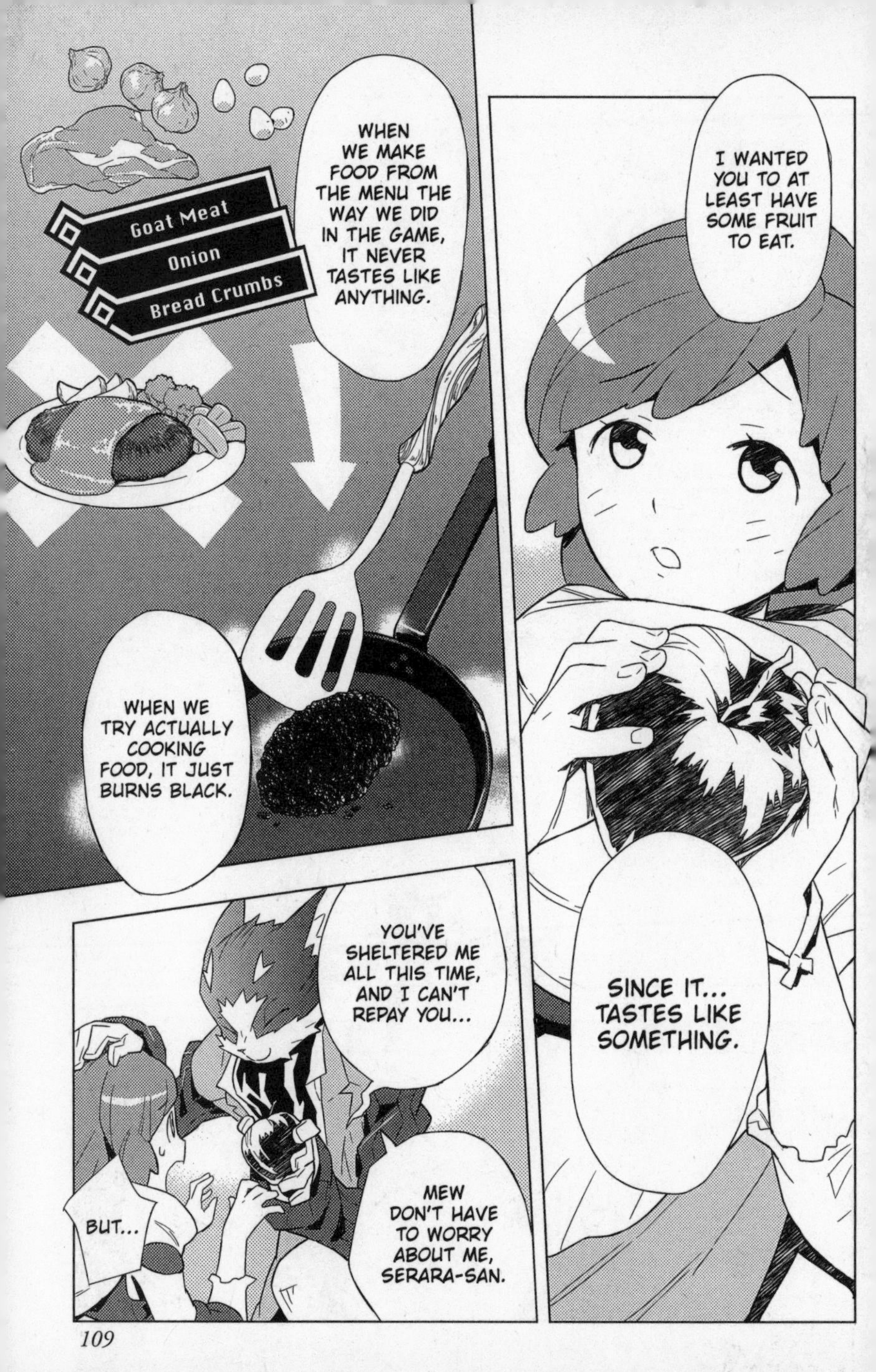
I WANTED YOU TO AT LEAST HAVE SOME FRUIT TO EAT.
SINCE IT... TASTES LIKE SOMETHING.
WHEN WE MAKE FOOD FROM THE MENU THE WAY WE DID IN THE GAME, IT NEVER TASTES LIKE ANYTHING.
Goat Meat
Onion
Bread Crumbs
WHEN WE TRY ACTUALLY COOKING FOOD, IT JUST BURNS BLACK.
YOU'VE SHELTERED ME ALL THIS TIME, AND I CAN'T REPAY YOU...
MEW DON'T HAVE TO WORRY ABOUT ME, SERARA-SAN.
BUT...

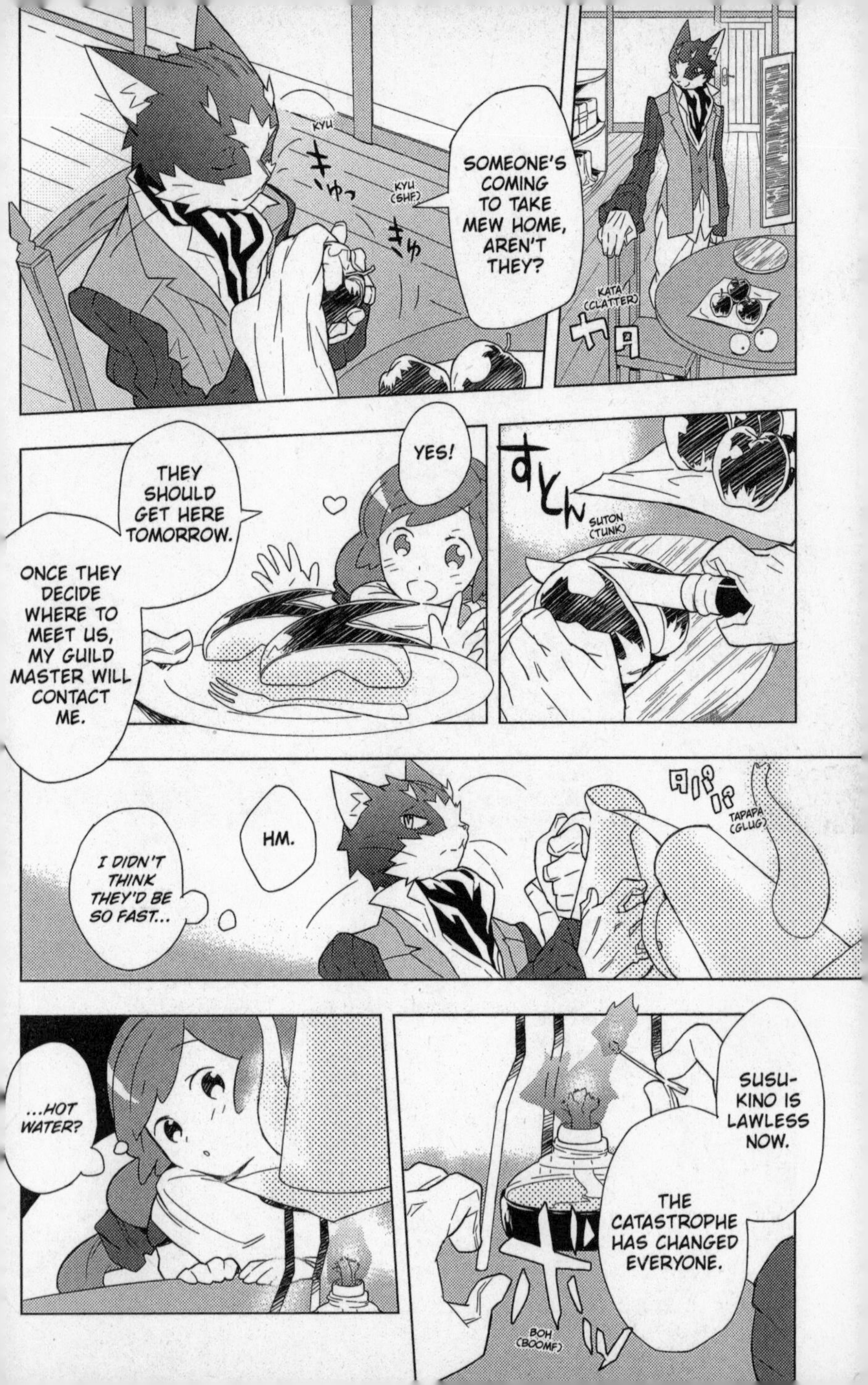
KATA (CLATTER)
SOMEONE'S COMING TO TAKE MEW HOME, AREN'T THEY?
KYU
KYU (SHF)
SUTON (TUNK)
YES!
THEY SHOULD GET HERE TOMORROW.
ONCE THEY DECIDE WHERE TO MEET US, MY GUILD MASTER WILL CONTACT ME.
TAPAPA (GLUG)
HM.
I DIDN'T THINK THEY'D BE SO FAST...
SUSU-KINO IS LAWLESS NOW.
THE CATASTROPHE HAS CHANGED EVERYONE.
BOH (BOOMF)
...HOT WATER?

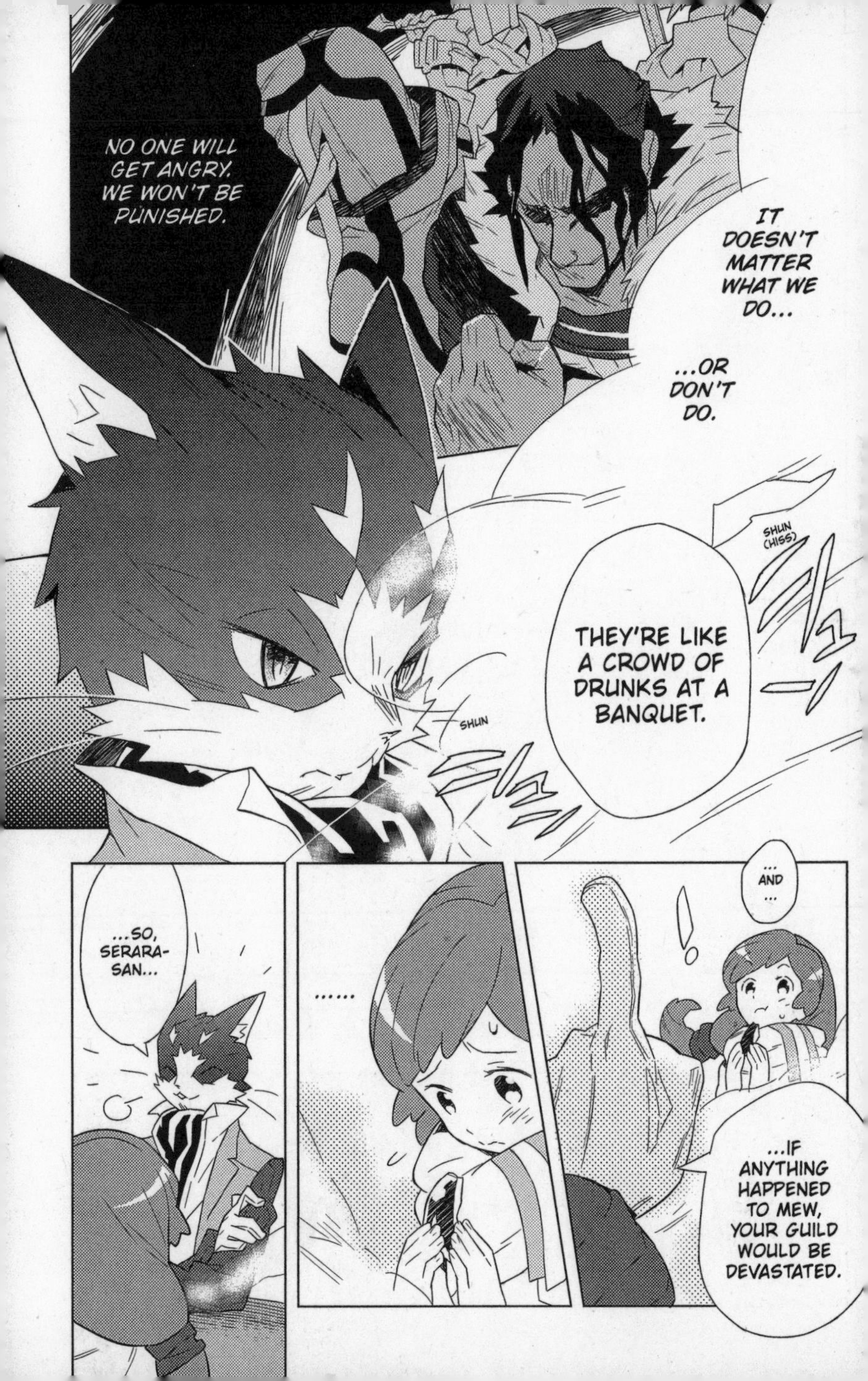
IT DOESN'T MATTER WHAT WE DO...
...OR DON'T DO.
NO ONE WILL GET ANGRY. WE WON'T BE PUNISHED.
SHUN (HISS)
THEY'RE LIKE A CROWD OF DRUNKS AT A BANQUET.
SHUN
...AND...
!
...IF ANYTHING HAPPENED TO MEW, YOUR GUILD WOULD BE DEVASTATED.
......
...SO, SERARA-SAN...

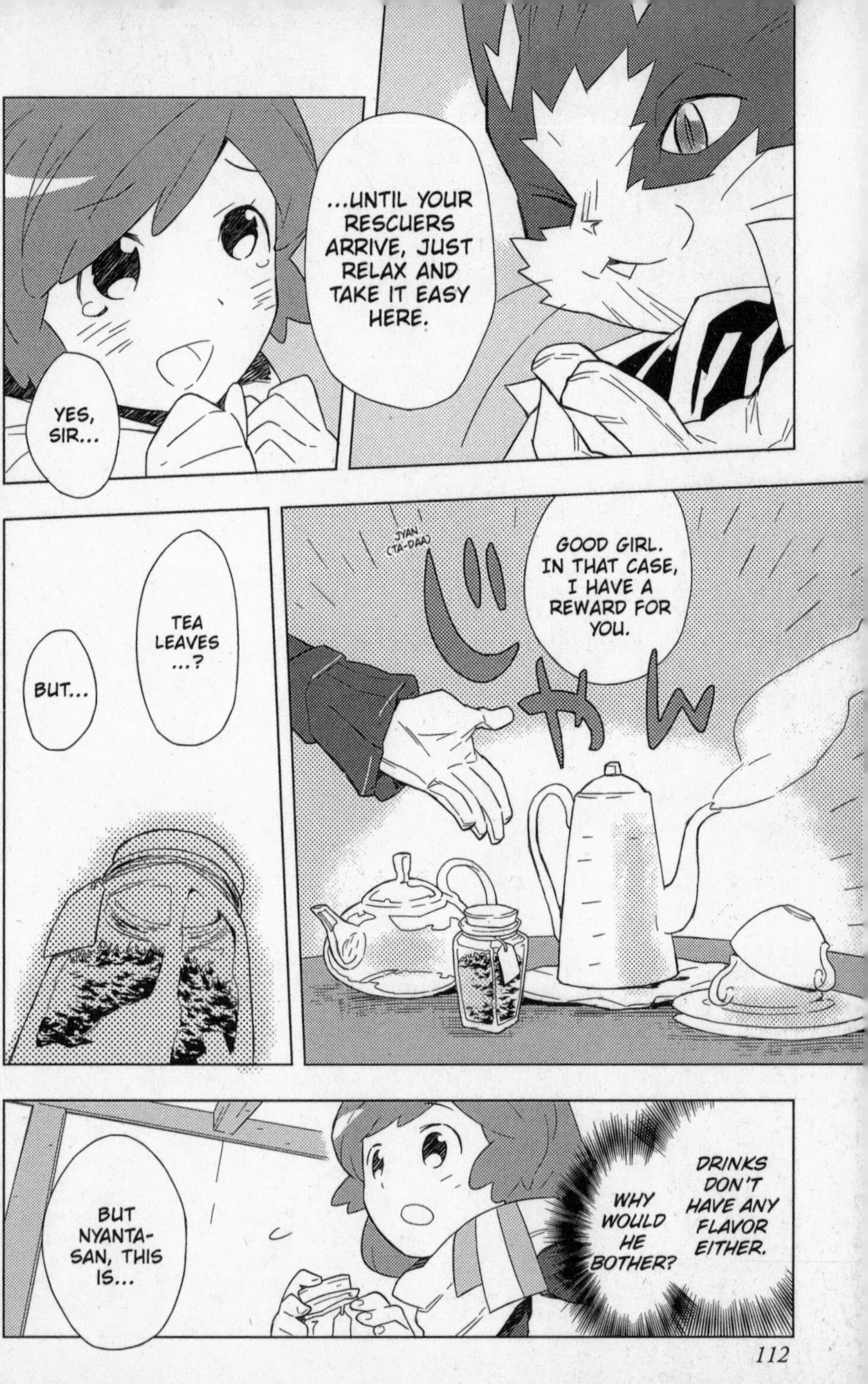
...UNTIL YOUR RESCUERS ARRIVE, JUST RELAX AND TAKE IT EASY HERE.
YES, SIR...
JYAN (TA-DAA)
GOOD GIRL. IN THAT CASE, I HAVE A REWARD FOR YOU.
TEA LEAVES ...?
BUT...
DRINKS DON'T HAVE ANY FLAVOR EITHER.
WHY WOULD HE BOTHER?
BUT NYANTA-SAN, THIS IS...

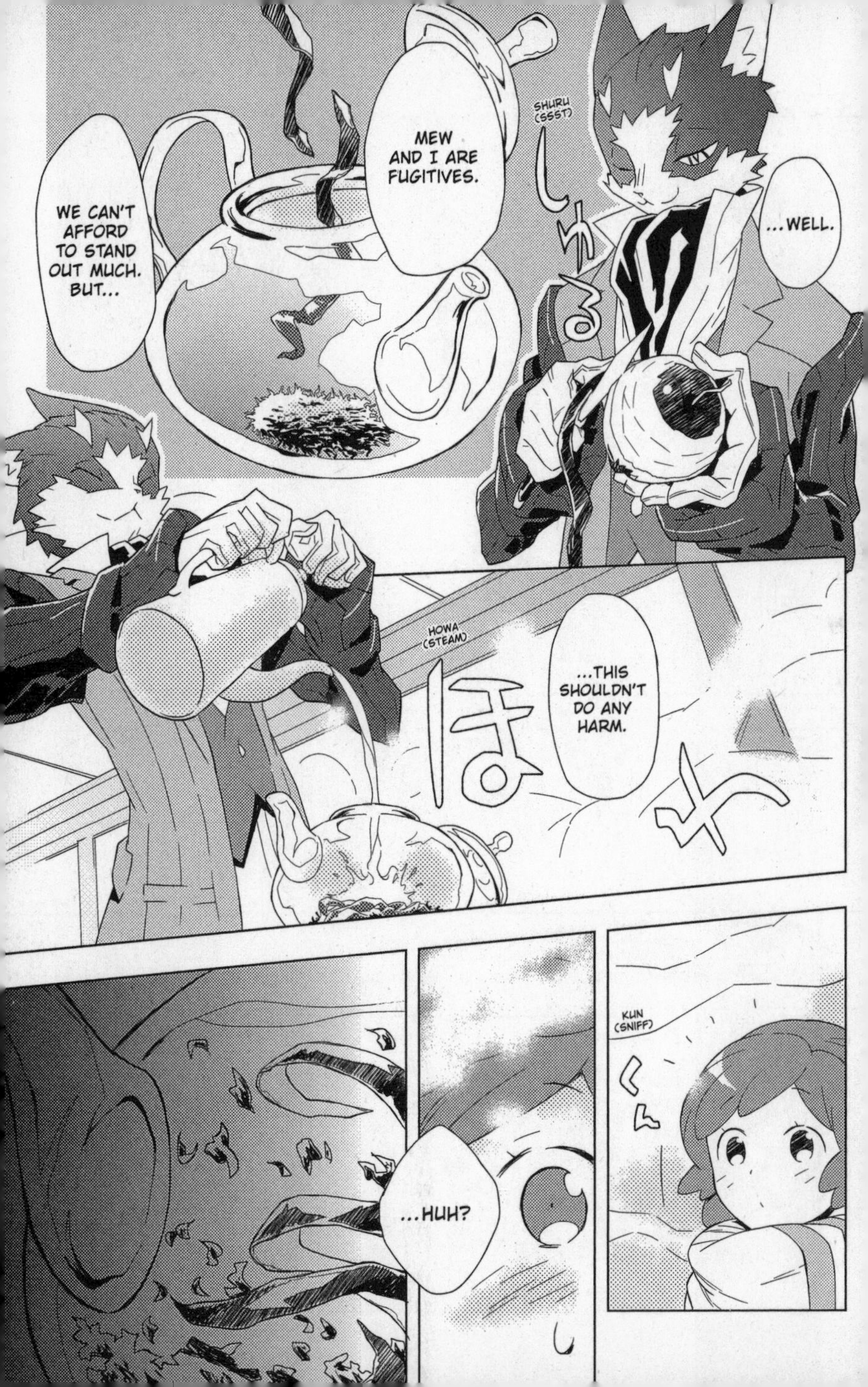
...WELL.
SHURU (SSST)
しゅる
MEW AND I ARE FUGITIVES.
WE CAN'T AFFORD TO STAND OUT MUCH. BUT...
...THIS SHOULDN'T DO ANY HARM.
HOWA (STEAM)
ほわ
KUN (SNIFF)
くん
...HUH?

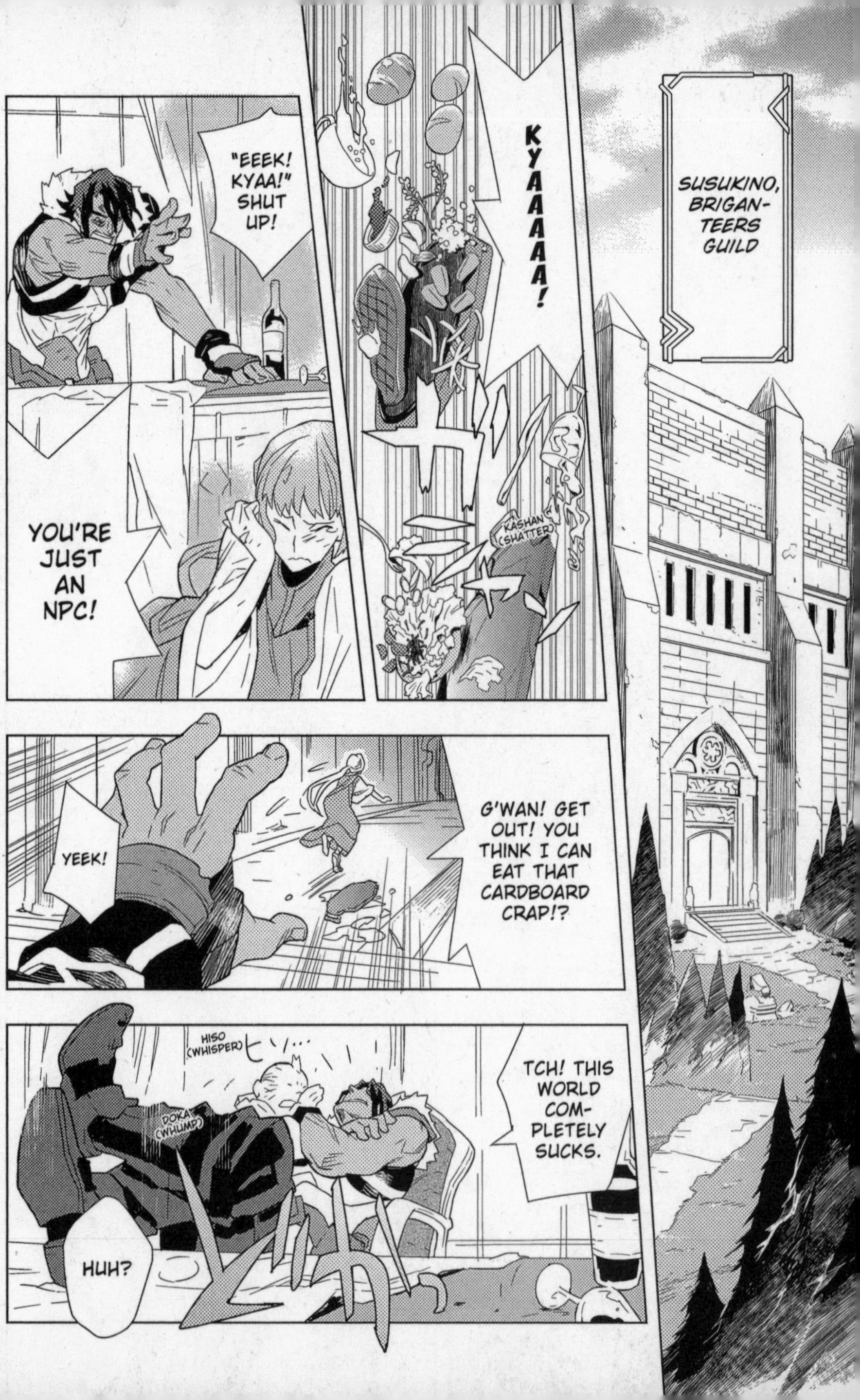
SUSUKINO, BRIGANTEERS GUILD
KYAAAAAA!
KASHAN (SHATTER)
"EEEK! KYAA!" SHUT UP!
YOU'RE JUST AN NPC!
G'WAN! GET OUT! YOU THINK I CAN EAT THAT CARDBOARD CRAP!?
YEEK!
TCH! THIS WORLD COMPLETELY SUCKS.
HISO (WHISPER)
DOKA (WHUMP)
HUH?

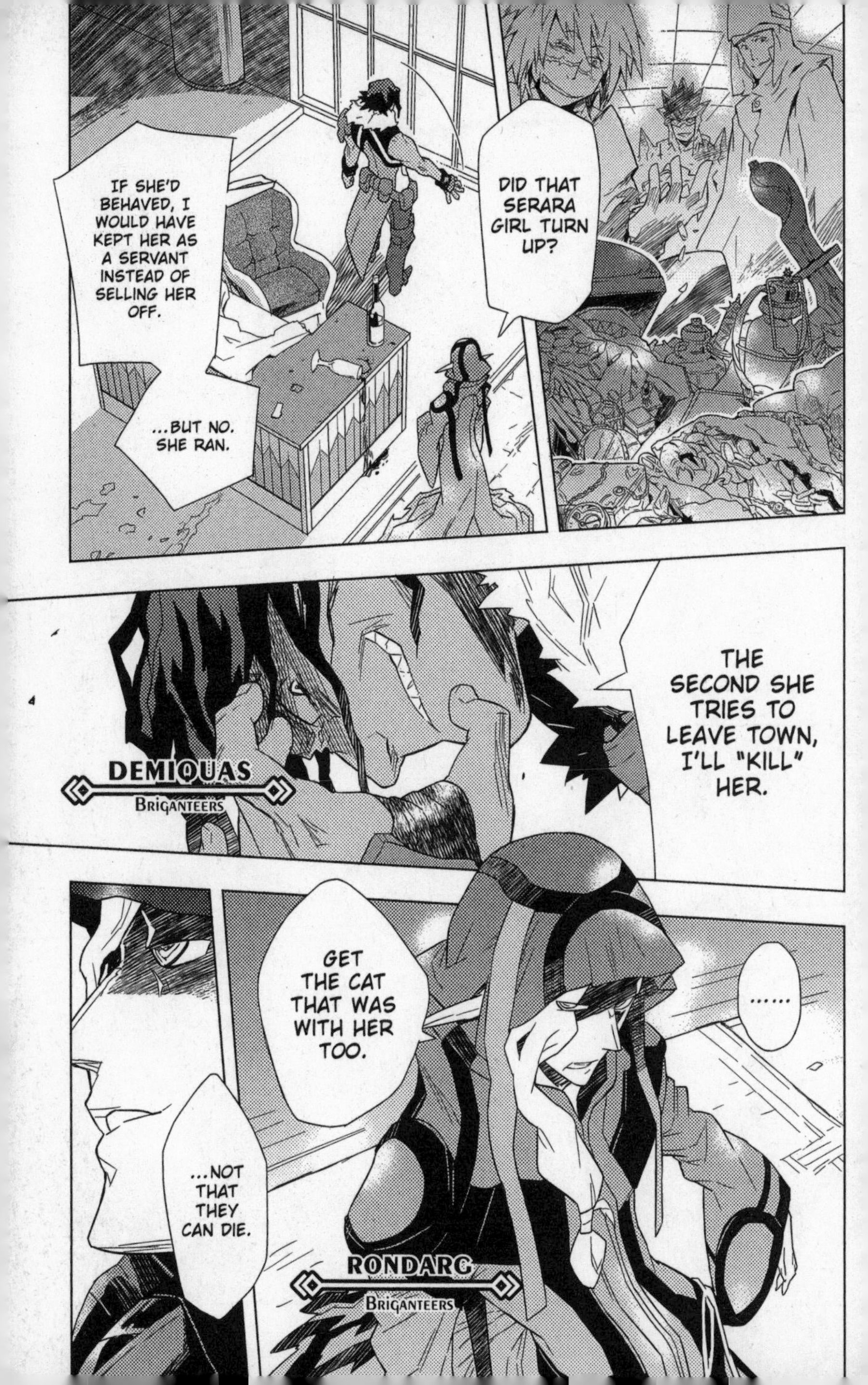
DID THAT SERARA GIRL TURN UP?
IF SHE'D BEHAVED, I WOULD HAVE KEPT HER AS A SERVANT INSTEAD OF SELLING HER OFF.
...BUT NO. SHE RAN.
THE SECOND SHE TRIES TO LEAVE TOWN, I'LL "KILL" HER.
DEMIQUAS
Briganteers
......
GET THE CAT THAT WAS WITH HER TOO.
...NOT THAT THEY CAN DIE.
RONDARC
Briganteers

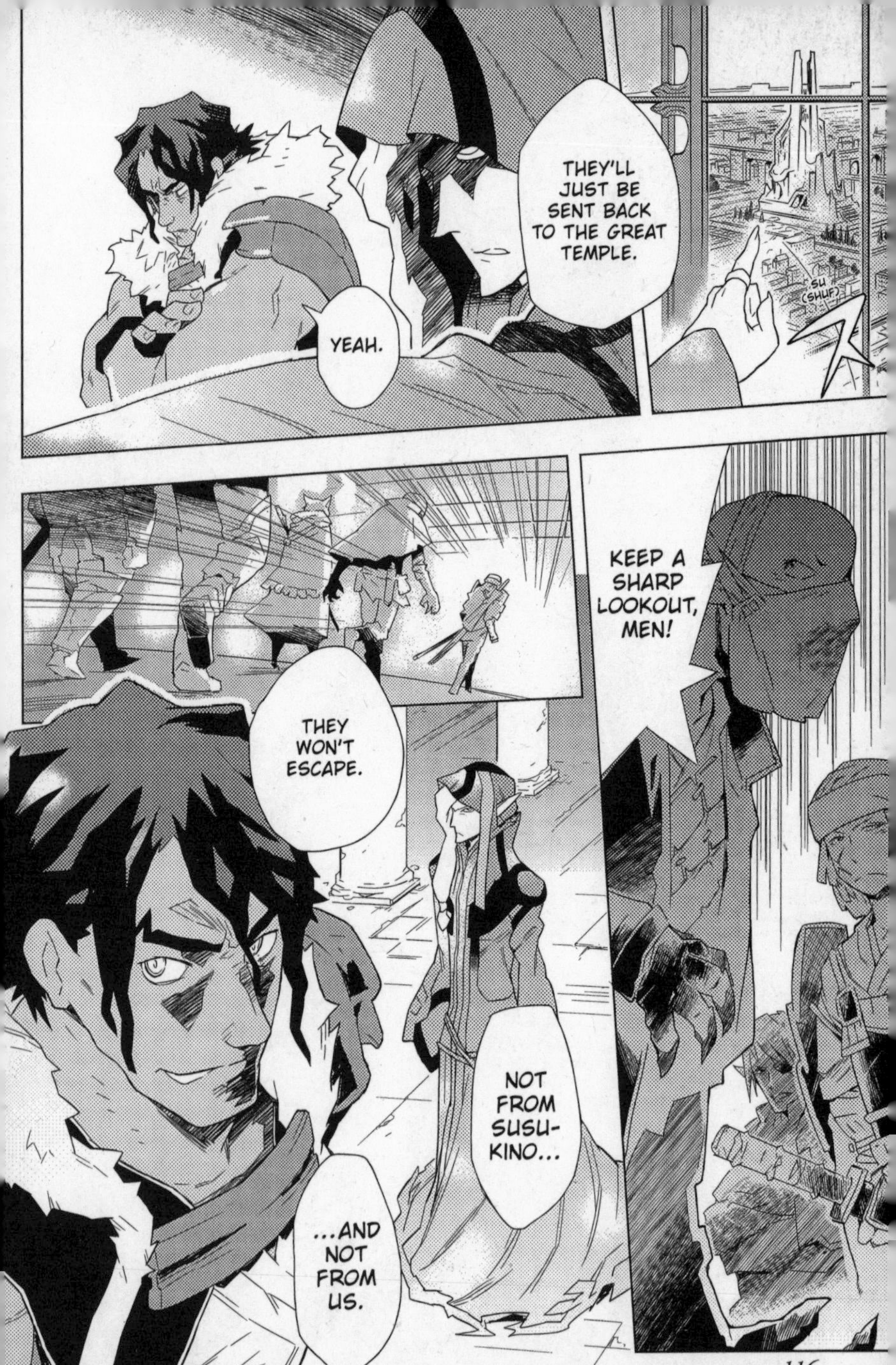
SU (SHUF)
THEY'LL JUST BE SENT BACK TO THE GREAT TEMPLE.
YEAH.
KEEP A SHARP LOOKOUT, MEN!
THEY WON'T ESCAPE.
NOT FROM SUSU-KINO...
...AND NOT FROM US.

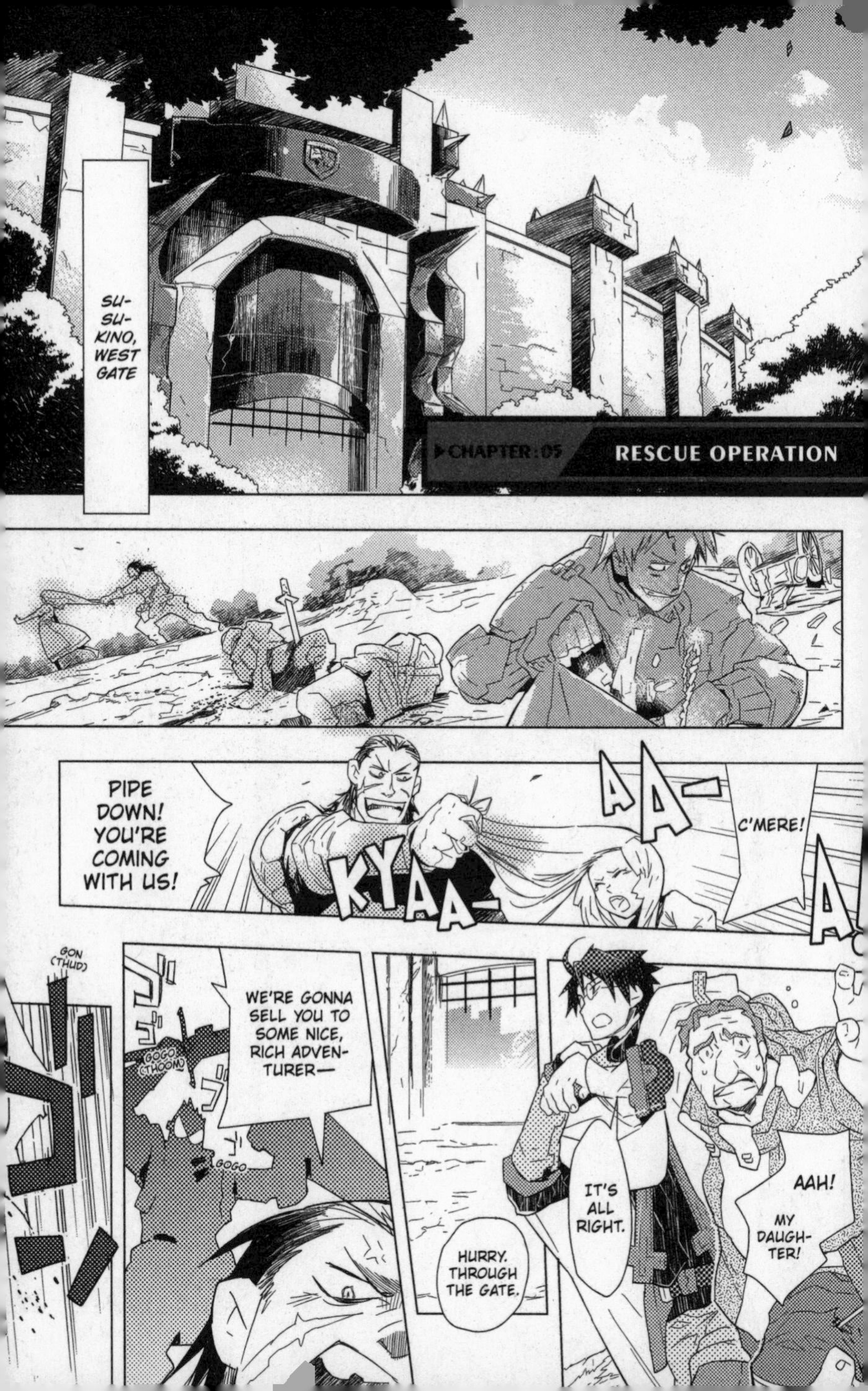
SU-SUKINO, WEST GATE
▶CHAPTER:05
RESCUE OPERATION
AA-A-A!
C'MERE!
KYAA-
PIPE DOWN! YOU'RE COMING WITH US!
AAH! MY DAUGHTER!
IT'S ALL RIGHT.
HURRY. THROUGH THE GATE.
WE'RE GONNA SELL YOU TO SOME NICE, RICH ADVENTURER—
GON (THUD)
GOGO (THOOM)
GOGO

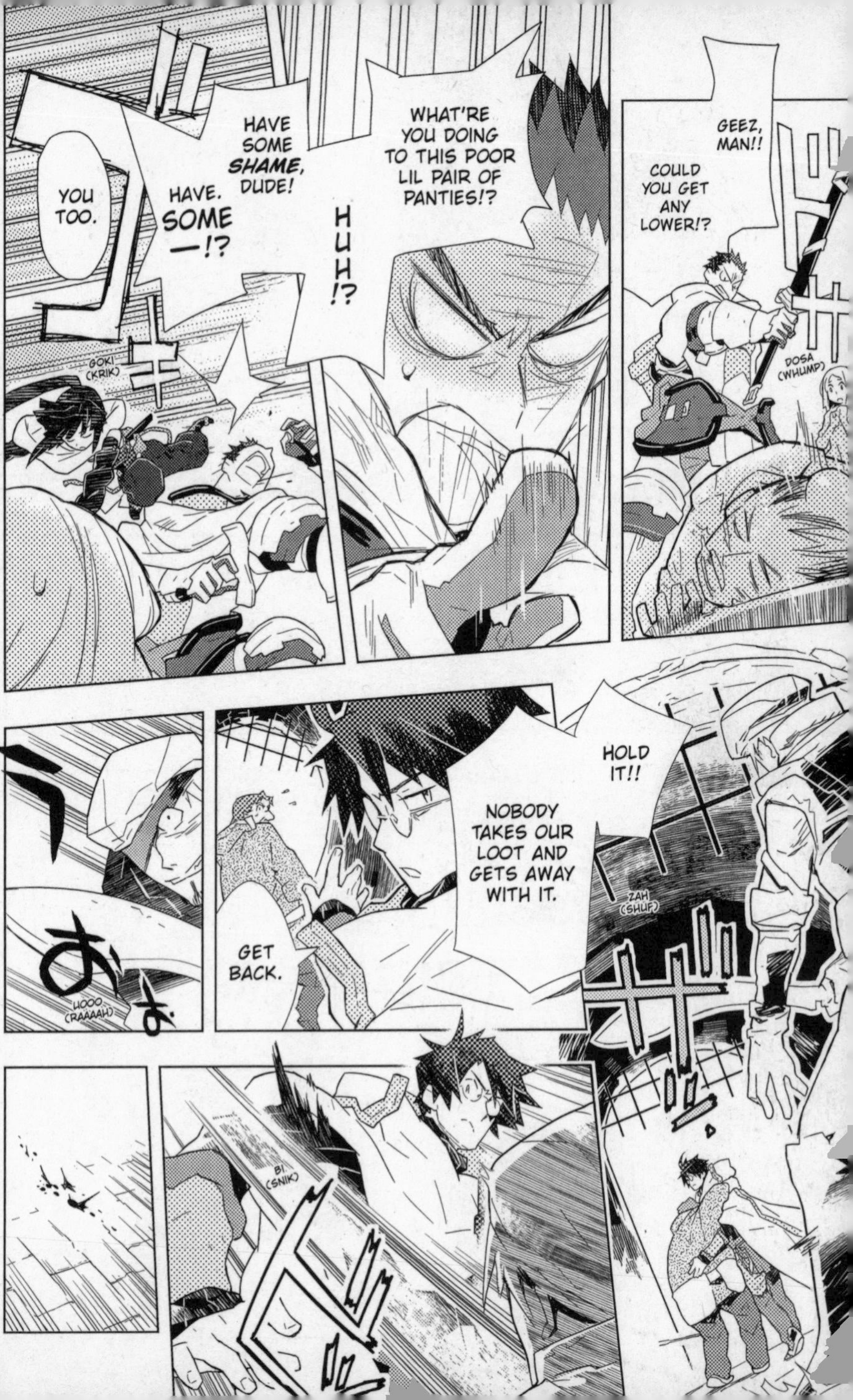
GEEZ, MAN!!
COULD YOU GET ANY LOWER!?
DOSA (WHUMP)
WHAT'RE YOU DOING TO THIS POOR LIL PAIR OF PANTIES!?
HUH!?
HAVE SOME *SHAME*, DUDE!
HAVE. SOME—!?
YOU TOO.
GOKI (KRIK)
HOLD IT!!
NOBODY TAKES OUR LOOT AND GETS AWAY WITH IT.
ZAH (SHUF)
GET BACK.
UOOO (RAAAAH)
BI (SNIK)

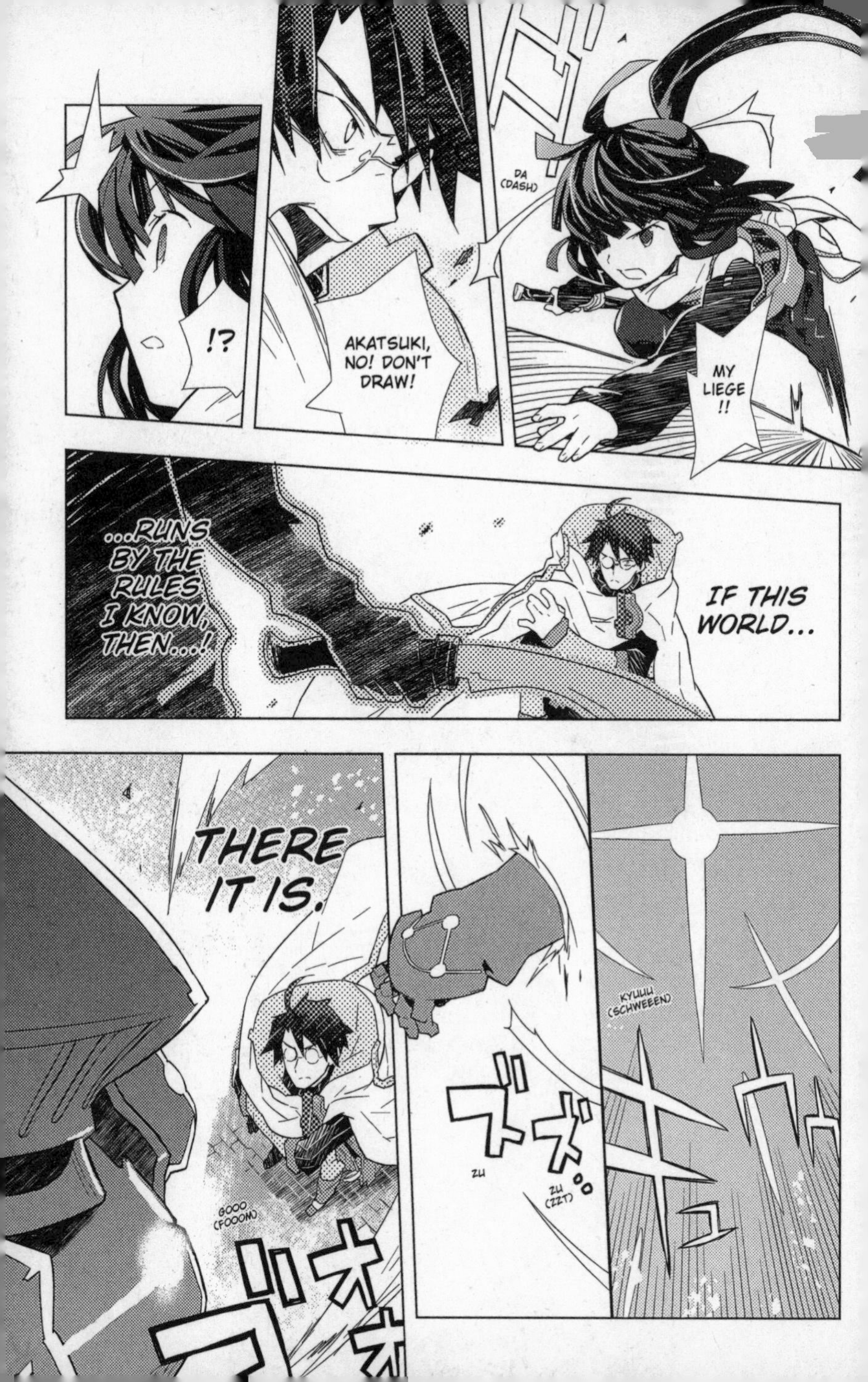
DA
(DASH)
MY LIEGE !!
AKATSUKI, NO! DON'T DRAW!
!?
IF THIS WORLD...
...RUNS BY THE RULES I KNOW, THEN...!
KYUUU
(SCHWEEEN)
ZU
ZU
(ZZT)
THERE IT IS.
GOOO
(FOOOM)

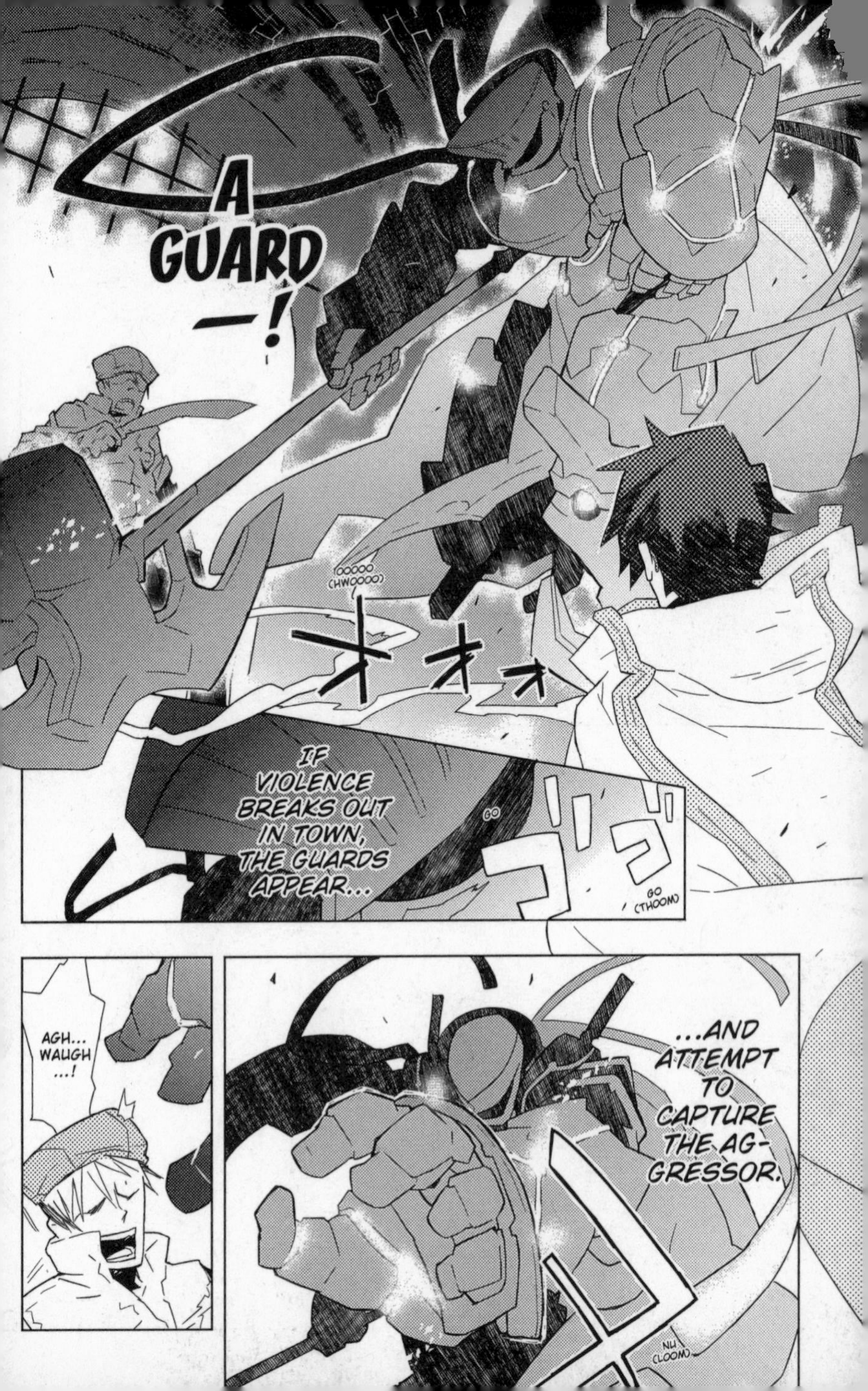
A GUARD—!
OOOOO (HWOOOO)
IF VIOLENCE BREAKS OUT IN TOWN, THE GUARDS APPEAR...
GO
GO (THOOM)
...AND ATTEMPT TO CAPTURE THE AG-GRESSOR.
NU (LOOM)
AGH... WAUGH ...!

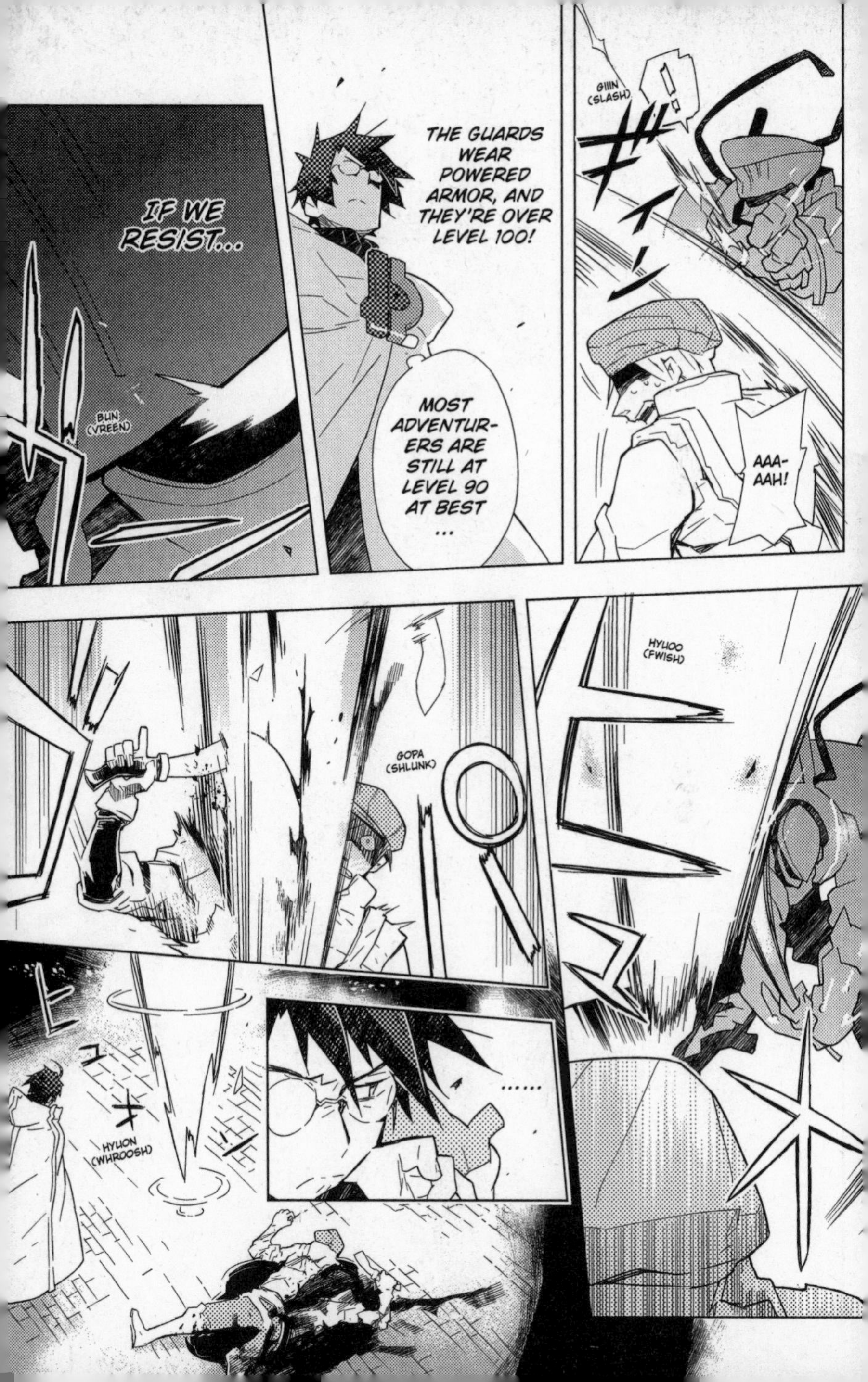
GIIIN (SLASH)
AAA-AAH!
THE GUARDS WEAR POWERED ARMOR, AND THEY'RE OVER LEVEL 100!
MOST ADVENTURERS ARE STILL AT LEVEL 90 AT BEST...
IF WE RESIST...
BUN (VREEN)
HYUOO (FWISH)
GOPA (SHLUNK)
......
HYUON (WHROOSH)

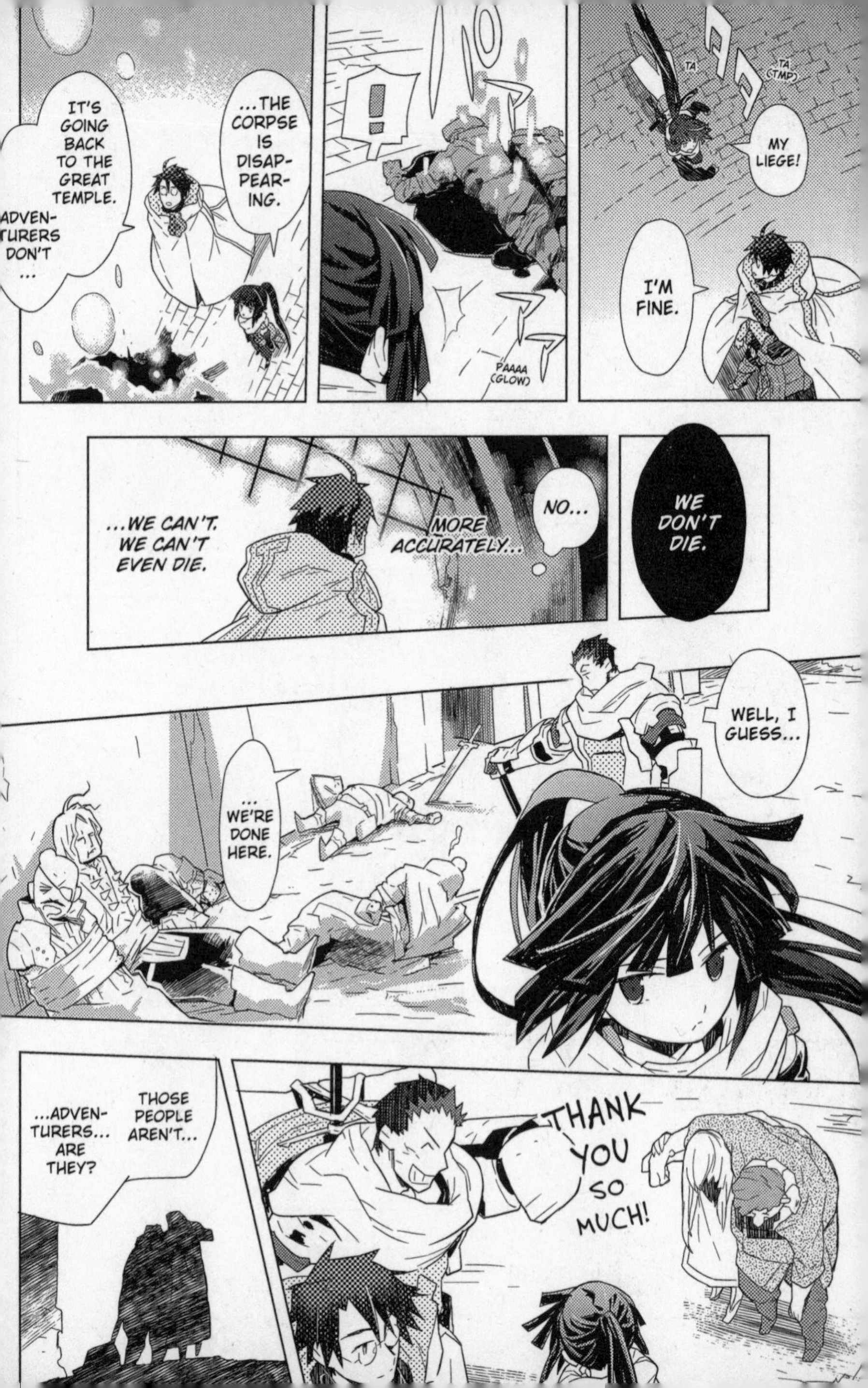
TA
TA (TMP)
MY LIEGE!
I'M FINE.
!
PAAAA (GLOW)
...THE CORPSE IS DISAPPEARING.
IT'S GOING BACK TO THE GREAT TEMPLE.
ADVENTURERS DON'T ...
WE DON'T DIE.
NO...
MORE ACCURATELY...
...WE CAN'T. WE CAN'T EVEN DIE.
WELL, I GUESS...
...WE'RE DONE HERE.
THANK YOU SO MUCH!
THOSE PEOPLE AREN'T...
...ADVENTURERS... ARE THEY?

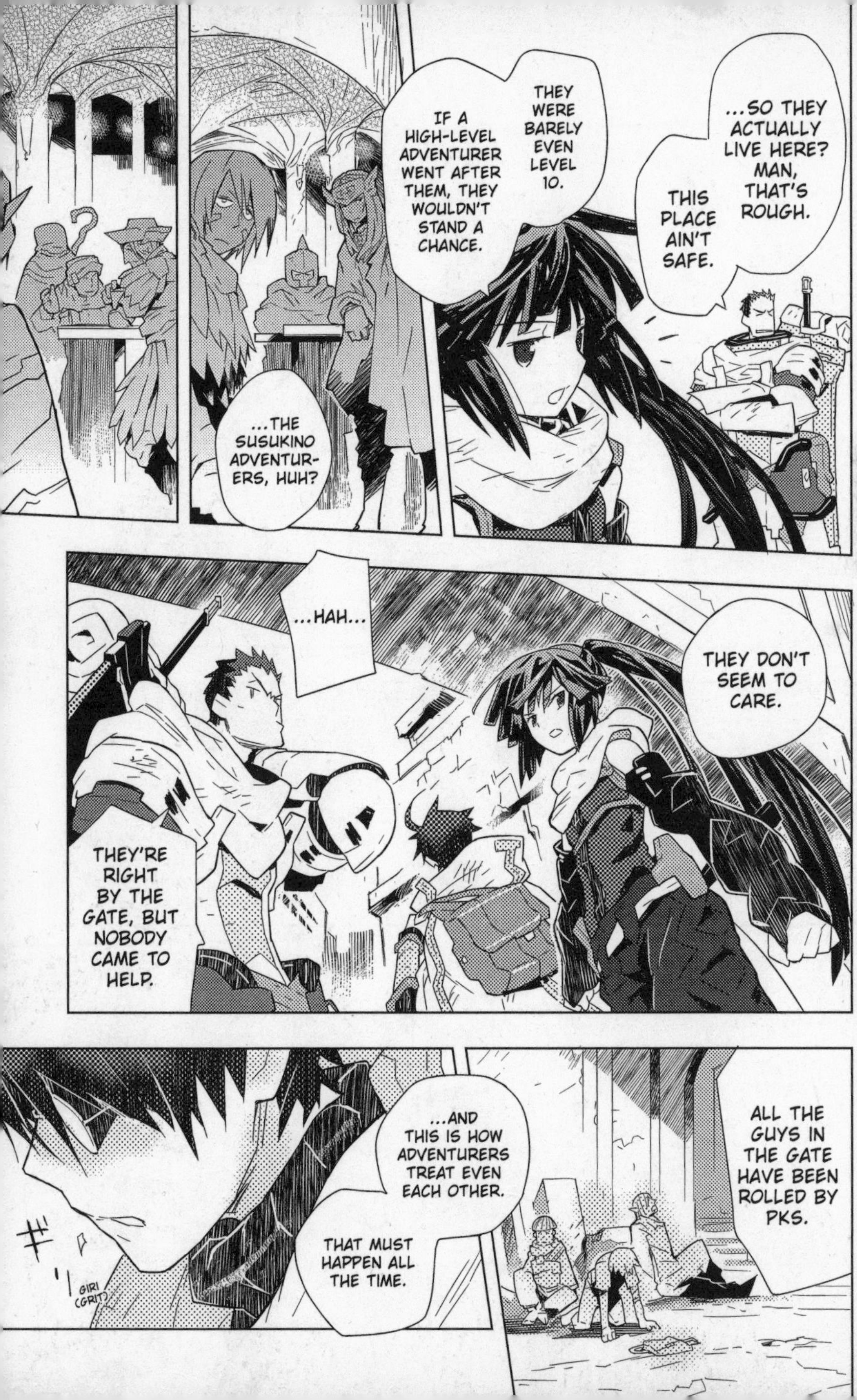
...SO THEY ACTUALLY LIVE HERE? MAN, THAT'S ROUGH.
THIS PLACE AIN'T SAFE.
THEY WERE BARELY EVEN LEVEL 10.
IF A HIGH-LEVEL ADVENTURER WENT AFTER THEM, THEY WOULDN'T STAND A CHANCE.
...THE SUSUKINO ADVENTURERS, HUH?
THEY DON'T SEEM TO CARE.
...HAH...
THEY'RE RIGHT BY THE GATE, BUT NOBODY CAME TO HELP.
ALL THE GUYS IN THE GATE HAVE BEEN ROLLED BY PKS.
...AND THIS IS HOW ADVENTURERS TREAT EVEN EACH OTHER.
THAT MUST HAPPEN ALL THE TIME.
GIRI (GRIT)

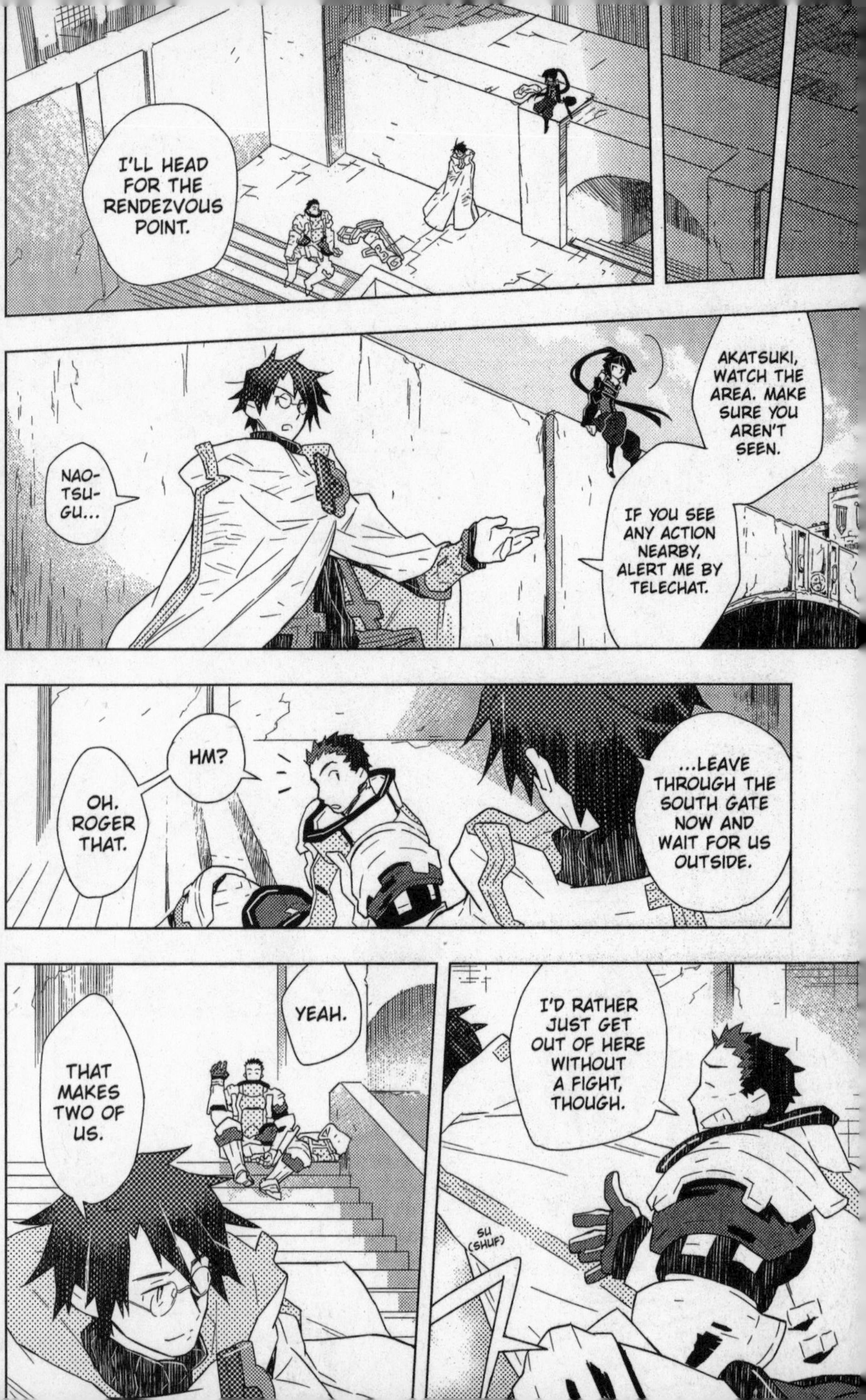
I'LL HEAD FOR THE RENDEZVOUS POINT.
AKATSUKI, WATCH THE AREA. MAKE SURE YOU AREN'T SEEN.
IF YOU SEE ANY ACTION NEARBY, ALERT ME BY TELECHAT.
NAO-TSU-GU...
...LEAVE THROUGH THE SOUTH GATE NOW AND WAIT FOR US OUTSIDE.
HM?
OH. ROGER THAT.
I'D RATHER JUST GET OUT OF HERE WITHOUT A FIGHT, THOUGH.
SU (SHUF)
YEAH.
THAT MAKES TWO OF US.

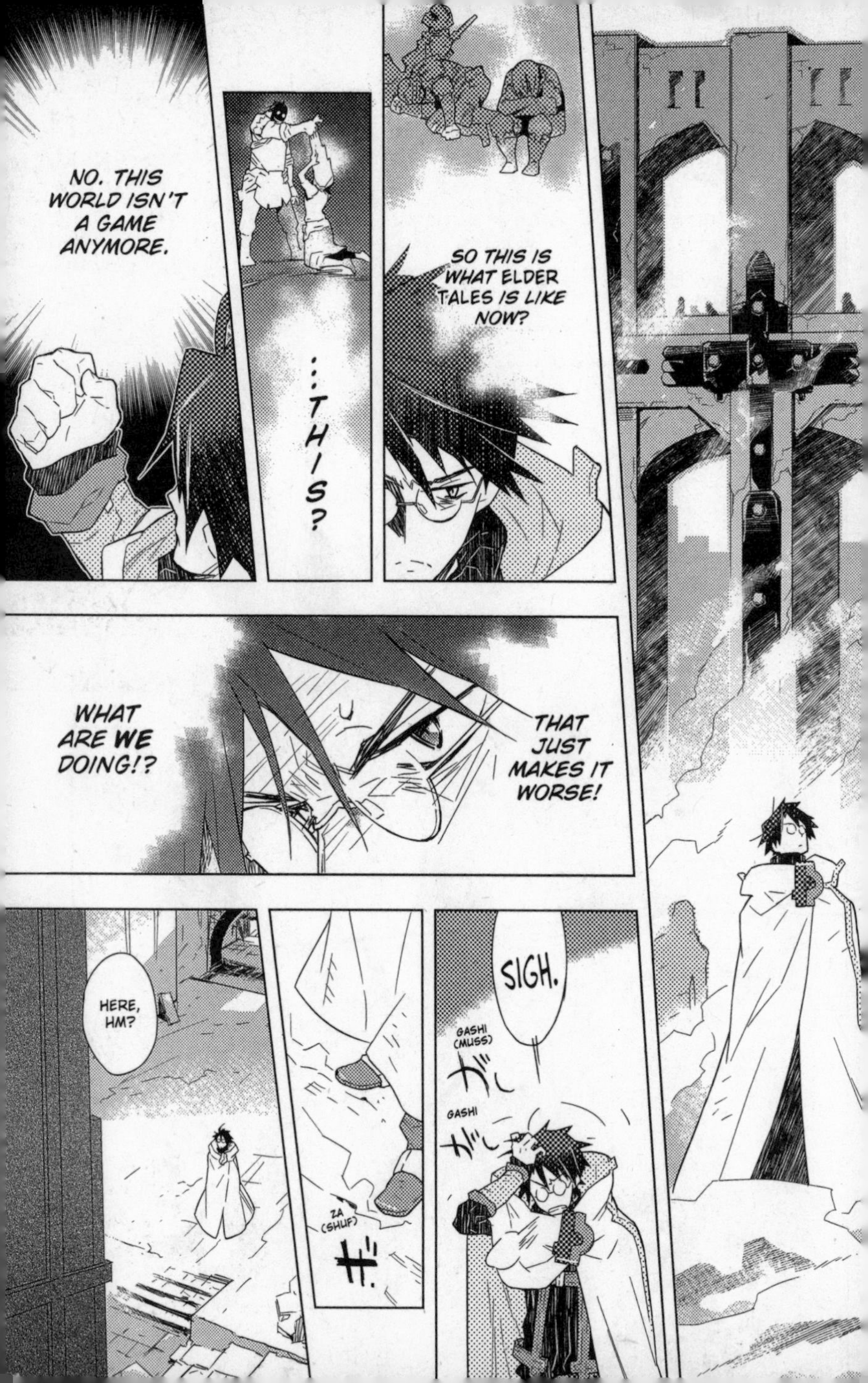
SO THIS IS WHAT ELDER TALES IS LIKE NOW?
...THIS?
NO. THIS WORLD ISN'T A GAME ANYMORE.
THAT JUST MAKES IT WORSE!
WHAT ARE WE DOING!?
SIGH.
GASHI (MUSS)
GASHI
ZA (SHUF)
HERE, HM?

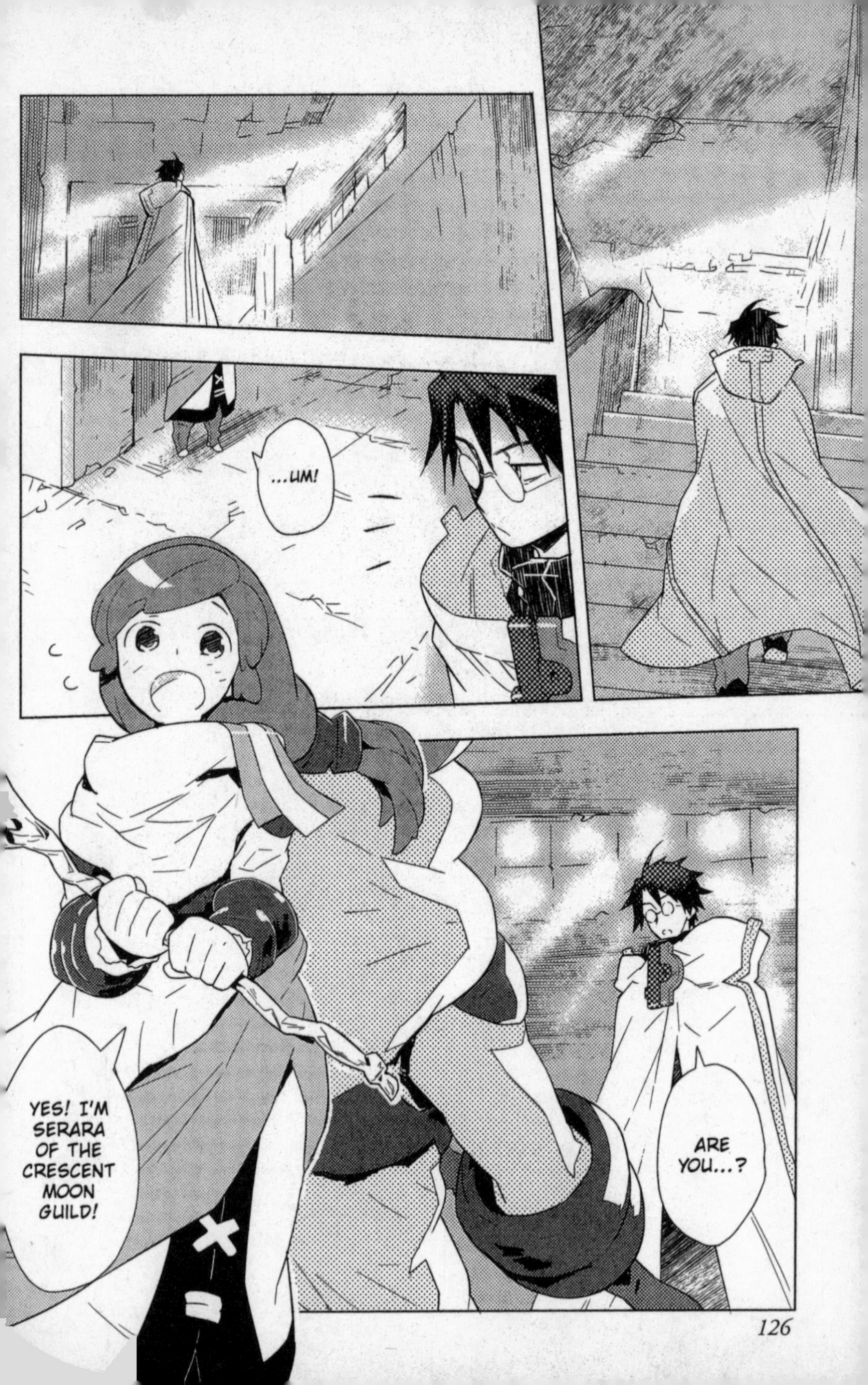
...UM!
ARE YOU...?
YES! I'M SERARA OF THE CRESCENT MOON GUILD!

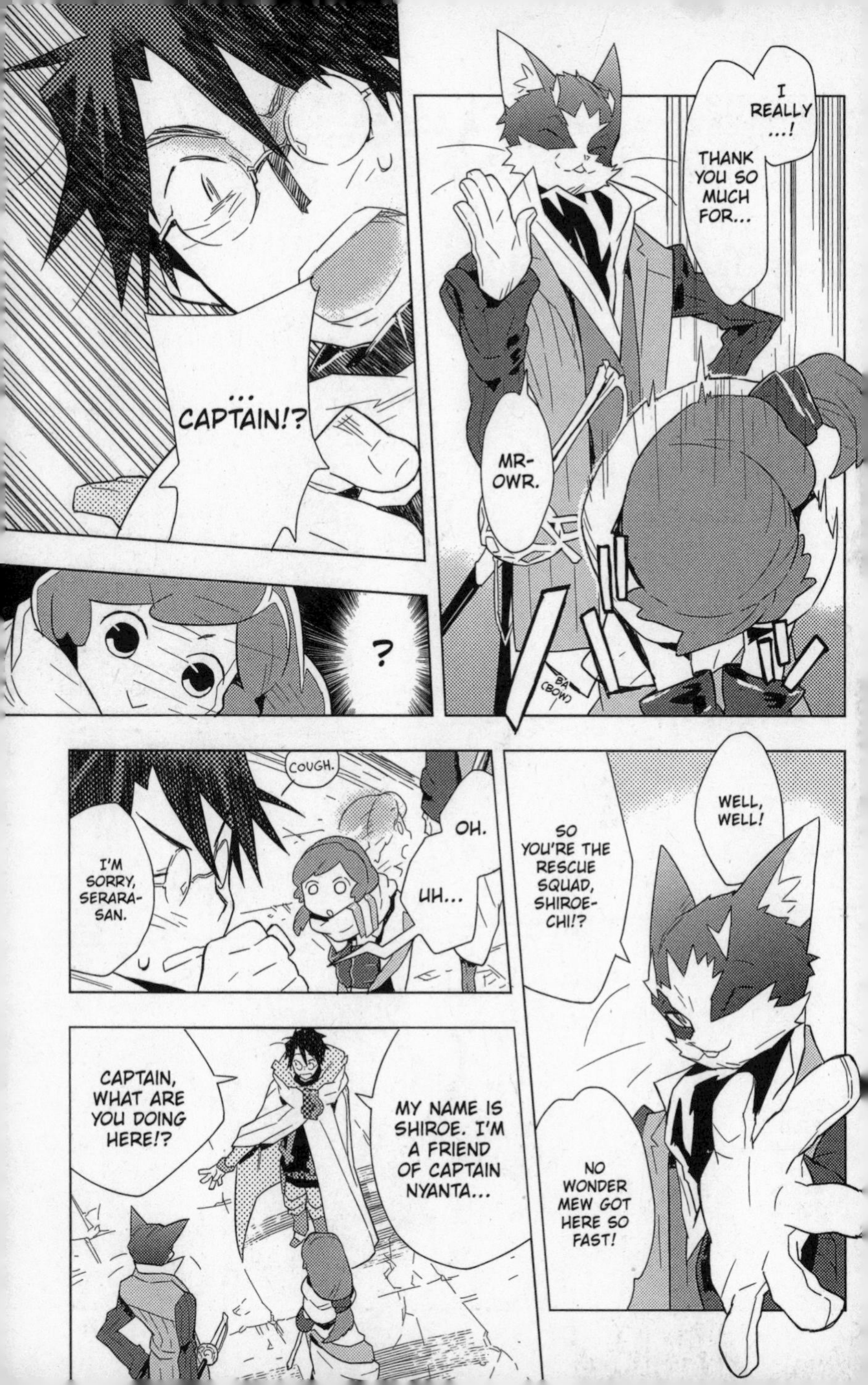
I REALLY ...!
THANK YOU SO MUCH FOR...
MR-OWR.
BA (BOW)
... CAPTAIN!?
?
WELL, WELL!
SO YOU'RE THE RESCUE SQUAD, SHIROE-CHI!?
NO WONDER MEW GOT HERE SO FAST!
COUGH.
OH.
UH...
I'M SORRY, SERARA-SAN.
MY NAME IS SHIROE. I'M A FRIEND OF CAPTAIN NYANTA...
CAPTAIN, WHAT ARE YOU DOING HERE!?

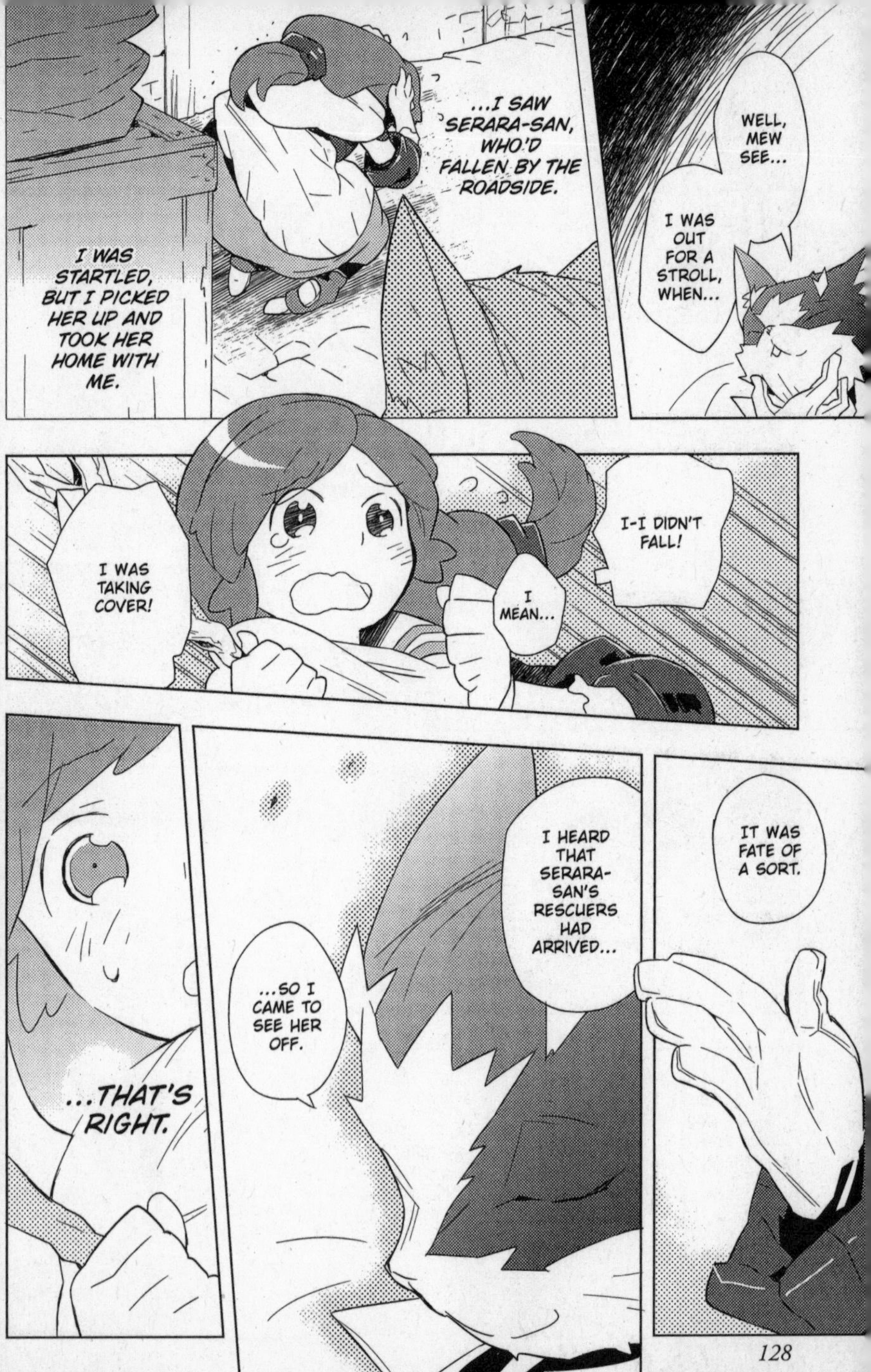
WELL, MEW SEE...
I WAS OUT FOR A STROLL, WHEN...
...I SAW SERARA-SAN, WHO'D FALLEN BY THE ROADSIDE.
I WAS STARTLED, BUT I PICKED HER UP AND TOOK HER HOME WITH ME.
I-I DIDN'T FALL!
I MEAN...
I WAS TAKING COVER!
IT WAS FATE OF A SORT.
I HEARD THAT SERARA-SAN'S RESCUERS HAD ARRIVED...
...SO I CAME TO SEE HER OFF.
...THAT'S RIGHT.

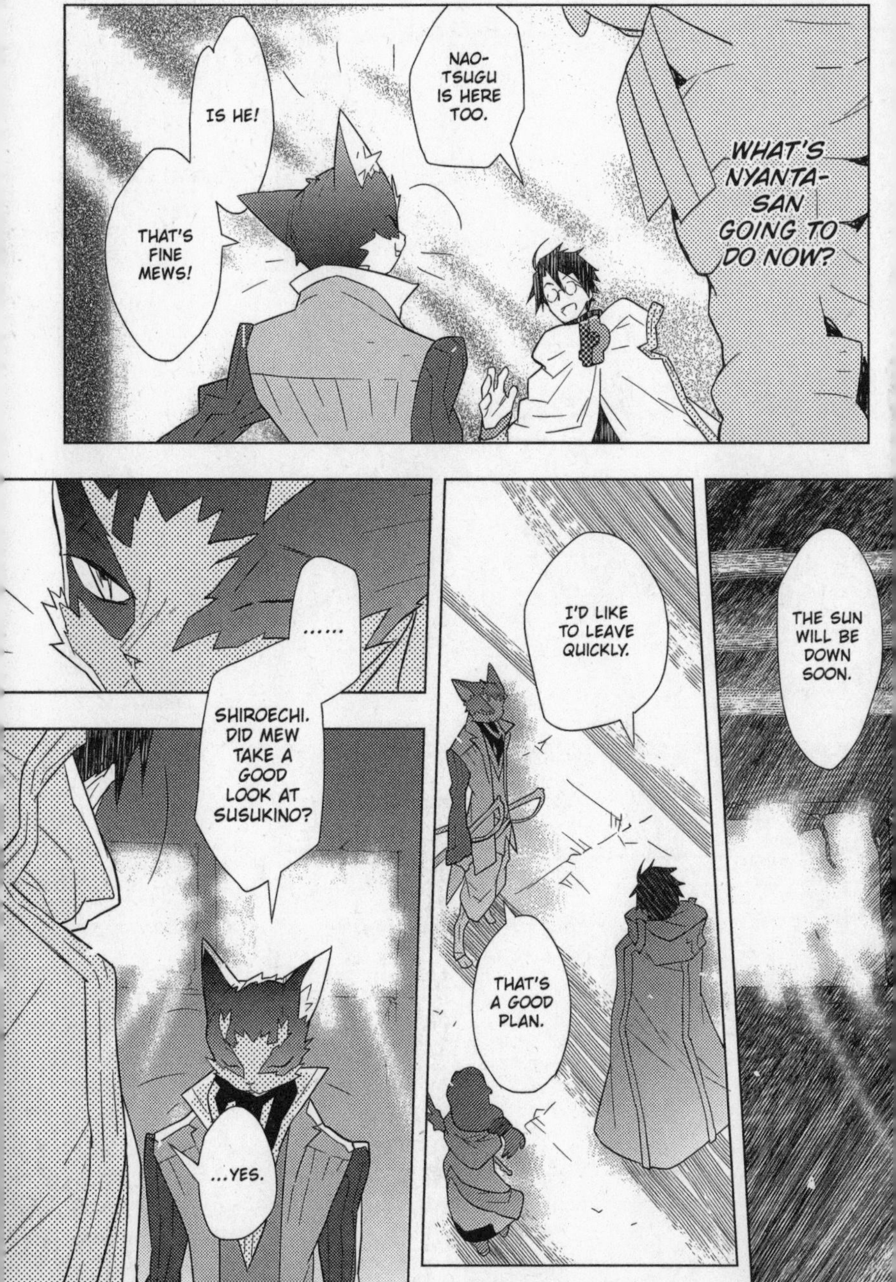
WHAT'S NYANTA-SAN GOING TO DO NOW?
NAO-TSUGU IS HERE TOO.
IS HE!
THAT'S FINE MEWS!
THE SUN WILL BE DOWN SOON.
I'D LIKE TO LEAVE QUICKLY.
THAT'S A GOOD PLAN.
......
SHIROECHI. DID MEW TAKE A GOOD LOOK AT SUSUKINO?
...YES.

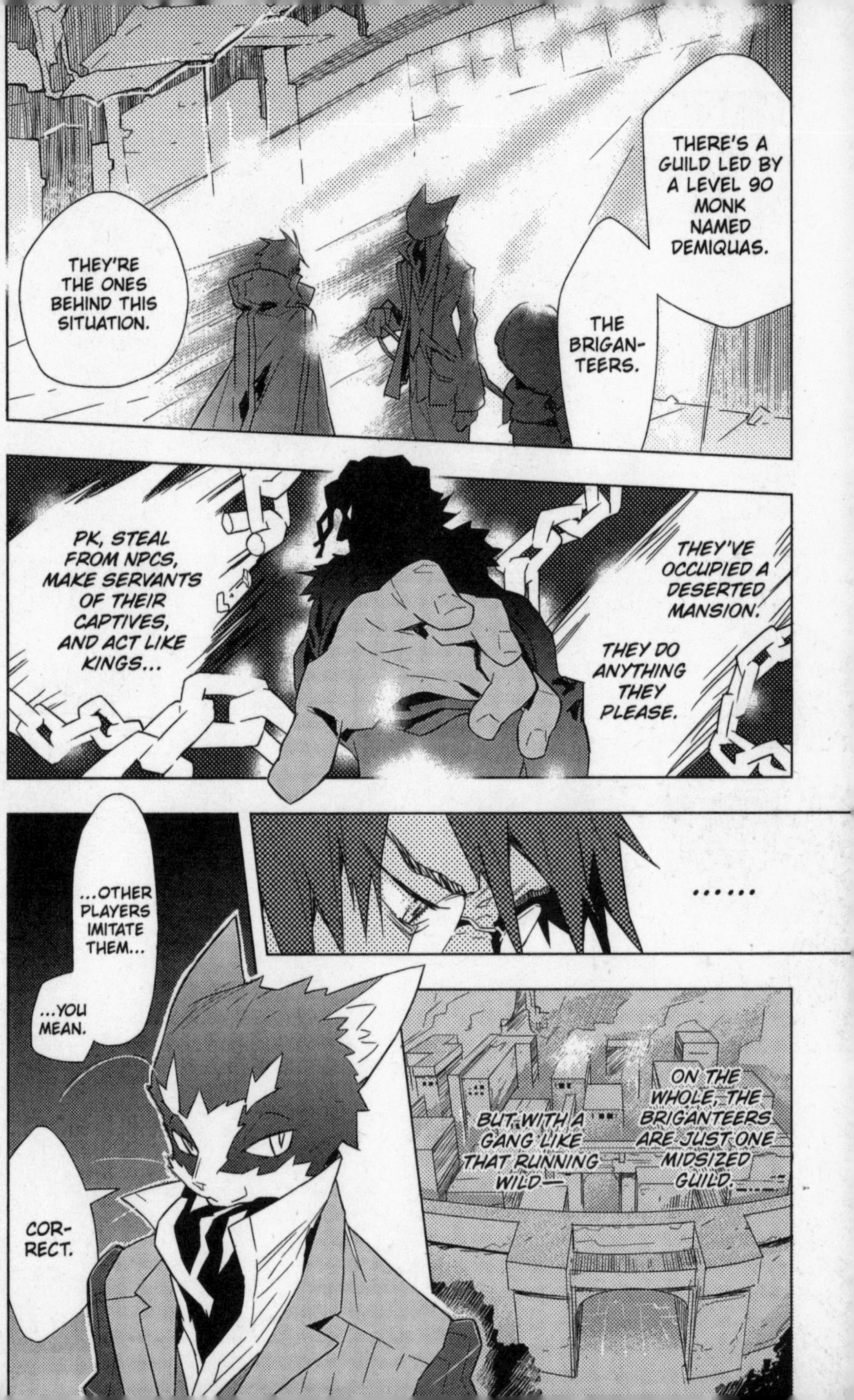
THERE'S A GUILD LED BY A LEVEL 90 MONK NAMED DEMIQUAS.
THE BRIGAN-TEERS.
THEY'RE THE ONES BEHIND THIS SITUATION.
THEY'VE OCCUPIED A DESERTED MANSION.
THEY DO ANYTHING THEY PLEASE.
PK, STEAL FROM NPCS, MAKE SERVANTS OF THEIR CAPTIVES, AND ACT LIKE KINGS...
......
ON THE WHOLE, THE BRIGANTEERS ARE JUST ONE MIDSIZED GUILD.
BUT WITH A GANG LIKE THAT RUNNING WILD—
...OTHER PLAYERS IMITATE THEM...
...YOU MEAN.
COR-RECT.

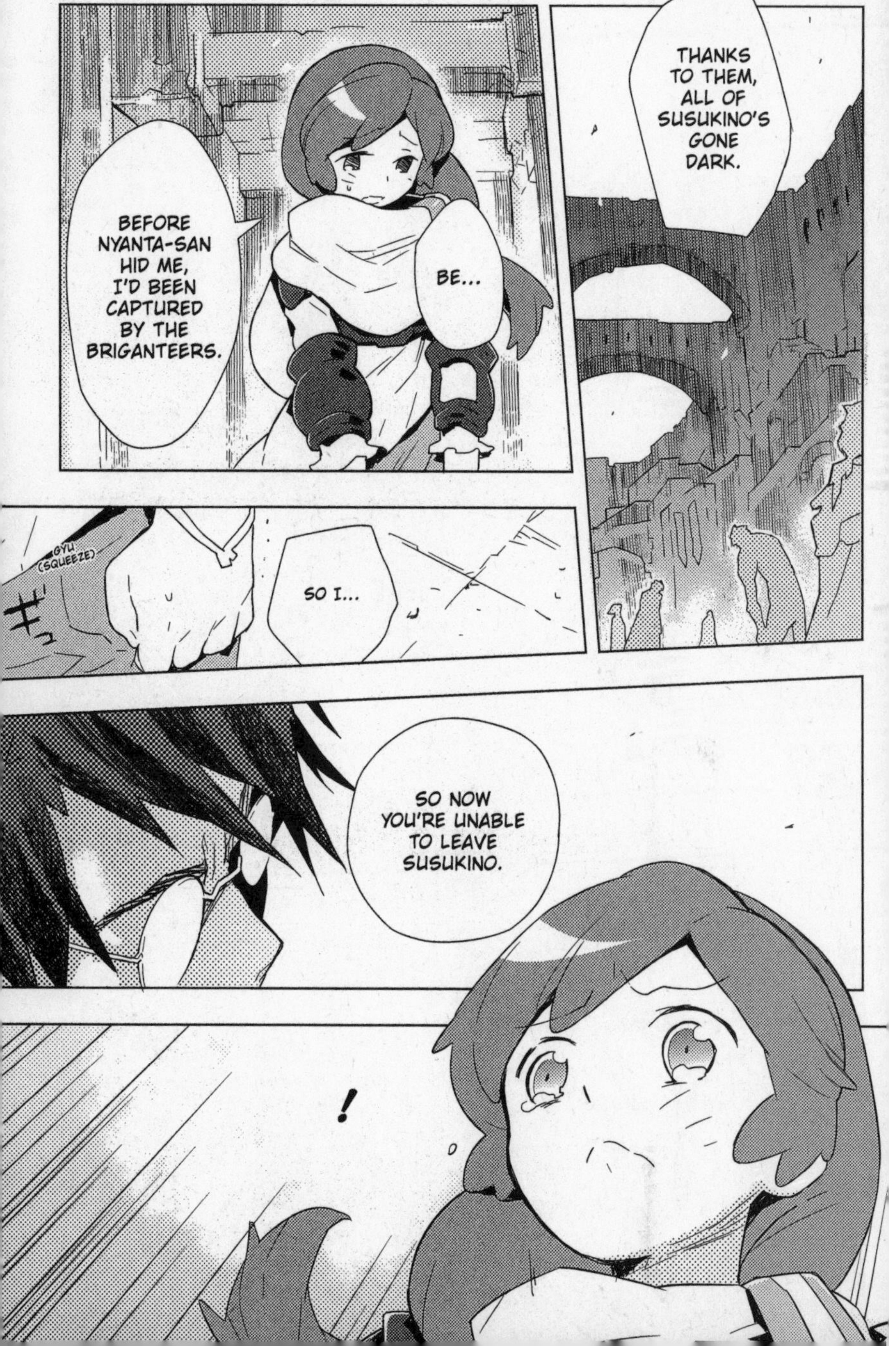
THANKS TO THEM, ALL OF SUSUKINO'S GONE DARK.
BE...
BEFORE NYANTA-SAN HID ME, I'D BEEN CAPTURED BY THE BRIGANTEERS.
SO I...
GYU (SQUEEZE)
SO NOW YOU'RE UNABLE TO LEAVE SUSUKINO.
!

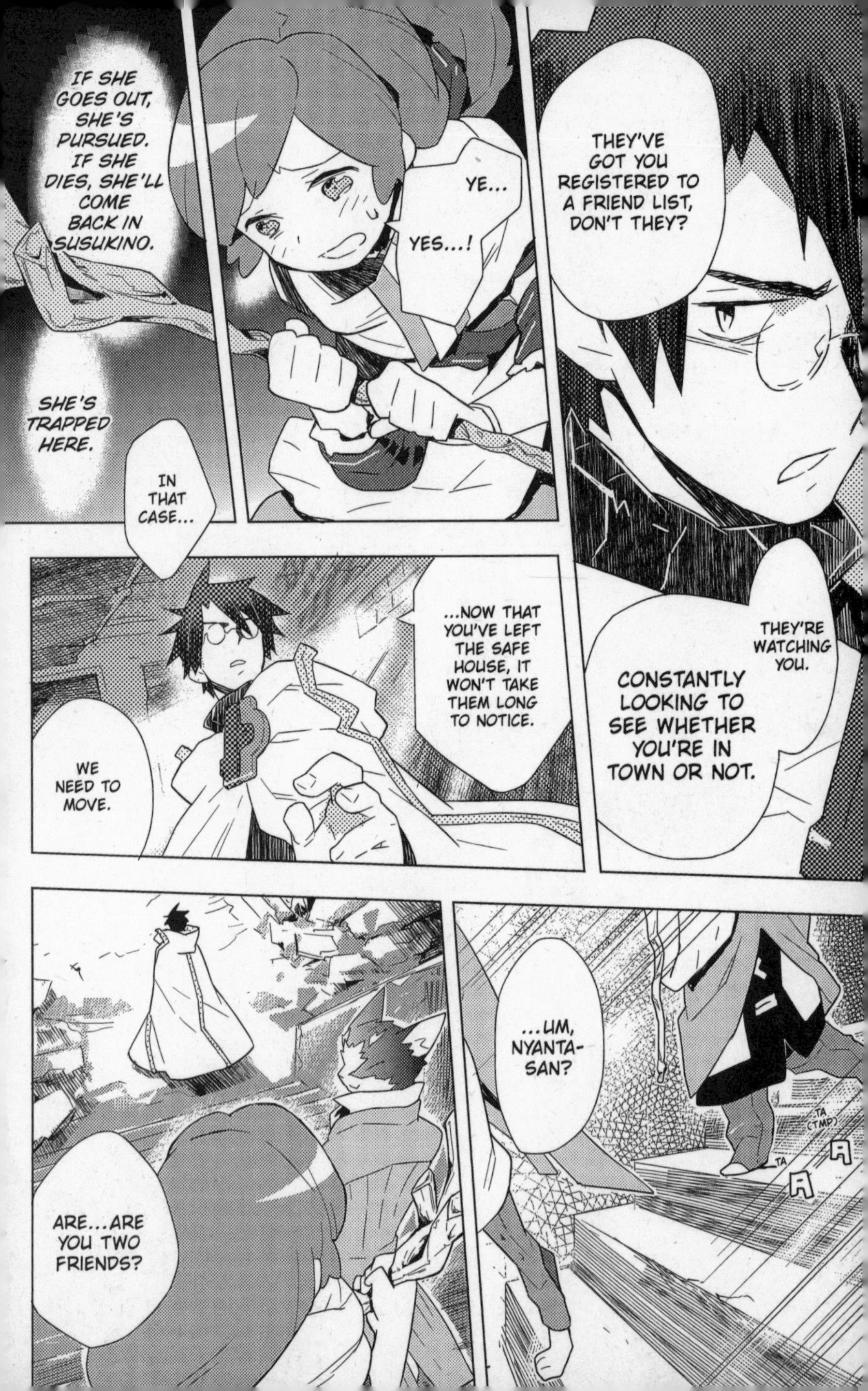
THEY'VE GOT YOU REGISTERED TO A FRIEND LIST, DON'T THEY?
THEY'RE WATCHING YOU.
CONSTANTLY LOOKING TO SEE WHETHER YOU'RE IN TOWN OR NOT.
YE...
YES...!
IF SHE GOES OUT, SHE'S PURSUED. IF SHE DIES, SHE'LL COME BACK IN SUSUKINO.
SHE'S TRAPPED HERE.
IN THAT CASE...
...NOW THAT YOU'VE LEFT THE SAFE HOUSE, IT WON'T TAKE THEM LONG TO NOTICE.
WE NEED TO MOVE.
...UM, NYANTA-SAN?
TA (TMP)
TA
ARE...ARE YOU TWO FRIENDS?

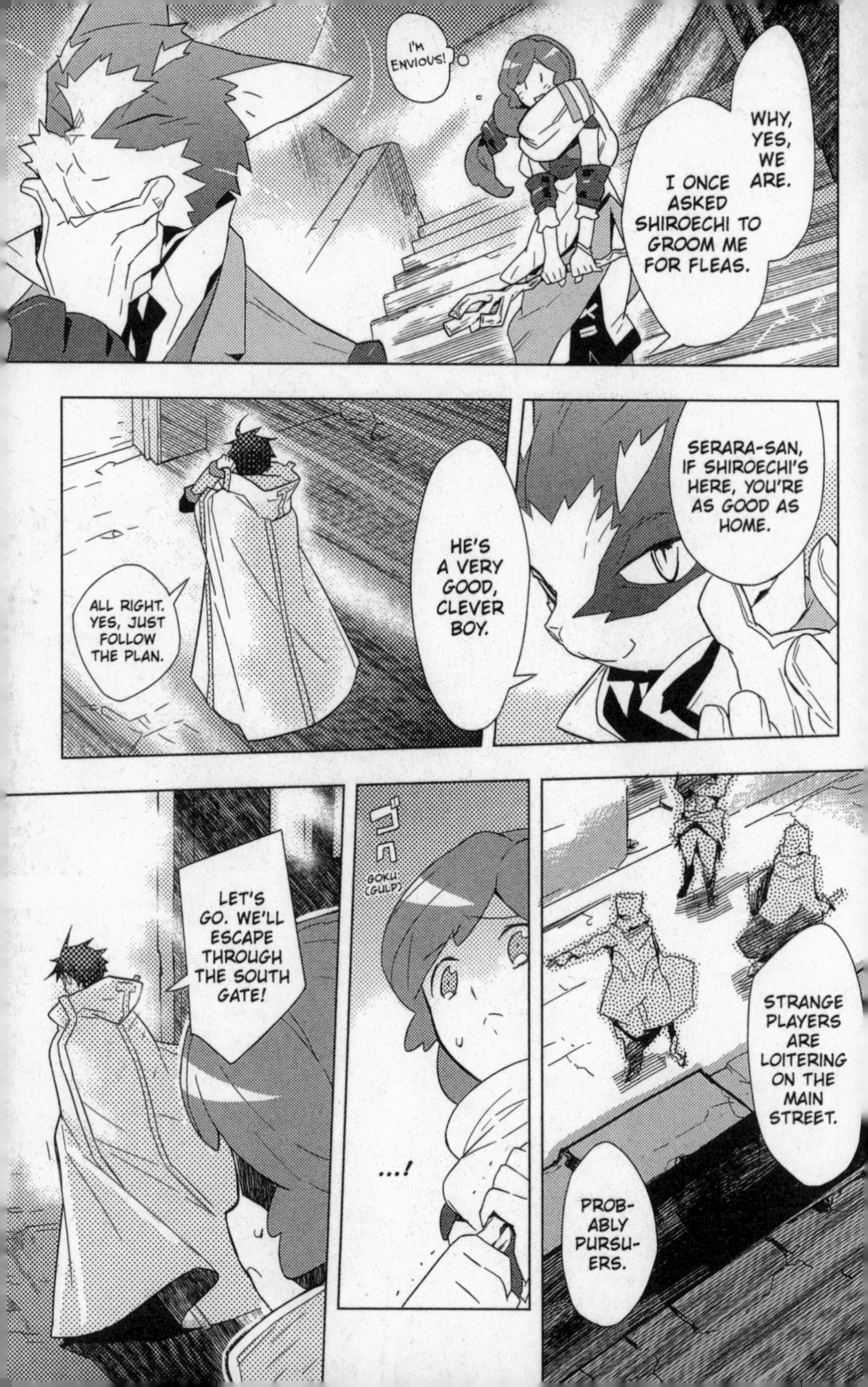
WHY, YES, WE ARE.
I ONCE ASKED SHIROECHI TO GROOM ME FOR FLEAS.
I'M ENVIOUS!
SERARA-SAN, IF SHIROECHI'S HERE, YOU'RE AS GOOD AS HOME.
HE'S A VERY GOOD, CLEVER BOY.
ALL RIGHT. YES, JUST FOLLOW THE PLAN.
STRANGE PLAYERS ARE LOITERING ON THE MAIN STREET.
PROB-ABLY PURSU-ERS.
GOKU (GULP)
...!
LET'S GO. WE'LL ESCAPE THROUGH THE SOUTH GATE!

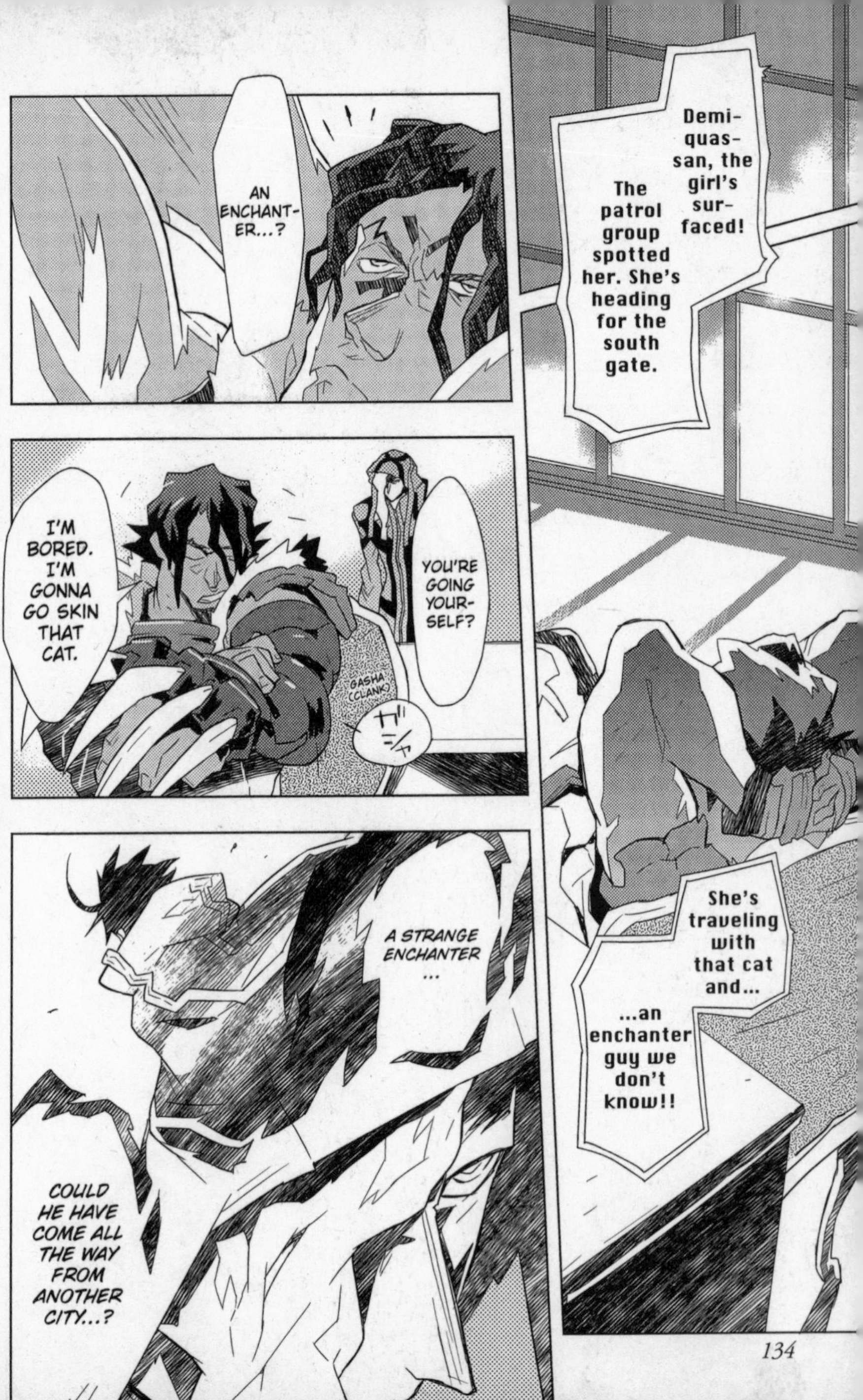
Demi-quas-san, the girl's sur-faced!
The patrol group spotted her. She's heading for the south gate.
She's traveling with that cat and...
...an enchanter guy we don't know!!
AN ENCHANT-ER...?
YOU'RE GOING YOUR-SELF?
ガシャ
GASHA (CLANK)
I'M BORED. I'M GONNA GO SKIN THAT CAT.
A STRANGE ENCHANTER ...
COULD HE HAVE COME ALL THE WAY FROM ANOTHER CITY...?

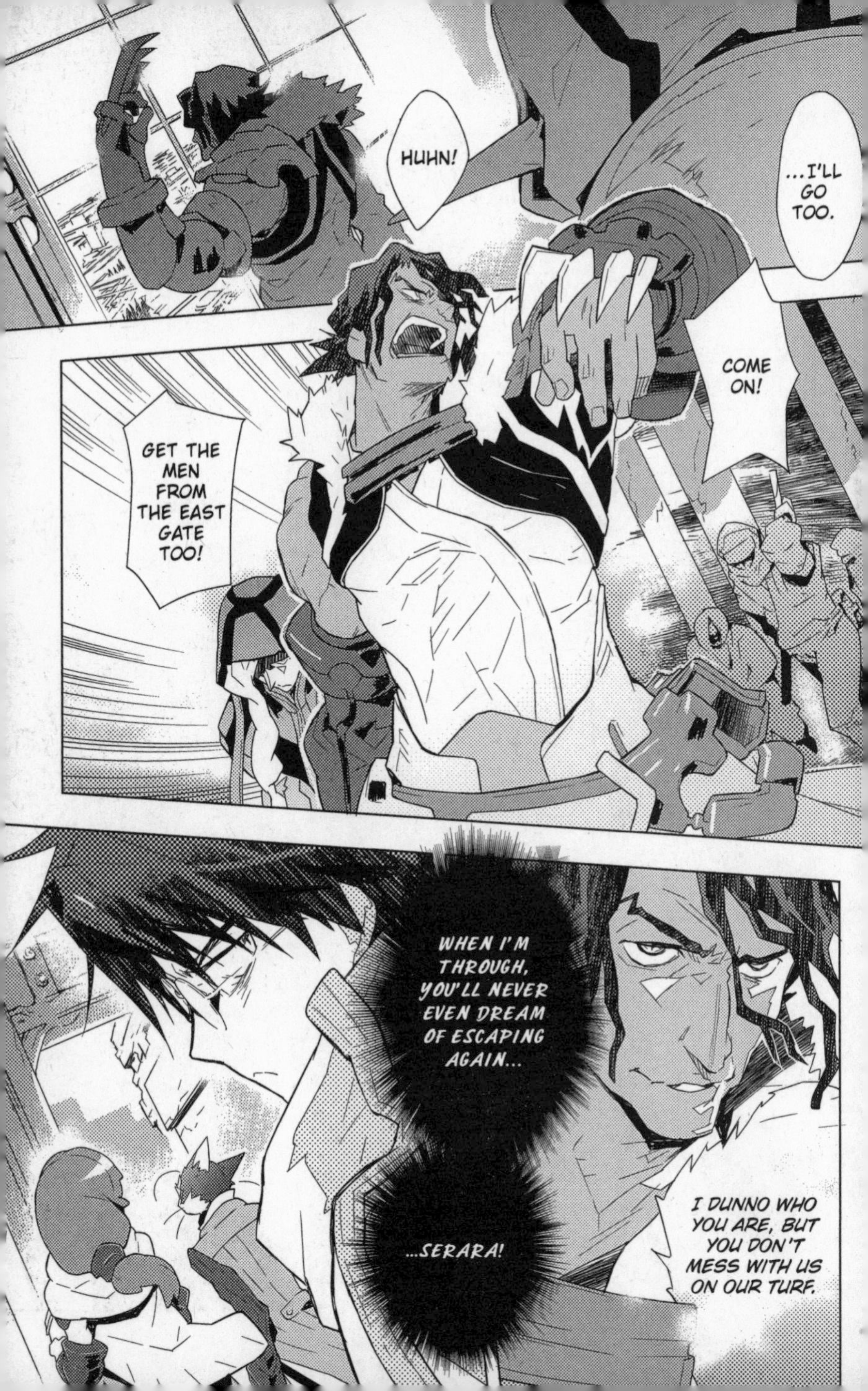
...I'LL GO TOO.
HUHN!
COME ON!
GET THE MEN FROM THE EAST GATE TOO!
WHEN I'M THROUGH, YOU'LL NEVER EVEN DREAM OF ESCAPING AGAIN...
...SERARA!
I DUNNO WHO YOU ARE, BUT YOU DON'T MESS WITH US ON OUR TURF.

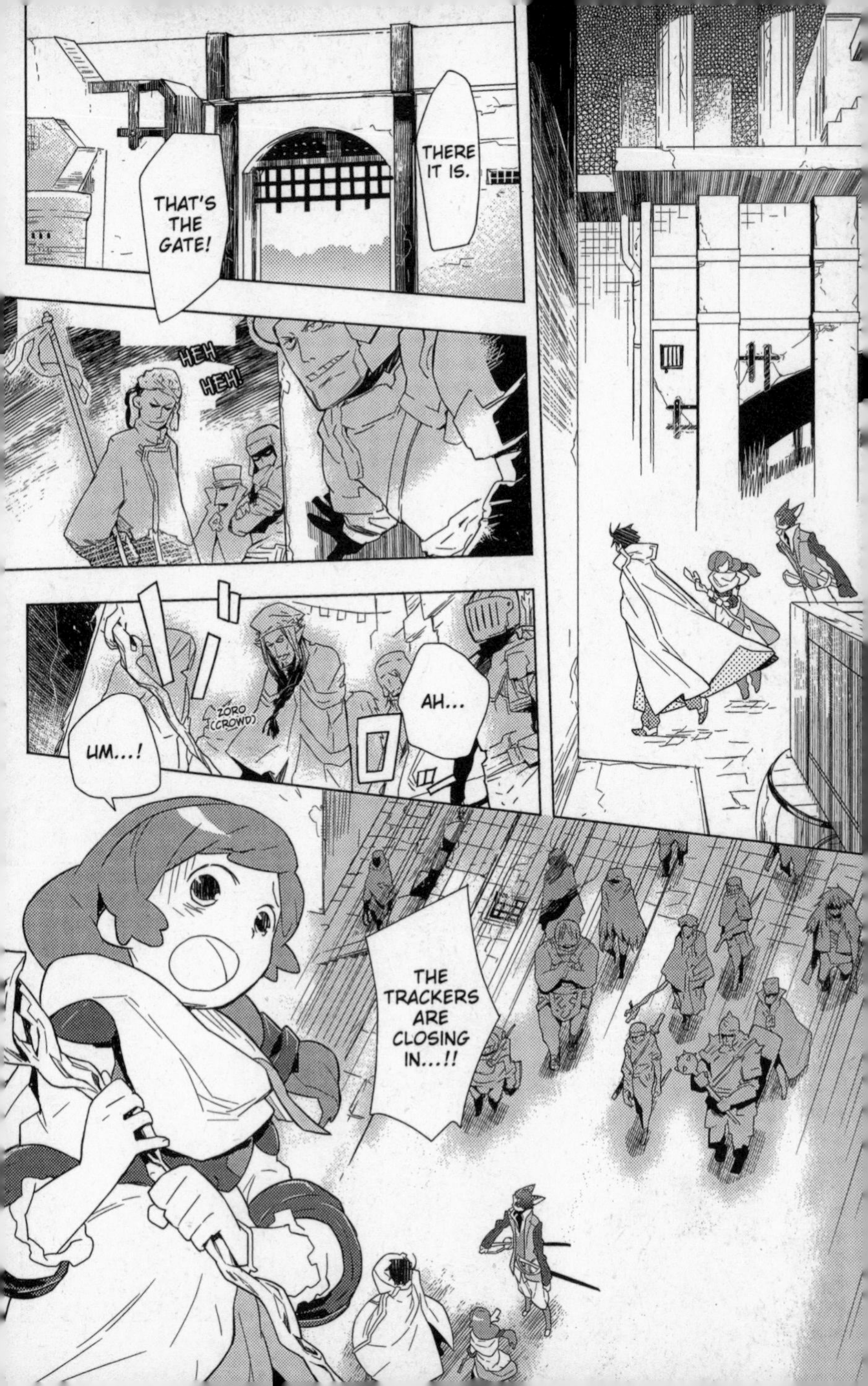
THERE IT IS.
THAT'S THE GATE!
HEH HEH!
AH...
ZORO (CROWD)
UM...!
THE TRACKERS ARE CLOSING IN...!!

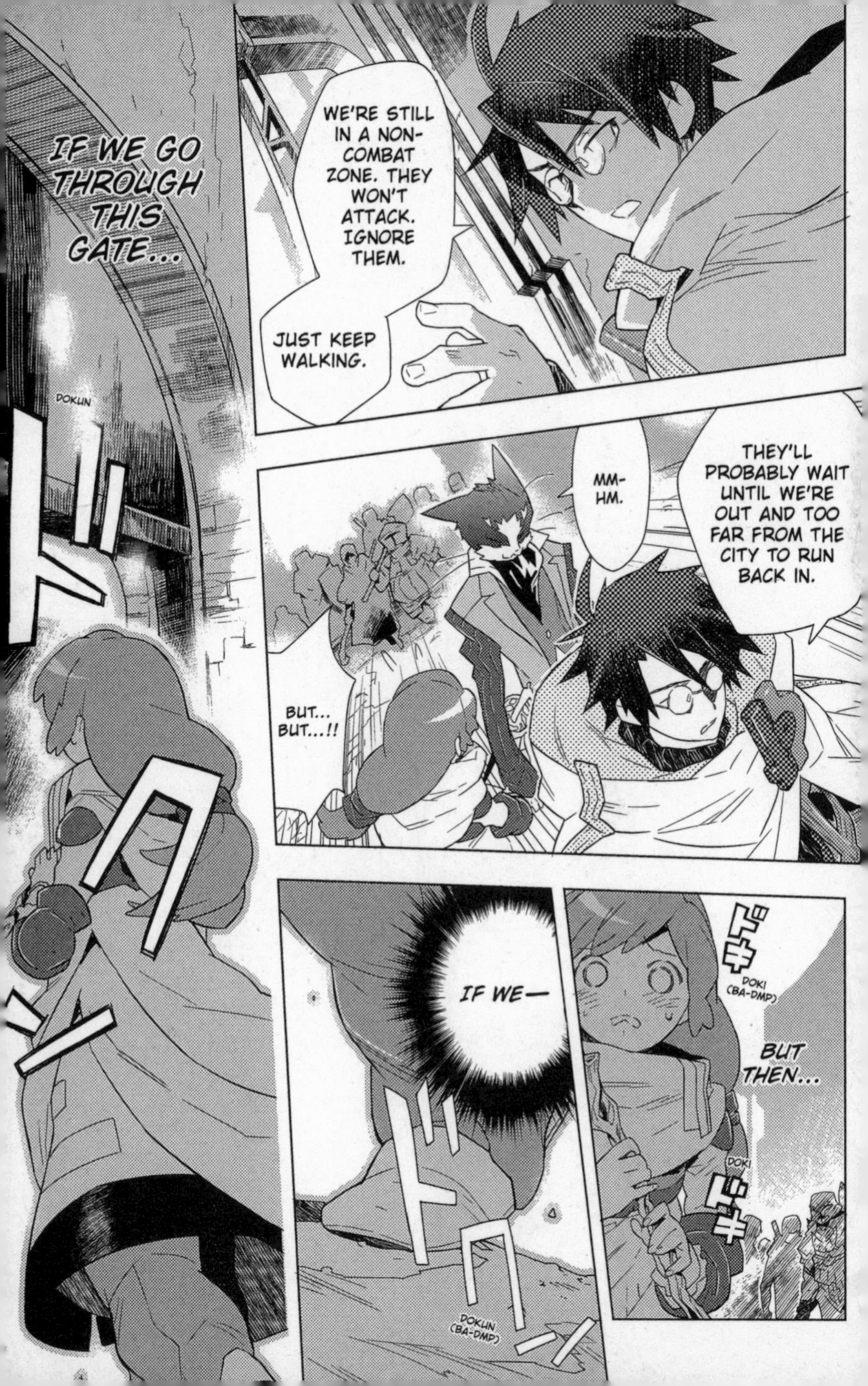
WE'RE STILL IN A NON-COMBAT ZONE. THEY WON'T ATTACK. IGNORE THEM.
JUST KEEP WALKING.
THEY'LL PROBABLY WAIT UNTIL WE'RE OUT AND TOO FAR FROM THE CITY TO RUN BACK IN.
MM-HM.
BUT... BUT...!!
DOKI (BA-DMP)
BUT THEN...
DOKI
IF WE—
DOKUN (BA-DMP)
IF WE GO THROUGH THIS GATE...
DOKUN

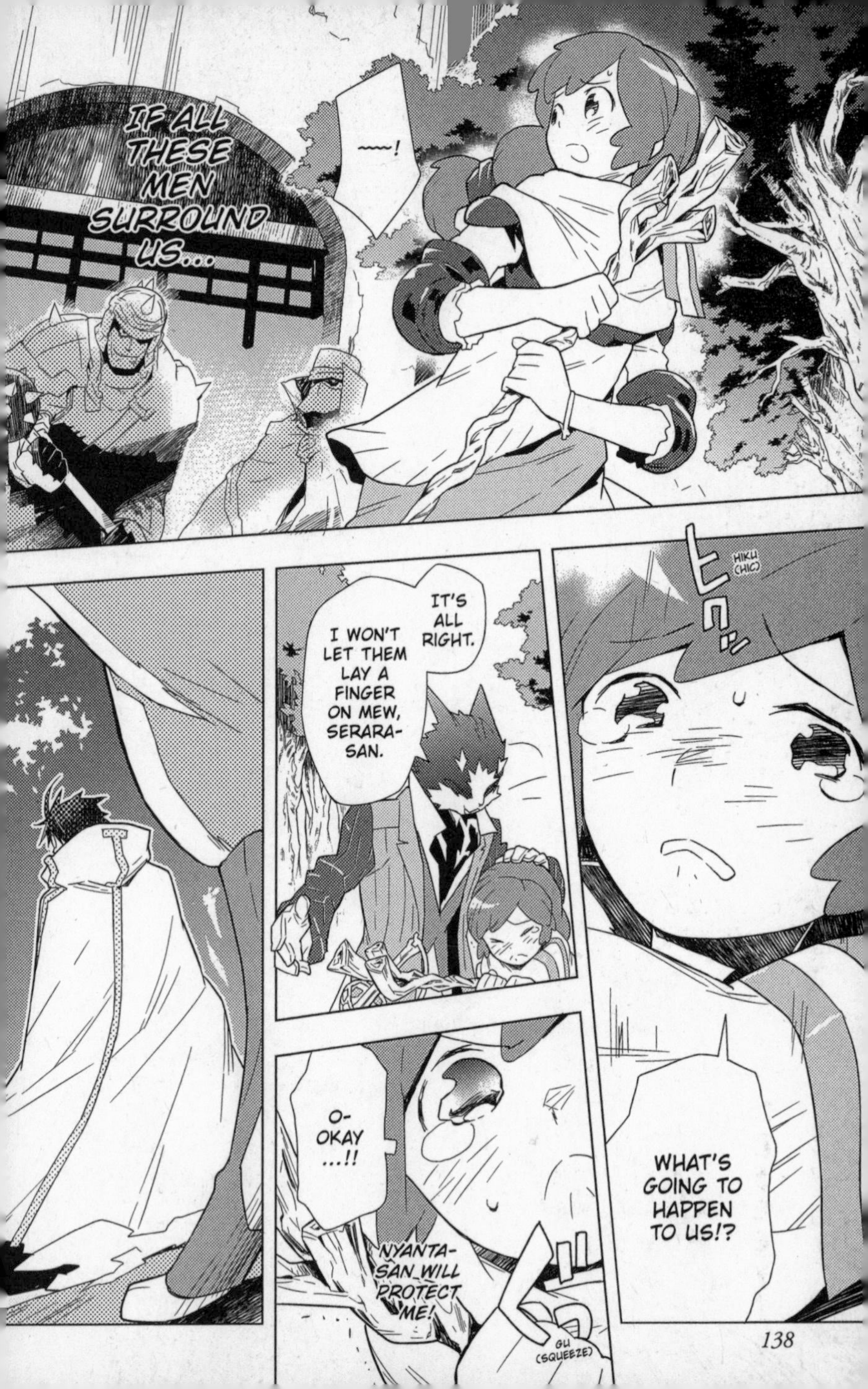

IF ALL THESE MEN SURROUND US...
HIKU (HIC)
WHAT'S GOING TO HAPPEN TO US!?
IT'S ALL RIGHT.
I WON'T LET THEM LAY A FINGER ON MEW, SERARA-SAN.
O-OKAY ...!!
NYANTA-SAN WILL PROTECT ME!
GU (SQUEEZE)

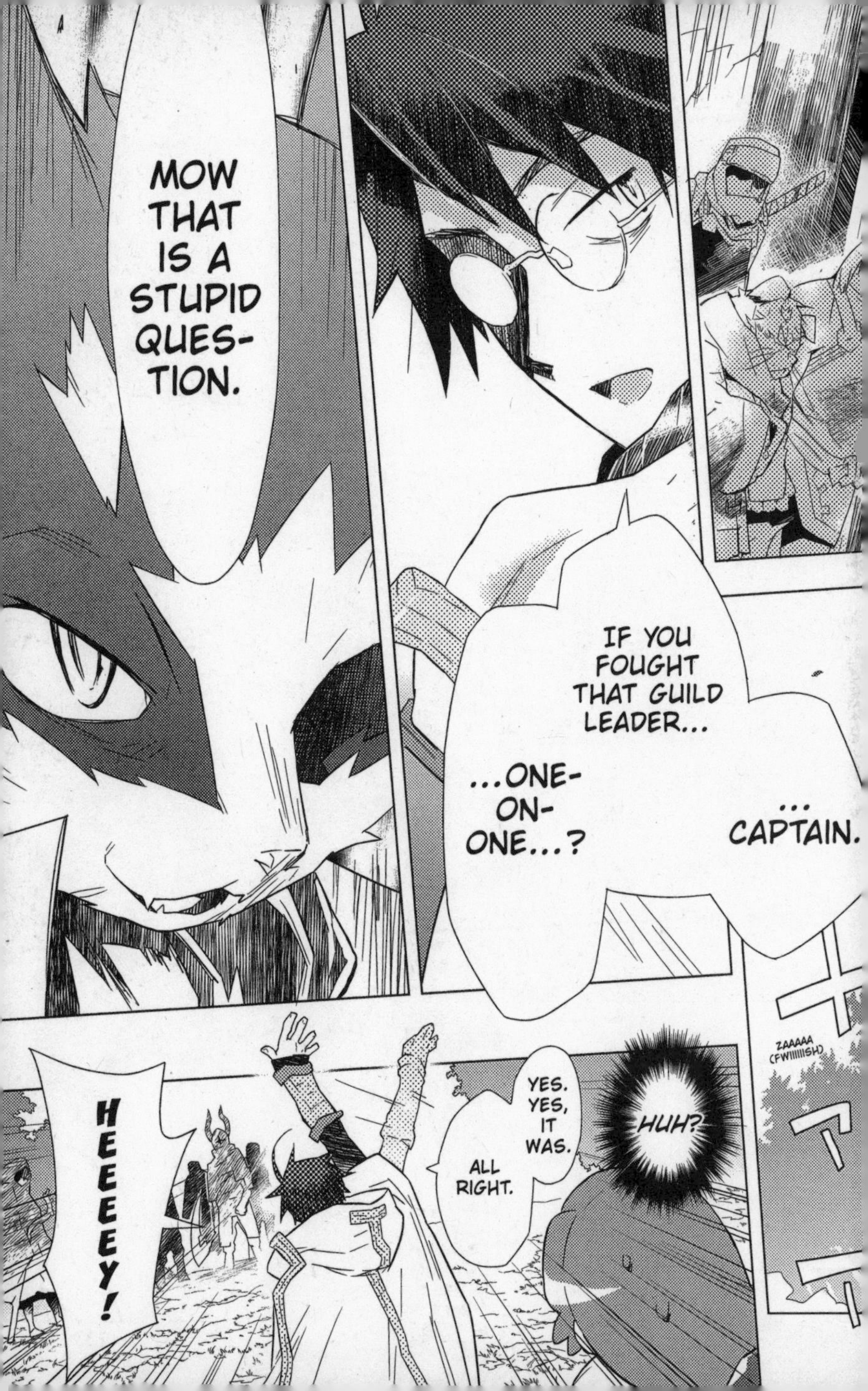

... CAPTAIN.
IF YOU FOUGHT THAT GUILD LEADER...
...ONE-ON-ONE...?
MOW THAT IS A STUPID QUES-TION.
ZAAAAA (FWIIIIISH)
HUH?
YES. YES, IT WAS.
ALL RIGHT.
HEEEEEY!

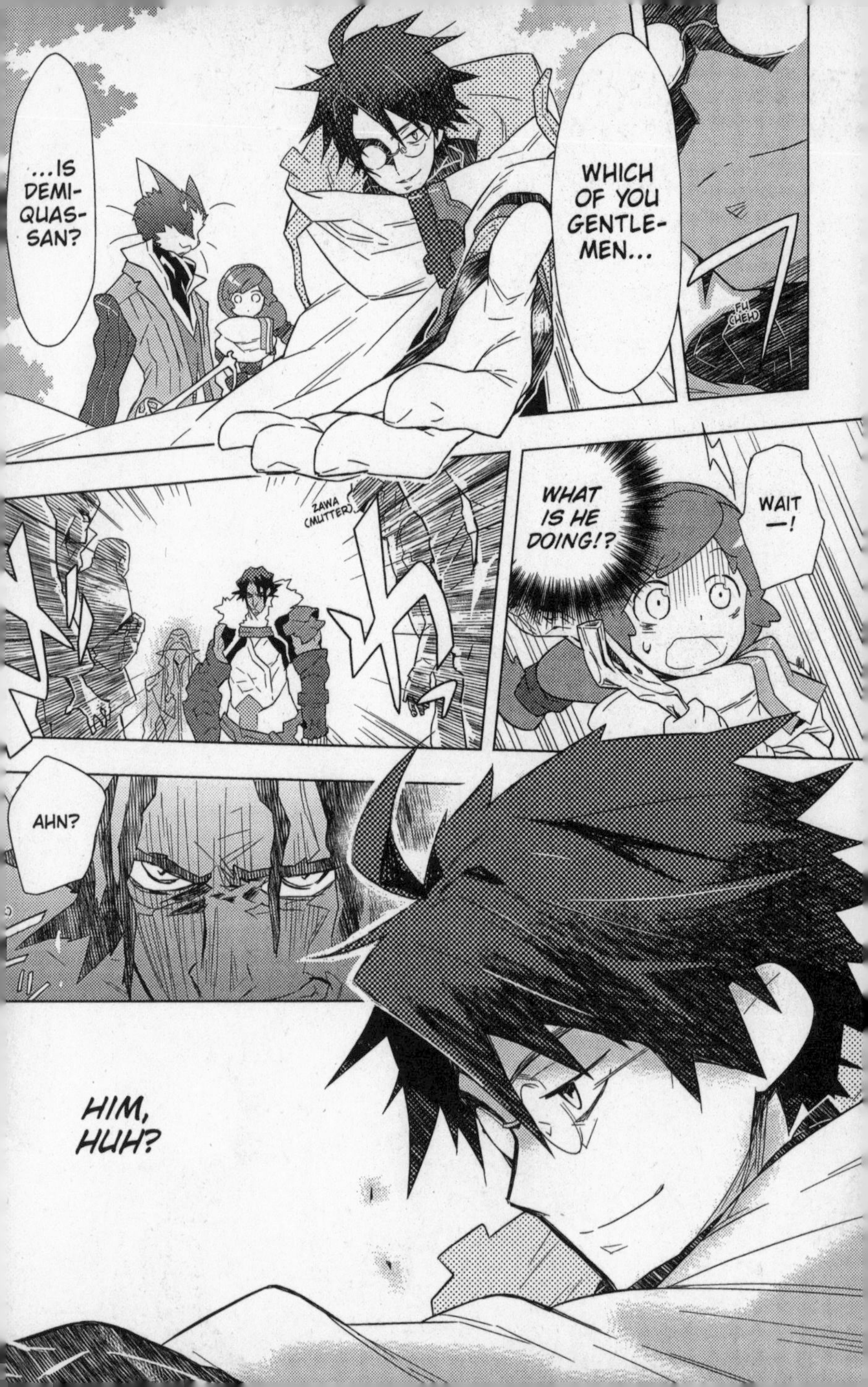
WHICH OF YOU GENTLE-MEN...
FU (HEH)
...IS DEMI-QUAS-SAN?
WAIT—!
WHAT IS HE DOING!?
ZAWA (MUTTER)
AHN?
HIM, HUH?

# CHAPTER : 06 STRATEGY

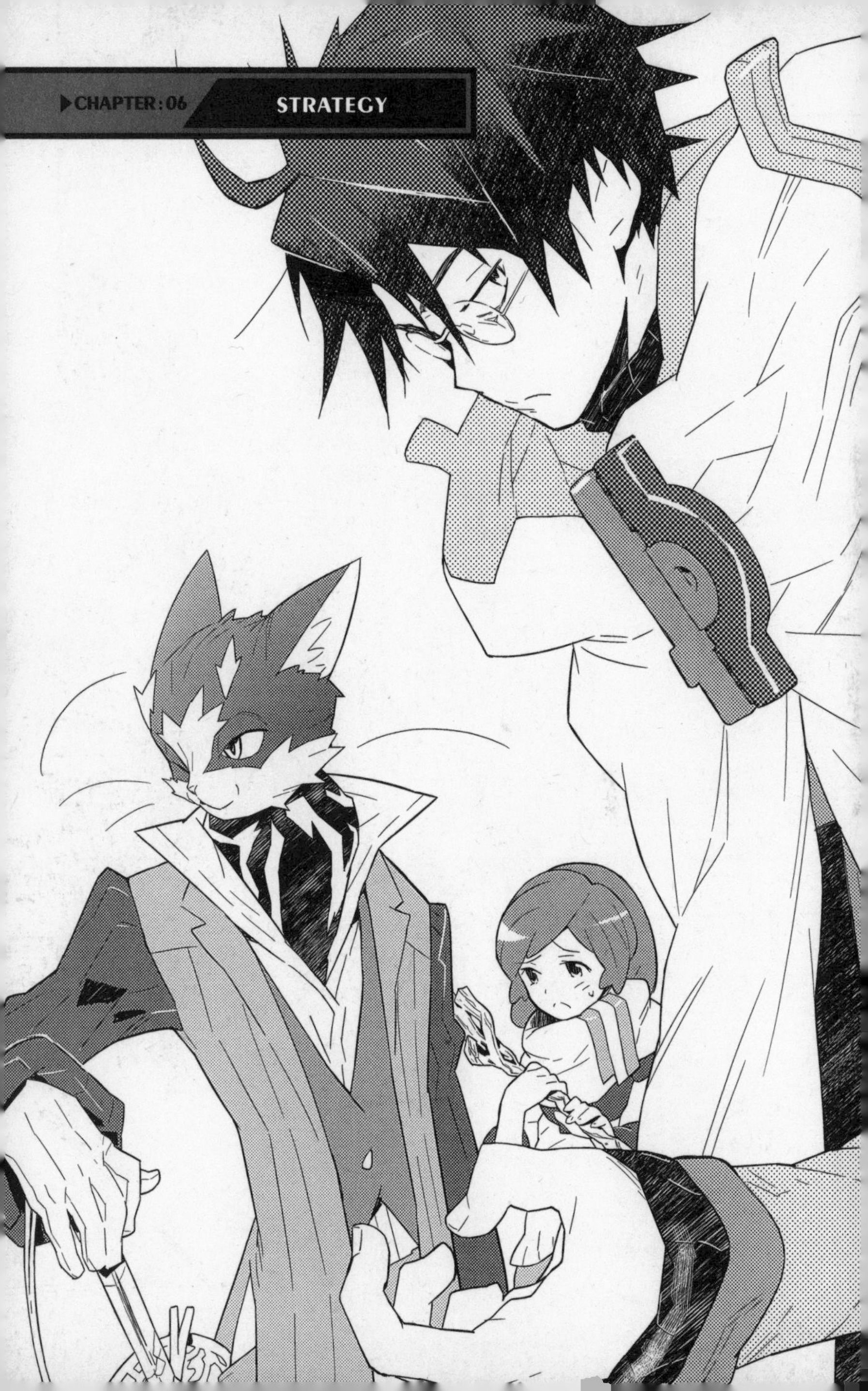

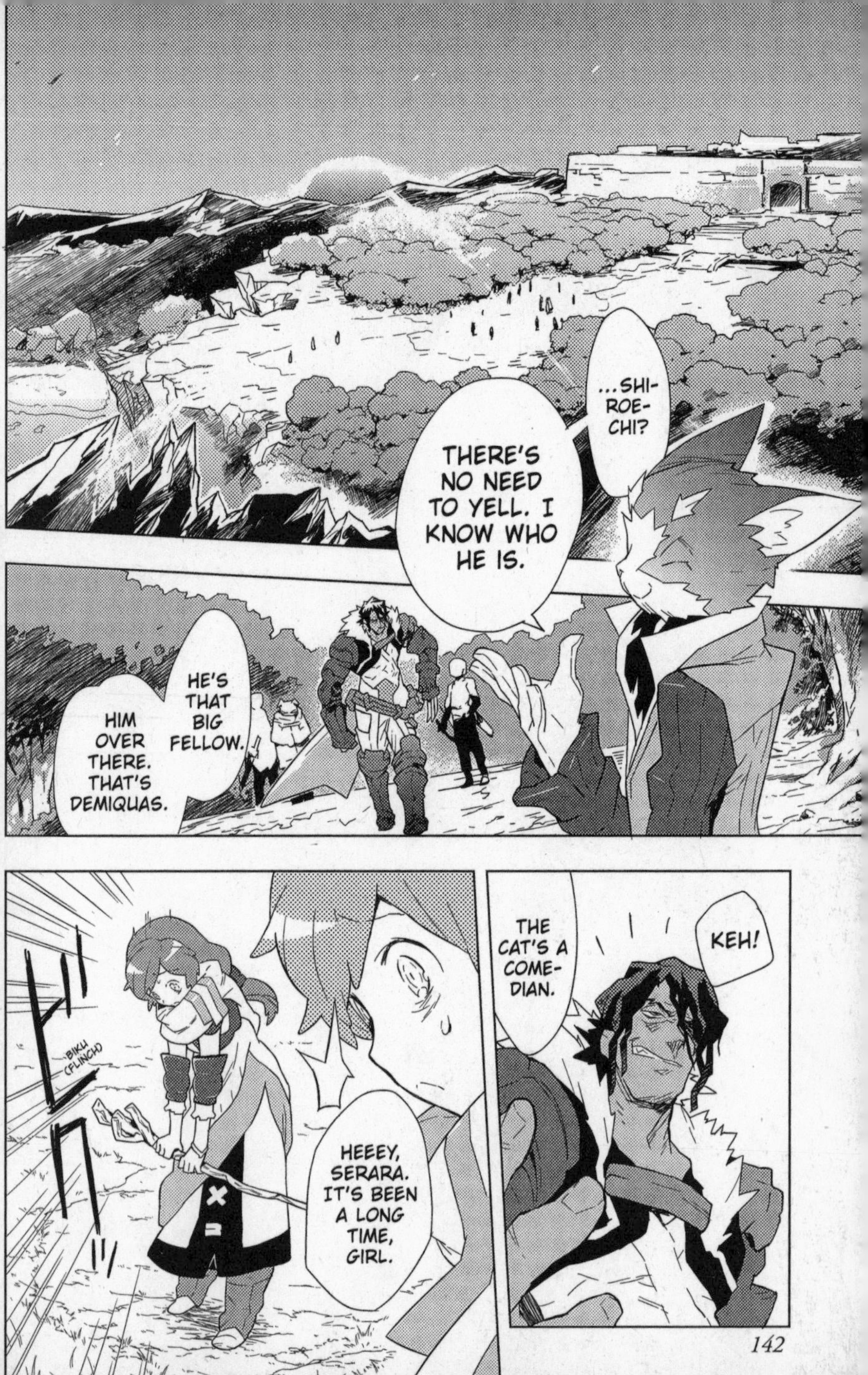
...SHIROE-CHI?
THERE'S NO NEED TO YELL. I KNOW WHO HE IS.
HE'S THAT BIG FELLOW.
HIM OVER THERE. THAT'S DEMIQUAS.
KEH!
THE CAT'S A COMEDIAN.
HEEEY, SERARA. IT'S BEEN A LONG TIME, GIRL.
BIKU (FLINCH)

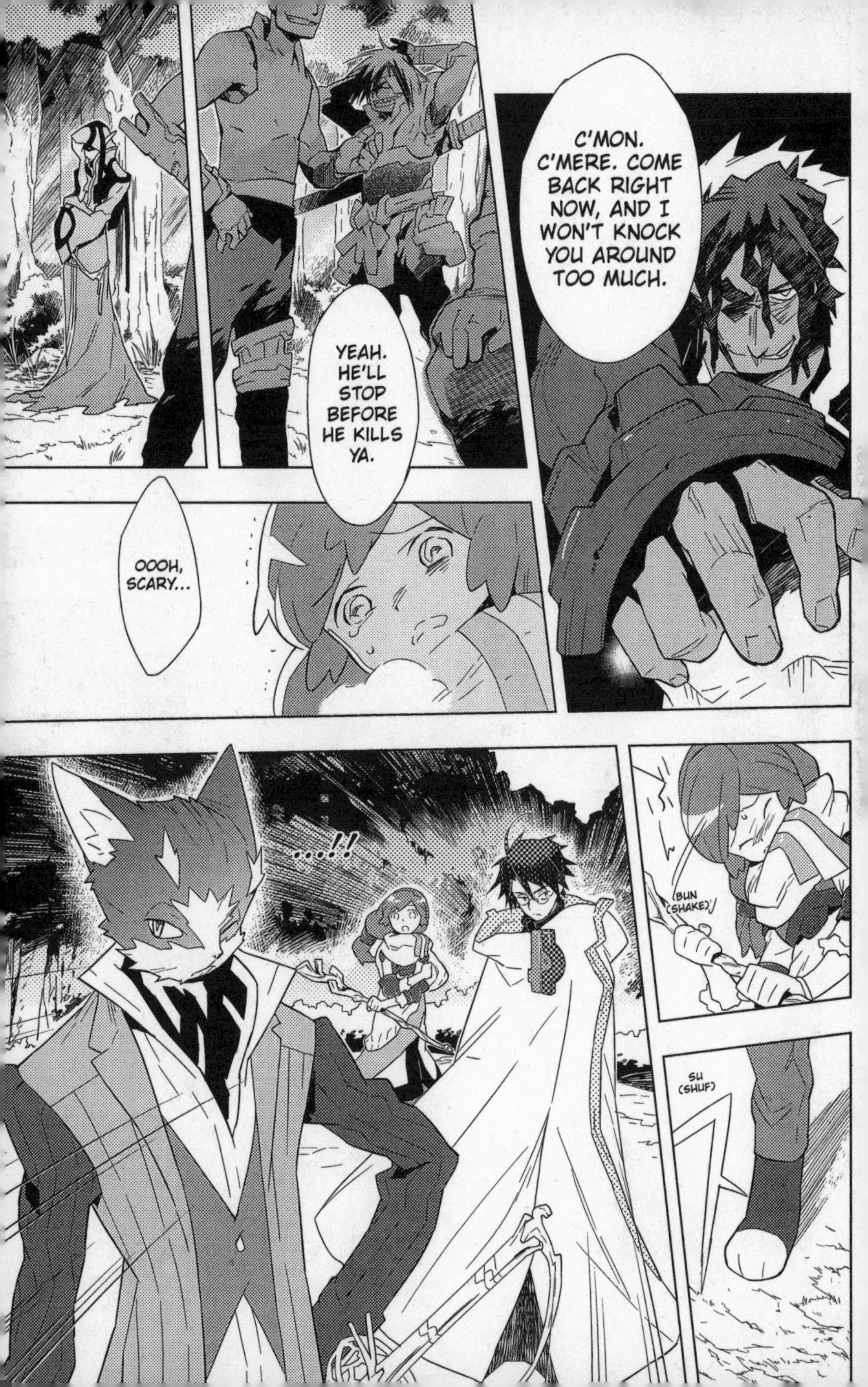
C'MON. C'MERE. COME BACK RIGHT NOW, AND I WON'T KNOCK YOU AROUND TOO MUCH.
YEAH. HE'LL STOP BEFORE HE KILLS YA.
OOOH, SCARY...
BUN (SHAKE)
SU (SHUF)
...!!

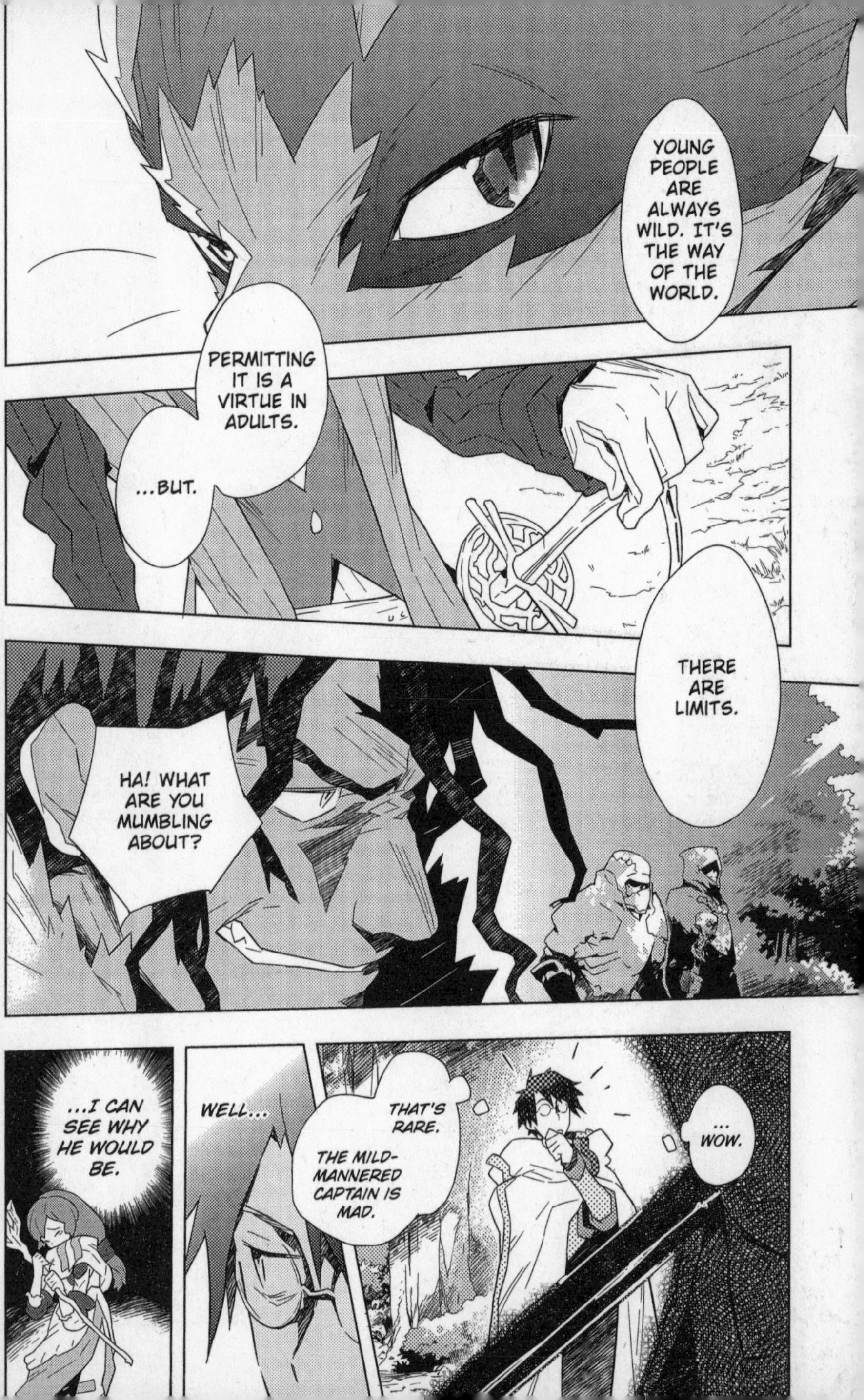
YOUNG PEOPLE ARE ALWAYS WILD. IT'S THE WAY OF THE WORLD.
PERMITTING IT IS A VIRTUE IN ADULTS.
...BUT.
THERE ARE LIMITS.
HA! WHAT ARE YOU MUMBLING ABOUT?
...WOW.
THAT'S RARE.
THE MILD-MANNERED CAPTAIN IS MAD.
WELL...
...I CAN SEE WHY HE WOULD BE.

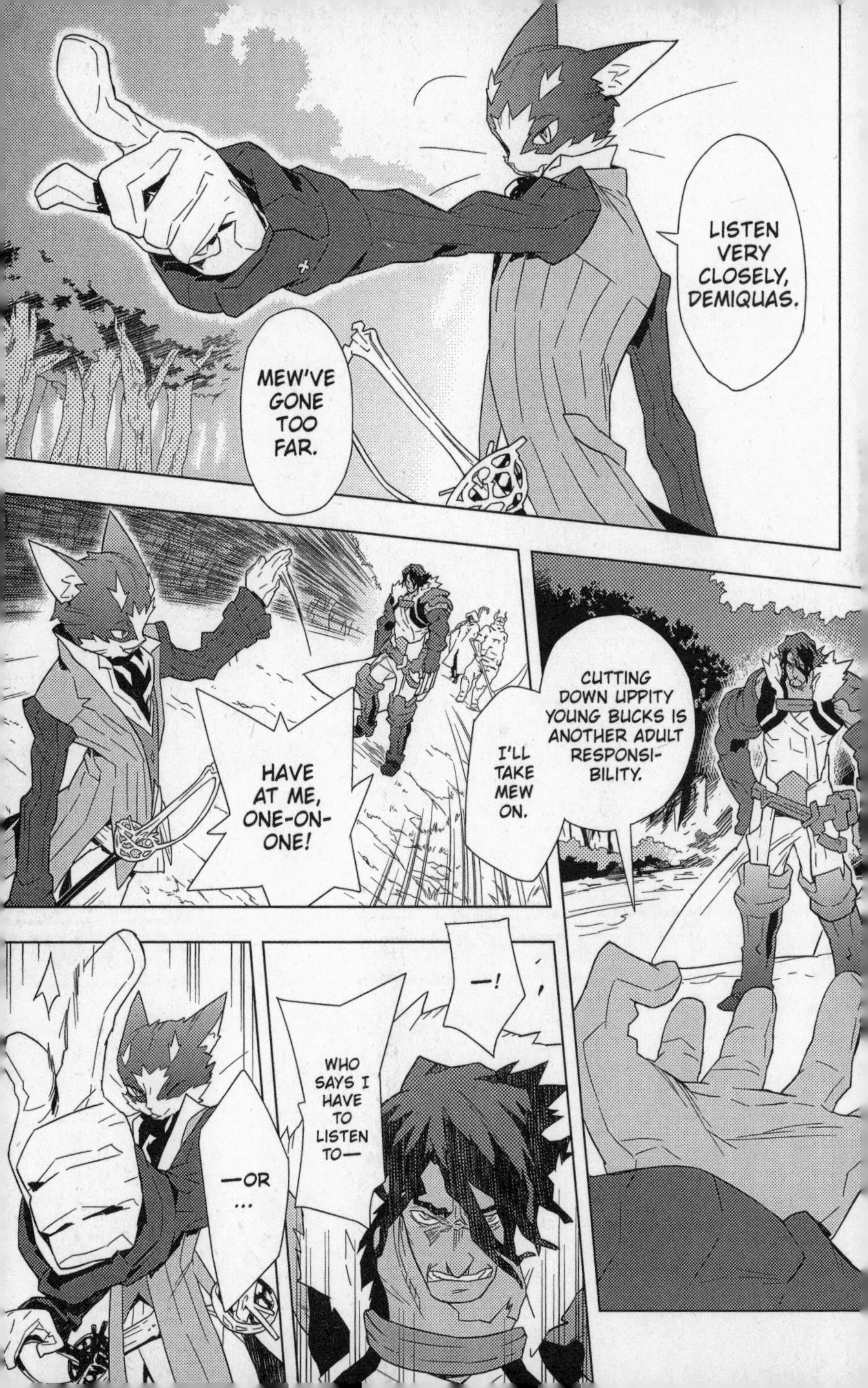
LISTEN VERY CLOSELY, DEMIQUAS.
MEW'VE GONE TOO FAR.
CUTTING DOWN UPPITY YOUNG BUCKS IS ANOTHER ADULT RESPONSI-BILITY.
I'LL TAKE MEW ON.
HAVE AT ME, ONE-ON-ONE!
—!
WHO SAYS I HAVE TO LISTEN TO—
—OR ...

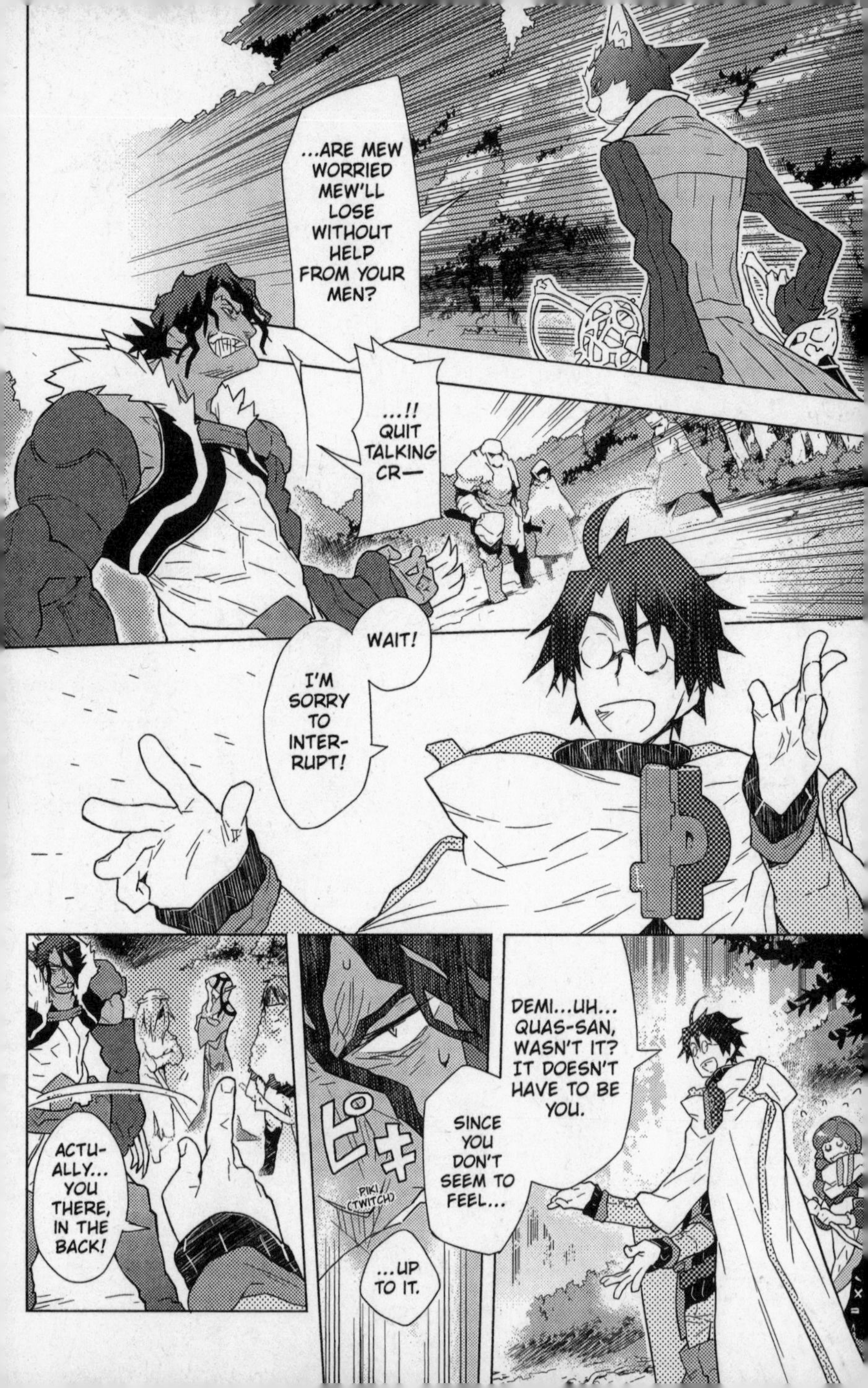
...ARE MEW WORRIED MEW'LL LOSE WITHOUT HELP FROM YOUR MEN?
...!! QUIT TALKING CR—
WAIT!
I'M SORRY TO INTERRUPT!
DEMI...UH... QUAS-SAN, WASN'T IT? IT DOESN'T HAVE TO BE YOU.
SINCE YOU DON'T SEEM TO FEEL...
ピキ
PIKI (TWITCH)
...UP TO IT.
ACTUALLY... YOU THERE, IN THE BACK!

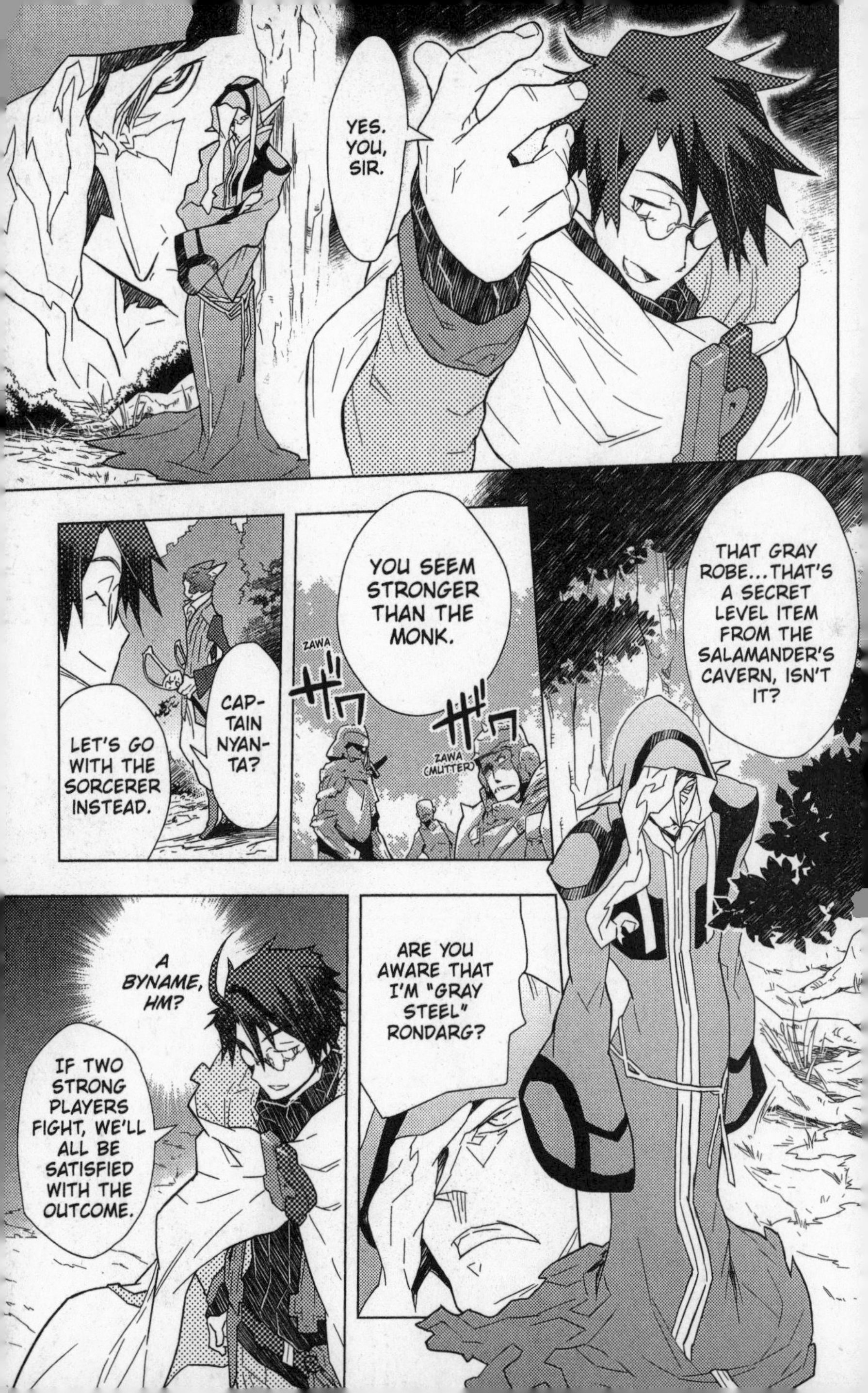
YES. YOU, SIR.
THAT GRAY ROBE...THAT'S A SECRET LEVEL ITEM FROM THE SALAMANDER'S CAVERN, ISN'T IT?
YOU SEEM STRONGER THAN THE MONK.
ザワ
ZAWA
ザワ
ZAWA (MUTTER)
CAP-TAIN NYAN-TA?
LET'S GO WITH THE SORCERER INSTEAD.
ARE YOU AWARE THAT I'M "GRAY STEEL" RONDARG?
A BYNAME, HM?
IF TWO STRONG PLAYERS FIGHT, WE'LL ALL BE SATISFIED WITH THE OUTCOME.

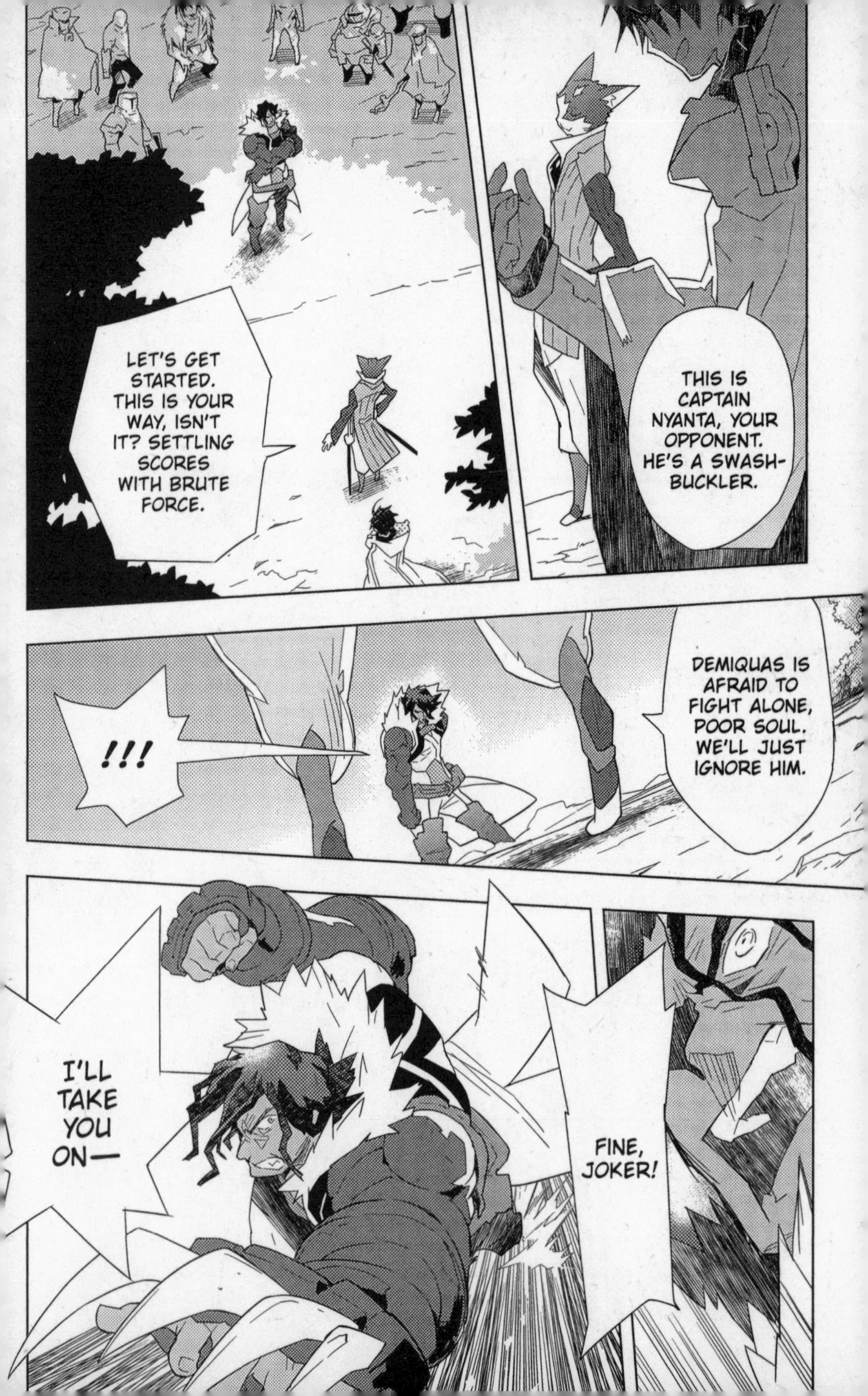
THIS IS CAPTAIN NYANTA, YOUR OPPONENT. HE'S A SWASH-BUCKLER.
LET'S GET STARTED. THIS IS YOUR WAY, ISN'T IT? SETTLING SCORES WITH BRUTE FORCE.
DEMIQUAS IS AFRAID TO FIGHT ALONE, POOR SOUL. WE'LL JUST IGNORE HIM.
!!!
I'LL TAKE YOU ON—
FINE, JOKER!

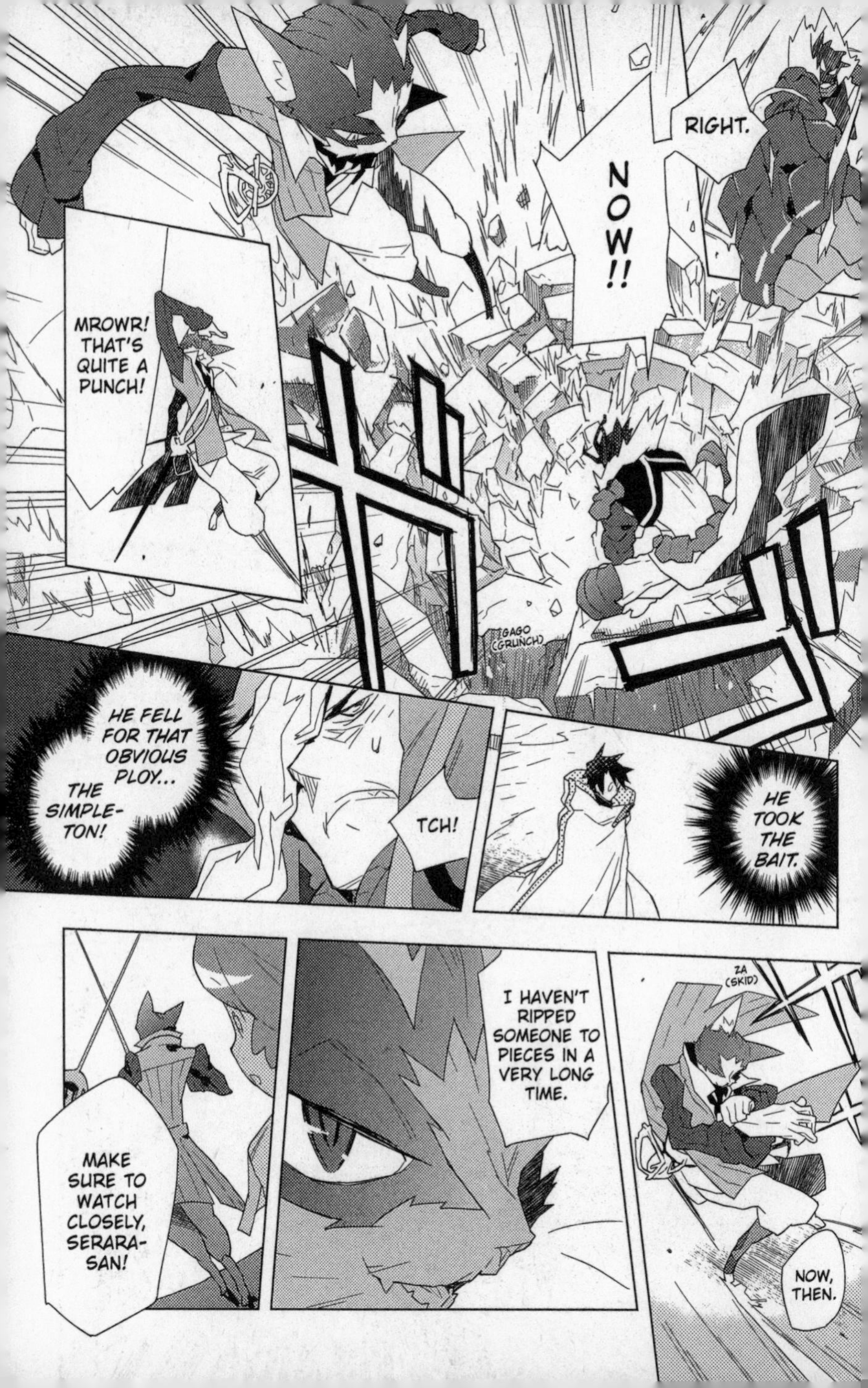
RIGHT.
NOW!!
MROWR! THAT'S QUITE A PUNCH!
GAGO (GRUNCH)
HE TOOK THE BAIT.
TCH!
HE FELL FOR THAT OBVIOUS PLOY... THE SIMPLETON!
ZA (SKID)
NOW, THEN.
I HAVEN'T RIPPED SOMEONE TO PIECES IN A VERY LONG TIME.
MAKE SURE TO WATCH CLOSELY, SERARA-SAN!

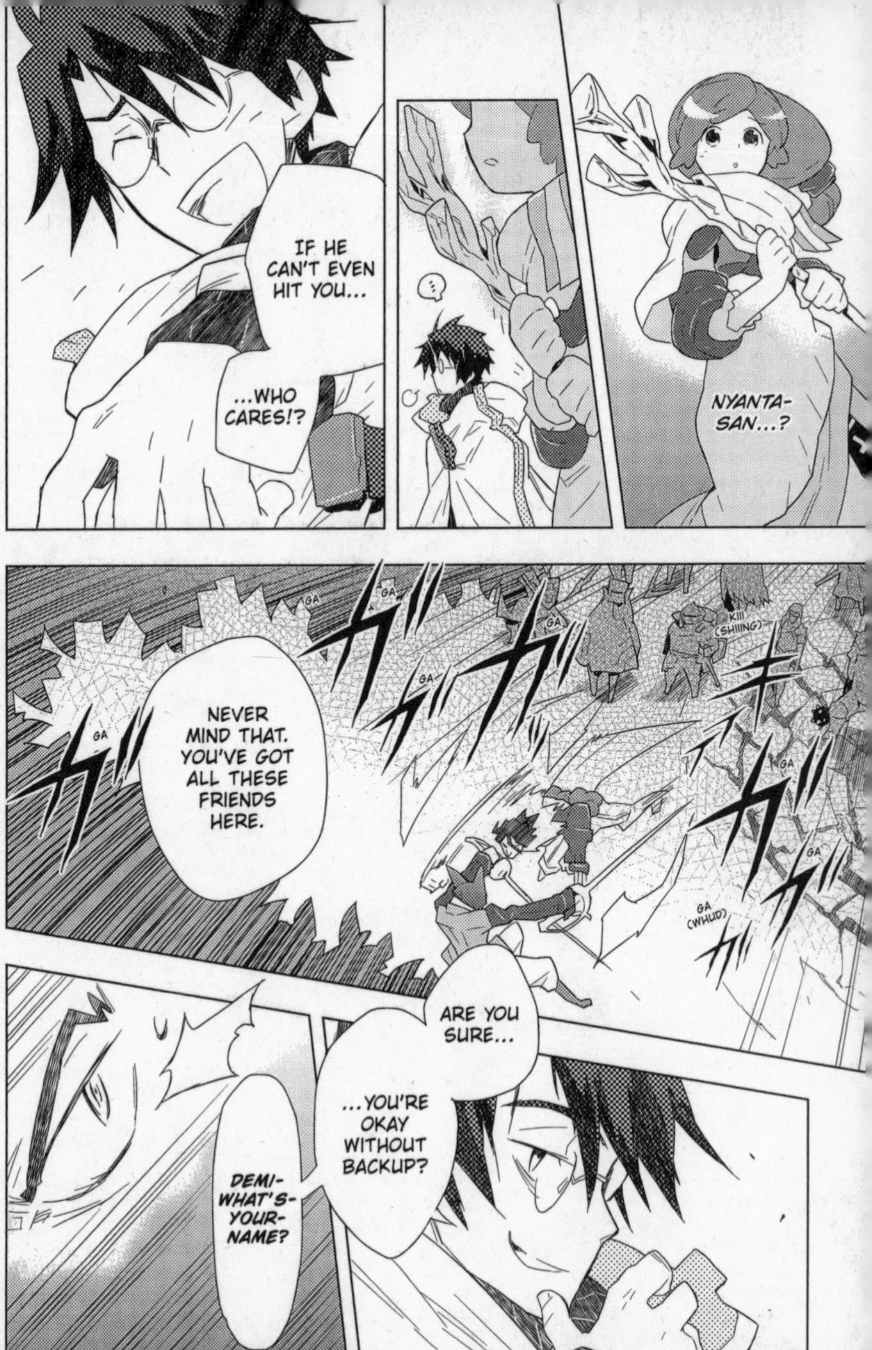
NYANTA-SAN...?
IF HE CAN'T EVEN HIT YOU...
...WHO CARES!?
GA
KIII (SHIIING)
GA
GA
NEVER MIND THAT. YOU'VE GOT ALL THESE FRIENDS HERE.
GA
GA
GA (WHUD)
GA
ARE YOU SURE...
...YOU'RE OKAY WITHOUT BACKUP?
DEMI-WHAT'S-YOUR-NAME?

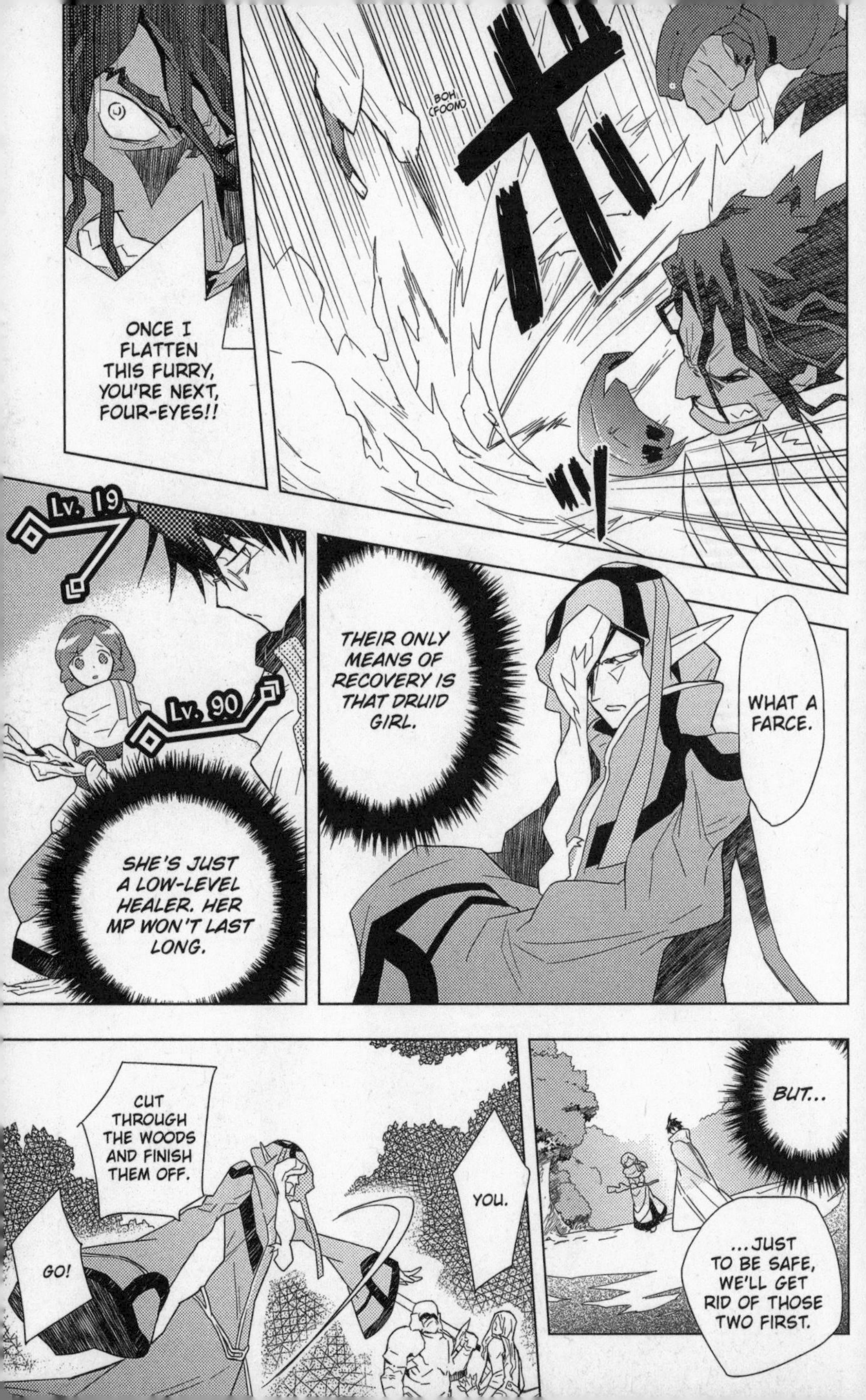
BOH
(FOOM)
ONCE I FLATTEN THIS FURRY, YOU'RE NEXT, FOUR-EYES!!
WHAT A FARCE.
THEIR ONLY MEANS OF RECOVERY IS THAT DRUID GIRL.
Lv. 19
Lv. 90
SHE'S JUST A LOW-LEVEL HEALER. HER MP WON'T LAST LONG.
BUT...
...JUST TO BE SAFE, WE'LL GET RID OF THOSE TWO FIRST.
YOU.
CUT THROUGH THE WOODS AND FINISH THEM OFF.
GO!

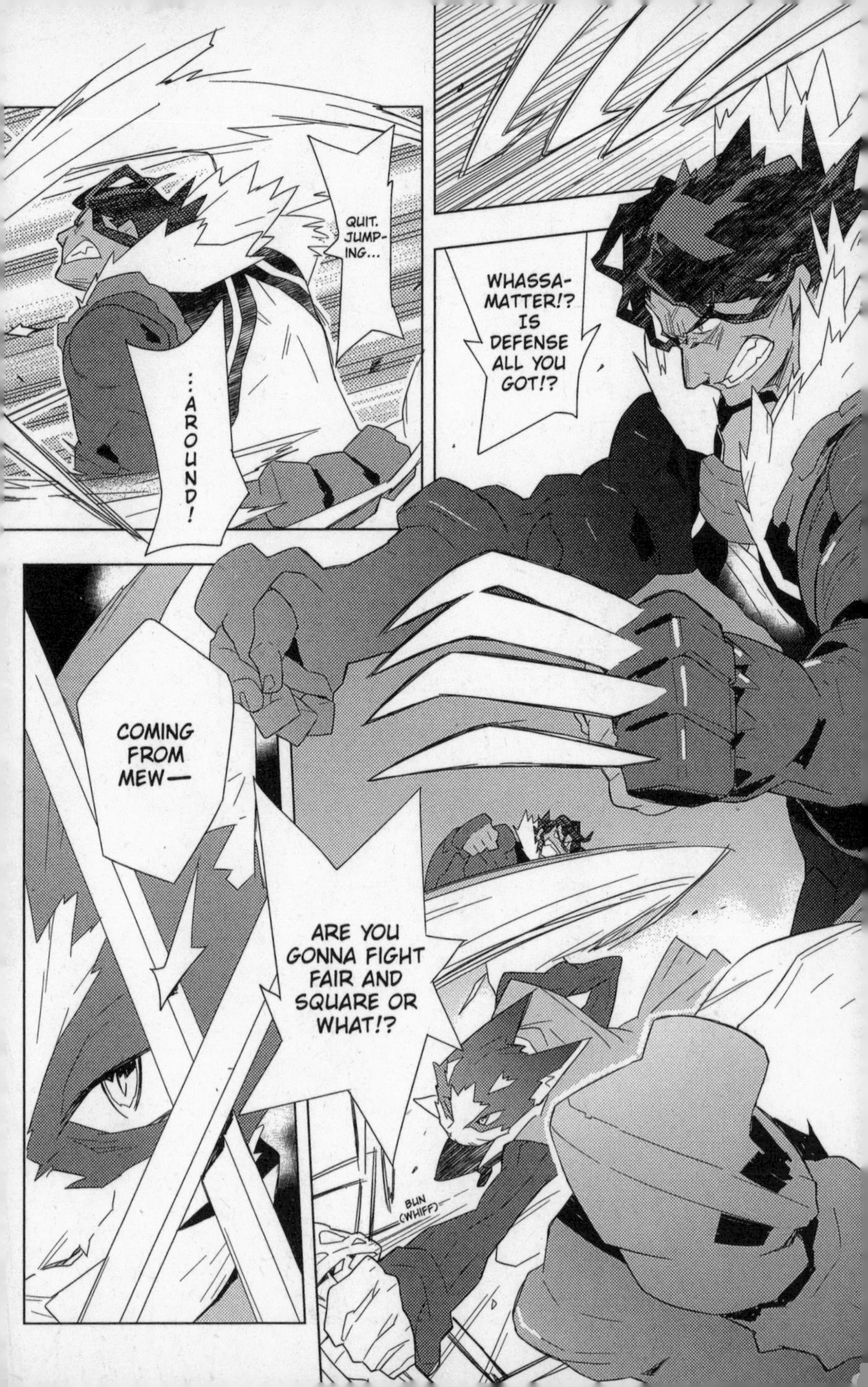
WHASSA-MATTER!? IS DEFENSE ALL YOU GOT!?
QUIT. JUMPING...
...AROUND!
ARE YOU GONNA FIGHT FAIR AND SQUARE OR WHAT!?
COMING FROM MEW—
BUN (WHIFF)

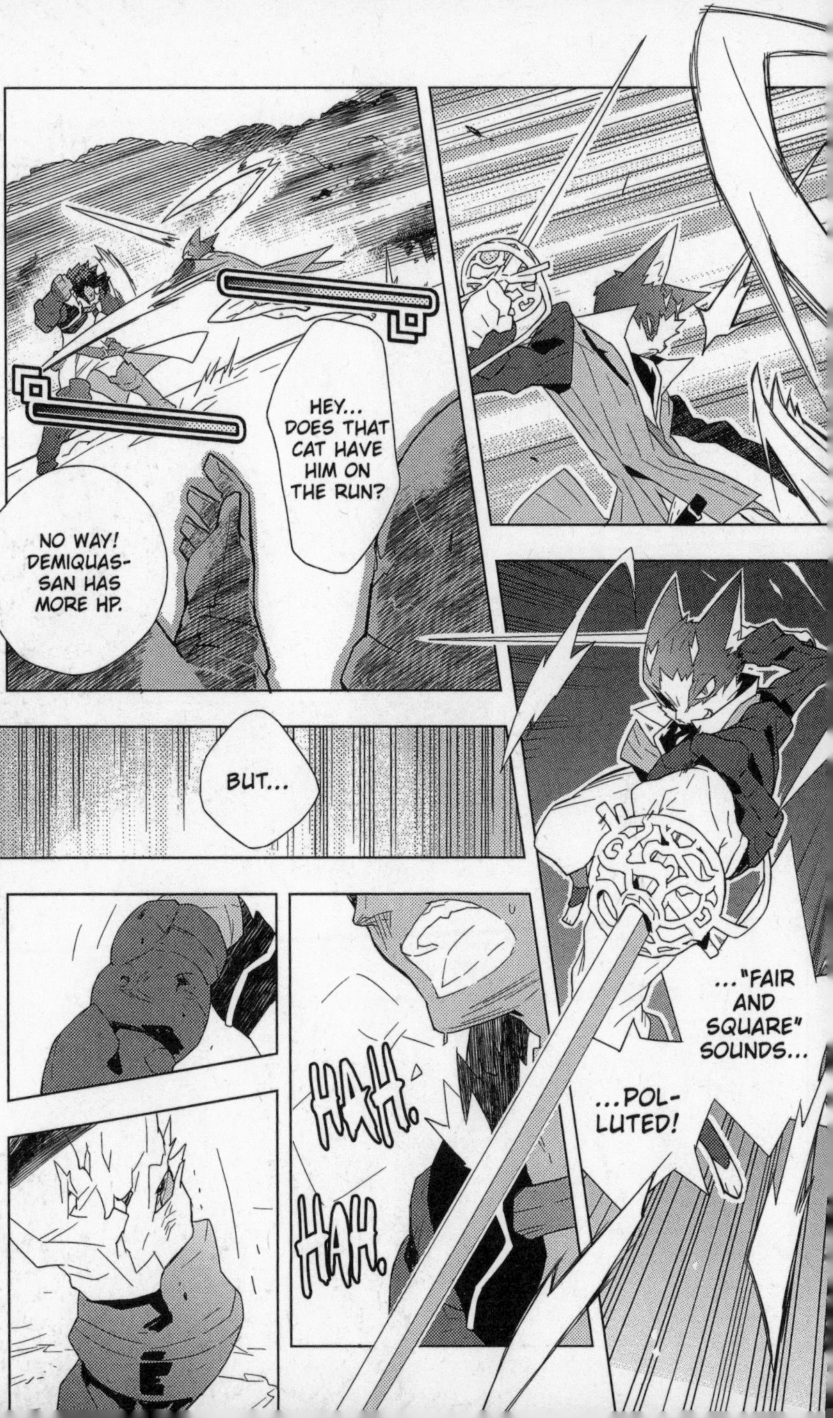
HEY... DOES THAT CAT HAVE HIM ON THE RUN?
NO WAY! DEMIQUAS-SAN HAS MORE HP.
..."FAIR AND SQUARE" SOUNDS...
...POL-LUTED!
BUT...
HAH.
HAH.

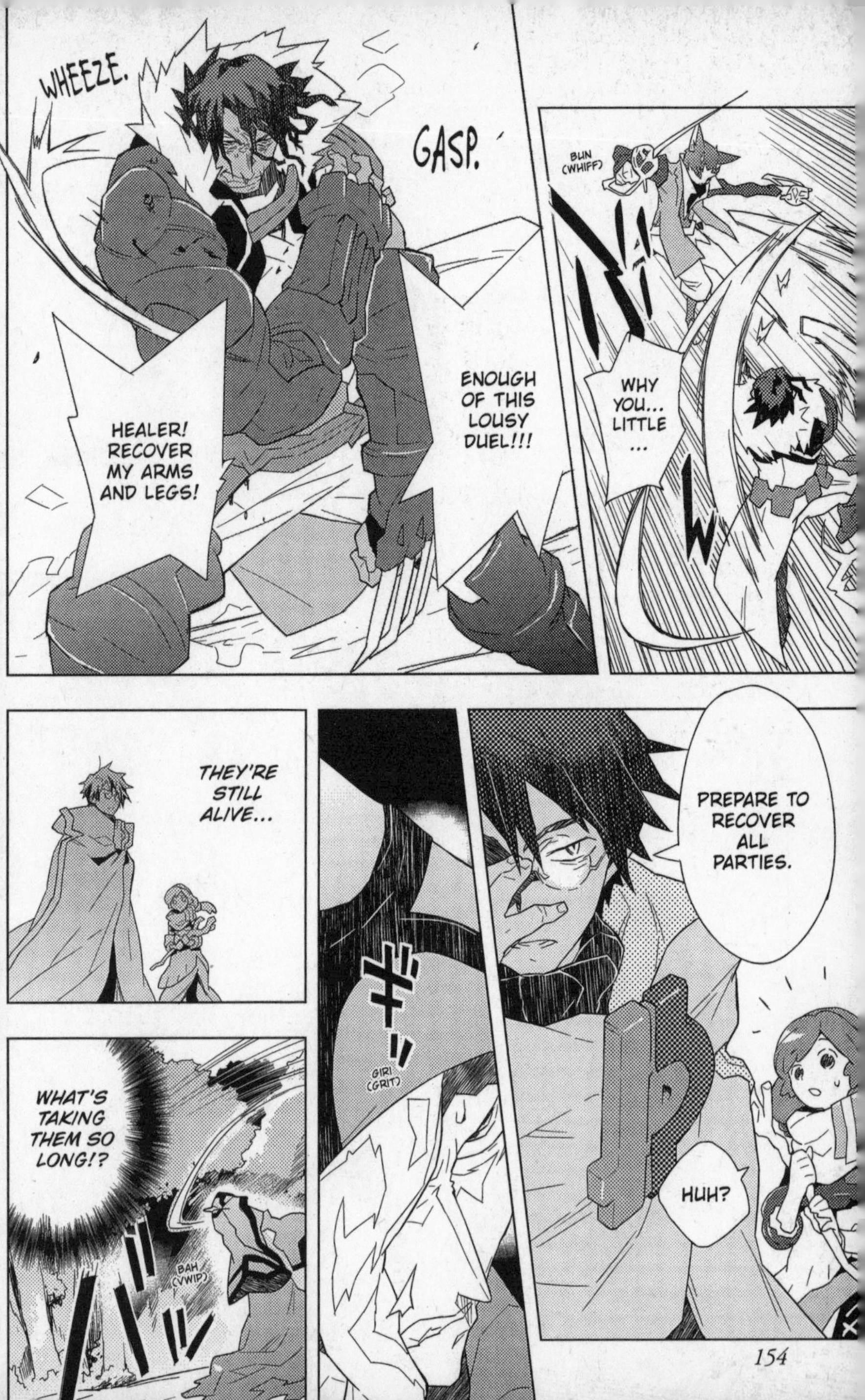
BUN (WHIFF)
WHY YOU... LITTLE ...
GASP.
WHEEZE.
ENOUGH OF THIS LOUSY DUEL!!!
HEALER! RECOVER MY ARMS AND LEGS!
PREPARE TO RECOVER ALL PARTIES.
GIRI (GRIT)
HUH?
THEY'RE STILL ALIVE...
WHAT'S TAKING THEM SO LONG!?
BAH (VWIP)

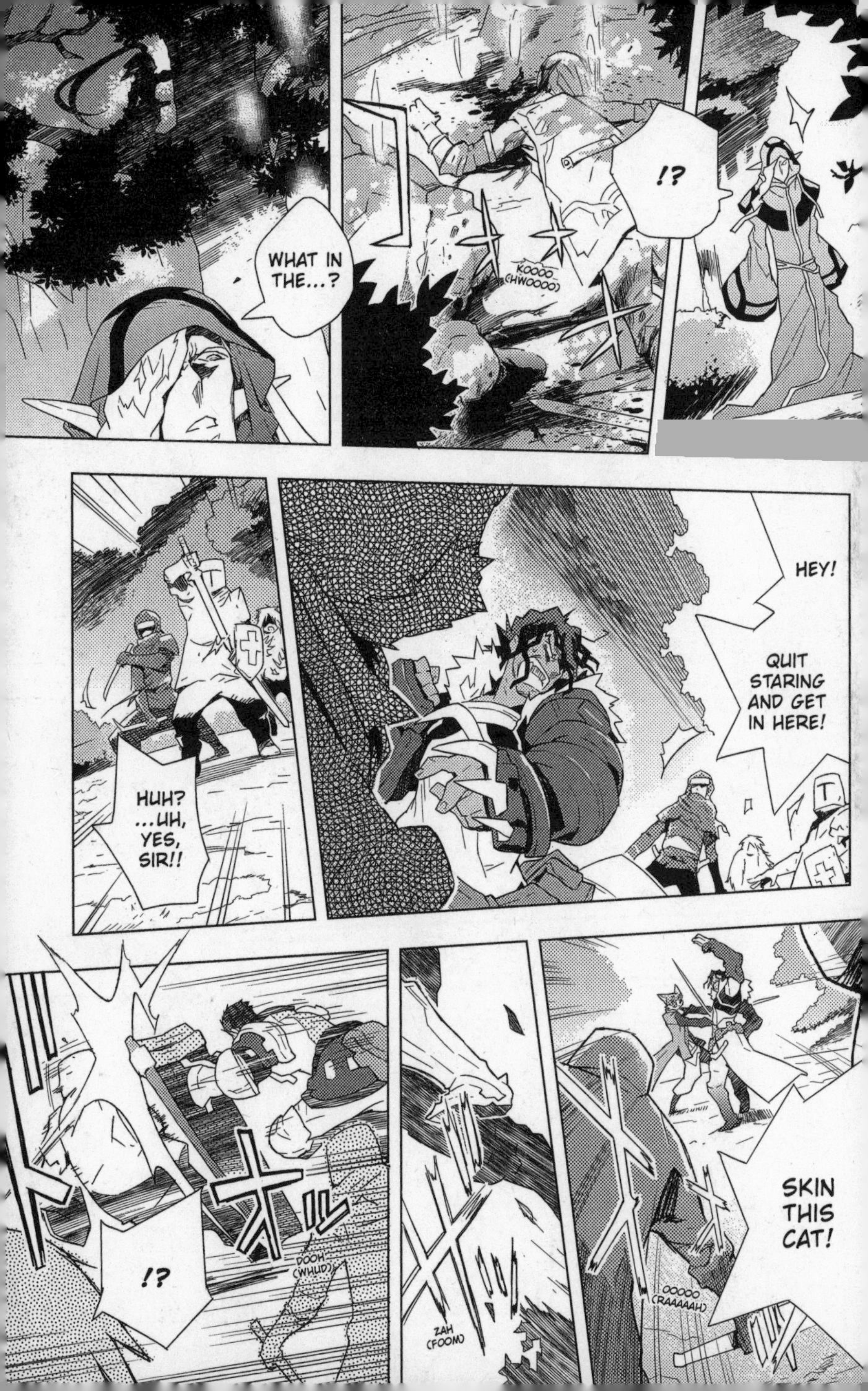
!?
KOOOO
(HWOOOO)
WHAT IN THE...?
HEY!
QUIT STARING AND GET IN HERE!
HUH? ...UH, YES, SIR!!
SKIN THIS CAT!
OOOOO
(RAAAAAH)
ZAH
(FOOM)
DOOH
(WHUD)
!?

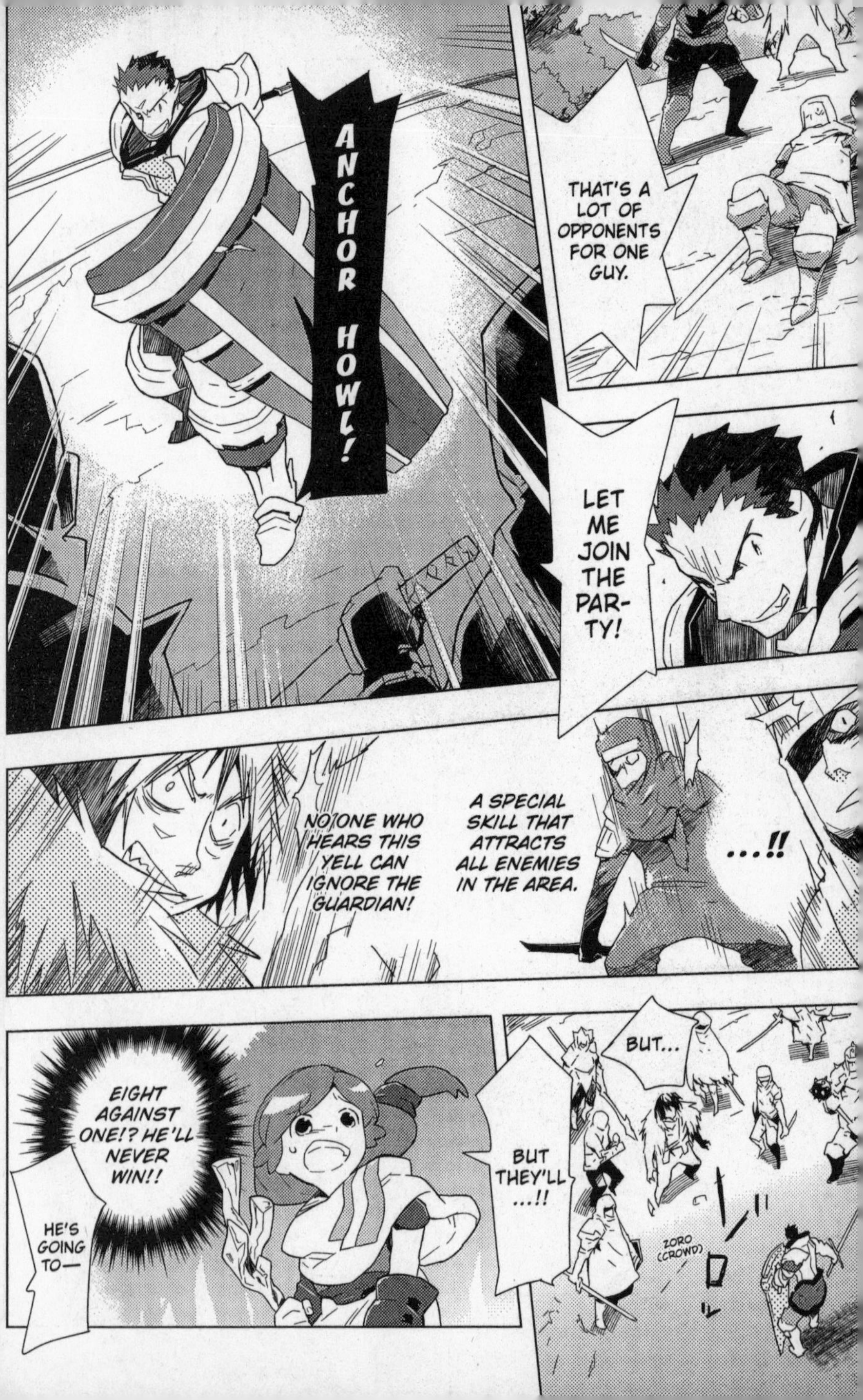
THAT'S A LOT OF OPPONENTS FOR ONE GUY.
LET ME JOIN THE PARTY!
ANCHOR HOWL!
...!!
A SPECIAL SKILL THAT ATTRACTS ALL ENEMIES IN THE AREA.
NO ONE WHO HEARS THIS YELL CAN IGNORE THE GUARDIAN!
BUT...
BUT THEY'LL ...!!
ZORO (CROWD)
EIGHT AGAINST ONE!? HE'LL NEVER WIN!!
HE'S GOING TO—

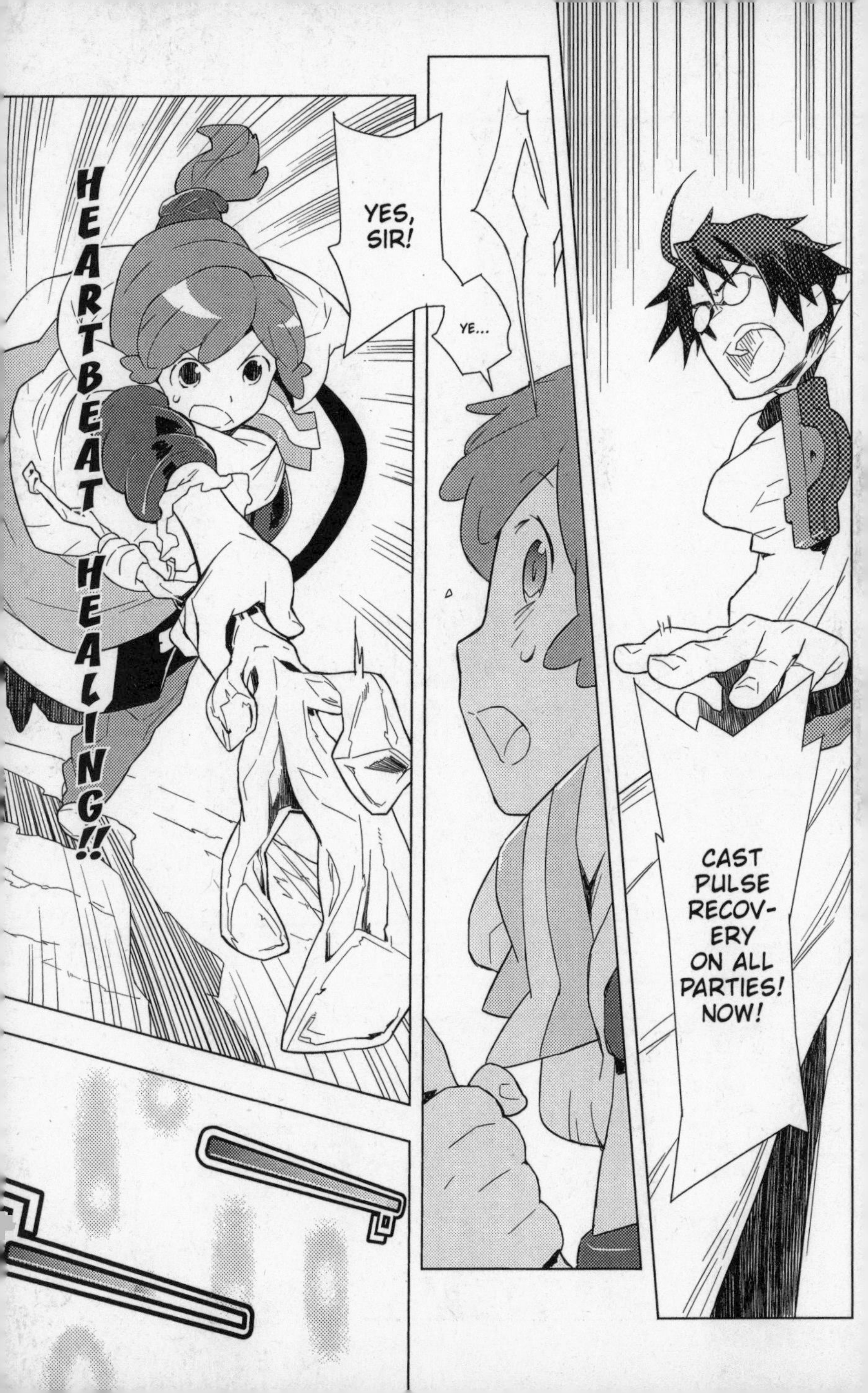
CAST PULSE RECOVERY ON ALL PARTIES! NOW!
YE...
YES, SIR!
HEARTBEAT HEALING!!

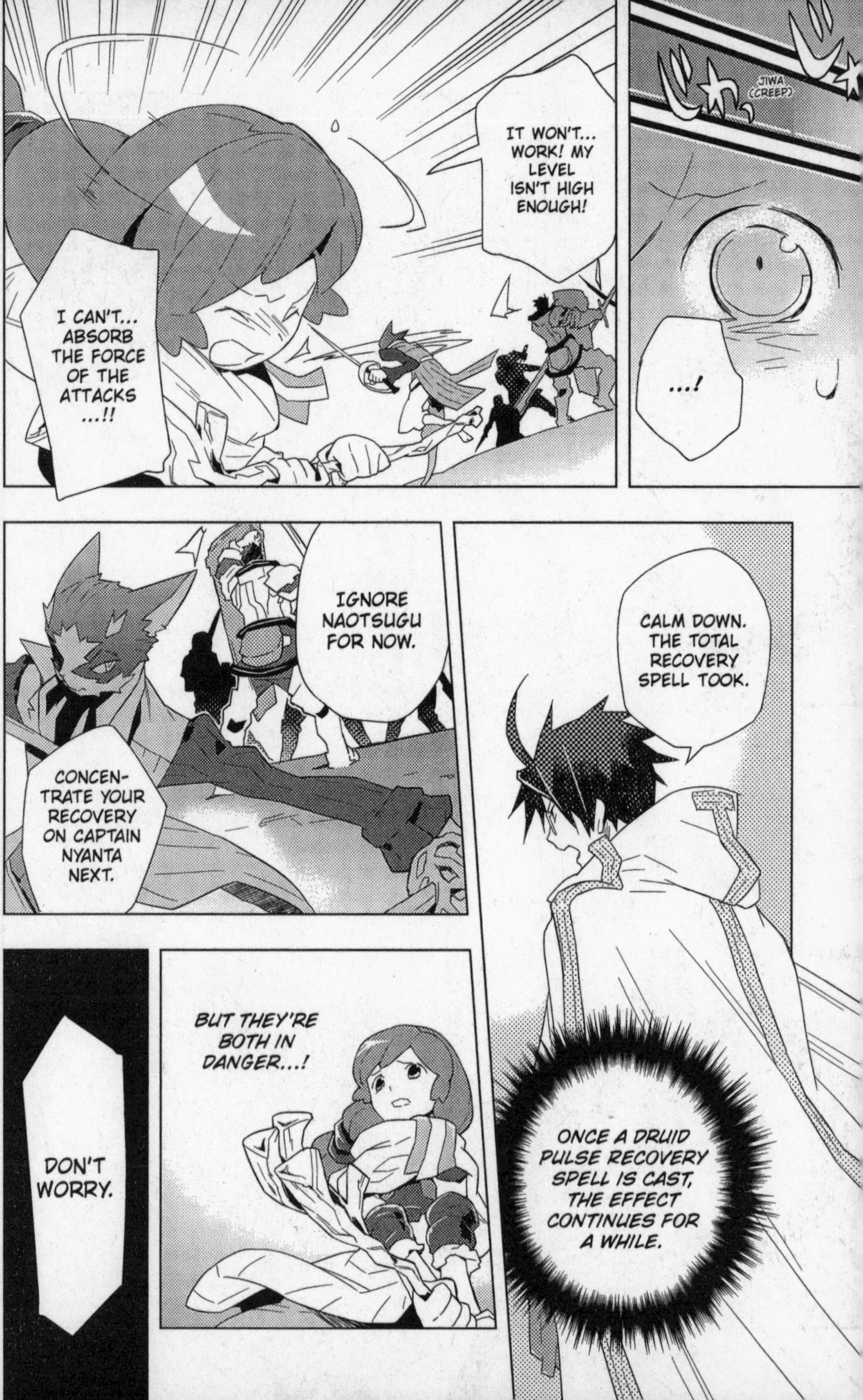
JIWA (CREEP)
...!
IT WON'T... WORK! MY LEVEL ISN'T HIGH ENOUGH!
I CAN'T... ABSORB THE FORCE OF THE ATTACKS ...!!
CALM DOWN. THE TOTAL RECOVERY SPELL TOOK.
ONCE A DRUID PULSE RECOVERY SPELL IS CAST, THE EFFECT CONTINUES FOR A WHILE.
IGNORE NAOTSUGU FOR NOW.
CONCEN-TRATE YOUR RECOVERY ON CAPTAIN NYANTA NEXT.
BUT THEY'RE BOTH IN DANGER...!
DON'T WORRY.

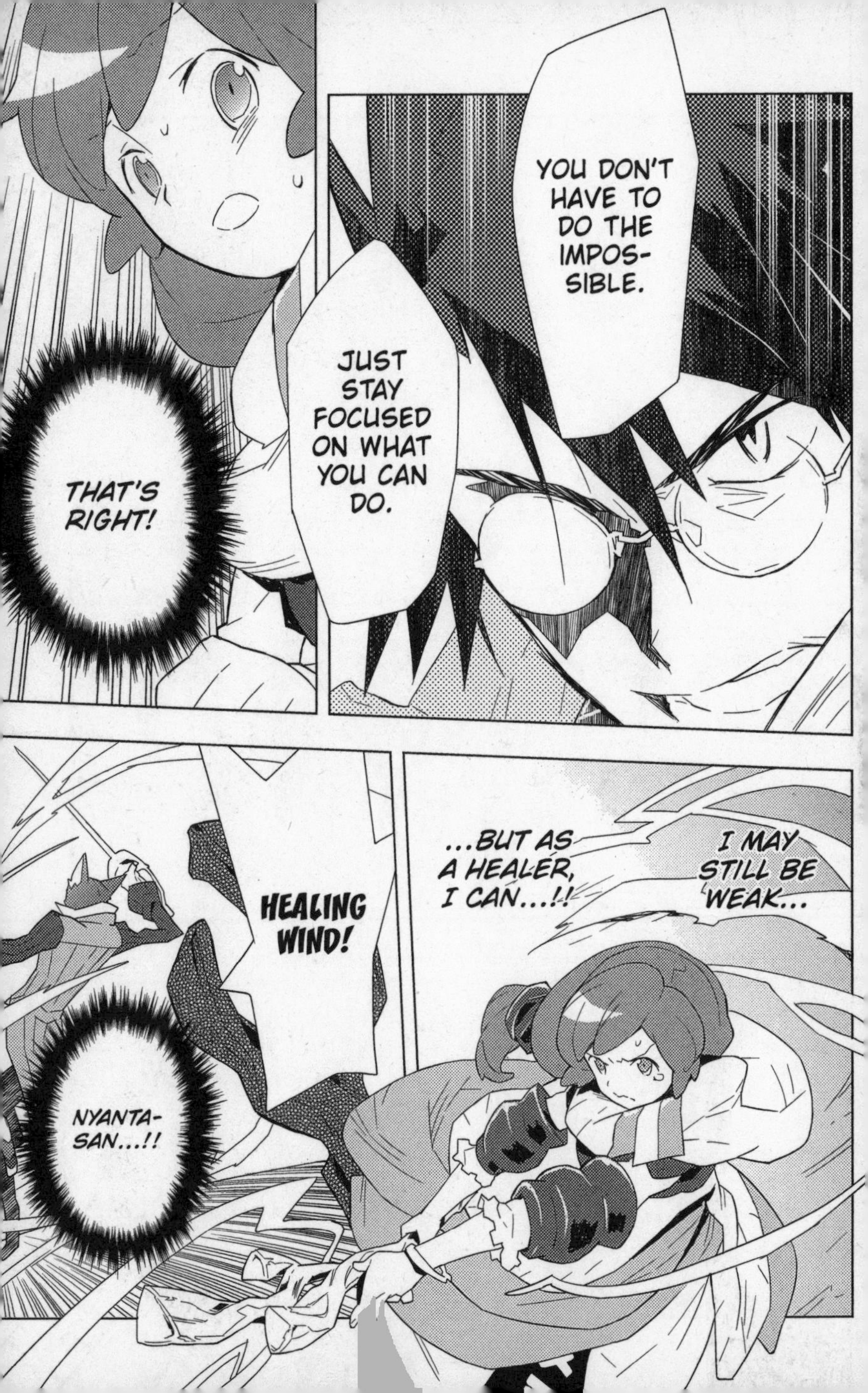
YOU DON'T HAVE TO DO THE IMPOS-SIBLE.
JUST STAY FOCUSED ON WHAT YOU CAN DO.
THAT'S RIGHT!
I MAY STILL BE WEAK...
...BUT AS A HEALER, I CAN...!!
HEALING WIND!
NYANTA-SAN...!!

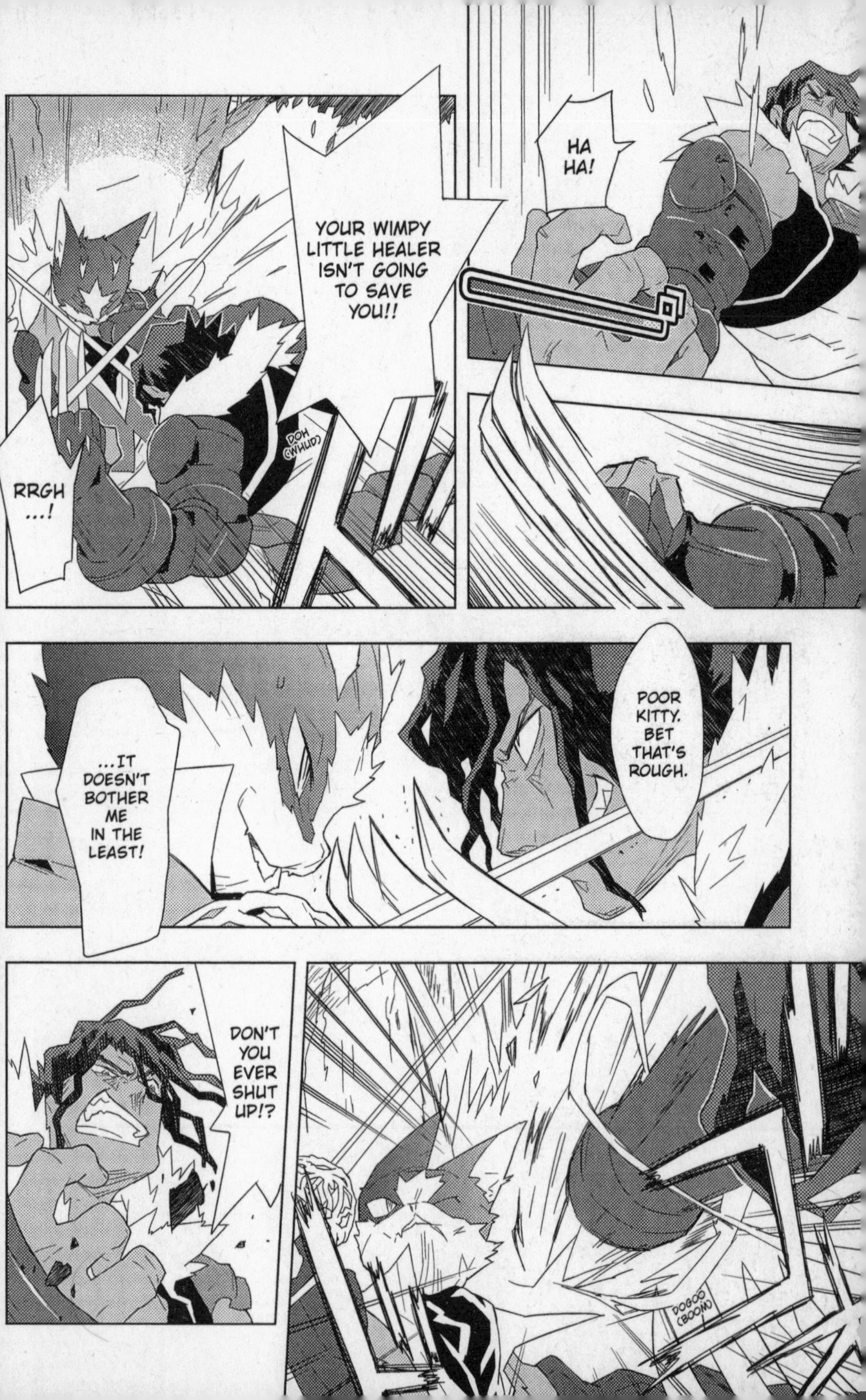
HA HA!
YOUR WIMPY LITTLE HEALER ISN'T GOING TO SAVE YOU!!
DOH (WHUD)
RRGH ...!
POOR KITTY. BET THAT'S ROUGH.
...IT DOESN'T BOTHER ME IN THE LEAST!
DOGOO (BOOM)
DON'T YOU EVER SHUT UP!?

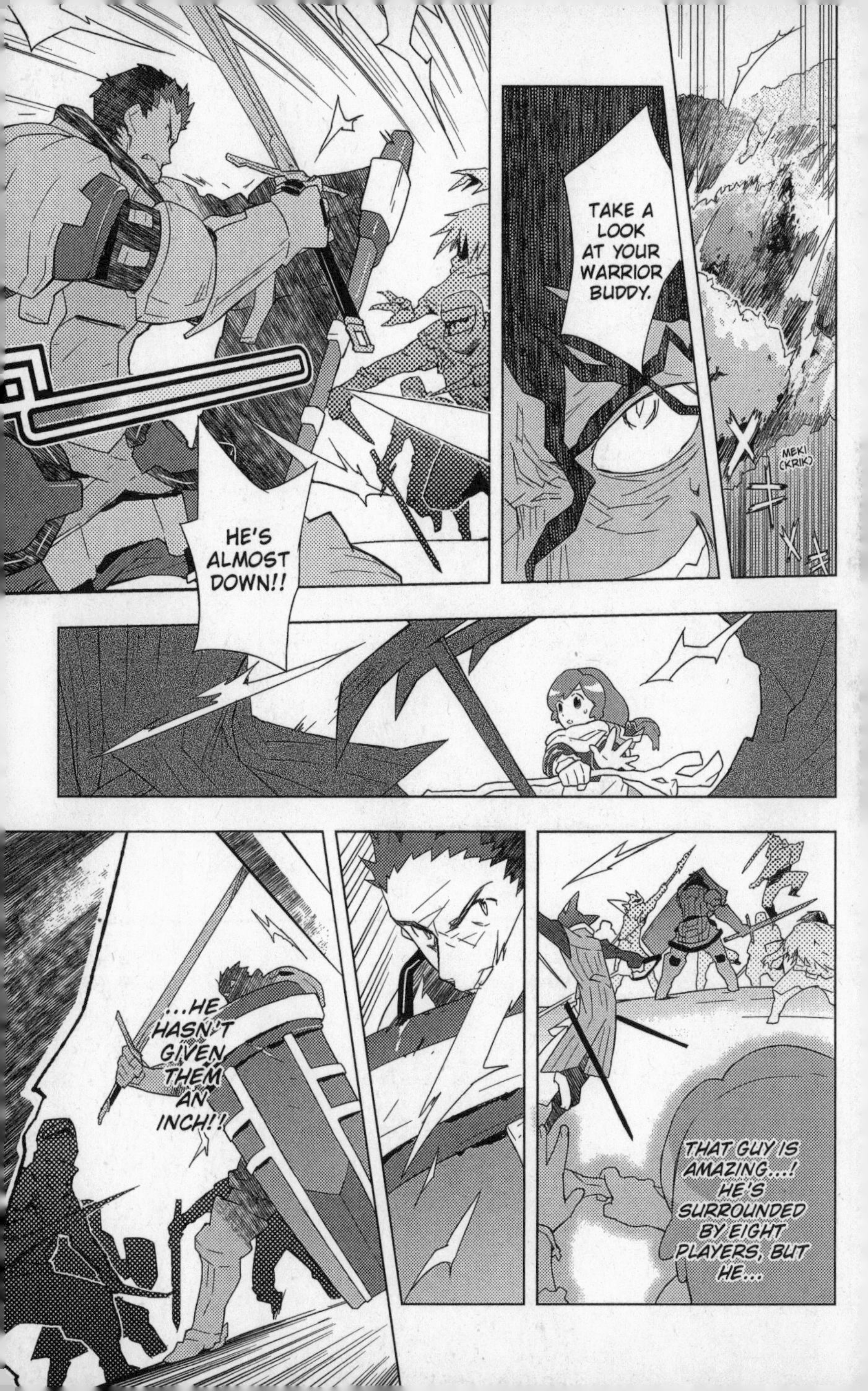
MEKI (KRIK)
TAKE A LOOK AT YOUR WARRIOR BUDDY.
HE'S ALMOST DOWN!!
THAT GUY IS AMAZING...! HE'S SURROUNDED BY EIGHT PLAYERS, BUT HE...
...HE HASN'T GIVEN THEM AN INCH!!

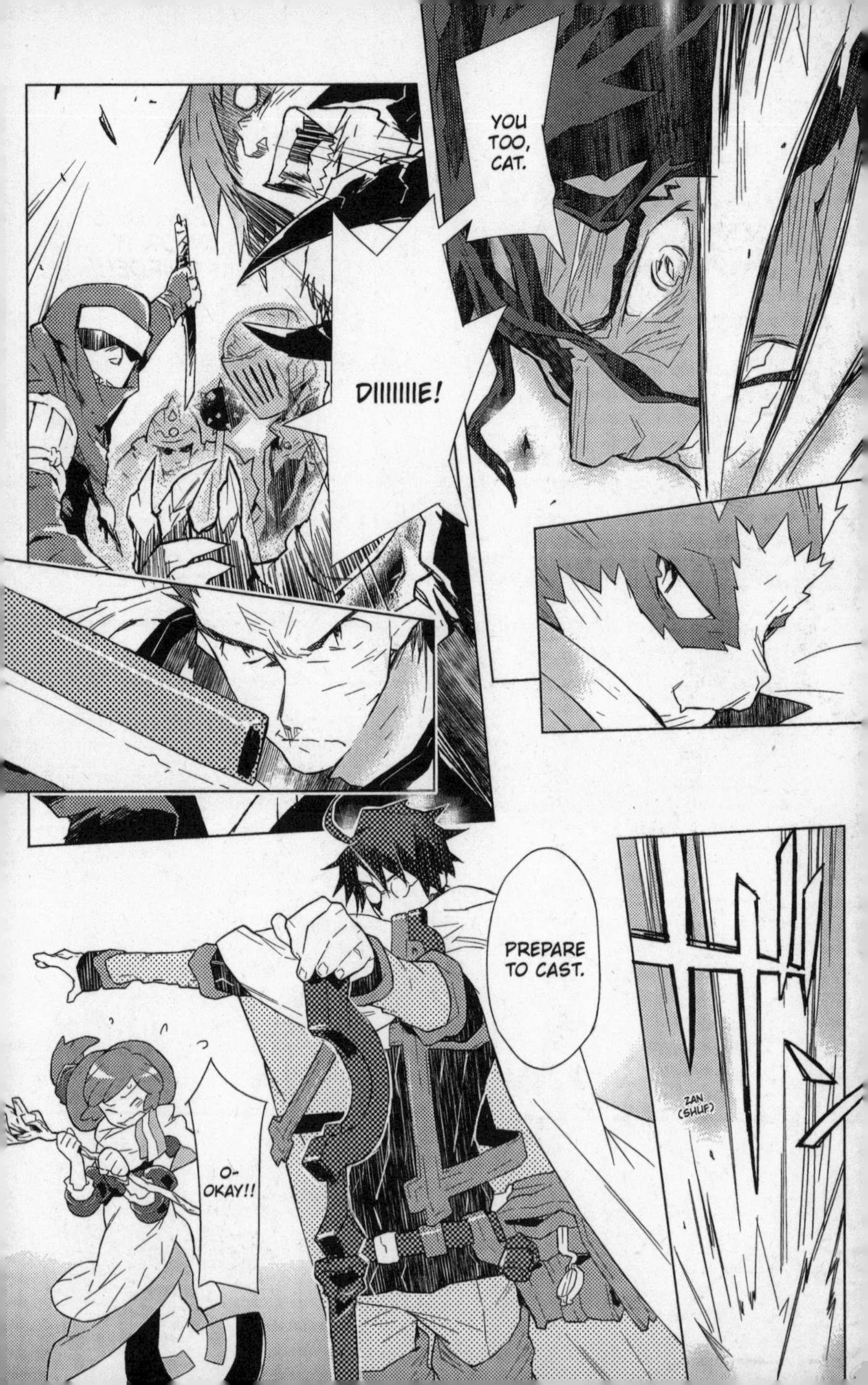
YOU TOO, CAT.
DIIIIIIIE!
PREPARE TO CAST.
ZAN (SHUF)
O-OKAY!!

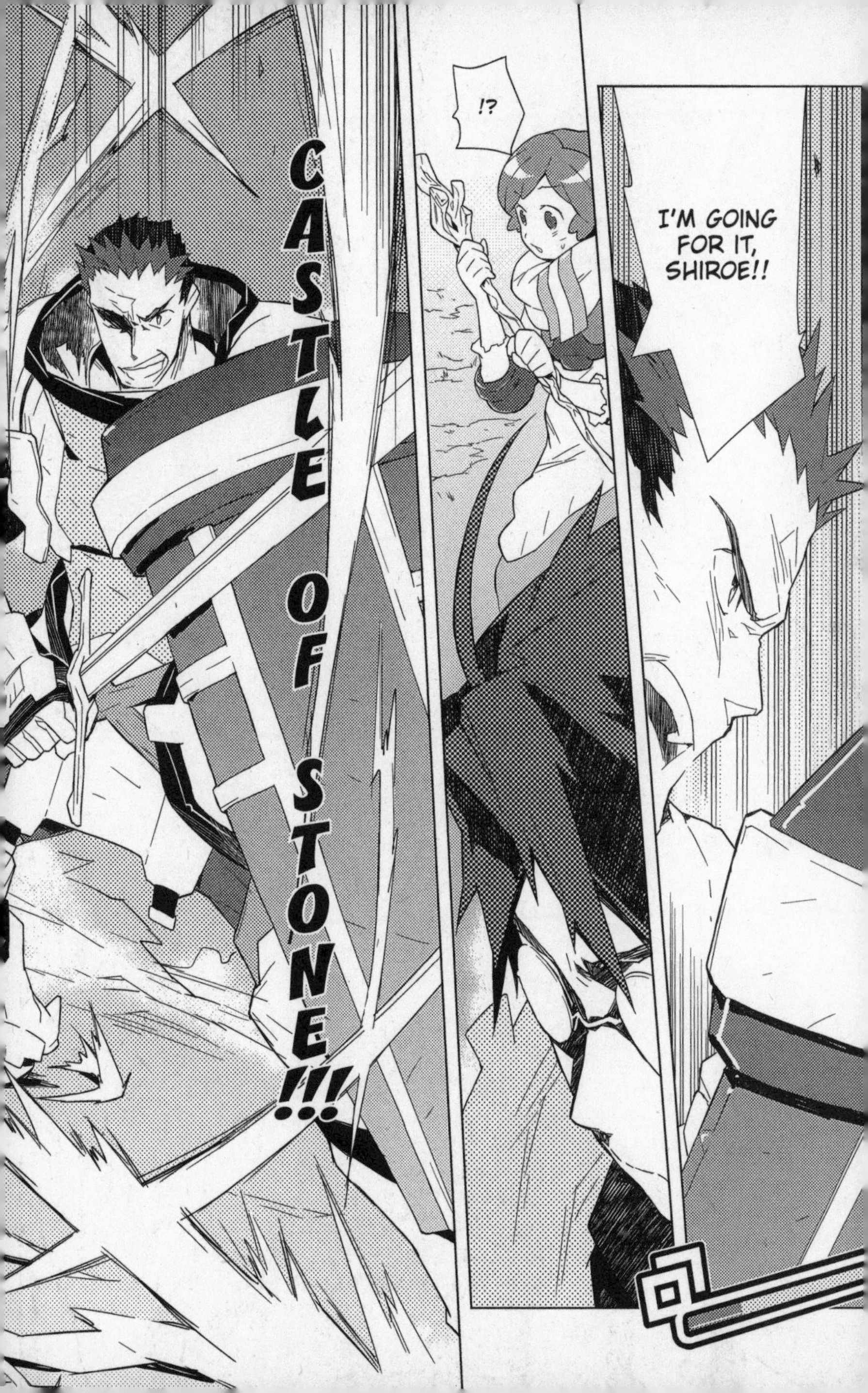
I'M GOING FOR IT, SHIROE!!
!?
CASTLE OF STONE!!!

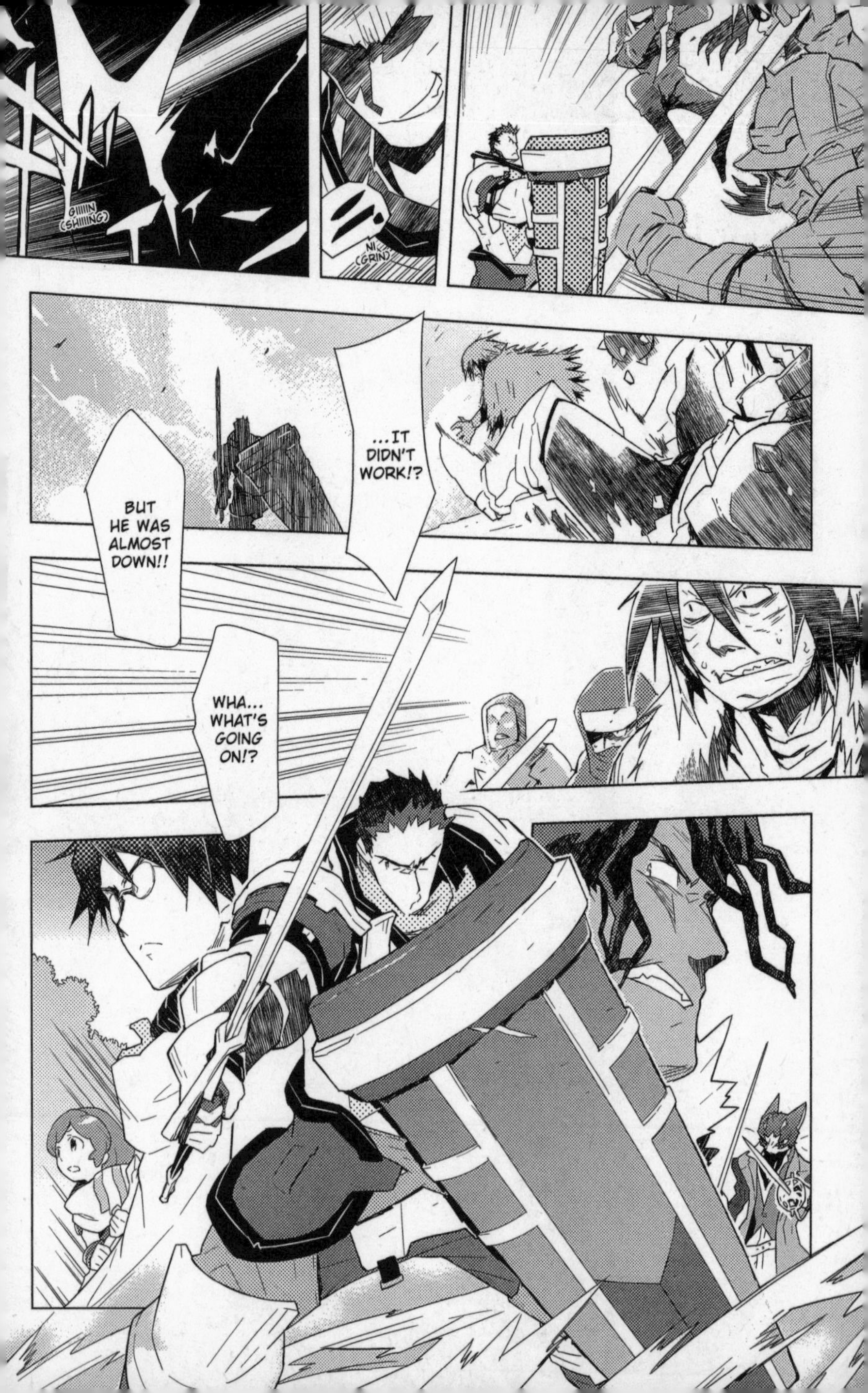
NI (GRIN)
GIIIIN (SHIIIING)
...IT DIDN'T WORK!?
BUT HE WAS ALMOST DOWN!!
WHA... WHAT'S GOING ON!?

# ▶CHAPTER:07 TEAM PLAY

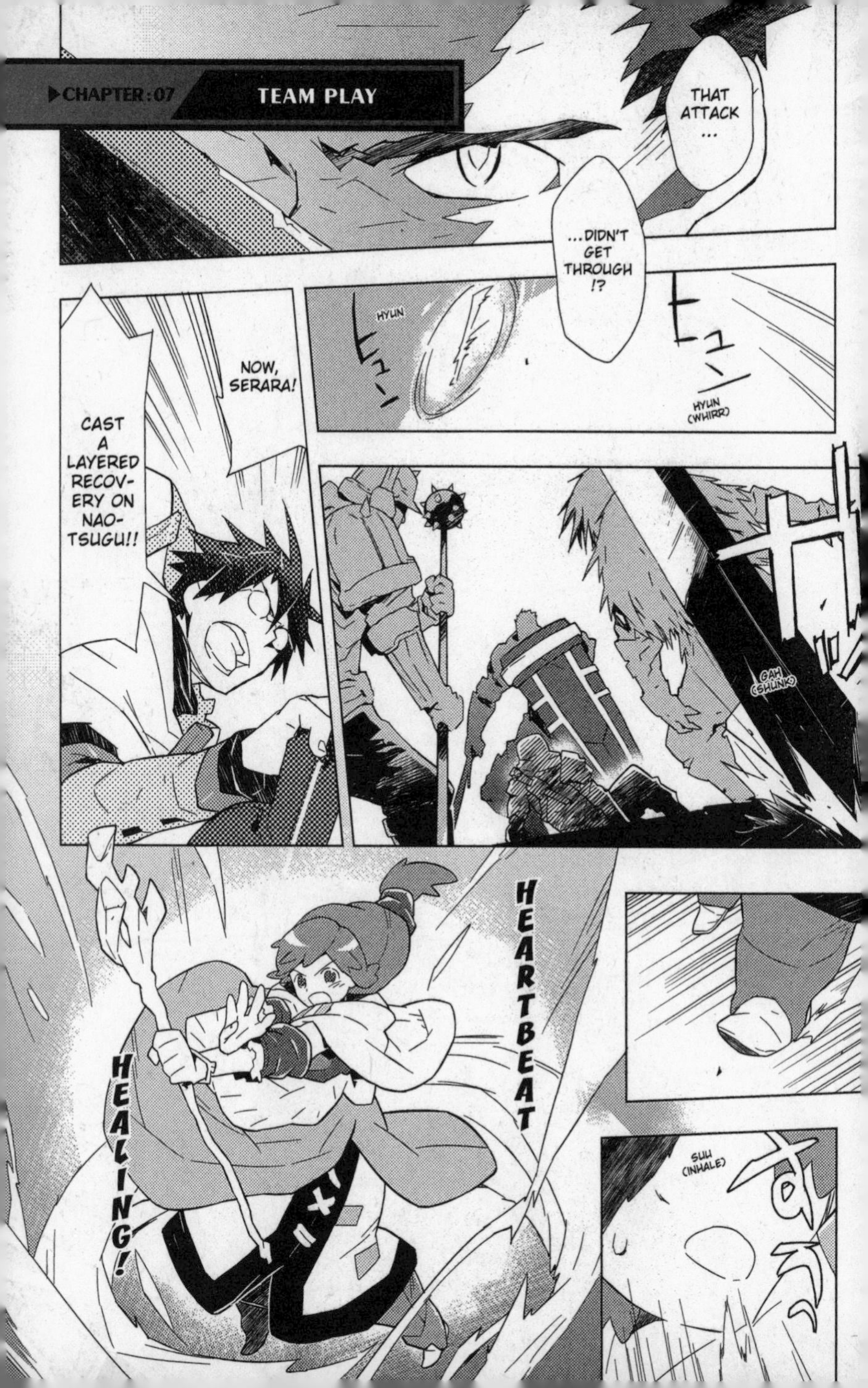
THAT ATTACK ...
...DIDN'T GET THROUGH !?
HYUN
HYUN (WHIRR)
GAH (SHUNK)
NOW, SERARA!
CAST A LAYERED RECOVERY ON NAO-TSUGU!!
SUH (INHALE)
HEARTBEAT
HEALING!

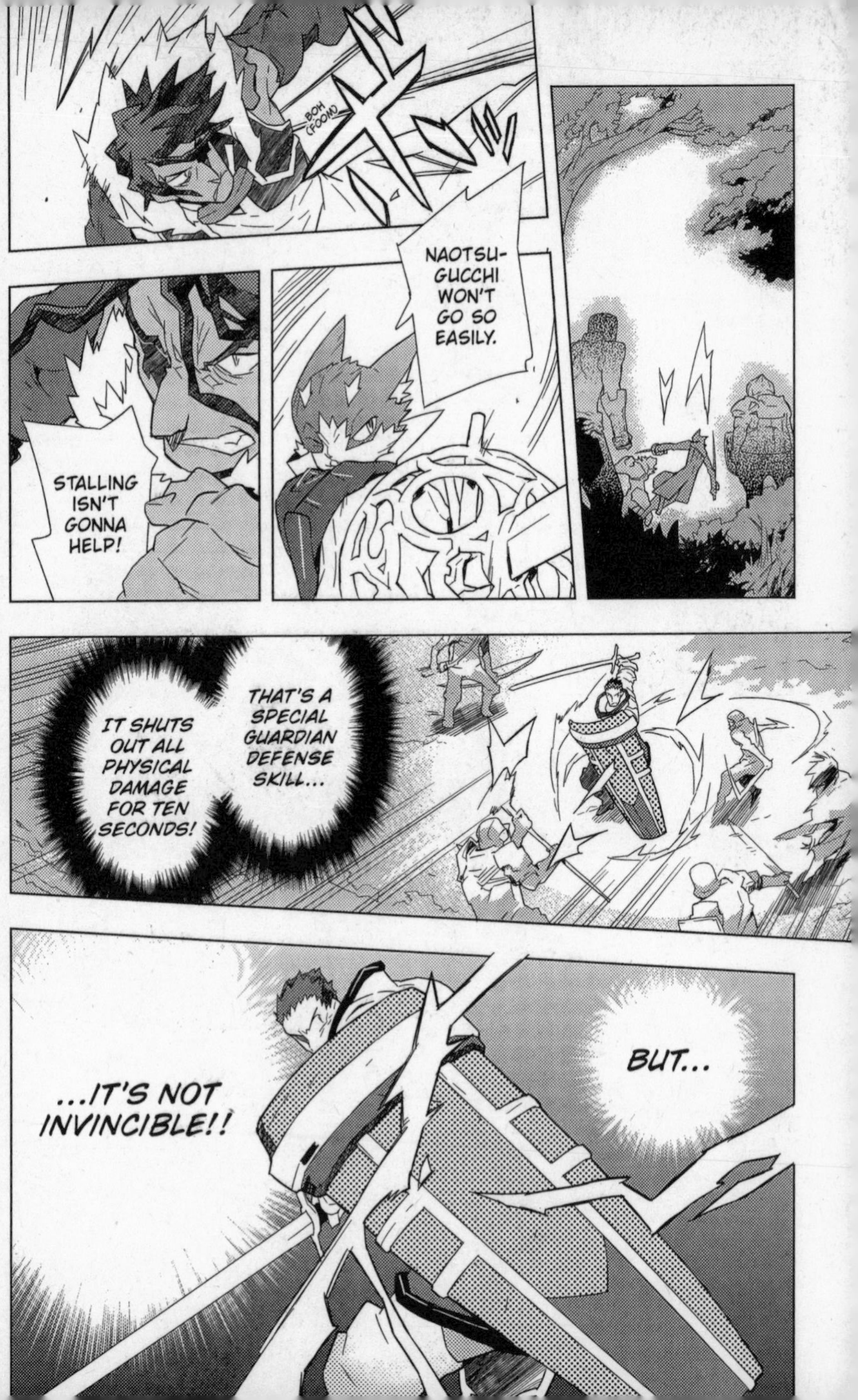
BOH (FOOM)
NAOTSU-GUCCHI WON'T GO SO EASILY.
STALLING ISN'T GONNA HELP!
THAT'S A SPECIAL GUARDIAN DEFENSE SKILL...
IT SHUTS OUT ALL PHYSICAL DAMAGE FOR TEN SECONDS!
BUT...
...IT'S NOT INVINCIBLE!!

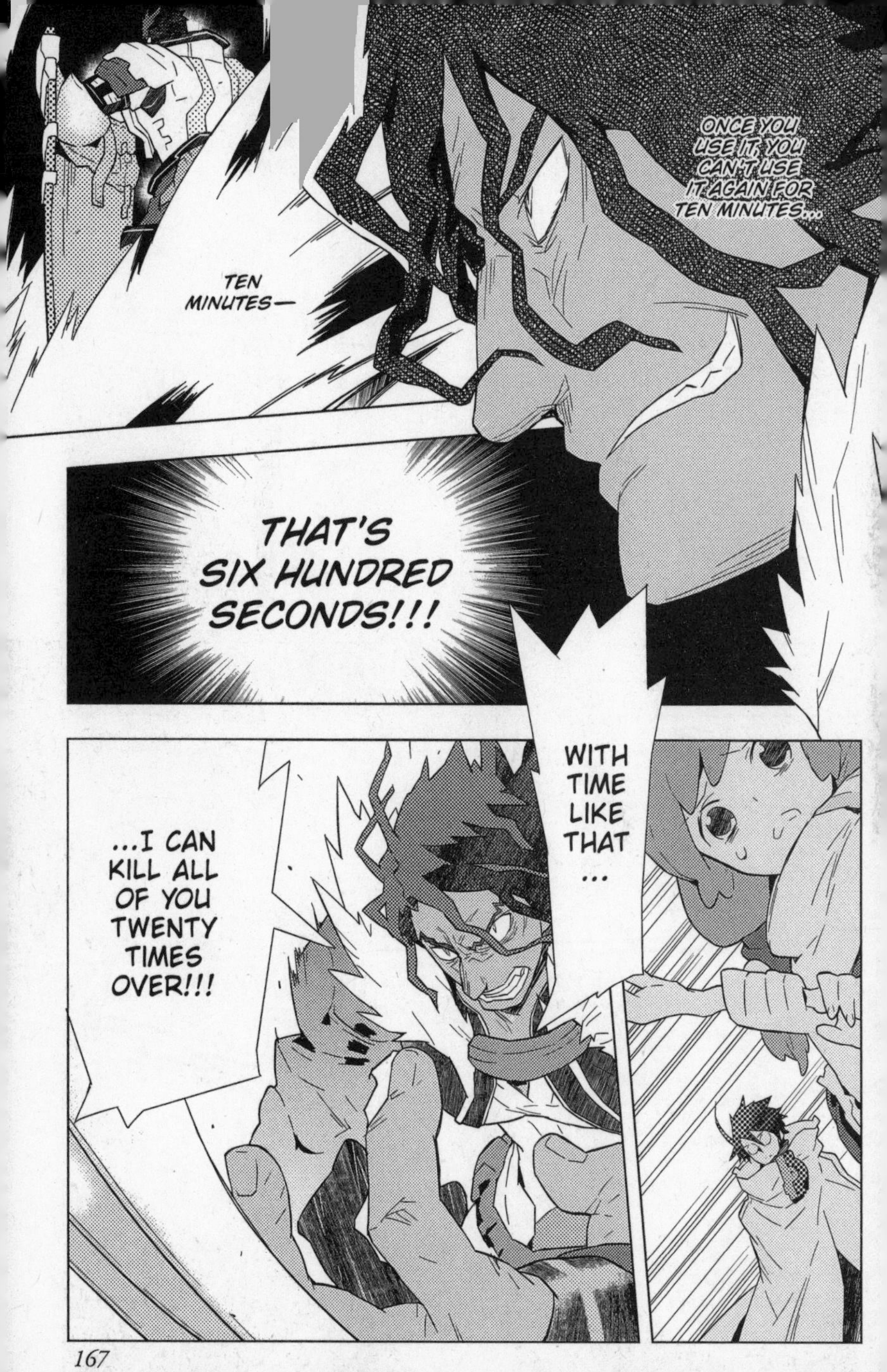
ONCE YOU USE IT, YOU CAN'T USE IT AGAIN FOR TEN MINUTES...
TEN MINUTES—
THAT'S SIX HUNDRED SECONDS!!!
WITH TIME LIKE THAT...
...I CAN KILL ALL OF YOU TWENTY TIMES OVER!!!

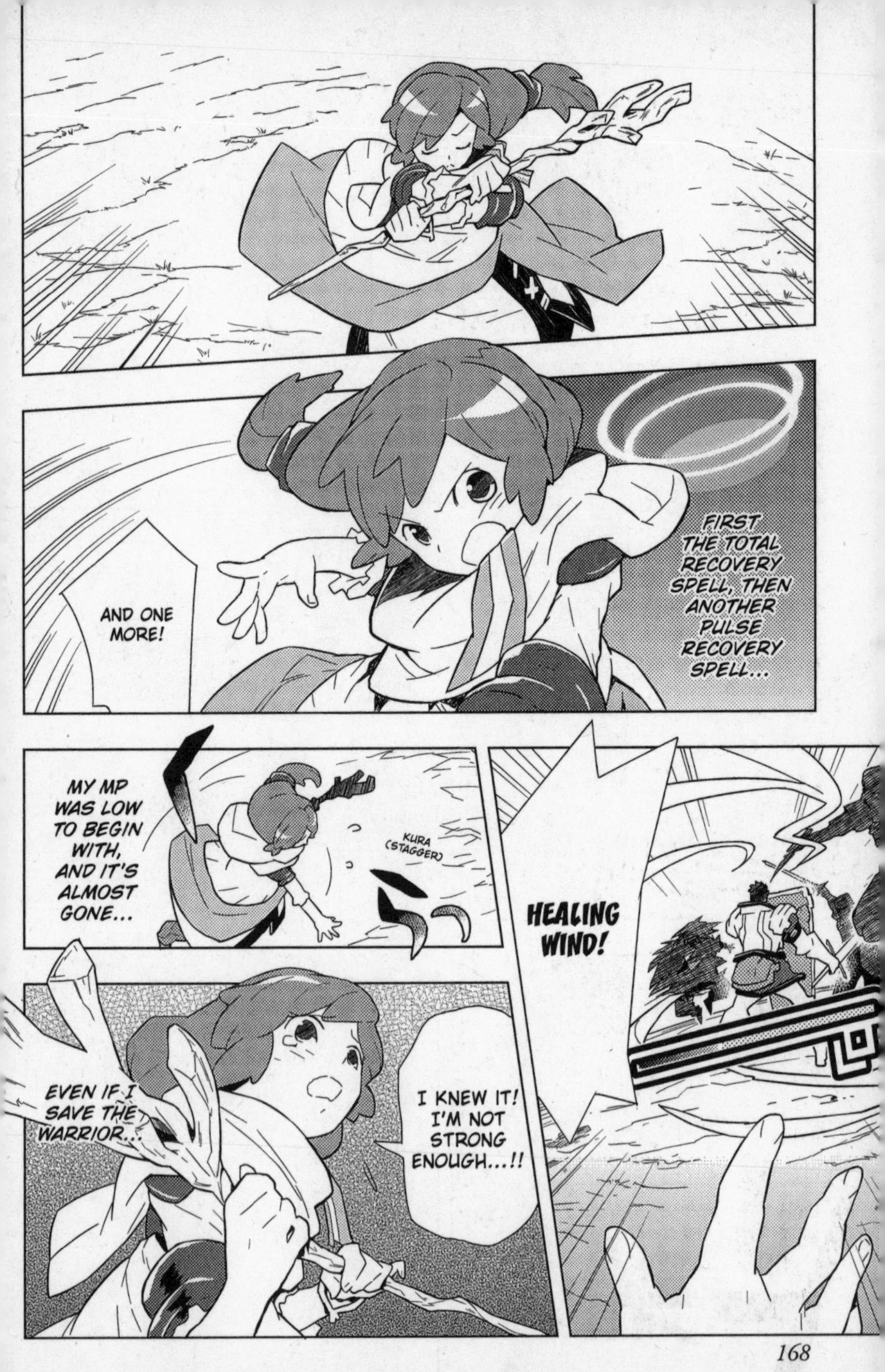
FIRST THE TOTAL RECOVERY SPELL, THEN ANOTHER PULSE RECOVERY SPELL...
AND ONE MORE!
HEALING WIND!
KURA (STAGGER)
MY MP WAS LOW TO BEGIN WITH, AND IT'S ALMOST GONE...
I KNEW IT! I'M NOT STRONG ENOUGH...!!
EVEN IF I SAVE THE WARRIOR...

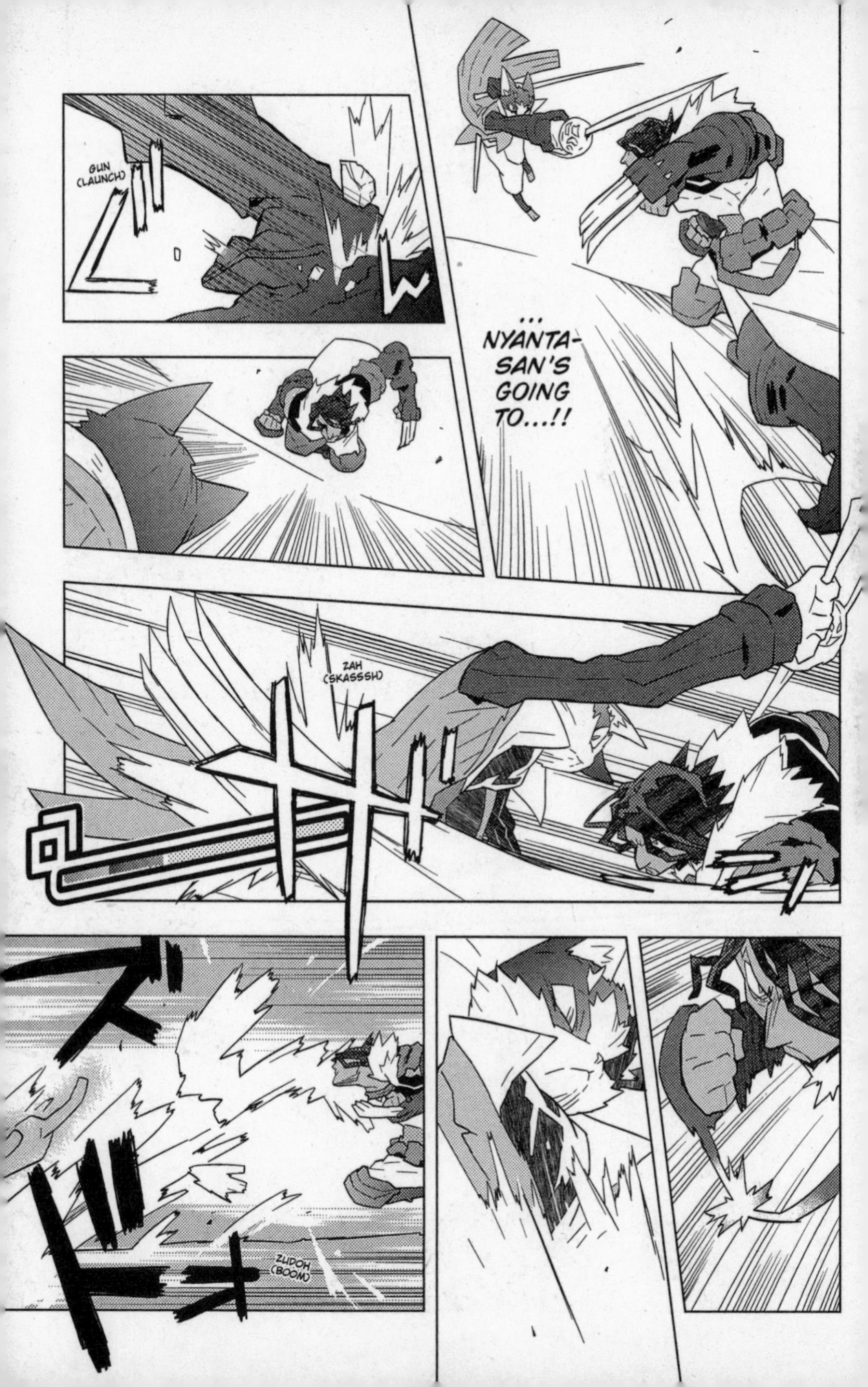
... NYANTA-SAN'S GOING TO...!!
GUN (LAUNCH)
ZAH (SKASSSH)
ZUDOH (BOOM)

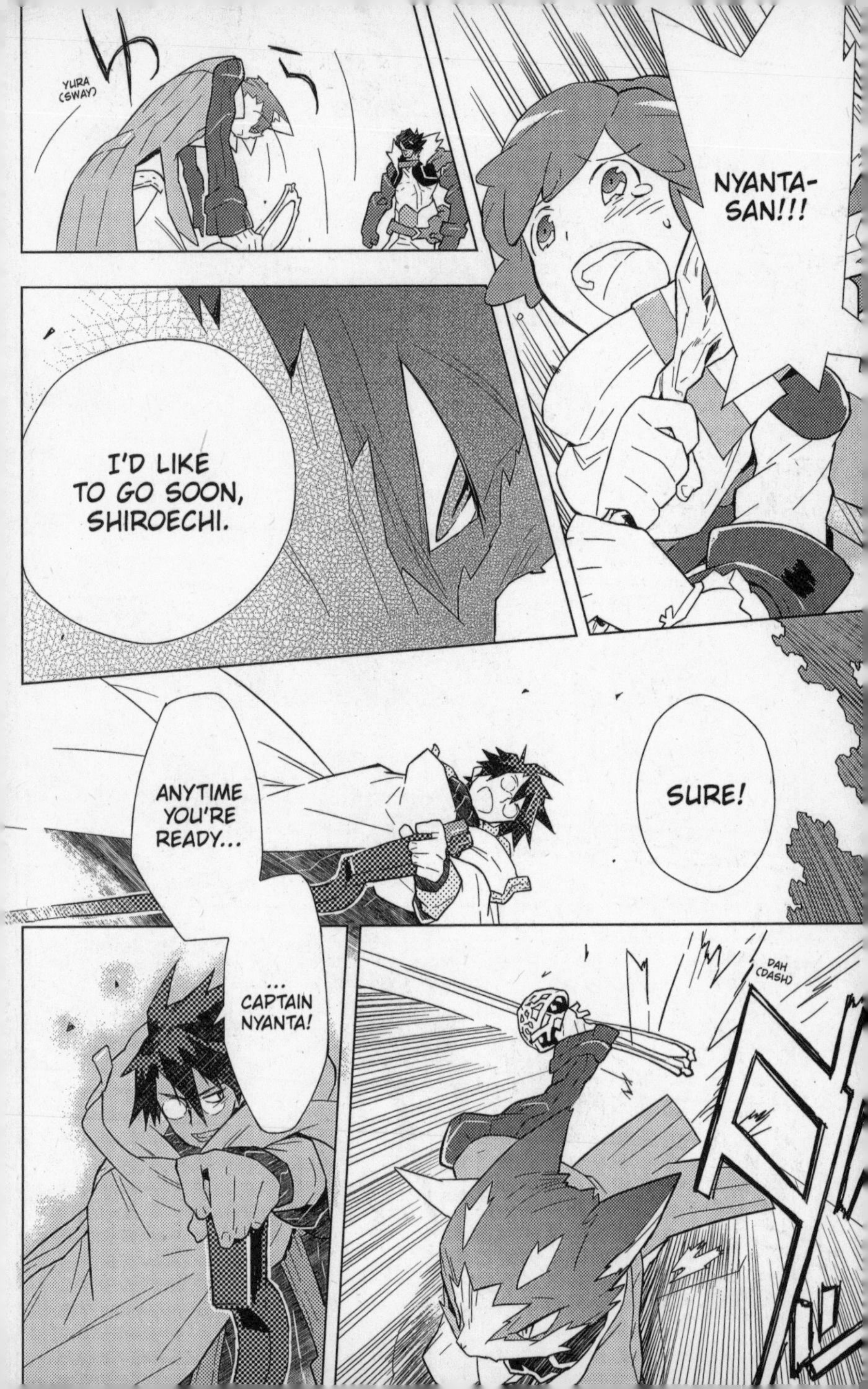
NYANTA-SAN!!!
YURA (SWAY)
I'D LIKE TO GO SOON, SHIROECHI.
SURE!
ANYTIME YOU'RE READY...
DAH (DASH)
... CAPTAIN NYANTA!

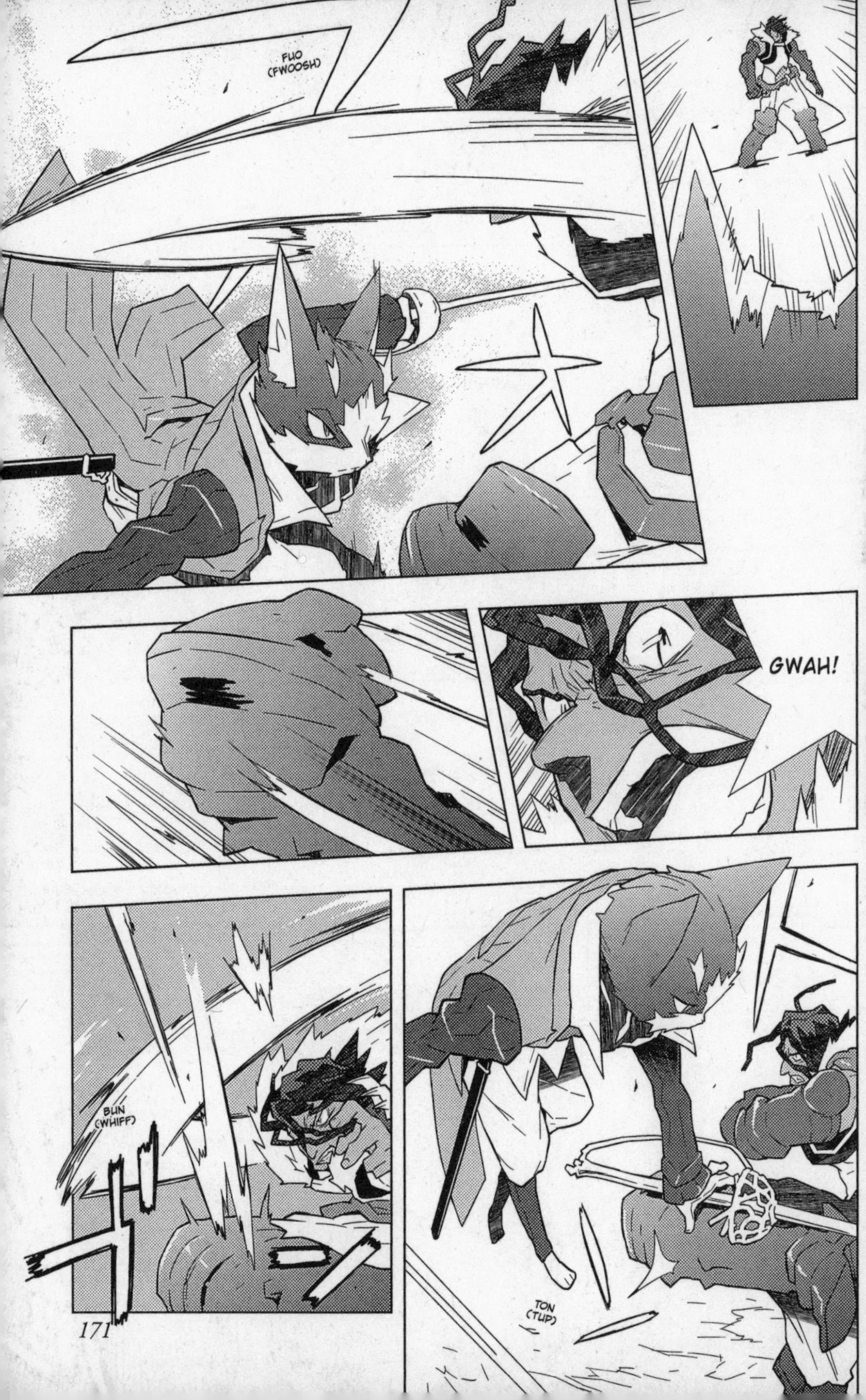
FUO
(FWOOSH)
GWAH!
TON
(TUP)
BUN
(WHIFF)

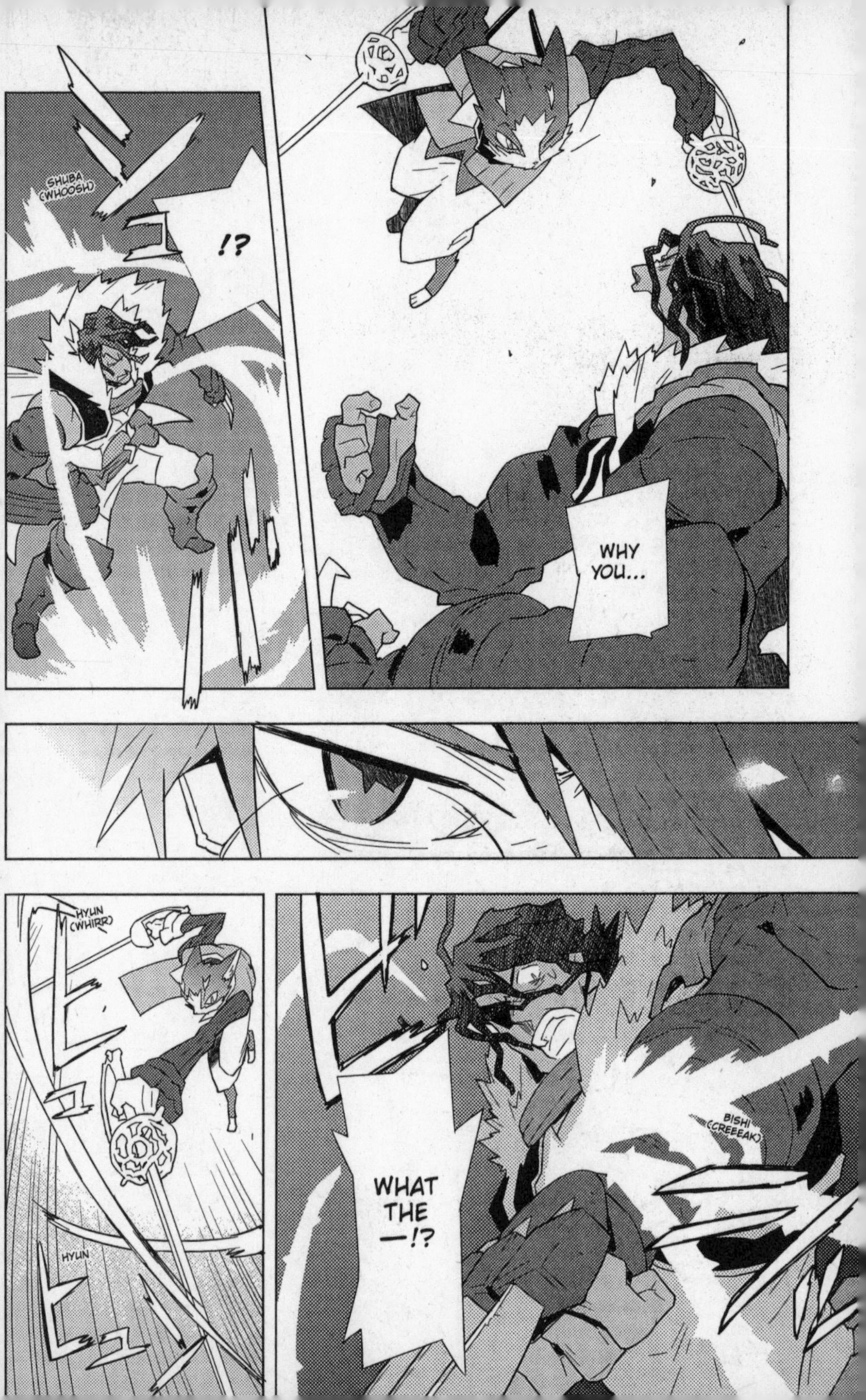
WHY YOU...
SHUBA (WHOOSH)
!?
BISHI (CREEEAK)
WHAT THE—!?
HYUN (WHIRR)
HYUN

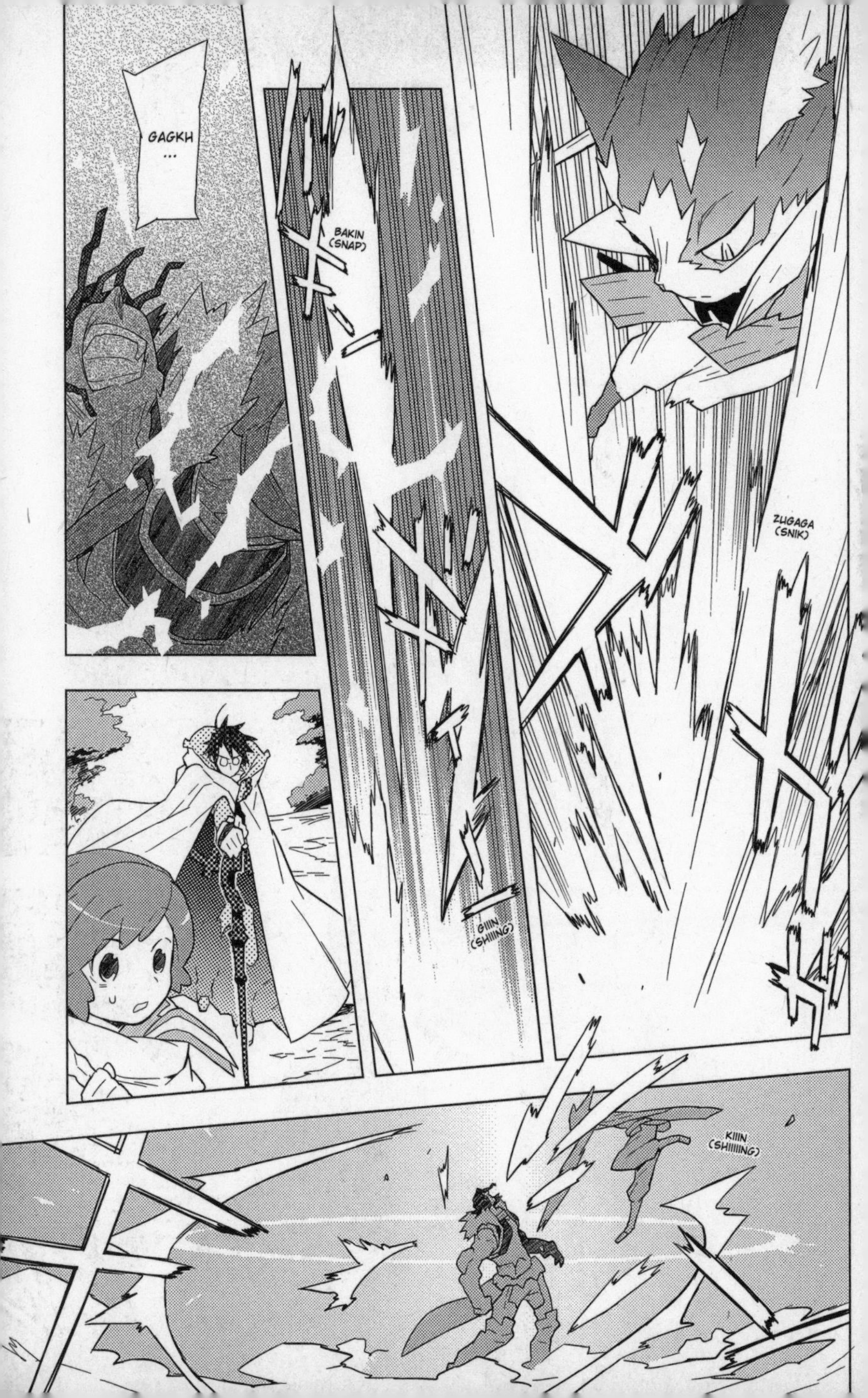
ZUGAGA (SNIK)
BAKIN (SNAP)
GIIIN (SHIIING)
GAGKH ...
KIIIN (SHIIIING)

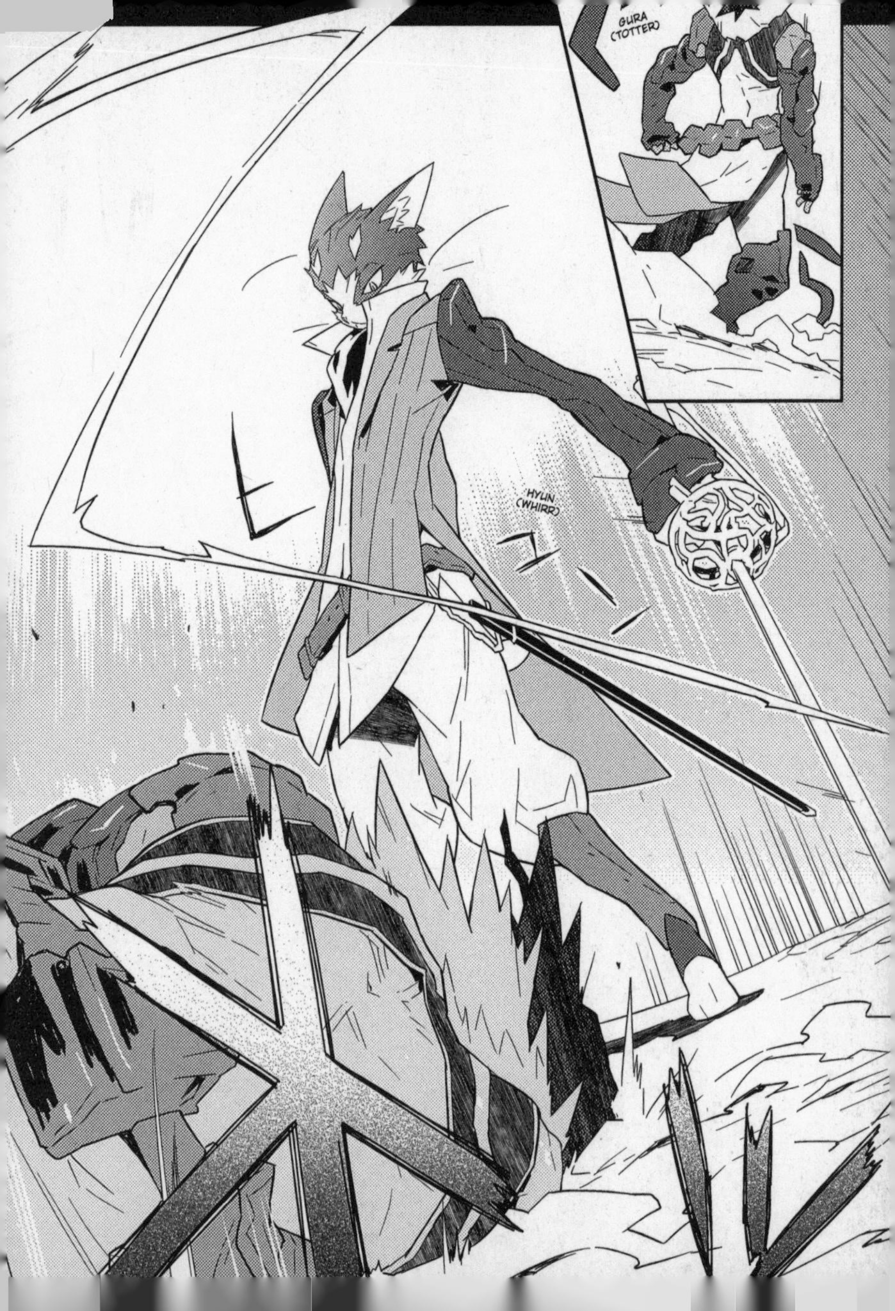
GURA (TOTTER)
HYUN (WHIRR)

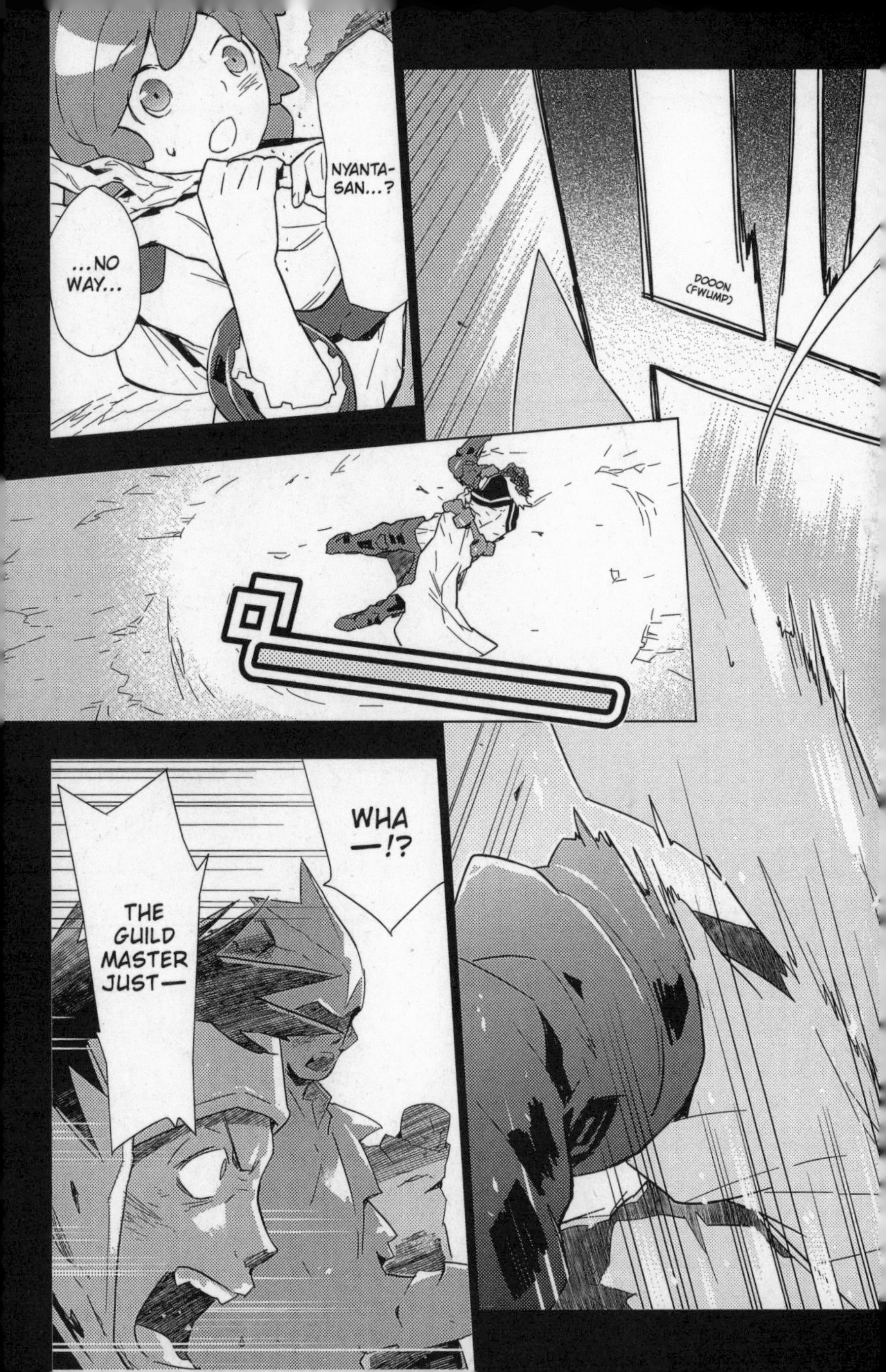
DOOON (FWUMP)
NYANTA-SAN...?
...NO WAY...
WHA—!?
THE GUILD MASTER JUST—

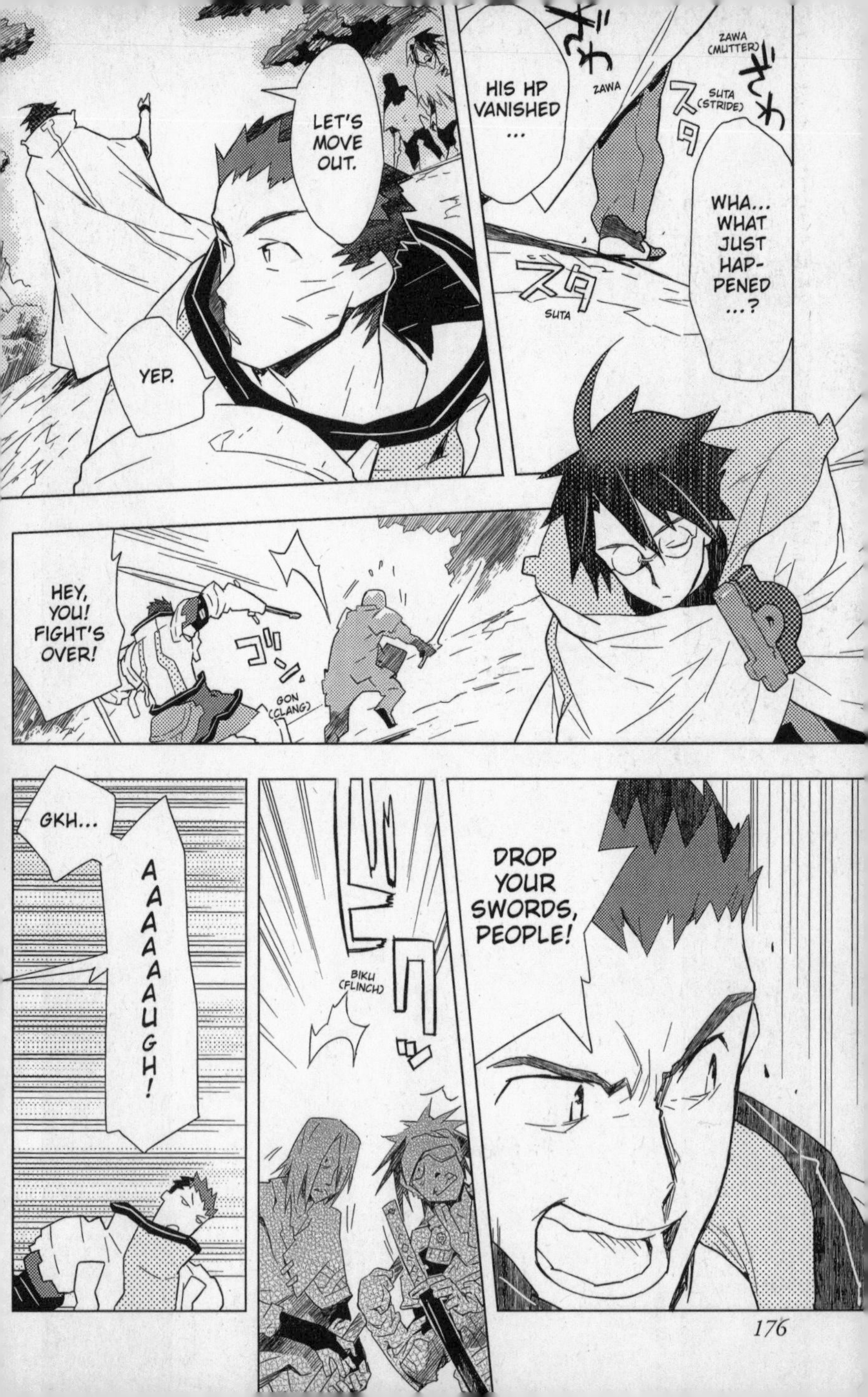
ZAWA (MUTTER)
SUTA (STRIDE)
WHA... WHAT JUST HAP-PENED ...?
HIS HP VANISHED ...
ZAWA
SUTA
LET'S MOVE OUT.
YEP.
HEY, YOU! FIGHT'S OVER!
GON (CLANG)
DROP YOUR SWORDS, PEOPLE!
BIKU (FLINCH)
GKH...
AAAAAAAUGH!

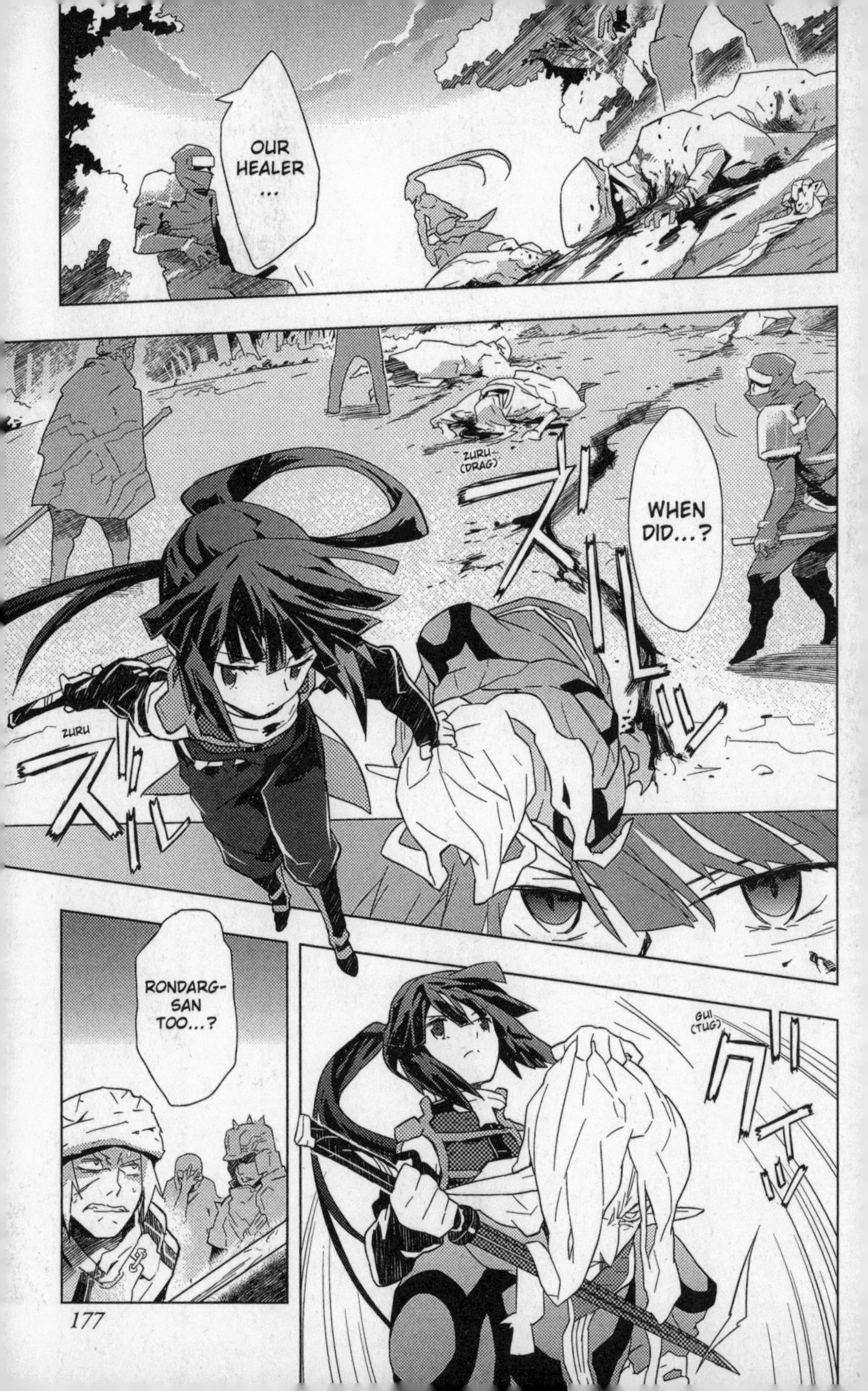
OUR HEALER ...
WHEN DID...?
ZURU (DRAG)
ZURU
GUI (TUG)
RONDARG-SAN TOO...?

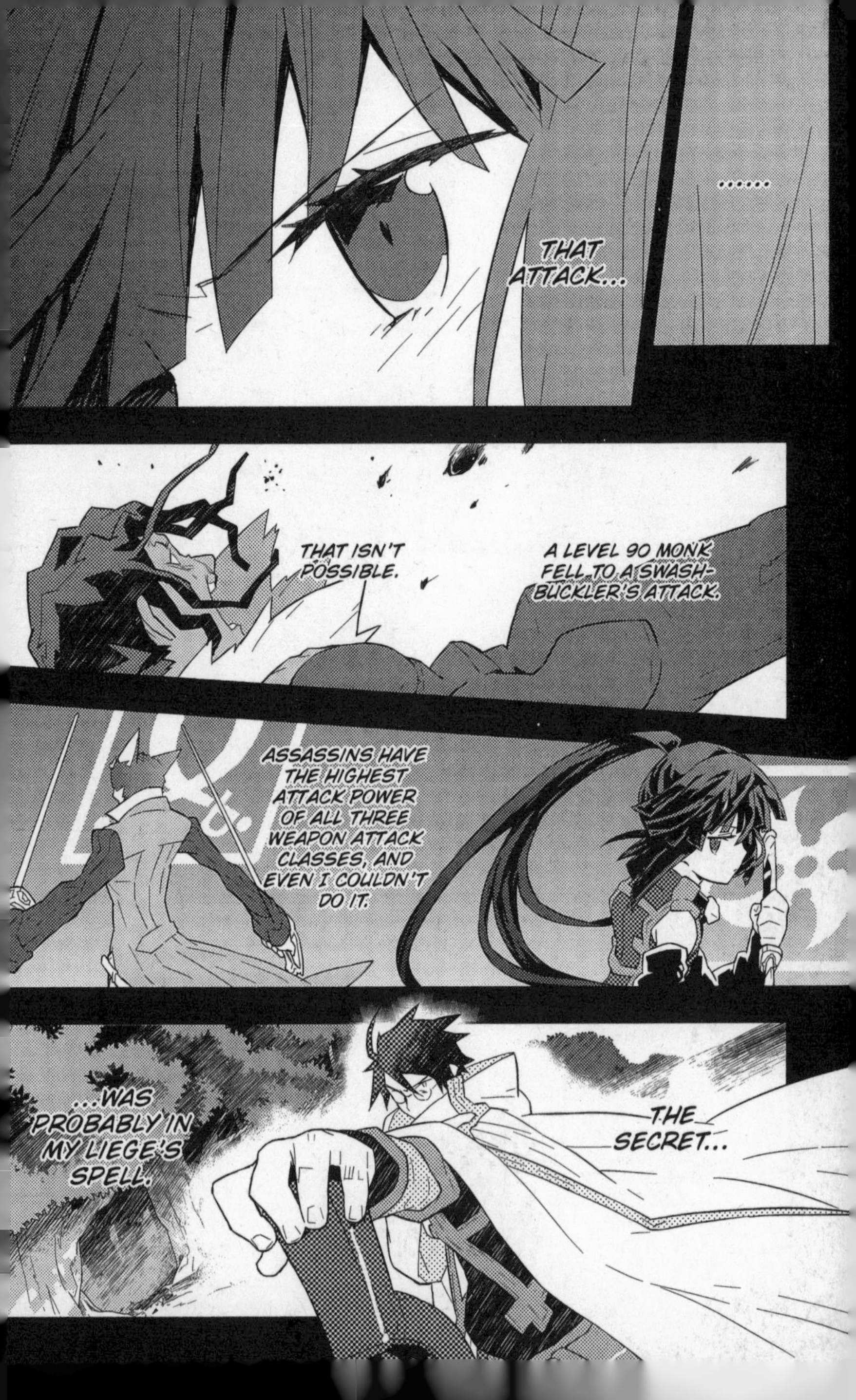
......
THAT ATTACK...
A LEVEL 90 MONK FELL TO A SWASH-BUCKLER'S ATTACK.
THAT ISN'T POSSIBLE.
ASSASSINS HAVE THE HIGHEST ATTACK POWER OF ALL THREE WEAPON ATTACK CLASSES, AND EVEN I COULDN'T DO IT.
THE SECRET...
...WAS PROBABLY IN MY LIEGE'S SPELL.

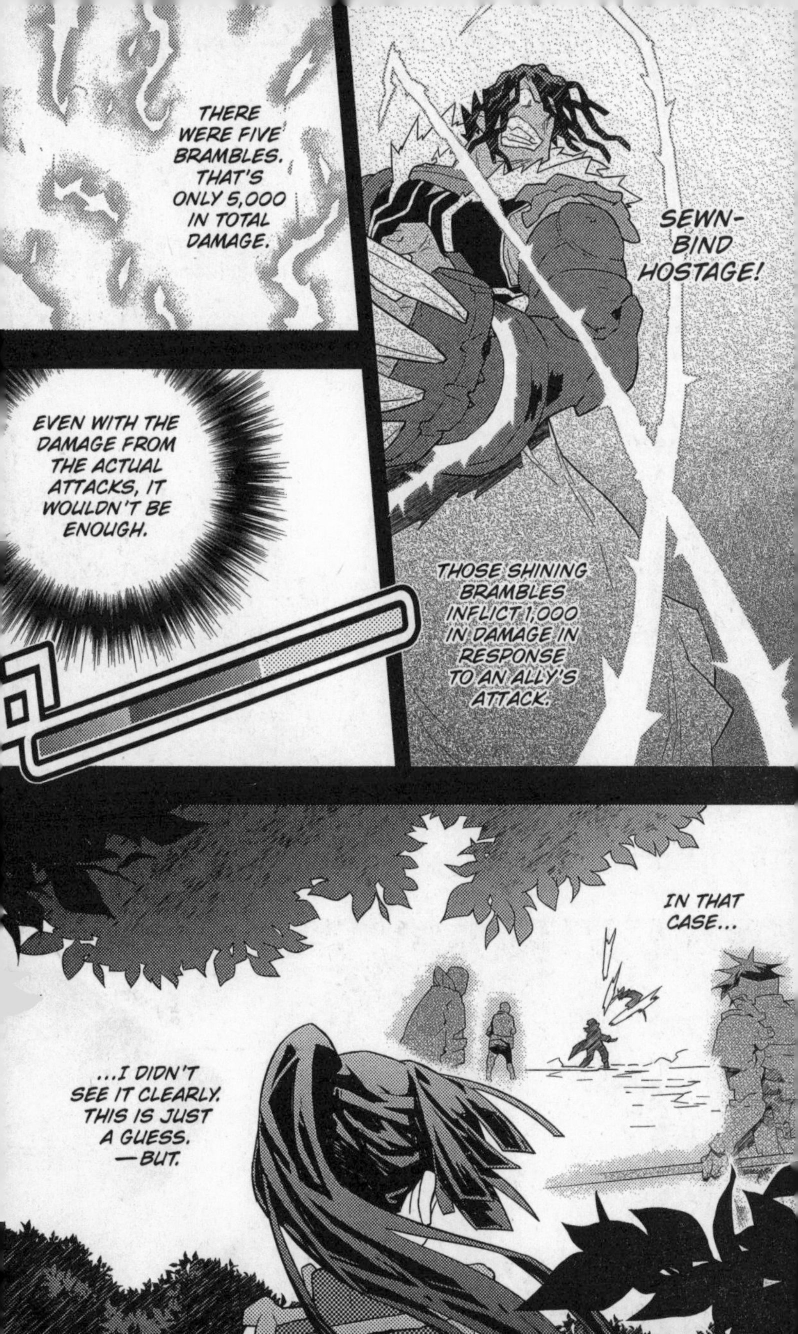
SEWN-BIND HOSTAGE!
THOSE SHINING BRAMBLES INFLICT 1,000 IN DAMAGE IN RESPONSE TO AN ALLY'S ATTACK.
THERE WERE FIVE BRAMBLES. THAT'S ONLY 5,000 IN TOTAL DAMAGE.
EVEN WITH THE DAMAGE FROM THE ACTUAL ATTACKS, IT WOULDN'T BE ENOUGH.
IN THAT CASE...
...I DIDN'T SEE IT CLEARLY. THIS IS JUST A GUESS. —BUT.

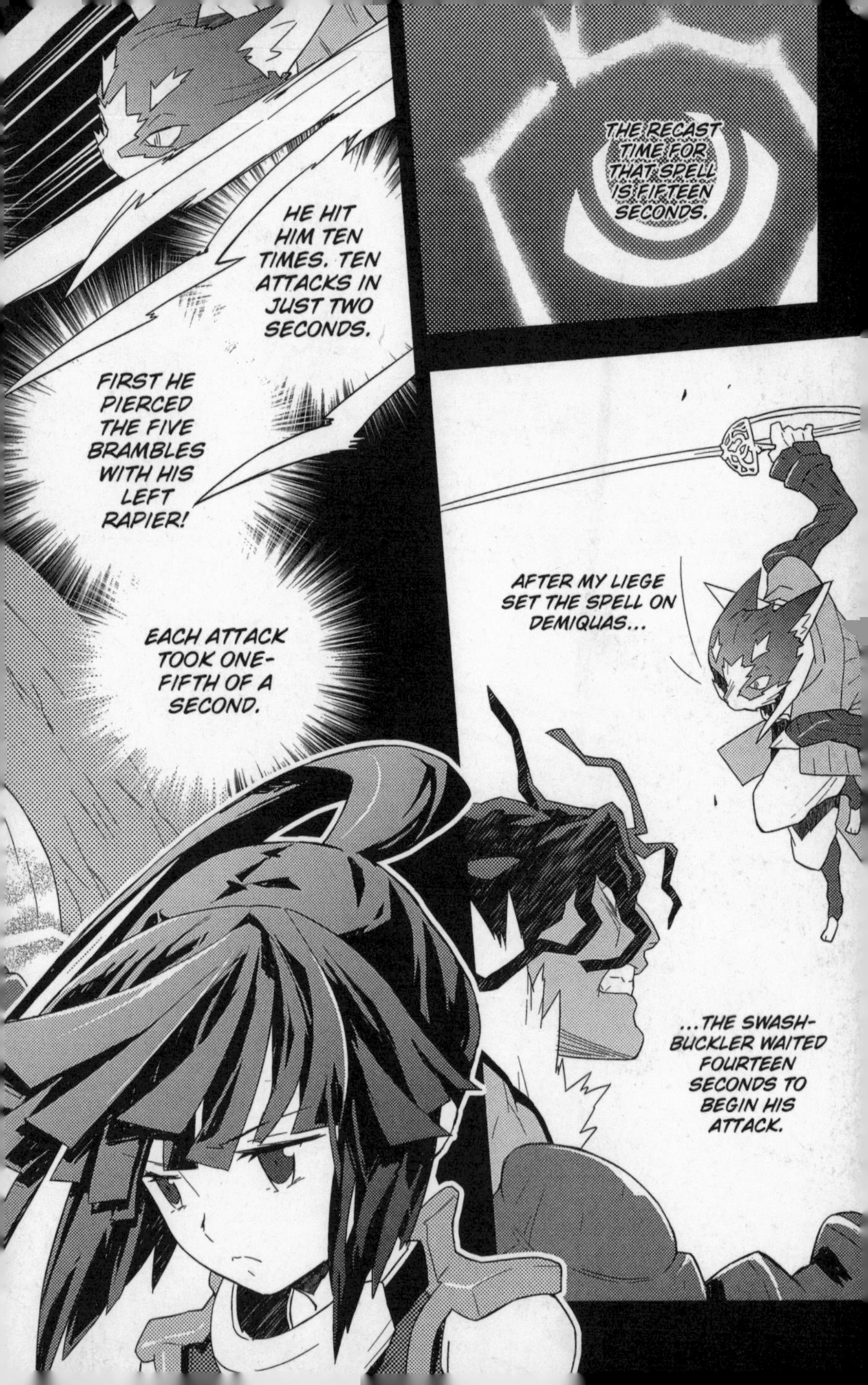
THE RECAST TIME FOR THAT SPELL IS FIFTEEN SECONDS.
AFTER MY LIEGE SET THE SPELL ON DEMIQUAS...
...THE SWASH-BUCKLER WAITED FOURTEEN SECONDS TO BEGIN HIS ATTACK.
HE HIT HIM TEN TIMES. TEN ATTACKS IN JUST TWO SECONDS.
FIRST HE PIERCED THE FIVE BRAMBLES WITH HIS LEFT RAPIER!
EACH ATTACK TOOK ONE-FIFTH OF A SECOND.

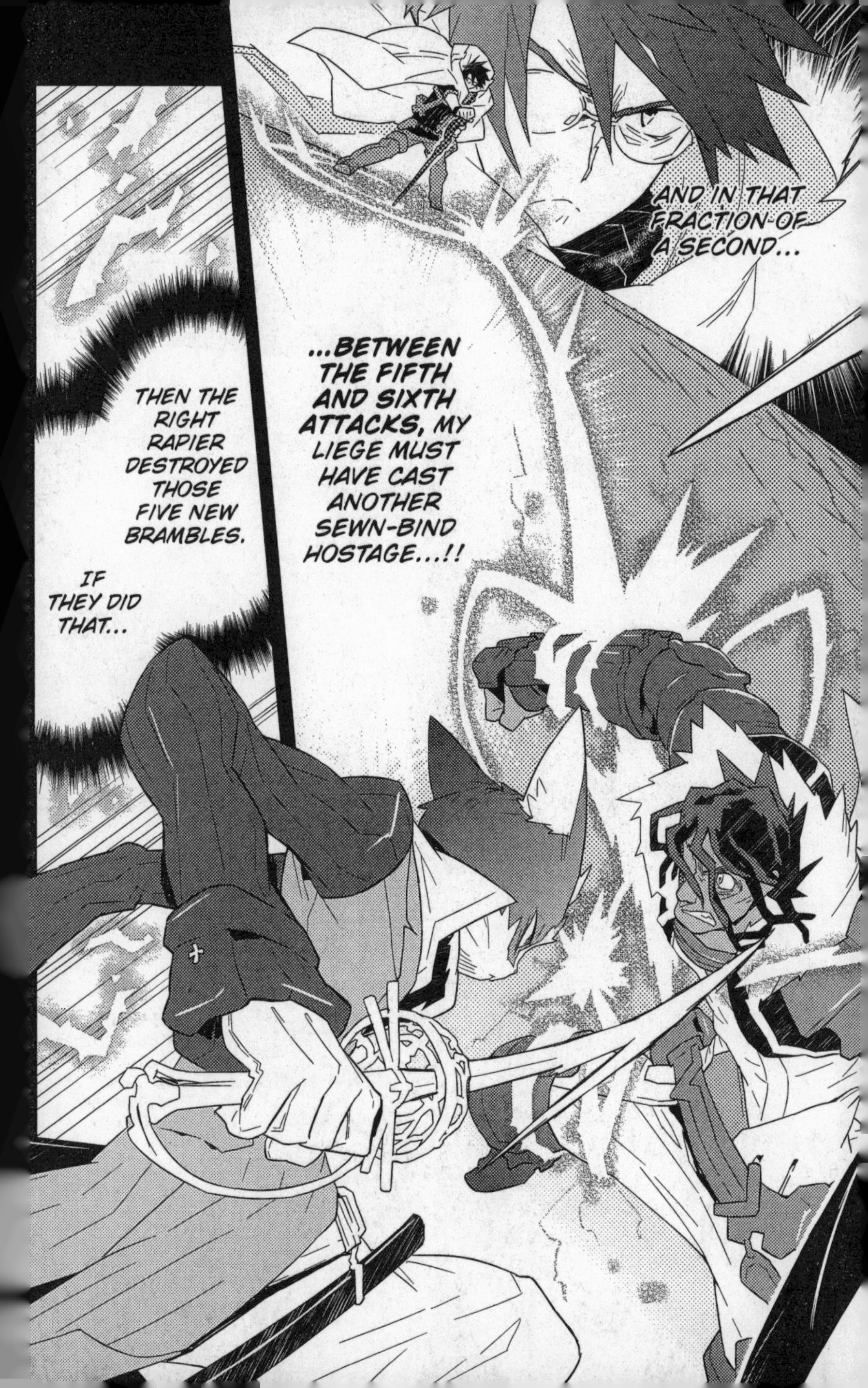
AND IN THAT FRACTION OF A SECOND...
...BETWEEN THE FIFTH AND SIXTH ATTACKS, MY LIEGE MUST HAVE CAST ANOTHER SEWN-BIND HOSTAGE...!!
THEN THE RIGHT RAPIER DESTROYED THOSE FIVE NEW BRAMBLES.
IF THEY DID THAT...

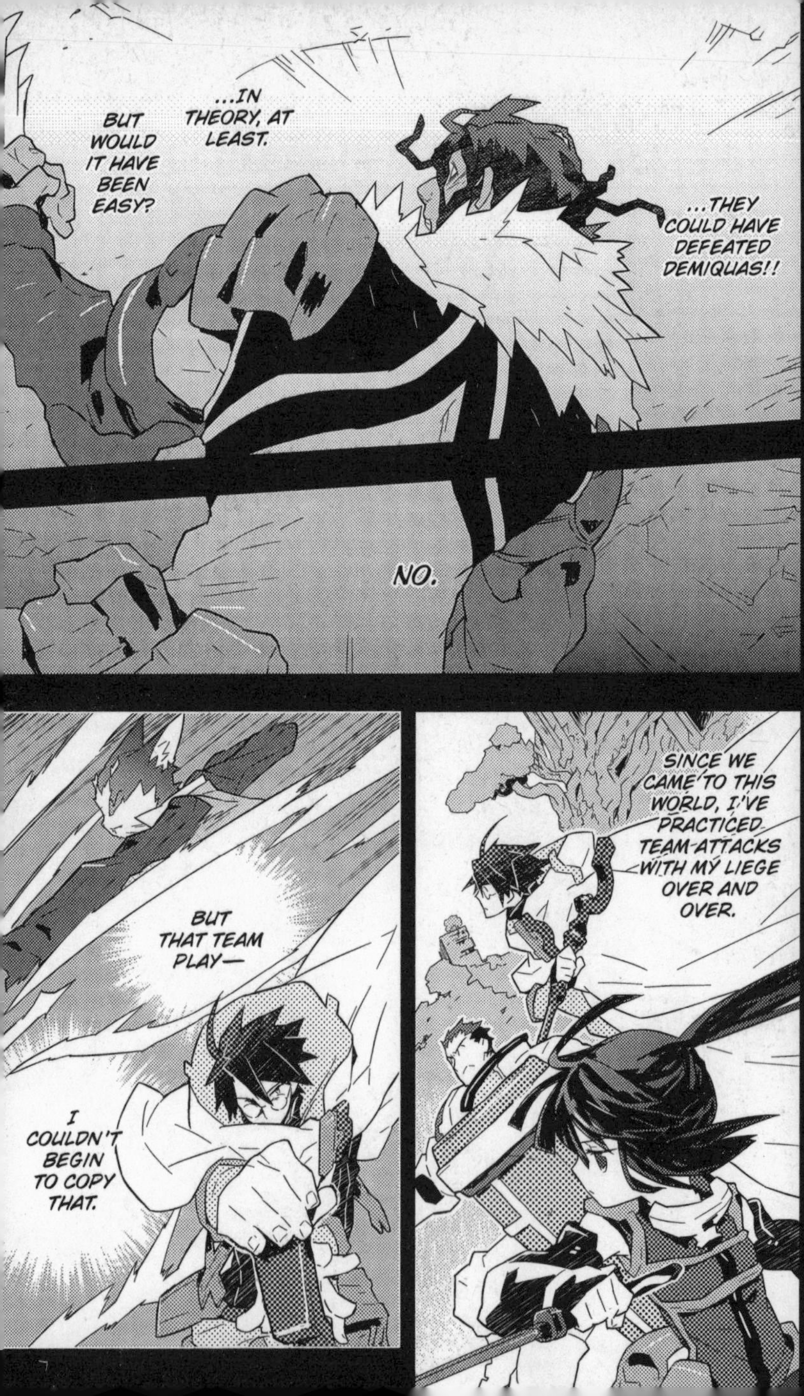
...THEY COULD HAVE DEFEATED DEMIQUAS!!
...IN THEORY, AT LEAST.
BUT WOULD IT HAVE BEEN EASY?
NO.
SINCE WE CAME TO THIS WORLD, I'VE PRACTICED TEAM-ATTACKS WITH MY LIEGE OVER AND OVER.
BUT THAT TEAM PLAY—
I COULDN'T BEGIN TO COPY THAT.

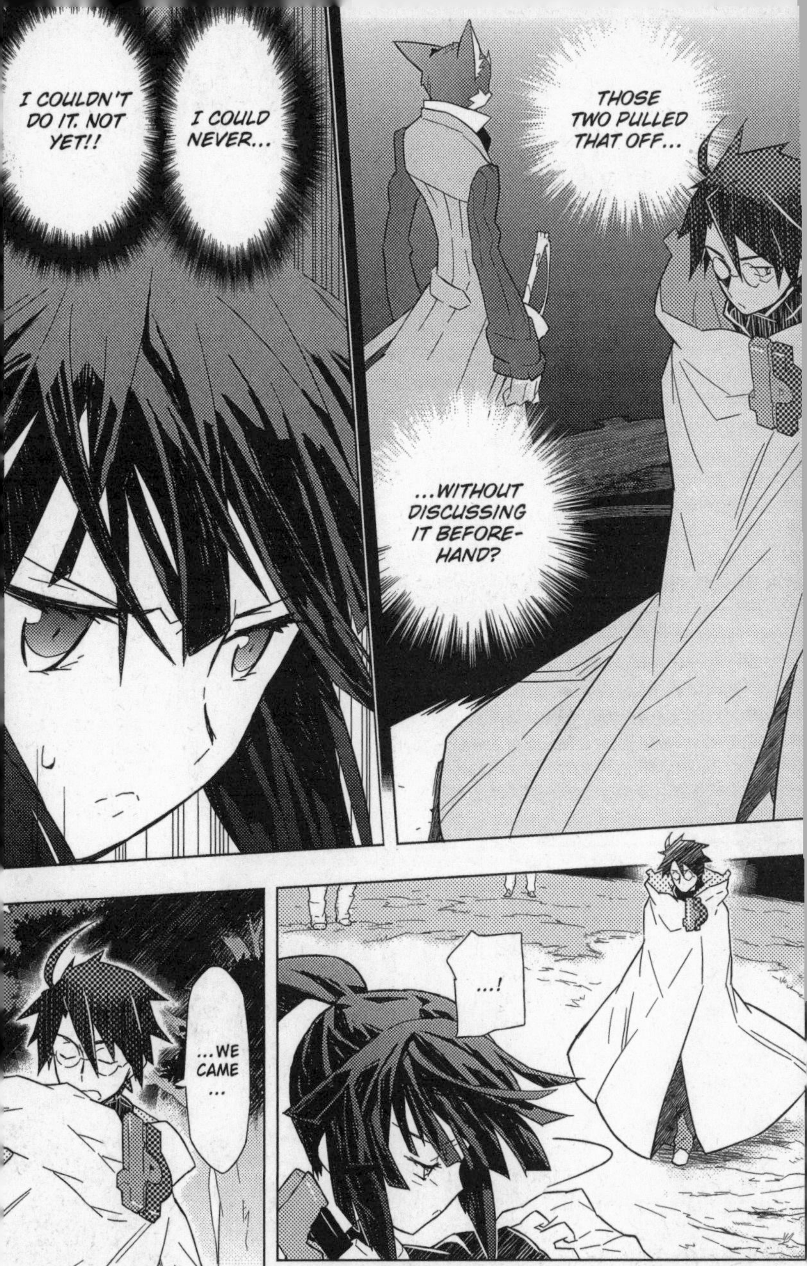
THOSE TWO PULLED THAT OFF...
...WITHOUT DISCUSSING IT BEFORE-HAND?
I COULD NEVER...
I COULDN'T DO IT. NOT YET!!
...!
...WE CAME ...

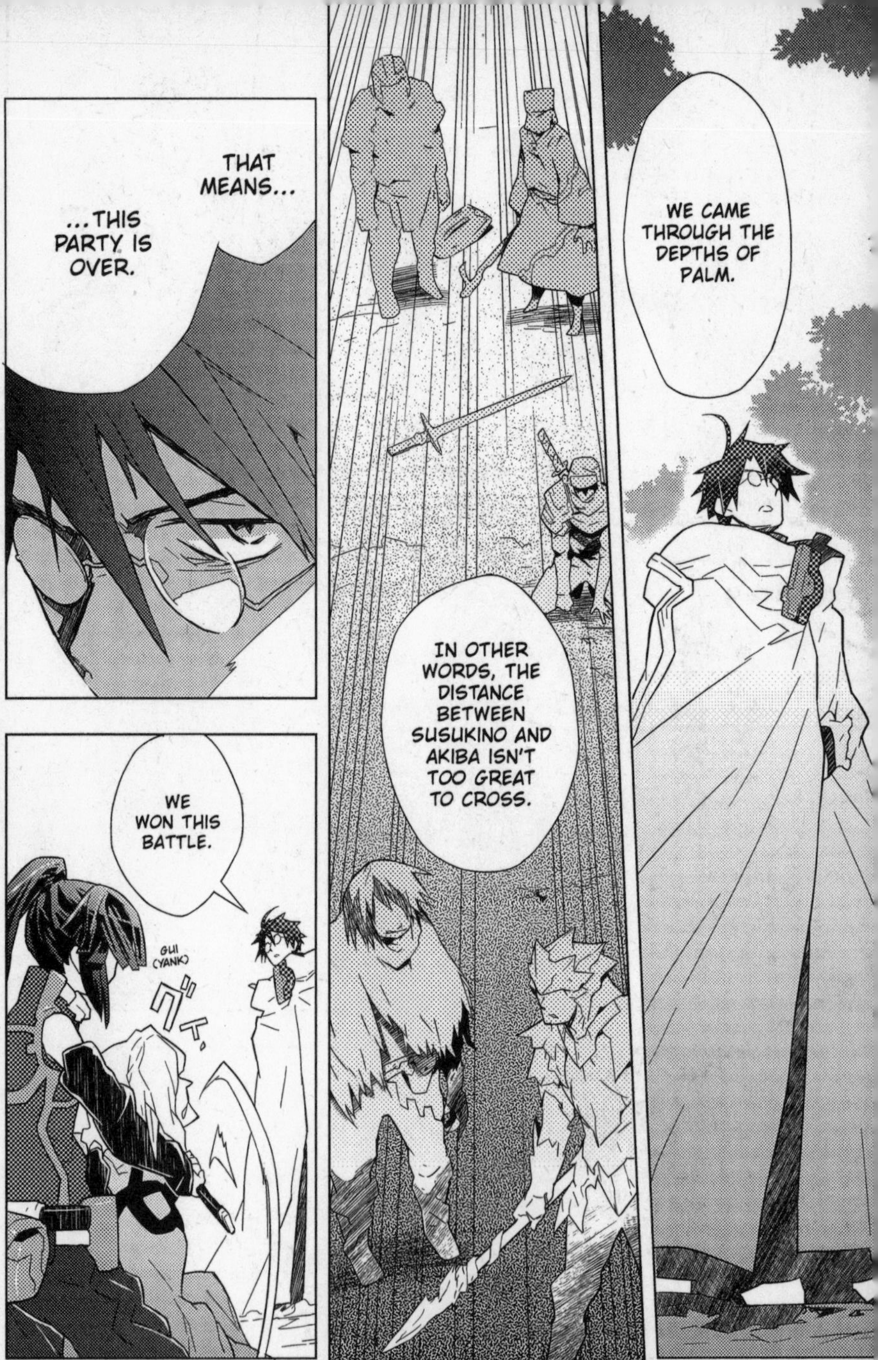
WE CAME THROUGH THE DEPTHS OF PALM.
IN OTHER WORDS, THE DISTANCE BETWEEN SUSUKINO AND AKIBA ISN'T TOO GREAT TO CROSS.
THAT MEANS...
...THIS PARTY IS OVER.
WE WON THIS BATTLE.
GUI (YANK)

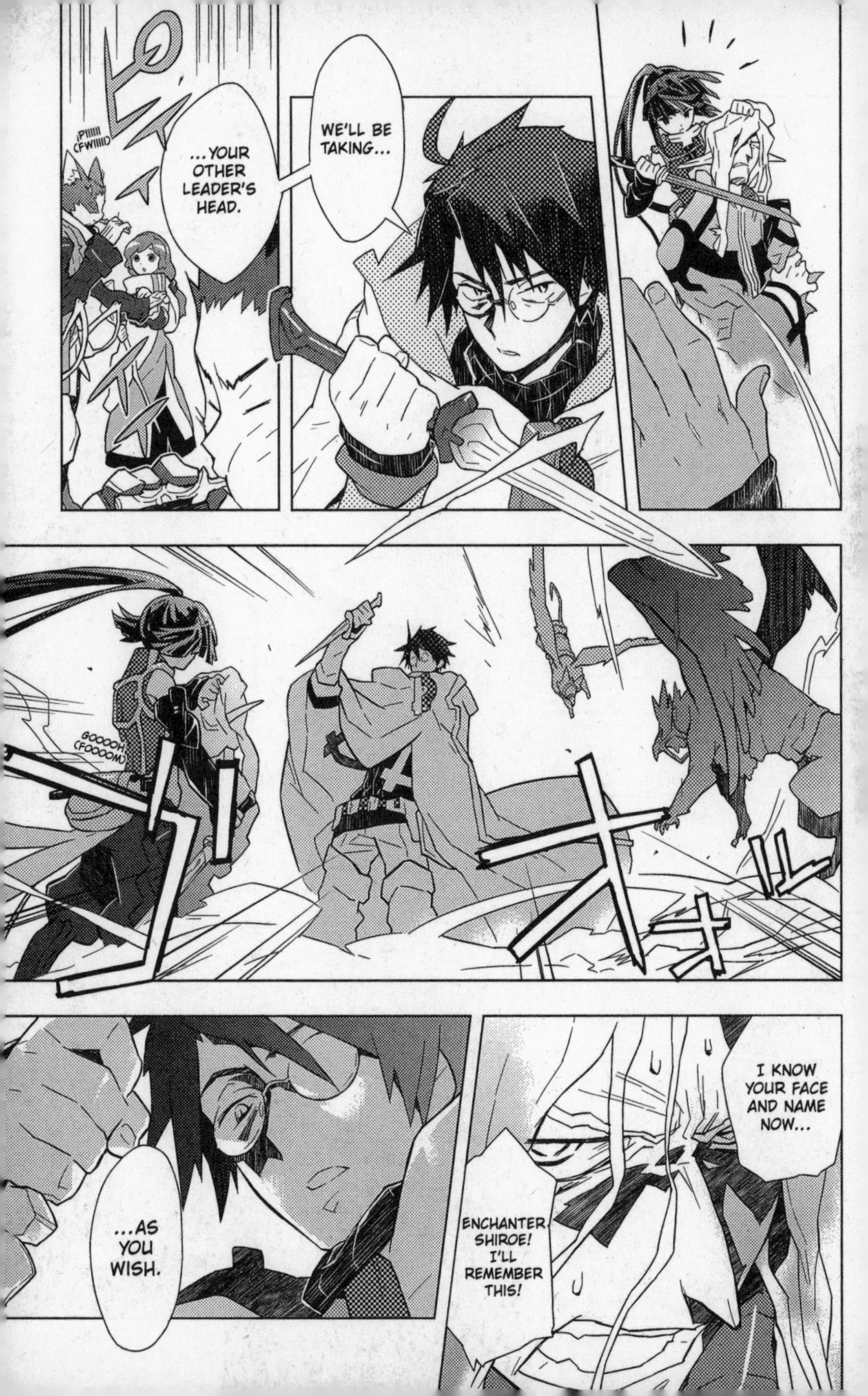
WE'LL BE TAKING...
...YOUR OTHER LEADER'S HEAD.
¡PIIIIII (FWIIIIII)
GOOOOH (FOOOOM)
I KNOW YOUR FACE AND NAME NOW...
ENCHANTER SHIROE! I'LL REMEMBER THIS!
...AS YOU WISH.

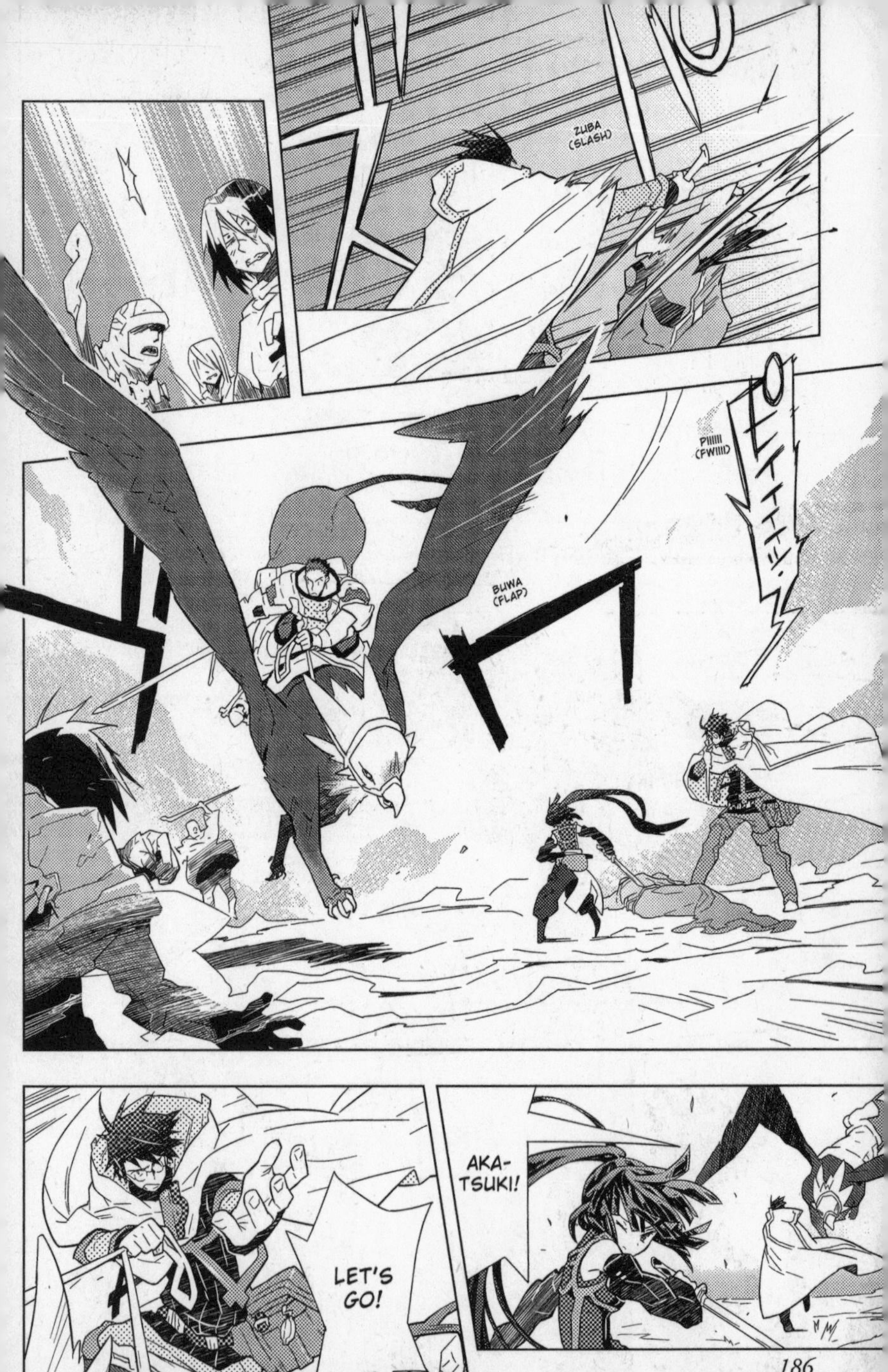
ZUBA
(SLASH)
PIIIIII
(FWIIII)
BUWA
(FLAP)
AKA-
TSUKI!
LET'S
GO!

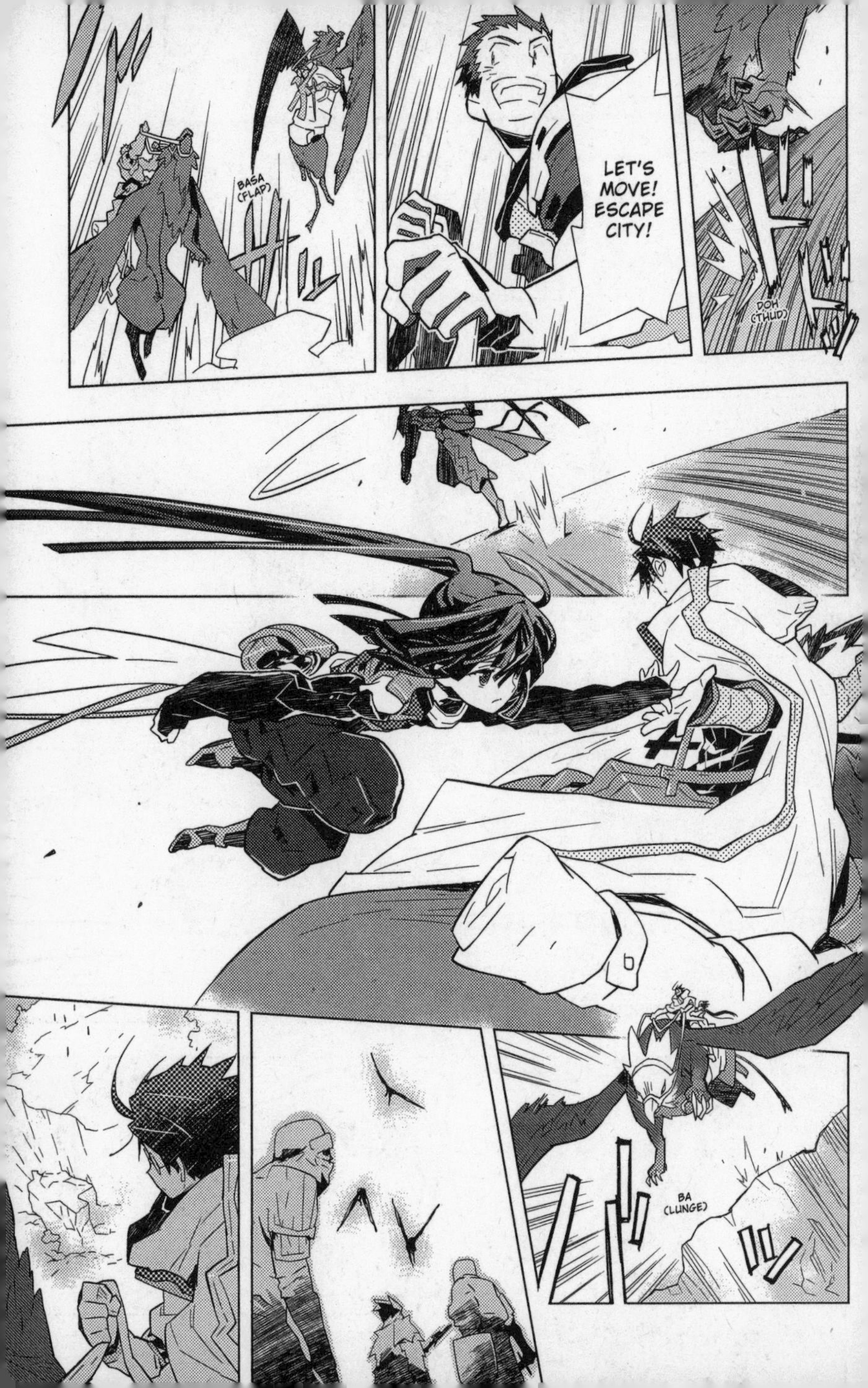
DOH (THUD)
LET'S MOVE! ESCAPE CITY!
BASA (FLAP)
BA (LUNGE)

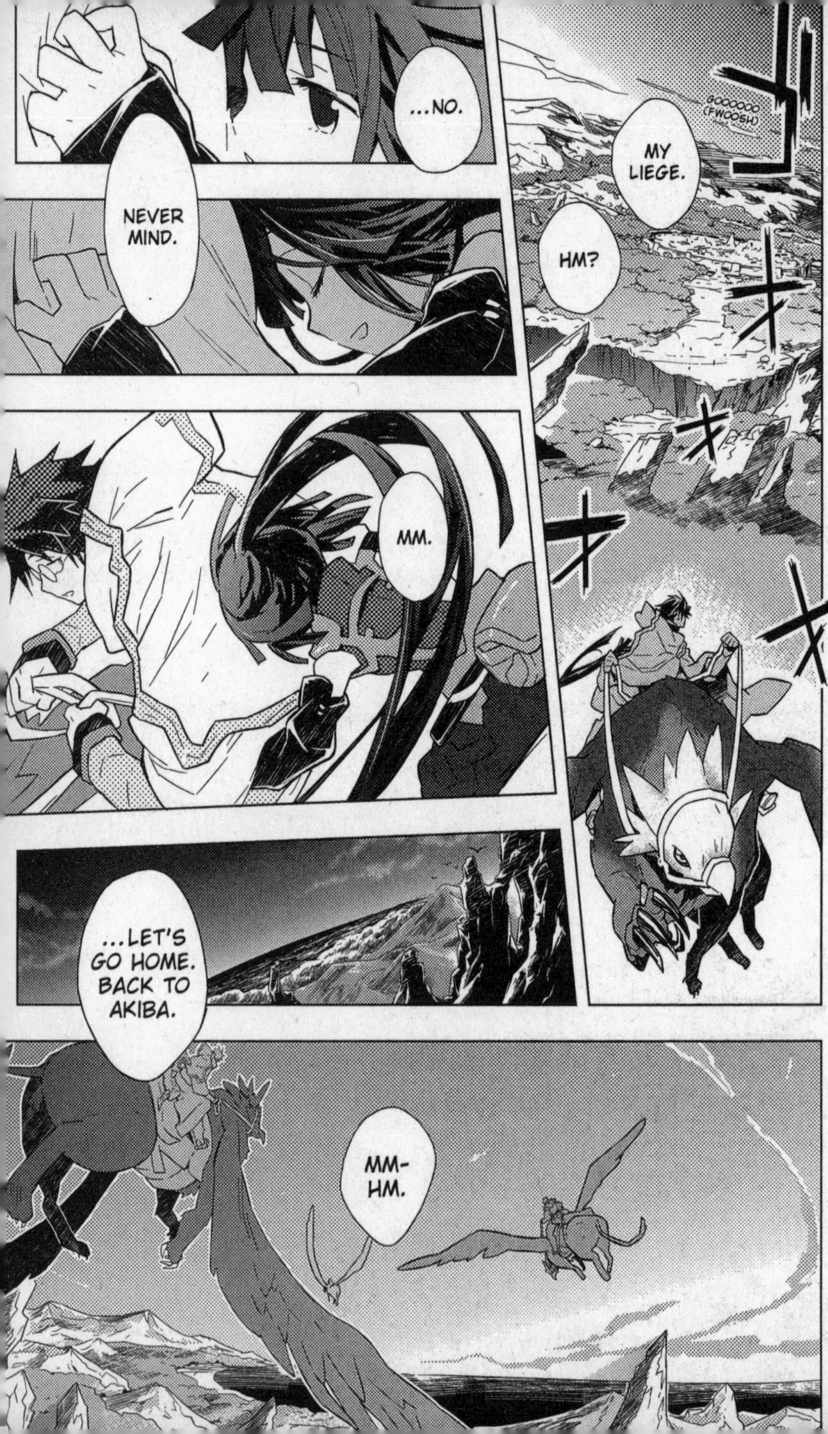
GOOOOOO (FWOOSH)
MY LIEGE.
HM?
...NO.
NEVER MIND.
MM.
...LET'S GO HOME. BACK TO AKIBA.
MM-HM.

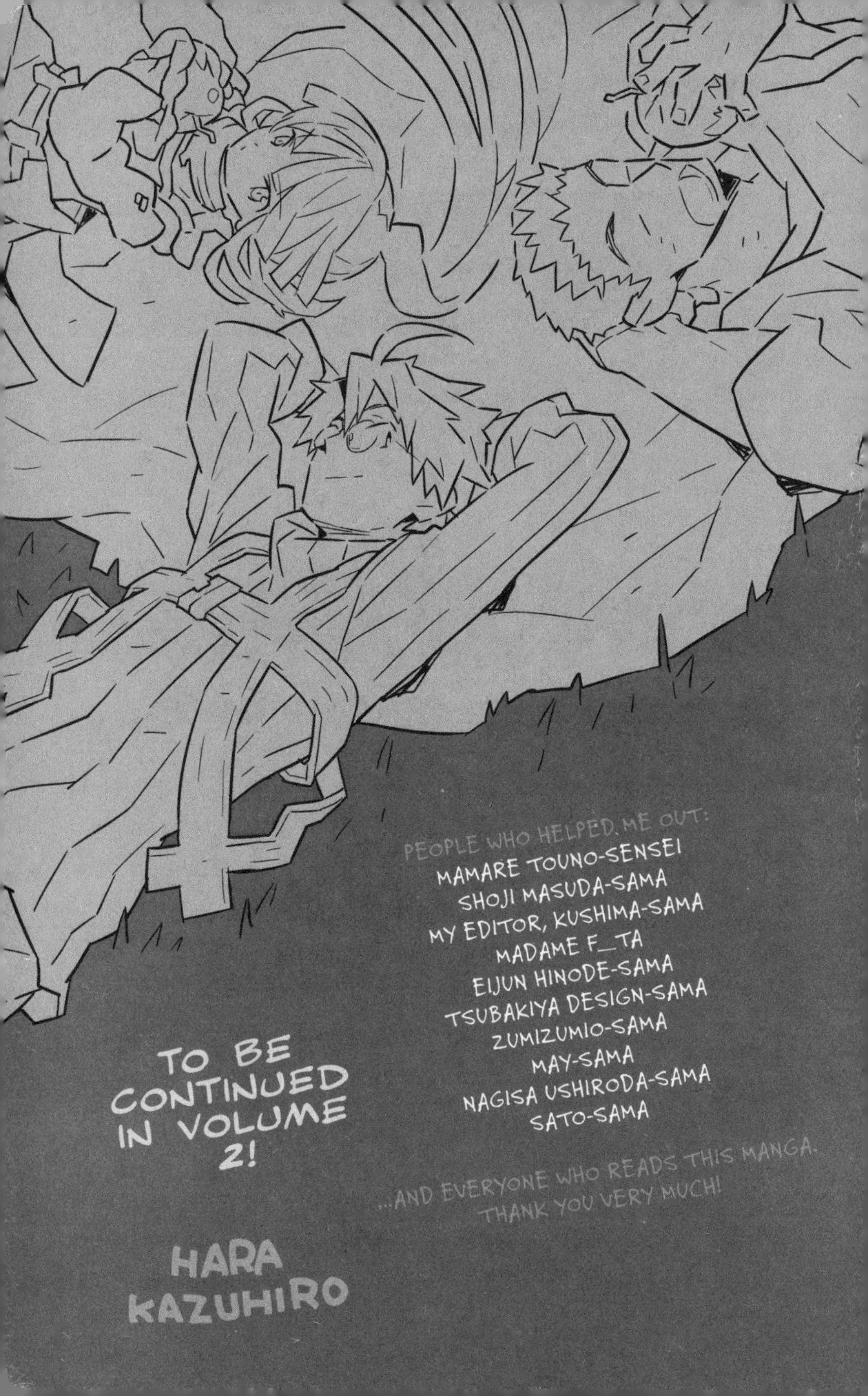
PEOPLE WHO HELPED ME OUT:
MAMARE TOUNO-SENSEI
SHOJI MASUDA-SAMA
MY EDITOR, KUSHIMA-SAMA
MADAME F_TA
EIJUN HINODE-SAMA
TSUBAKIYA DESIGN-SAMA
ZUMIZUMIO-SAMA
MAY-SAMA
NAGISA USHIRODA-SAMA
SATO-SAMA
TO BE CONTINUED IN VOLUME 2!
...AND EVERYONE WHO READS THIS MANGA. THANK YOU VERY MUCH!
HARA KAZUHIRO

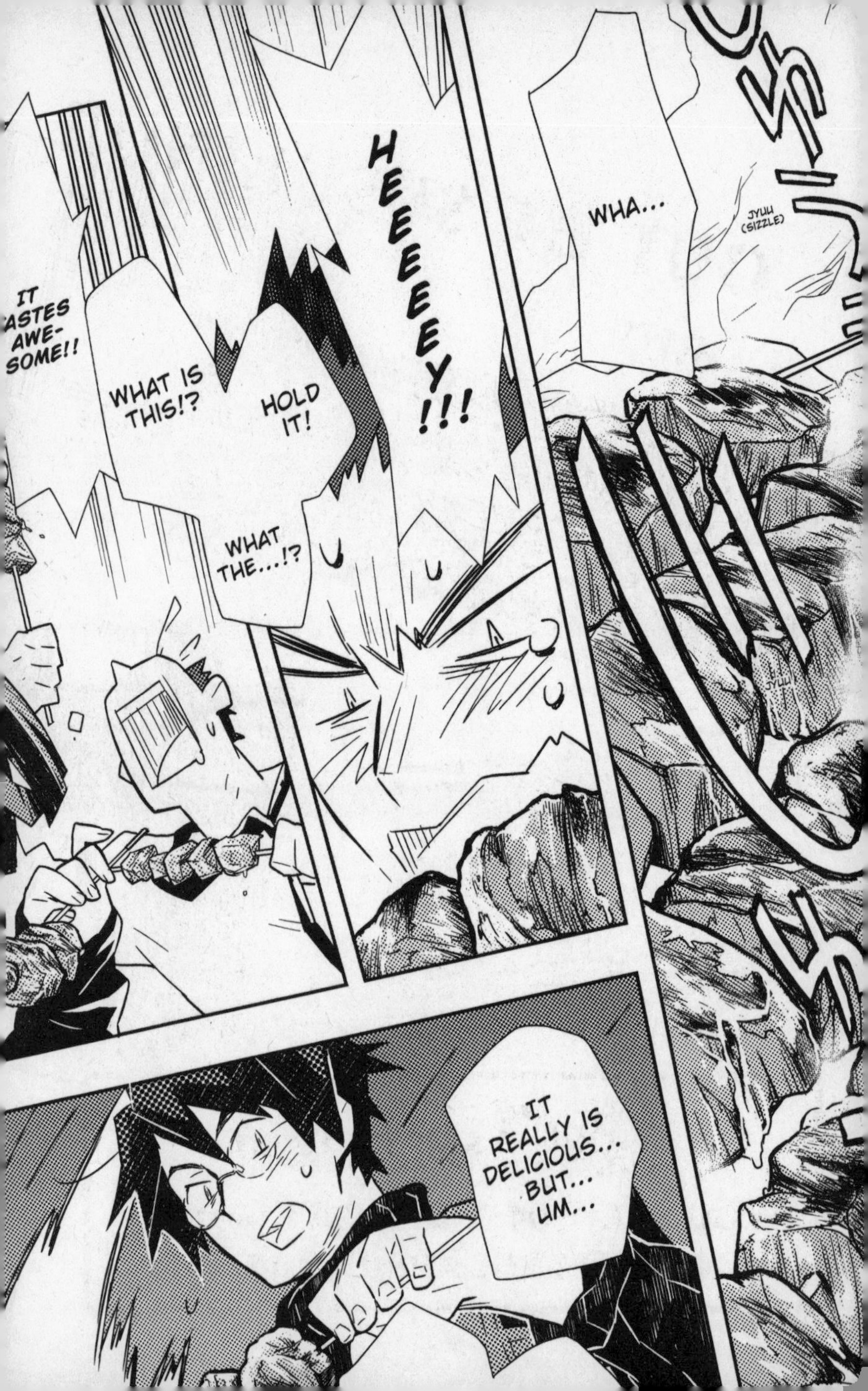
WHA...
JYUU (SIZZLE)
JYUU
HEEEEEEY!!!
HOLD IT!
WHAT THE...!?
WHAT IS THIS!?
IT ASTES AWE-SOME!!
IT REALLY IS DELICIOUS... BUT... UM...

# OUT OF SUSUKINO!!

## ...BUT...

## ...HOW COME THE FOOD...

## ...TASTES SO GOOD!?

IT DOES! THIS IS... AMAZING.

MMF!

UMPH!

Shiroe and company rescued Serara of the Crescent Moon guild and made their escape from Susukino.

On the way back to Akiba, Captain Nyanta shows them the answer to one of this world's questions!

Will tasty food transform Akiba!? Shifty Machiavelli-with-glasses Shiroe shows what he's made of!!

# LOG HORIZON

## VOLUME 1 OF THE LIGHT NOVEL IN STORES APRIL 2015!

# LOG HORIZON 1

▶ART: **KAZUHIRO HARA**

▶ORIGINAL STORY: **MAMARE TOUNO**

▶SUPERVISION: **SHOJI MASUDA**

▶TRANSLATION: **TAYLOR ENGEL**

▶LETTERING: **BRNDN BLAKESLEE & LYS BLAKESLEE**

LOG HORIZON Volume 1
© 2013 Hara Kazuhiro
© 2013 Touno Mamare
All rights reserved.
First published in Japan in 2013 by
KADOKAWA CORPORATION ENTERBRAIN
English translation rights arranged with
KADOKAWA CORPORATION ENTERBRAIN
through Tuttle-Mori Agency, Inc., Tokyo.

English translation © 2015 by Hachette Book Group, Inc.

Yen Press
Hachette Book Group
1290 Avenue of the Americas
New York, NY 10104

www.HachetteBookGroup.com
www.YenPress.com

Yen Press is an imprint of Hachette Book Group, Inc. The Yen Press name and logo are trademarks of Hachette Book Group, Inc.

The publisher is not responsible for websites (or their content) that are not owned by the publisher.

First Yen Press Edition: March 2015

ISBN: 978-0-316-38306-6

10 9 8 7 6 5 4 3 2 1

BVG

Printed in the United States of America